ZATCH BELL!™

ZATCH BELL!

Vol. 9

STORY AND ART BY
MAKOTO RAIKU

Translation/David Ury
Touch-up Art & Lettering/Gabe Crate
Design/Izumi Hirayama
Special Thanks/Jessica Villat, Miki Macaluso, Mitsuko Kitajima, and Akane Matsuo
Editor/Kit Fox

Managing Editor/Annette Roman
Editorial Director/Elizabeth Kawasaki
Editor in Chief/Alvin Lu
Sr. Director of Acquisitions/Rika Inouye
Sr. VP of Marketing/Liza Coppola
Exec. VP of Sales & Marketing/John Easum
Publisher/Hyoe Narita

Printed in the U.S.A.

Published by VIZ Media, LLC
P.O. Box 77010
San Francisco, CA 94107

10 9 8 7 6 5 4 3 2 1
First printing, October 2006

RATED T FOR TEEN

PARENTAL ADVISORY
ZATCH BELL! is rated T for Teen and is recommended for ages 13 and up. This volume contains realistic and fantasy violence.

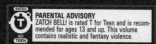

www.viz.com
store.viz.com

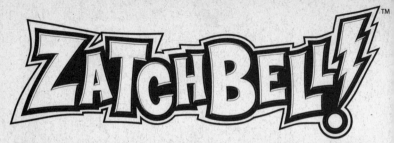

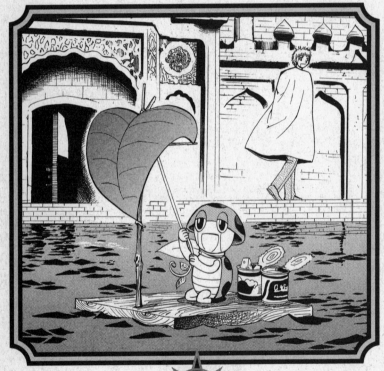

STORY AND ART BY

MAKOTO RAIKU

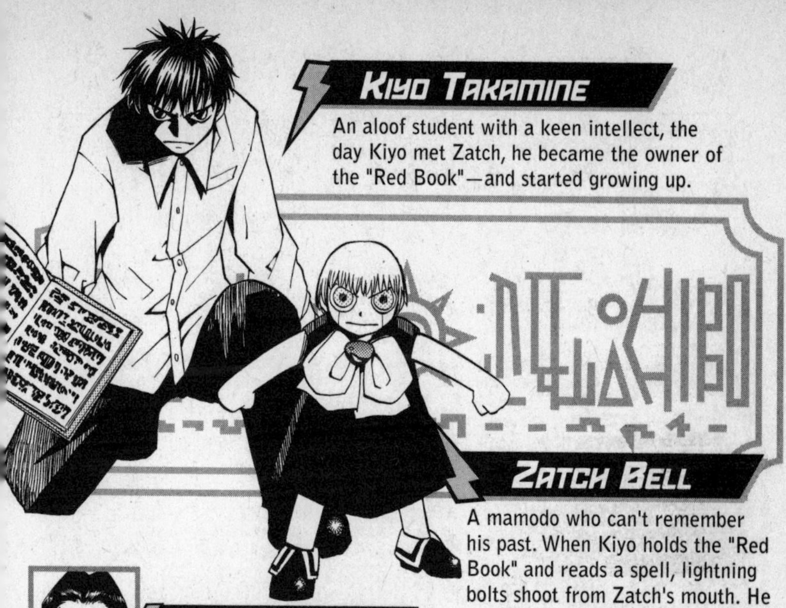

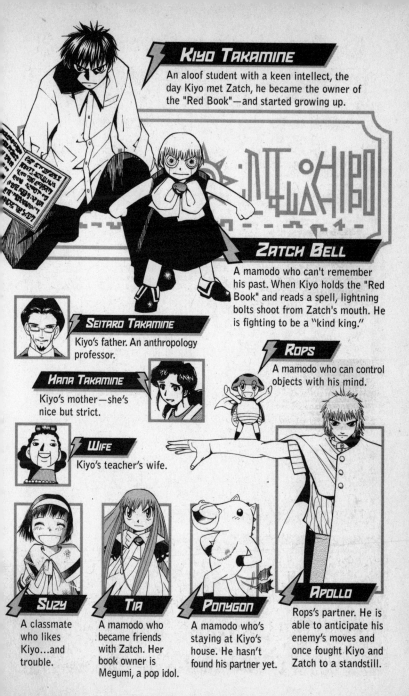

Kiyo Takamine

An aloof student with a keen intellect, the day Kiyo met Zatch, he became the owner of the "Red Book"—and started growing up.

Zatch Bell

A mamodo who can't remember his past. When Kiyo holds the "Red Book" and reads a spell, lightning bolts shoot from Zatch's mouth. He is fighting to be a "kind king."

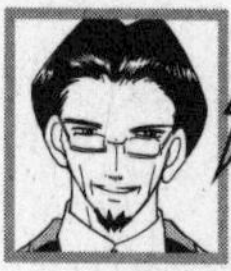

Seitaro Takamine

Kiyo's father. An anthropology professor.

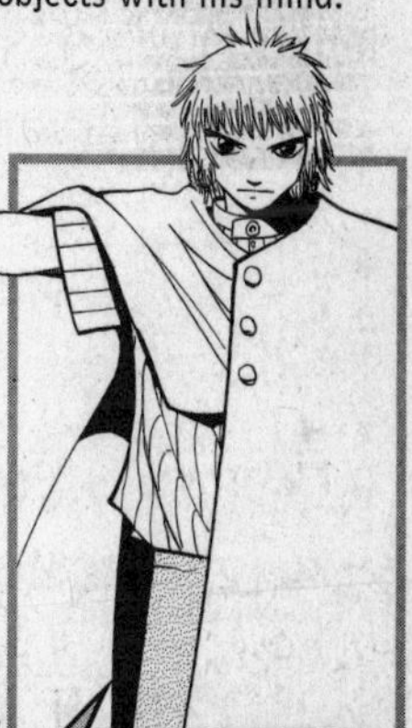

Rops

A mamodo who can control objects with his mind.

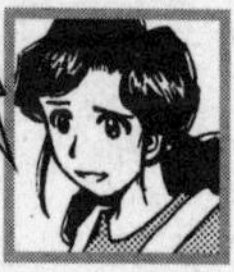

Hana Takamine

Kiyo's mother—she's nice but strict.

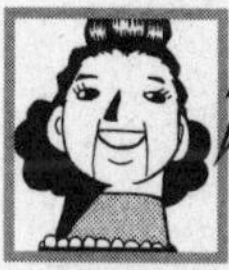

Wife

Kiyo's teacher's wife.

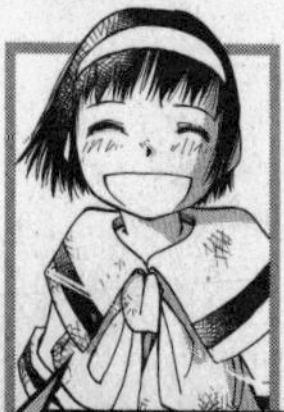

Suzy

A classmate who likes Kiyo...and trouble.

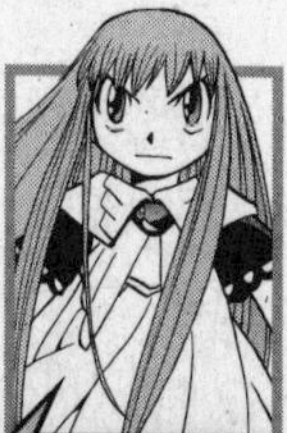

Tia

A mamodo who became friends with Zatch. Her book owner is Megumi, a pop idol.

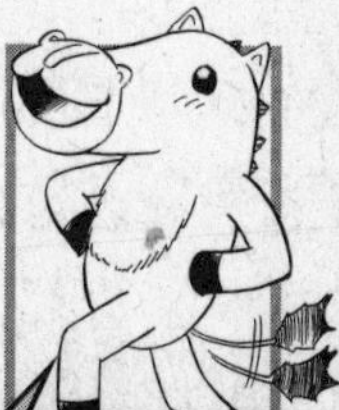

Ponygon

A mamodo who's staying at Kiyo's house. He hasn't found his partner yet.

Apollo

Rops's partner. He is able to anticipate his enemy's moves and once fought Kiyo and Zatch to a standstill.

ZATCH'S PAST OPPONENTS

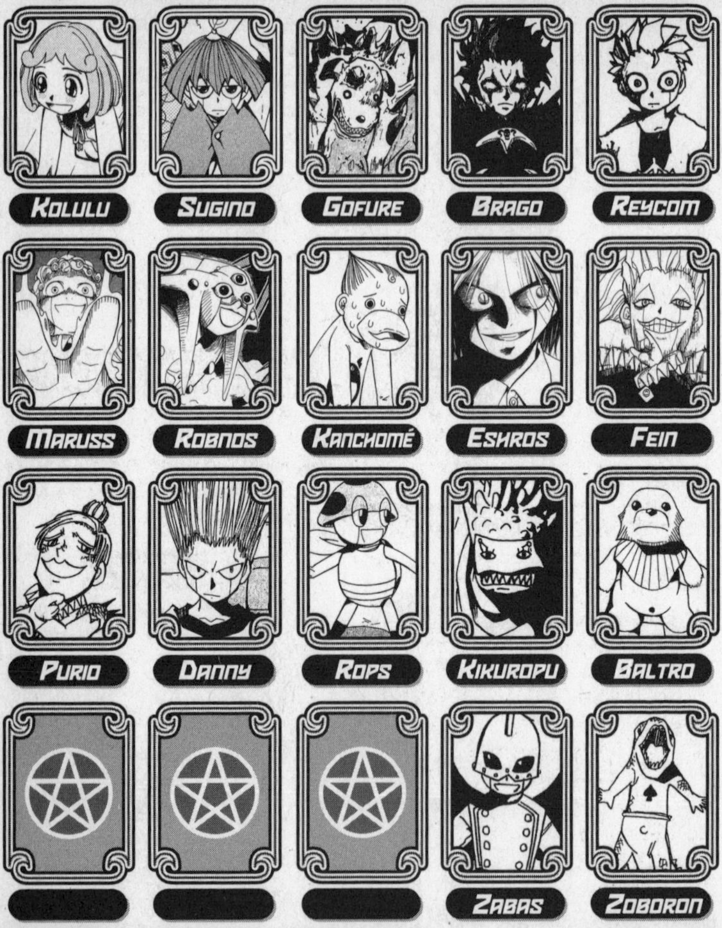

KOLULU
SUGINO
GOFURE
BRAGO
REYCOM
MARUSS
ROBNOS
KANCHOMÉ
ESHROS
FEIN
PURIO
DANNY
ROPS
KIKUROPU
BALTRO
ZABAS
ZOBORON

THE STORY THUS FAR

The battle to determine who will be the next king of the mamodo world takes place every 1,000 years in the human world. Each mamodo owns a "book" which increases its unique powers, and they must team up with a human in order to fight for their own survival. Zatch is one of 100 mamodo chosen to fight in this battle, and his partner is Kiyo, a junior high school student. The bond between Zatch and Kiyo deepens as they continue to survive through many harsh battles. Zatch swears, "I will fight to become a kind king."

ZATCH BELL!™ 9

CONTENTS

LEVEL 75: Zatch's Cold

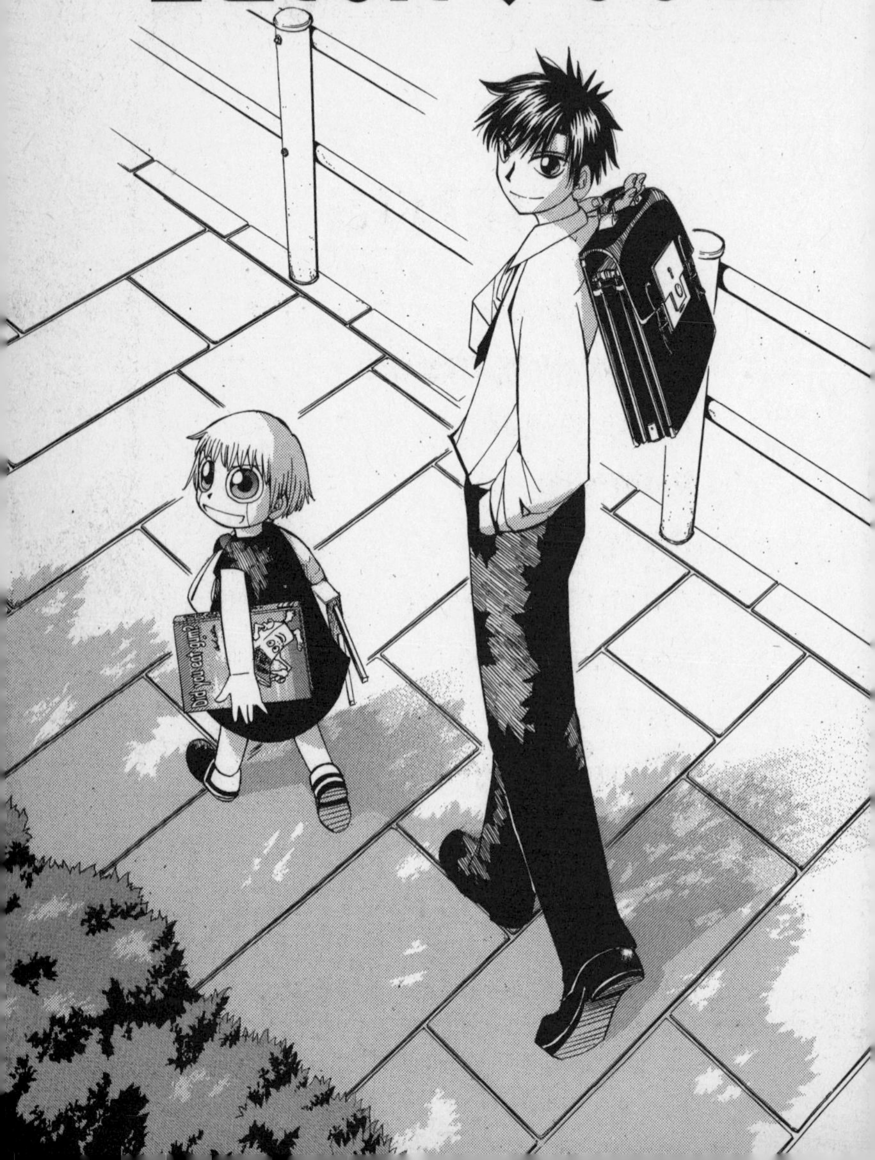
Did you eat gum?

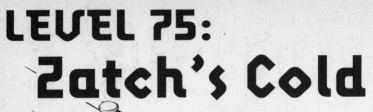

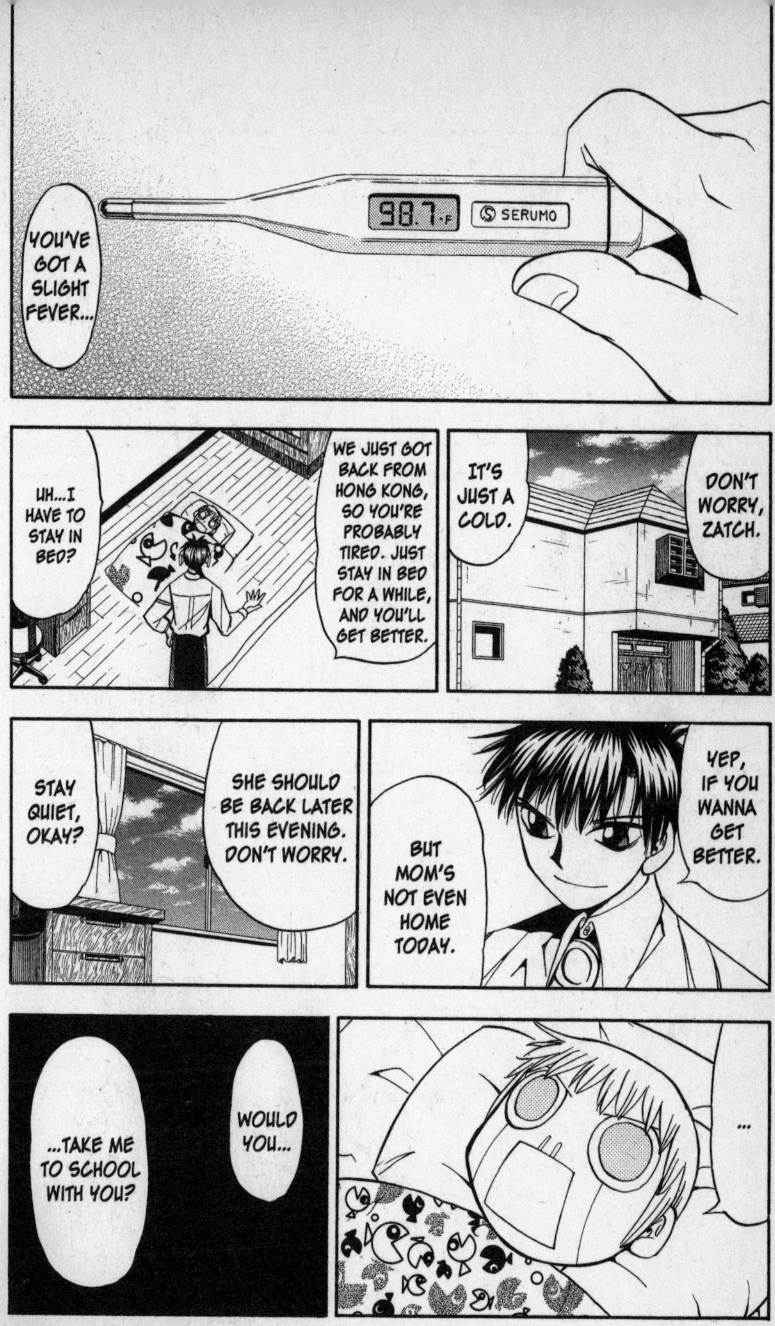
98.7 °F
SERUMO
YOU'VE GOT A SLIGHT FEVER...
DON'T WORRY, ZATCH.
IT'S JUST A COLD.
WE JUST GOT BACK FROM HONG KONG, SO YOU'RE PROBABLY TIRED. JUST STAY IN BED FOR A WHILE, AND YOU'LL GET BETTER.
UH...I HAVE TO STAY IN BED?
YEP, IF YOU WANNA GET BETTER.
BUT MOM'S NOT EVEN HOME TODAY.
SHE SHOULD BE BACK LATER THIS EVENING. DON'T WORRY.
STAY QUIET, OKAY?
...
WOULD YOU...
...TAKE ME TO SCHOOL WITH YOU?

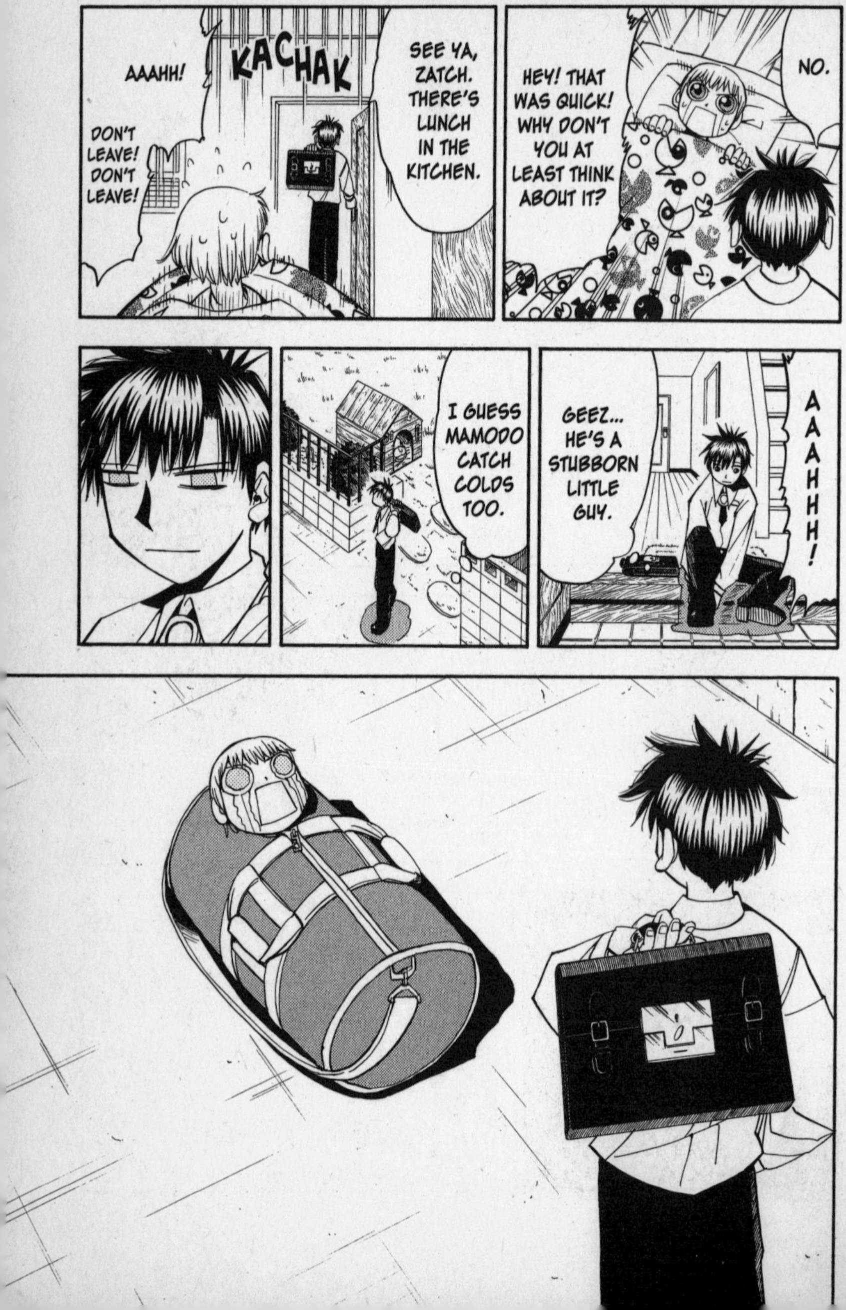
NO.
HEY! THAT WAS QUICK! WHY DON'T YOU AT LEAST THINK ABOUT IT?
SEE YA, ZATCH. THERE'S LUNCH IN THE KITCHEN.
KACHAK
AAAHH!
DON'T LEAVE! DON'T LEAVE!
AAAHHH!
GEEZ... HE'S A STUBBORN LITTLE GUY.
I GUESS MAMODO CATCH COLDS TOO.

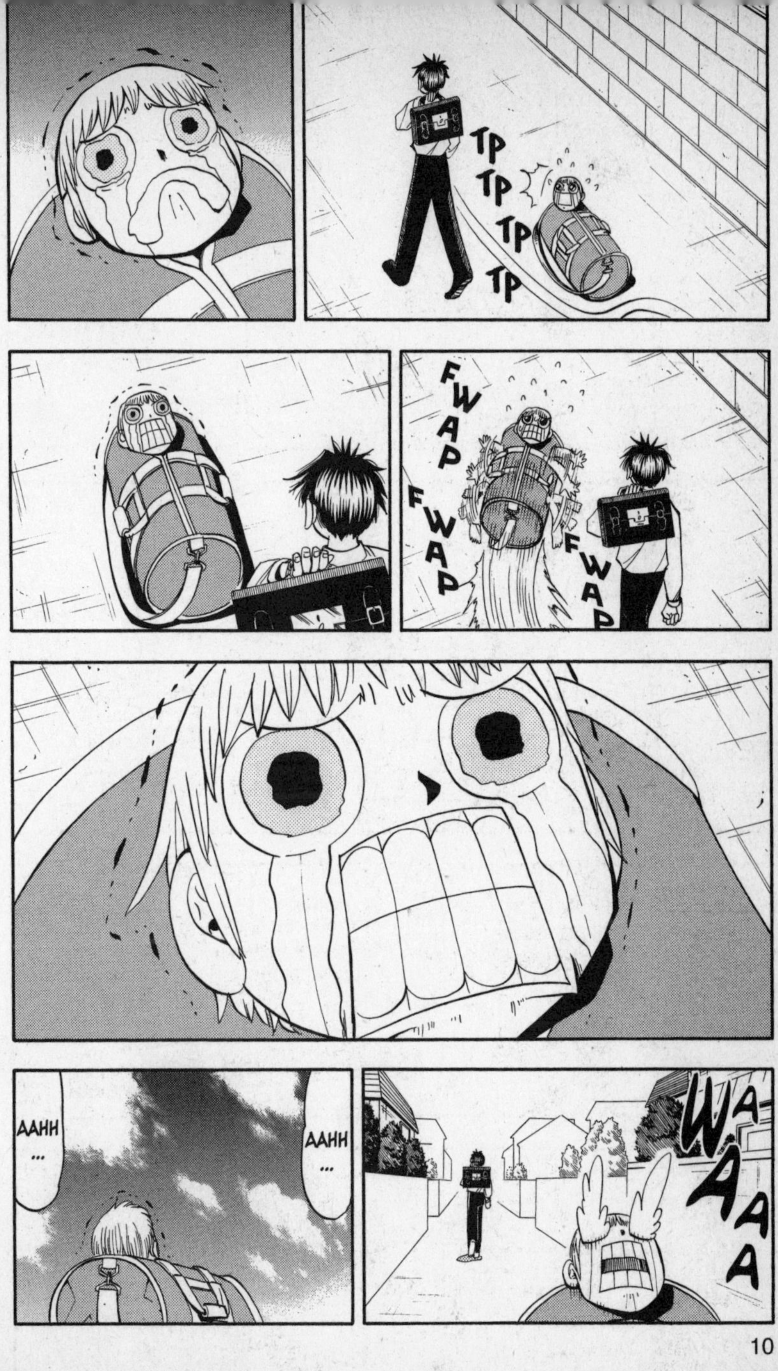
TP TP TP TP
FWAP FWAP FWAP
WA-AAAA
AAHH...
AAHH...

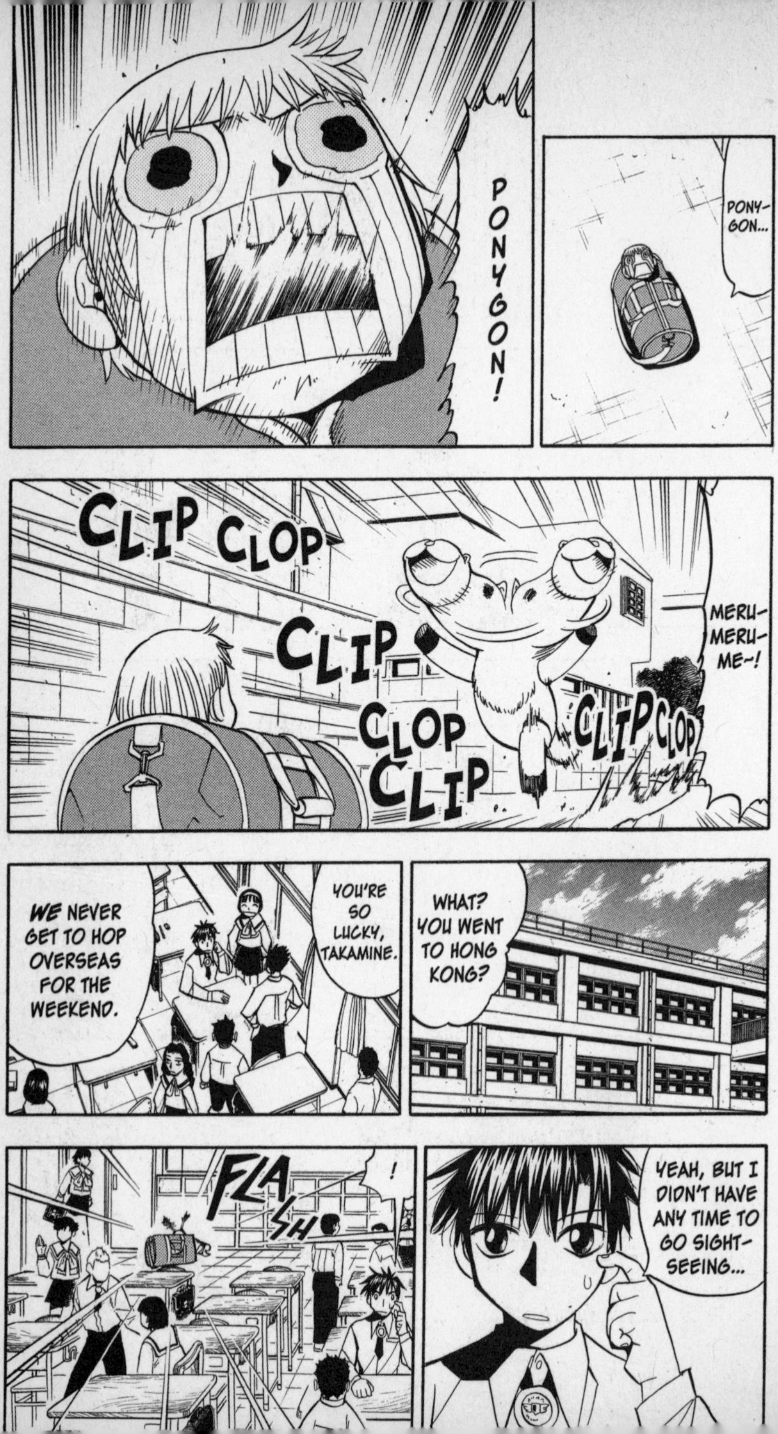
PONY-GON...
PONYGON!
MERU-MERU-ME~!
CLIP CLOP
CLIP
CLOP
CLIP
CLIP CLOP
WHAT? YOU WENT TO HONG KONG?
YOU'RE SO LUCKY, TAKAMINE.
WE NEVER GET TO HOP OVERSEAS FOR THE WEEKEND.
YEAH, BUT I DIDN'T HAVE ANY TIME TO GO SIGHT-SEEING...
!
FLASH

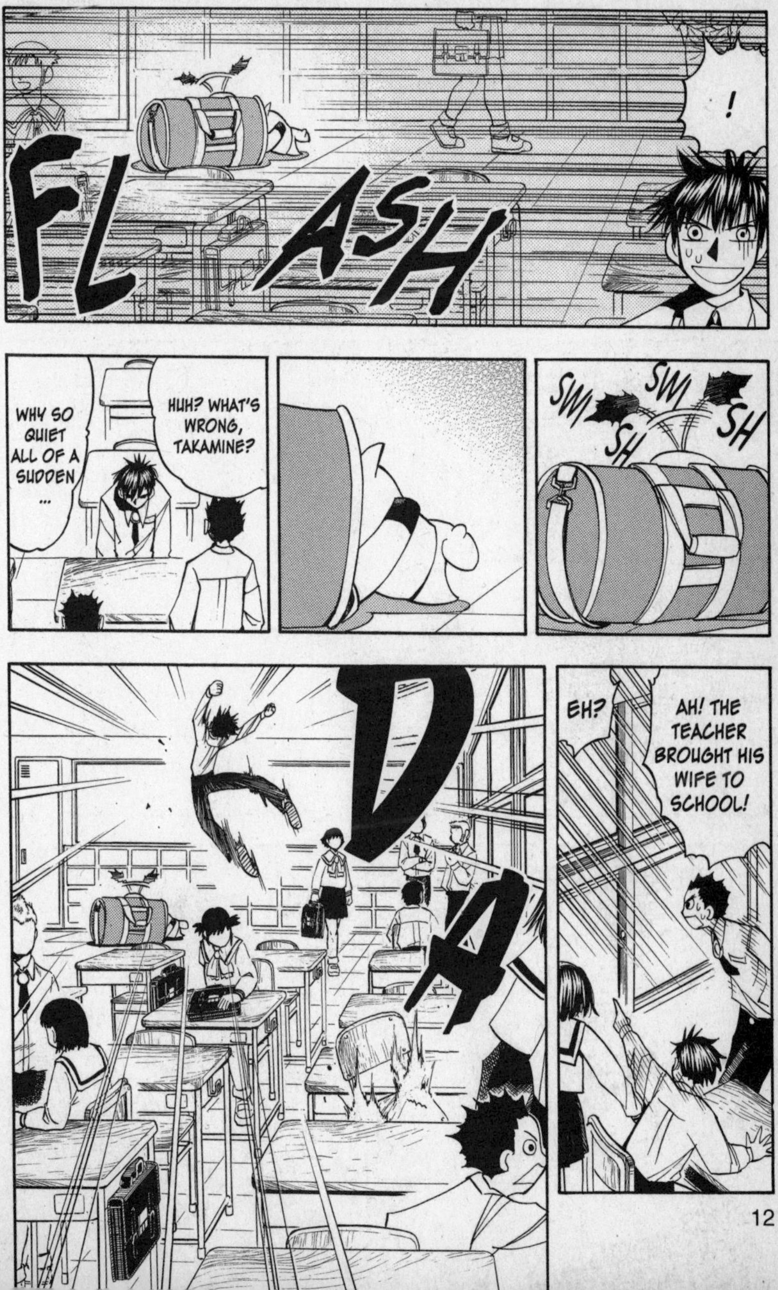
!
FLASH
SWISH SWISH
HUH? WHAT'S WRONG, TAKAMINE?
WHY SO QUIET ALL OF A SUDDEN ...
AH! THE TEACHER BROUGHT HIS WIFE TO SCHOOL!
EH?
DA

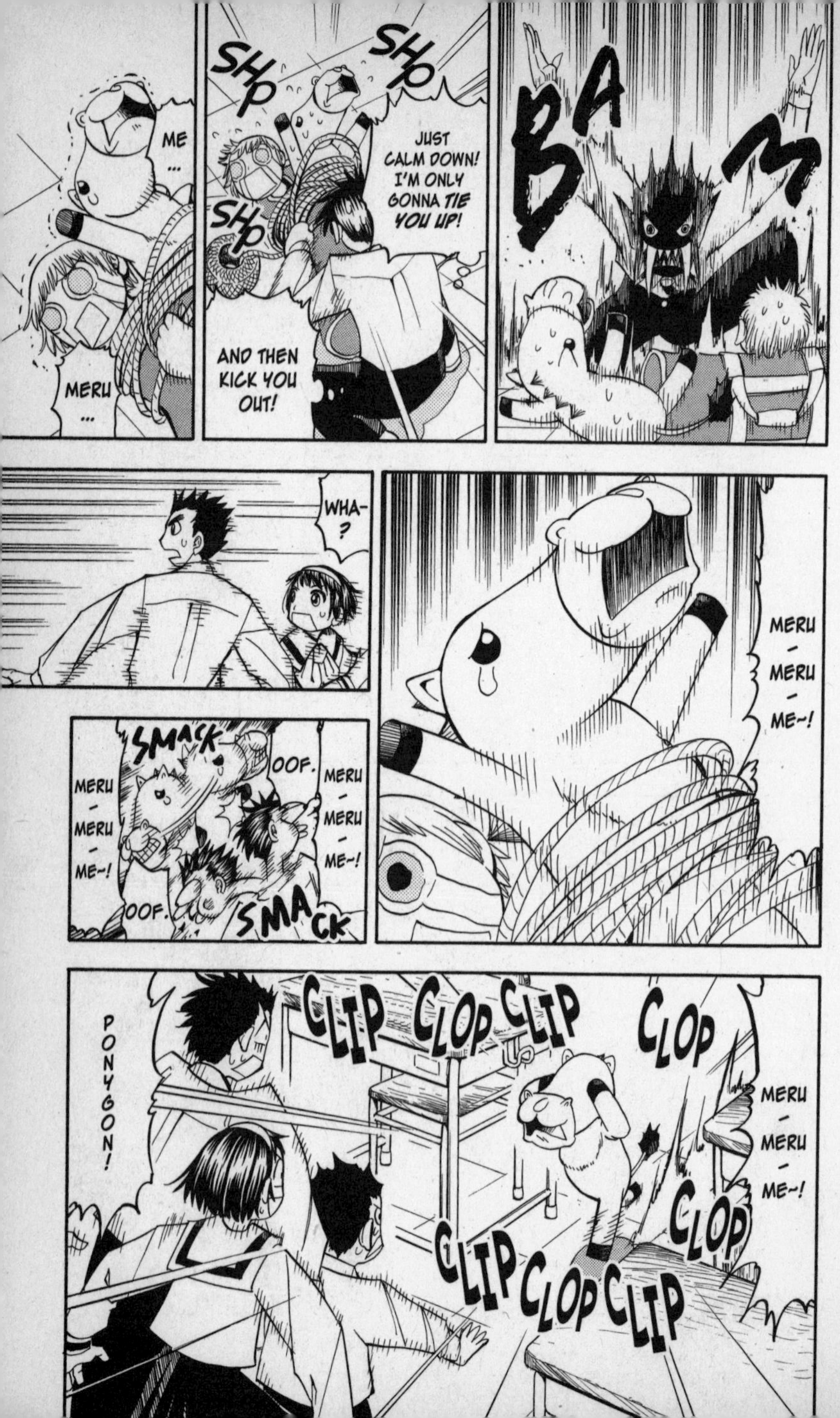
BAM
SHP
SHP
JUST CALM DOWN! I'M ONLY GONNA TIE YOU UP!
SHP
AND THEN KICK YOU OUT!
ME...
MERU...
MERU-MERU-ME~!
WHA-?
SMACK
OOF.
MERU-MERU-ME~!
MERU-MERU-ME~!
OOF.
SMACK
CLOP
CLIP CLOP CLIP
MERU-MERU-ME~!
CLOP
CLIP CLOP CLIP
PONYGON!

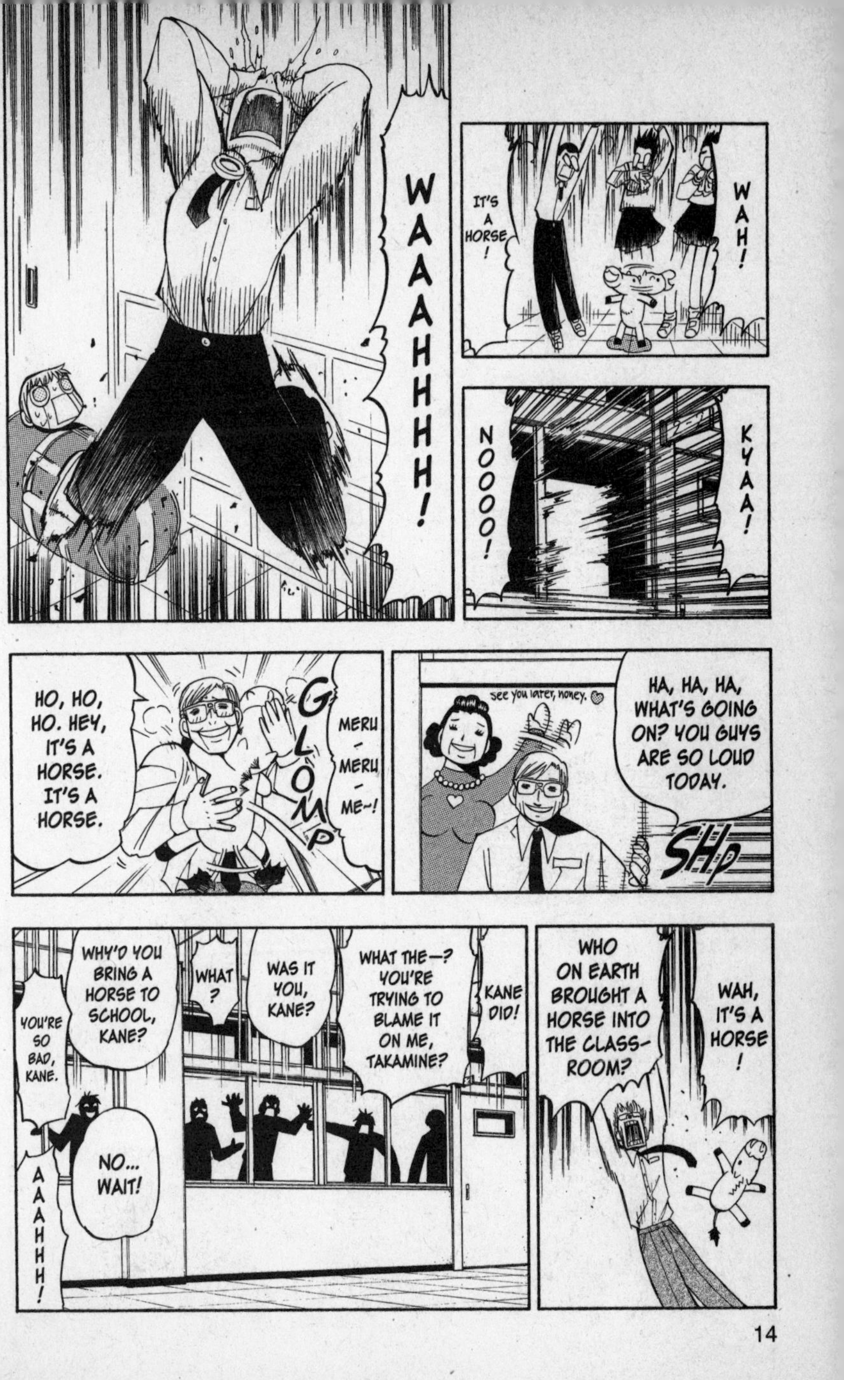
WAH!
IT'S A HORSE!
KYAAA!
NOOOO!
WAAAAHHHHH!
HA, HA, HA, WHAT'S GOING ON? YOU GUYS ARE SO LOUD TODAY.
see you later, honey.
SHP
MERU-MERU-ME~!
GLOMP
HO, HO, HO. HEY, IT'S A HORSE. IT'S A HORSE.
WAH, IT'S A HORSE!
WHO ON EARTH BROUGHT A HORSE INTO THE CLASS-ROOM?
KANE DID!
WHAT THE—? YOU'RE TRYING TO BLAME IT ON ME, TAKAMINE?
WAS IT YOU, KANE?
WHAT?
WHY'D YOU BRING A HORSE TO SCHOOL, KANE?
YOU'RE SO BAD, KANE.
NO... WAIT!
AAAHHHH!

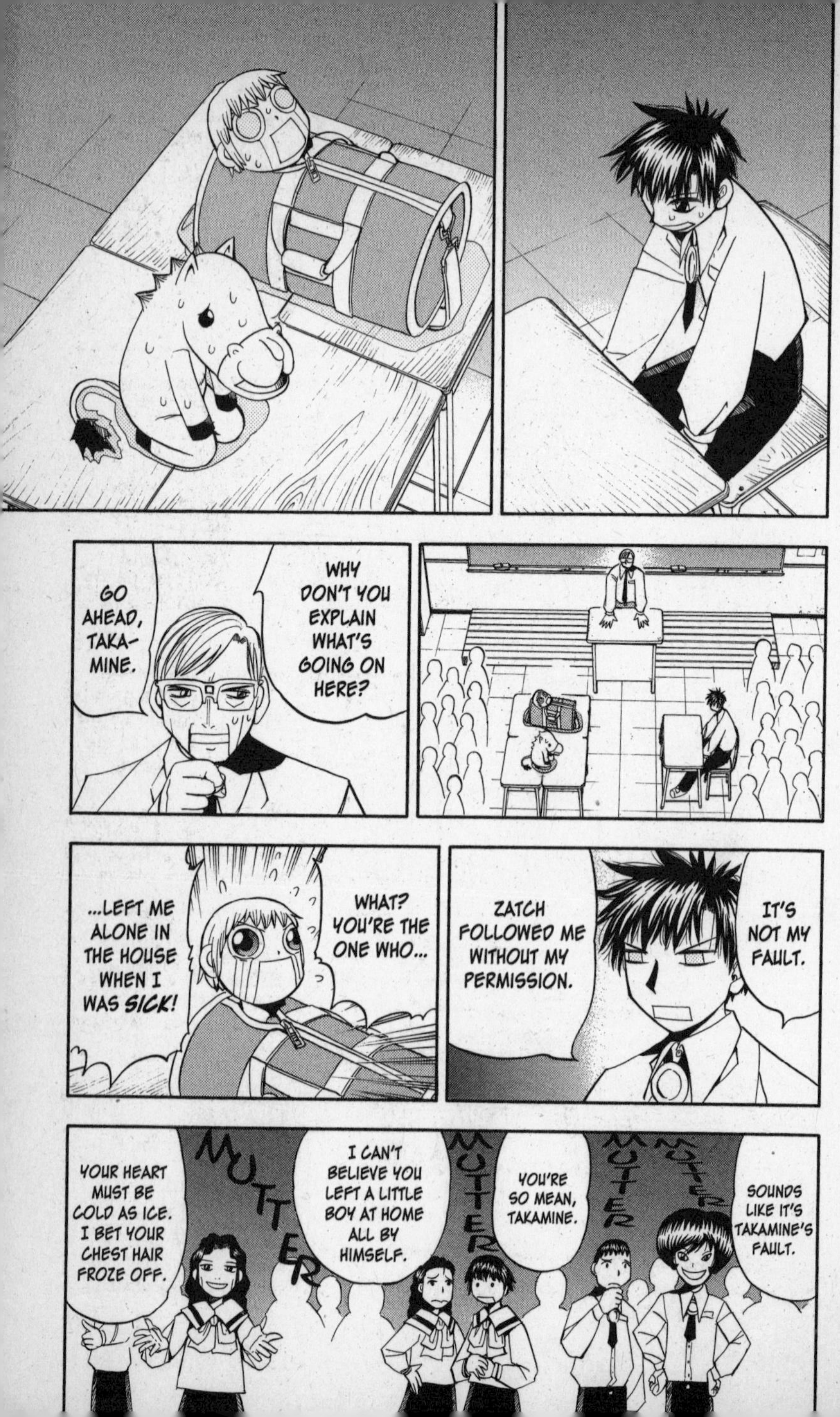
WHY DON'T YOU EXPLAIN WHAT'S GOING ON HERE?
GO AHEAD, TAKAMINE.
IT'S NOT MY FAULT.
ZATCH FOLLOWED ME WITHOUT MY PERMISSION.
WHAT? YOU'RE THE ONE WHO...
...LEFT ME ALONE IN THE HOUSE WHEN I WAS *SICK*!
SOUNDS LIKE IT'S TAKAMINE'S FAULT.
MUTTER
MUTTER
YOU'RE SO MEAN, TAKAMINE.
MUTTER
I CAN'T BELIEVE YOU LEFT A LITTLE BOY AT HOME ALL BY HIMSELF.
MUTTER
YOUR HEART MUST BE COLD AS ICE. I BET YOUR CHEST HAIR FROZE OFF.

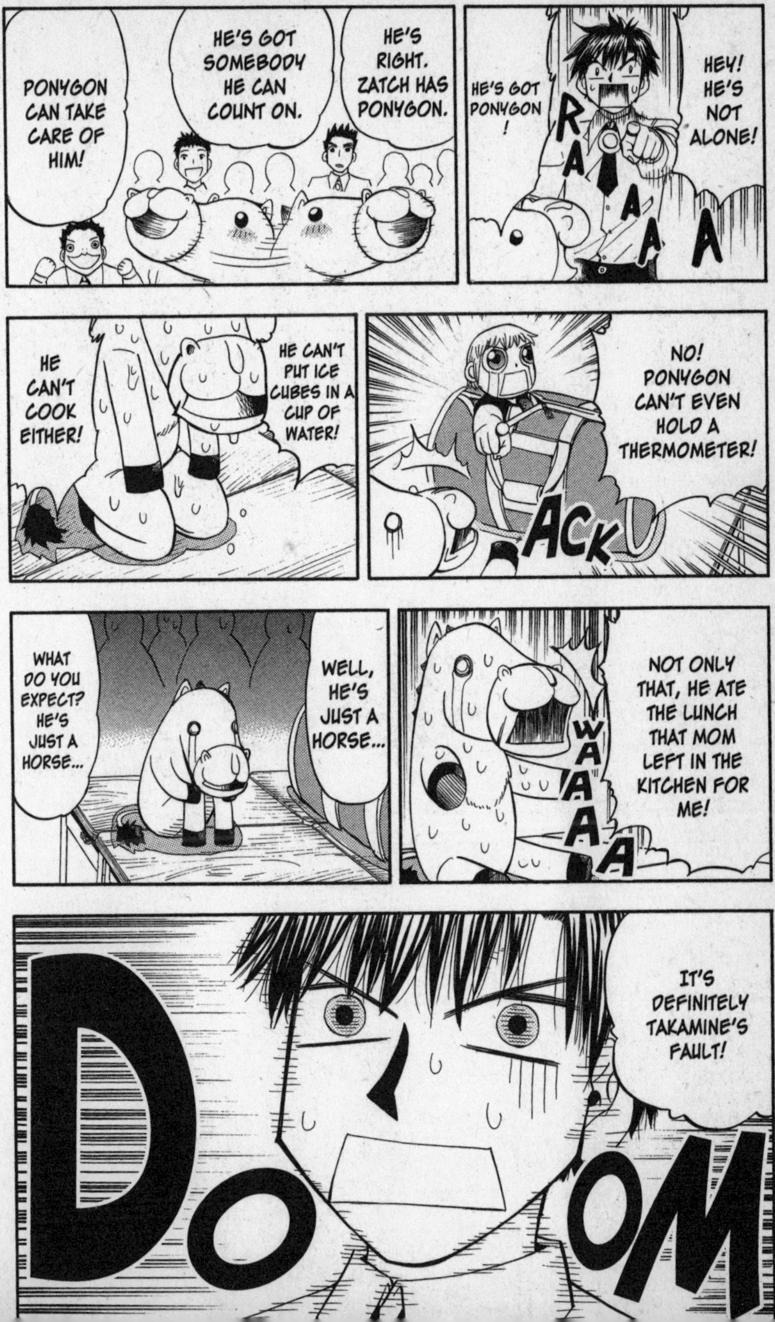
HEY! HE'S NOT ALONE!
HE'S GOT PONYGON!
RAAAAA
HE'S RIGHT. ZATCH HAS PONYGON.
HE'S GOT SOMEBODY HE CAN COUNT ON.
PONYGON CAN TAKE CARE OF HIM!
NO! PONYGON CAN'T EVEN HOLD A THERMOMETER!
ACK
HE CAN'T PUT ICE CUBES IN A CUP OF WATER!
HE CAN'T COOK EITHER!
NOT ONLY THAT, HE ATE THE LUNCH THAT MOM LEFT IN THE KITCHEN FOR ME!
WAAAAA
WELL, HE'S JUST A HORSE...
WHAT DO YOU EXPECT? HE'S JUST A HORSE...
IT'S DEFINITELY TAKAMINE'S FAULT!
DOOM

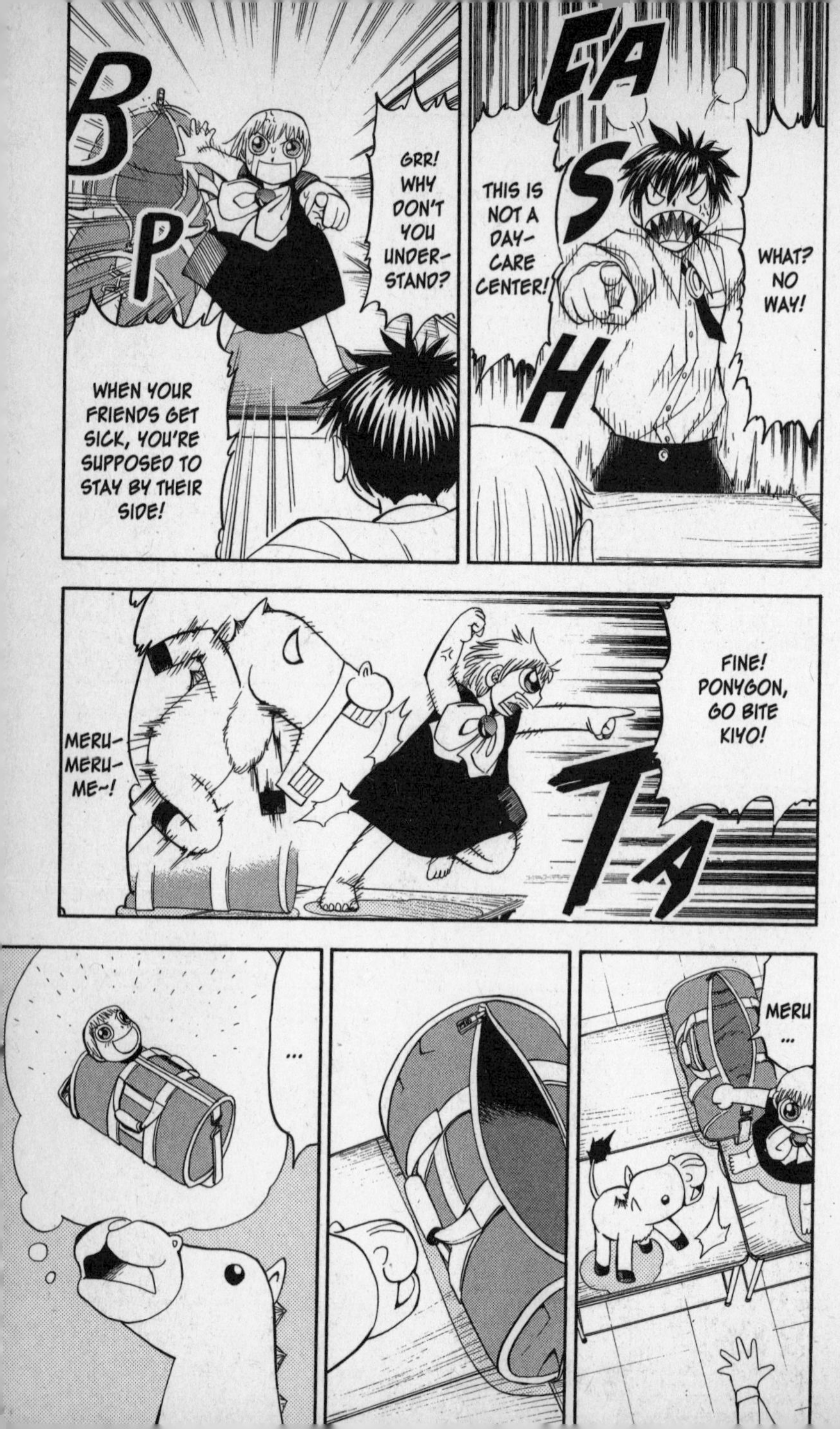
FASH
WHAT? NO WAY!
THIS IS NOT A DAY-CARE CENTER!
BP
GRR! WHY DON'T YOU UNDER-STAND?
WHEN YOUR FRIENDS GET SICK, YOU'RE SUPPOSED TO STAY BY THEIR SIDE!
FINE! PONYGON, GO BITE KIYO!
TA
MERU-MERU-ME~!
MERU...
...

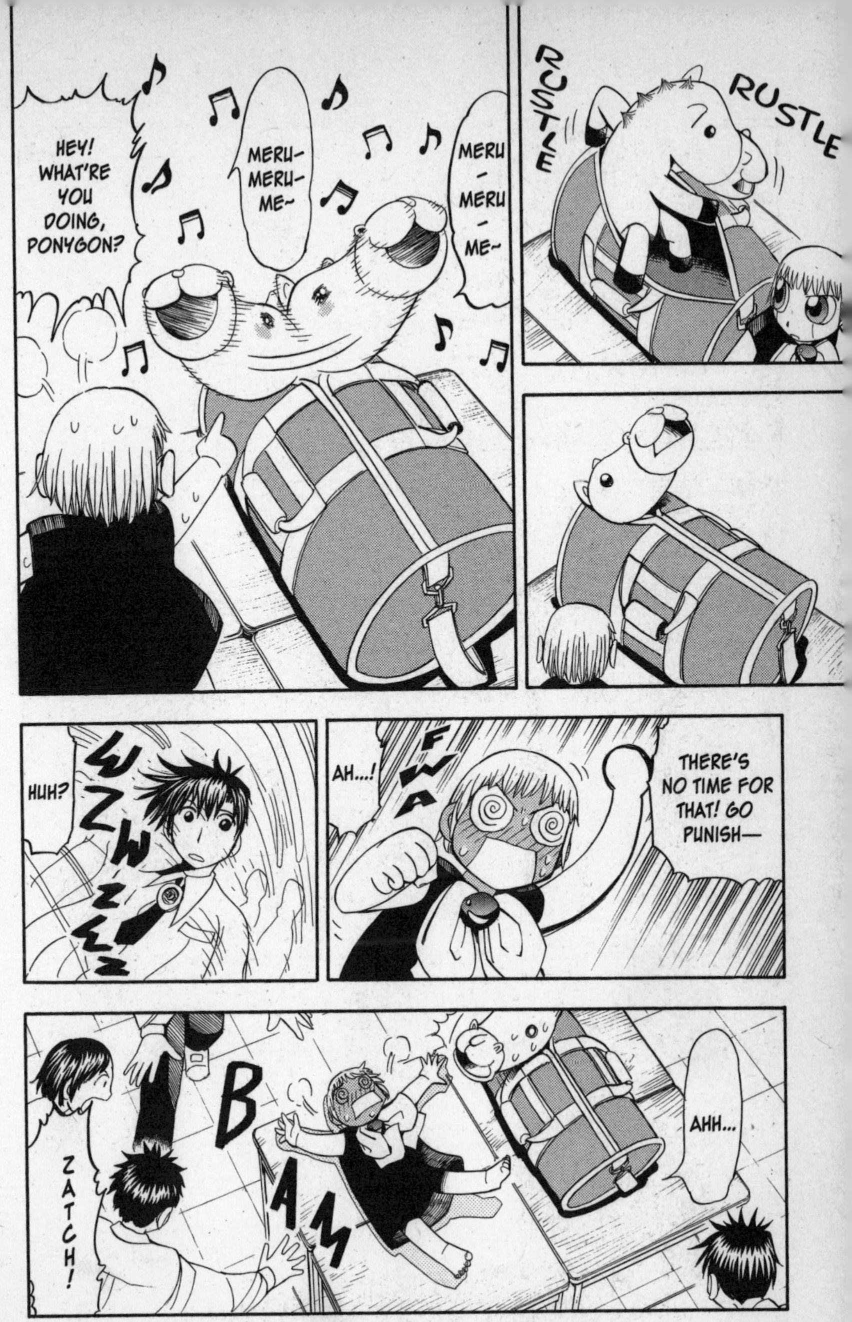
RUSTLE
RUSTLE
MERU-MERU-ME~
MERU-MERU-ME~
HEY! WHAT'RE YOU DOING, PONYGON?
THERE'S NO TIME FOR THAT! GO PUNISH—
FWA
AH...!
WZWZZZ
HUH?
AHH...
BAM
ZATCH!

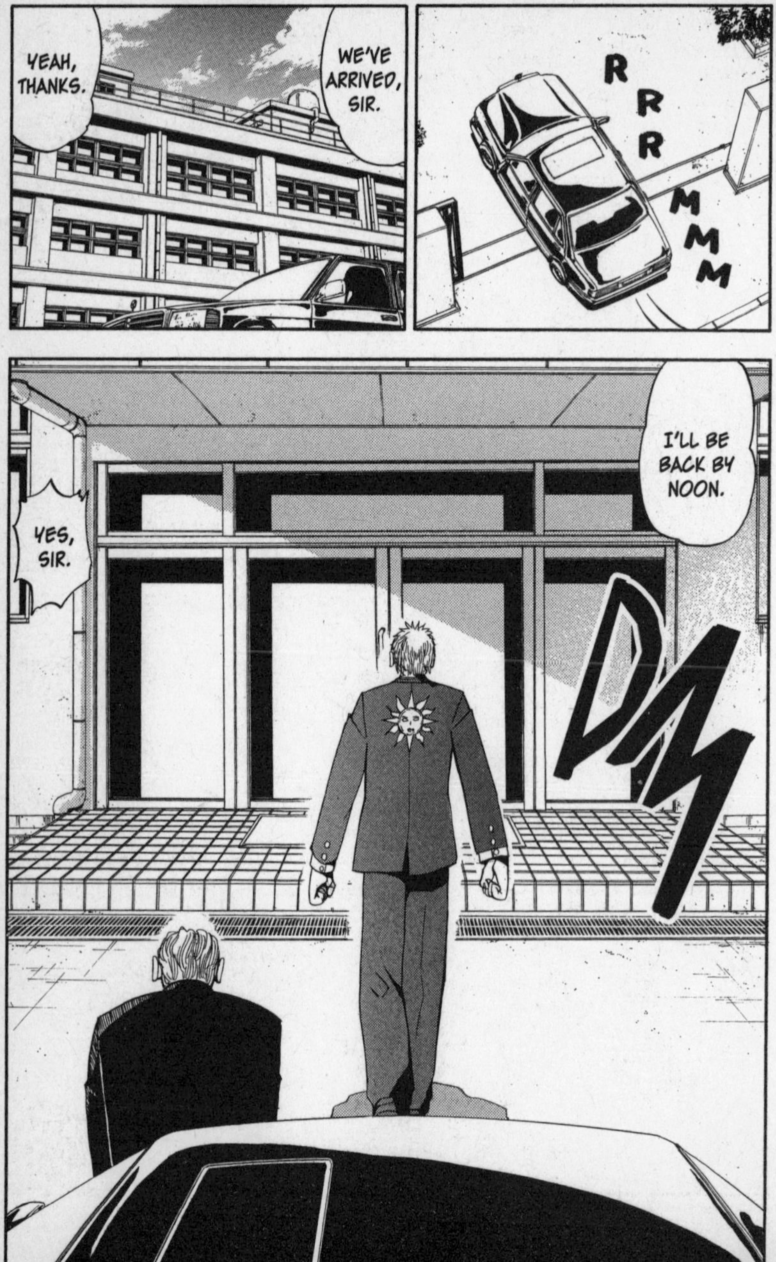
RRRMMM
WE'VE ARRIVED, SIR.
YEAH, THANKS.
I'LL BE BACK BY NOON.
YES, SIR.
DM

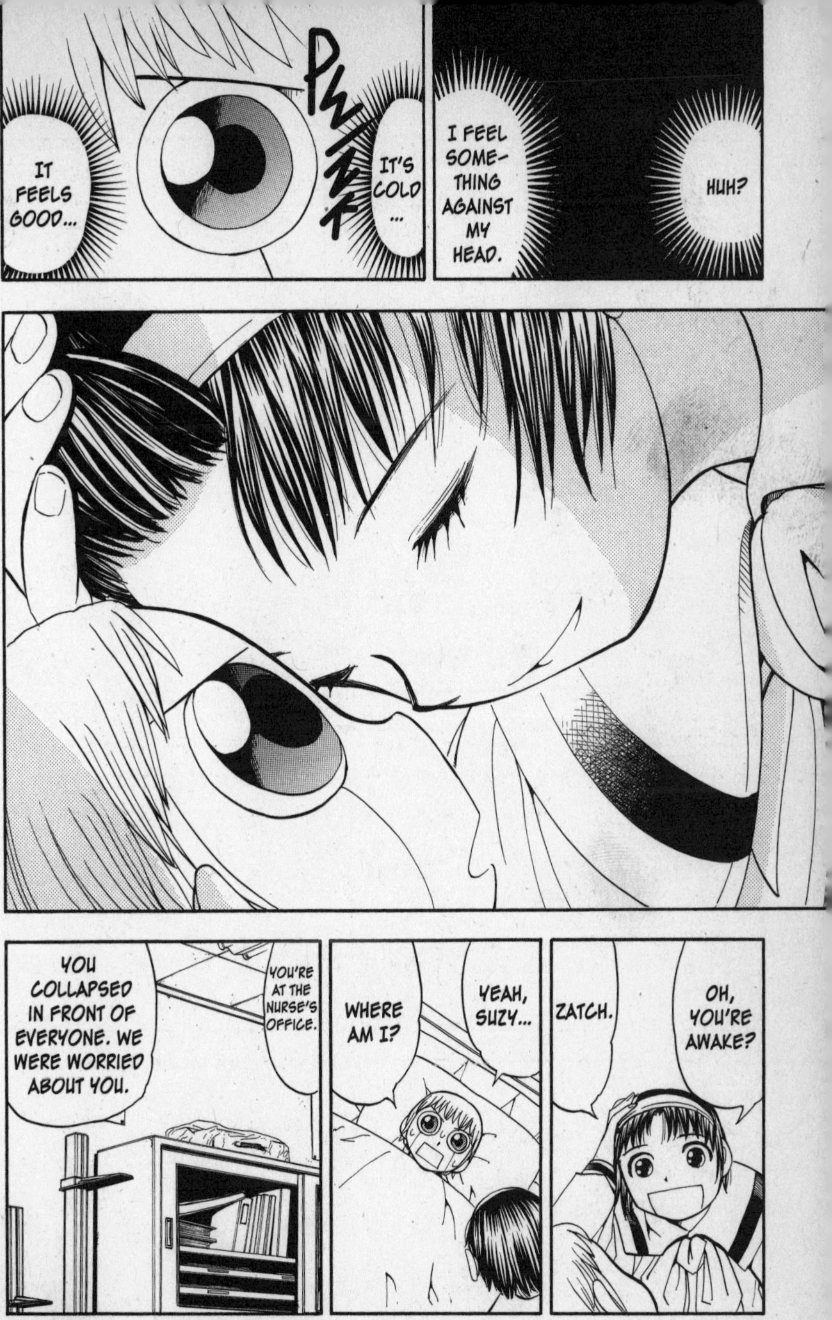
HUH?
I FEEL SOME-THING AGAINST MY HEAD.
IT'S COLD ...
PWINK
IT FEELS GOOD...
OH, YOU'RE AWAKE?
ZATCH.
YEAH, SUZY...
WHERE AM I?
YOU'RE AT THE NURSE'S OFFICE.
YOU COLLAPSED IN FRONT OF EVERYONE. WE WERE WORRIED ABOUT YOU.

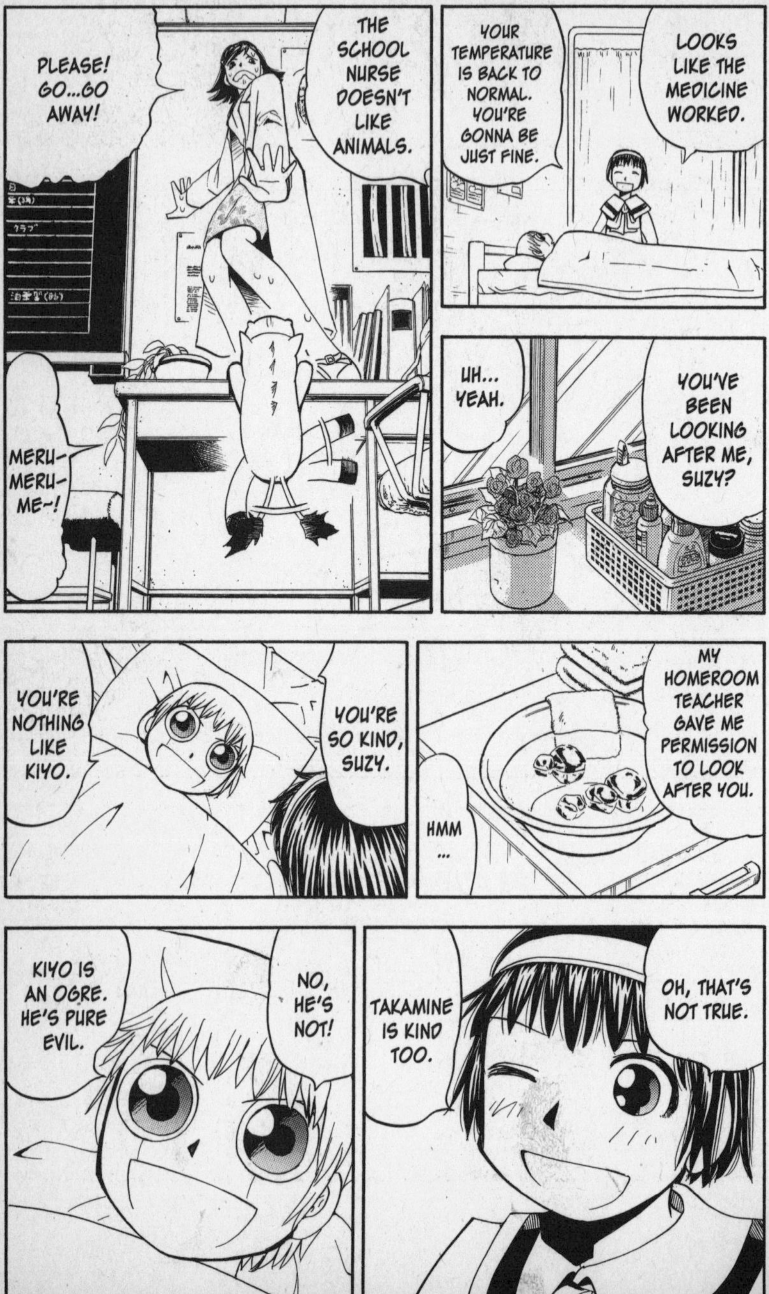
LOOKS LIKE THE MEDICINE WORKED.
YOUR TEMPERATURE IS BACK TO NORMAL. YOU'RE GONNA BE JUST FINE.
YOU'VE BEEN LOOKING AFTER ME, SUZY?
UH... YEAH.
THE SCHOOL NURSE DOESN'T LIKE ANIMALS.
PLEASE! GO...GO AWAY!
MERU-MERU-ME~!
MY HOMEROOM TEACHER GAVE ME PERMISSION TO LOOK AFTER YOU.
HMM...
YOU'RE SO KIND, SUZY.
YOU'RE NOTHING LIKE KIYO.
OH, THAT'S NOT TRUE.
TAKAMINE IS KIND TOO.
NO, HE'S NOT!
KIYO IS AN OGRE. HE'S PURE EVIL.

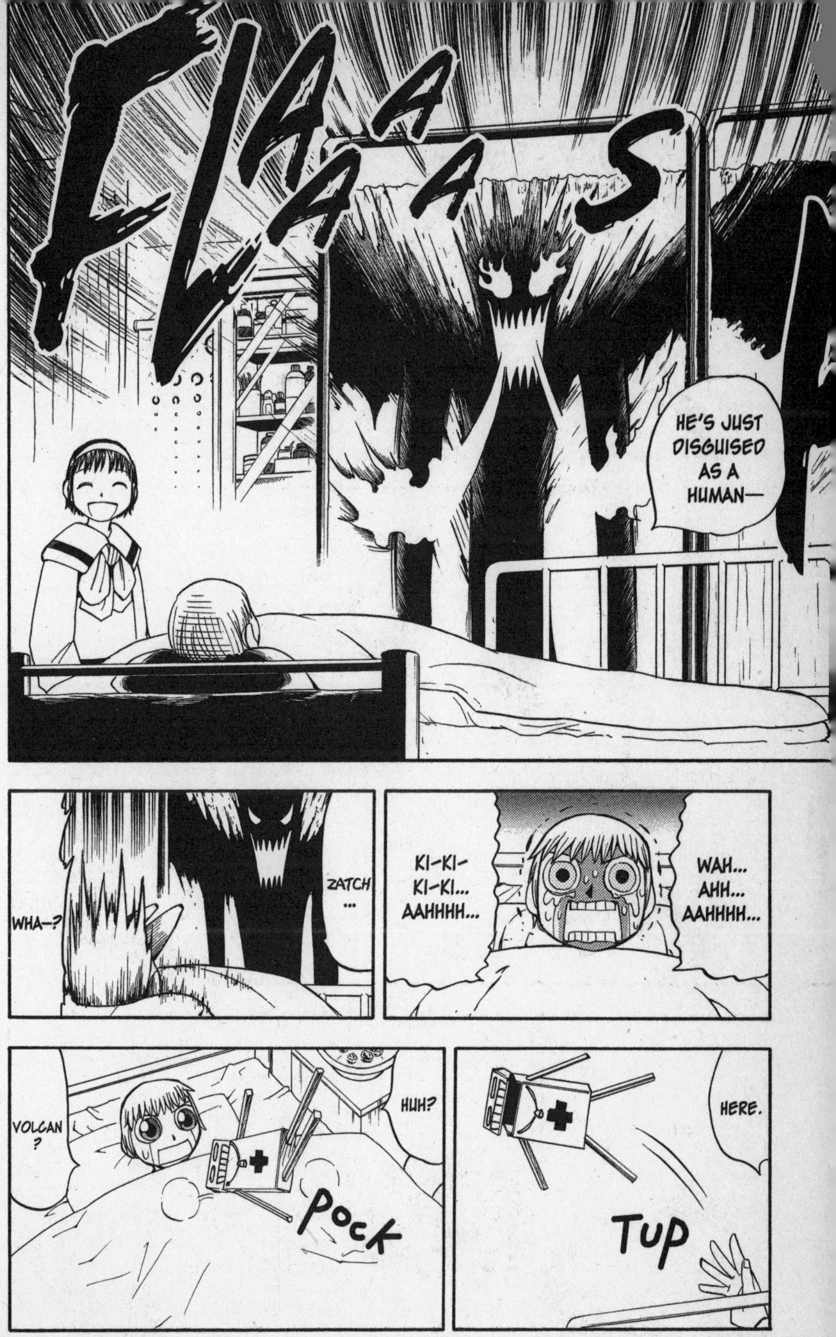
FLAAAAS
HE'S JUST DISGUISED AS A HUMAN—
WAH... AHH... AAHHHH...
KI-KI-KI-KI... AAHHHH...
ZATCH ...
WHA–?
HERE.
TUP
HUH?
VOLCAN ?
POCK

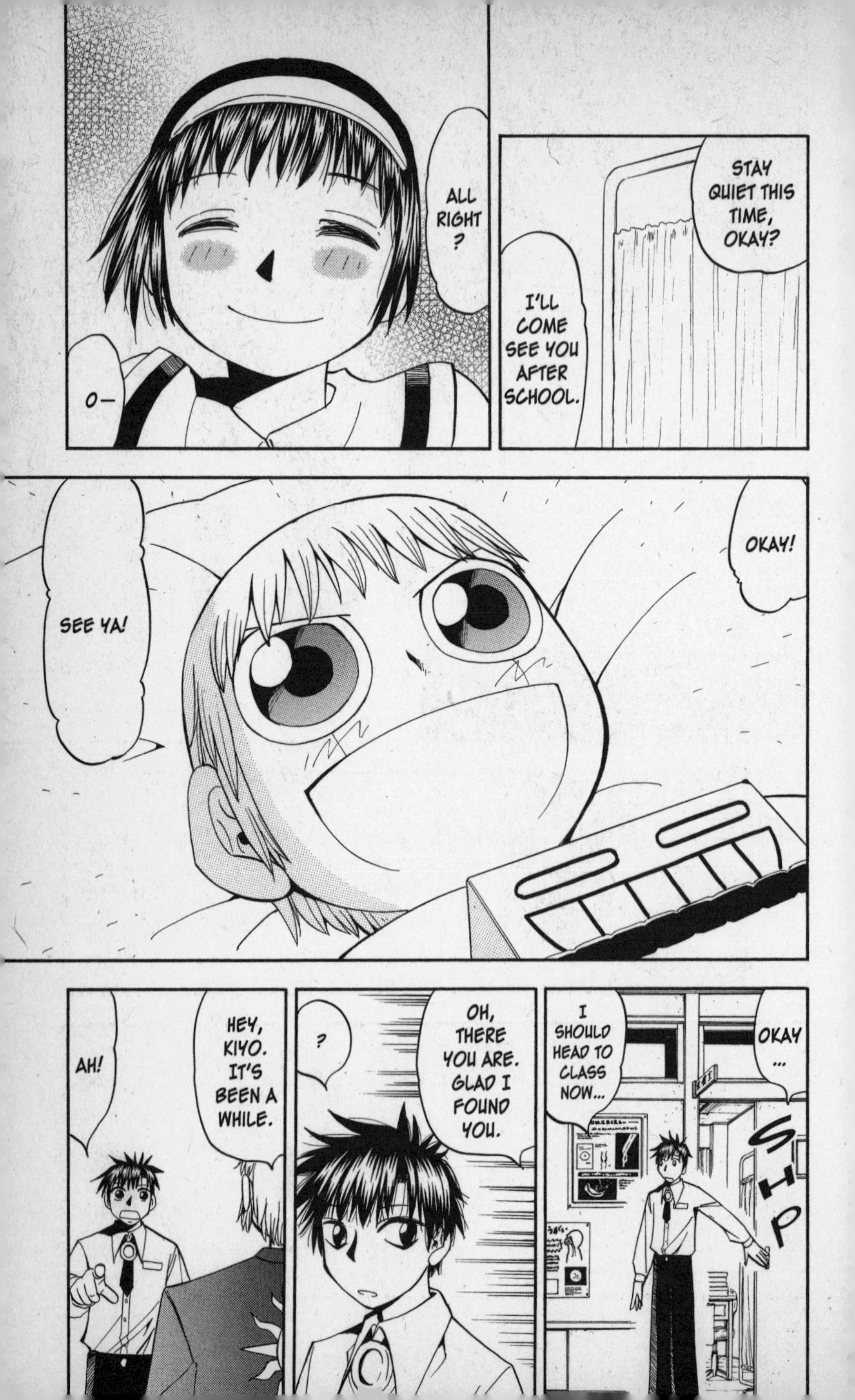
STAY QUIET THIS TIME, OKAY?
I'LL COME SEE YOU AFTER SCHOOL.
ALL RIGHT?
O—
OKAY!
SEE YA!
OKAY...
I SHOULD HEAD TO CLASS NOW...
SHP
OH, THERE YOU ARE. GLAD I FOUND YOU.
?
HEY, KIYO. IT'S BEEN A WHILE.
AH!

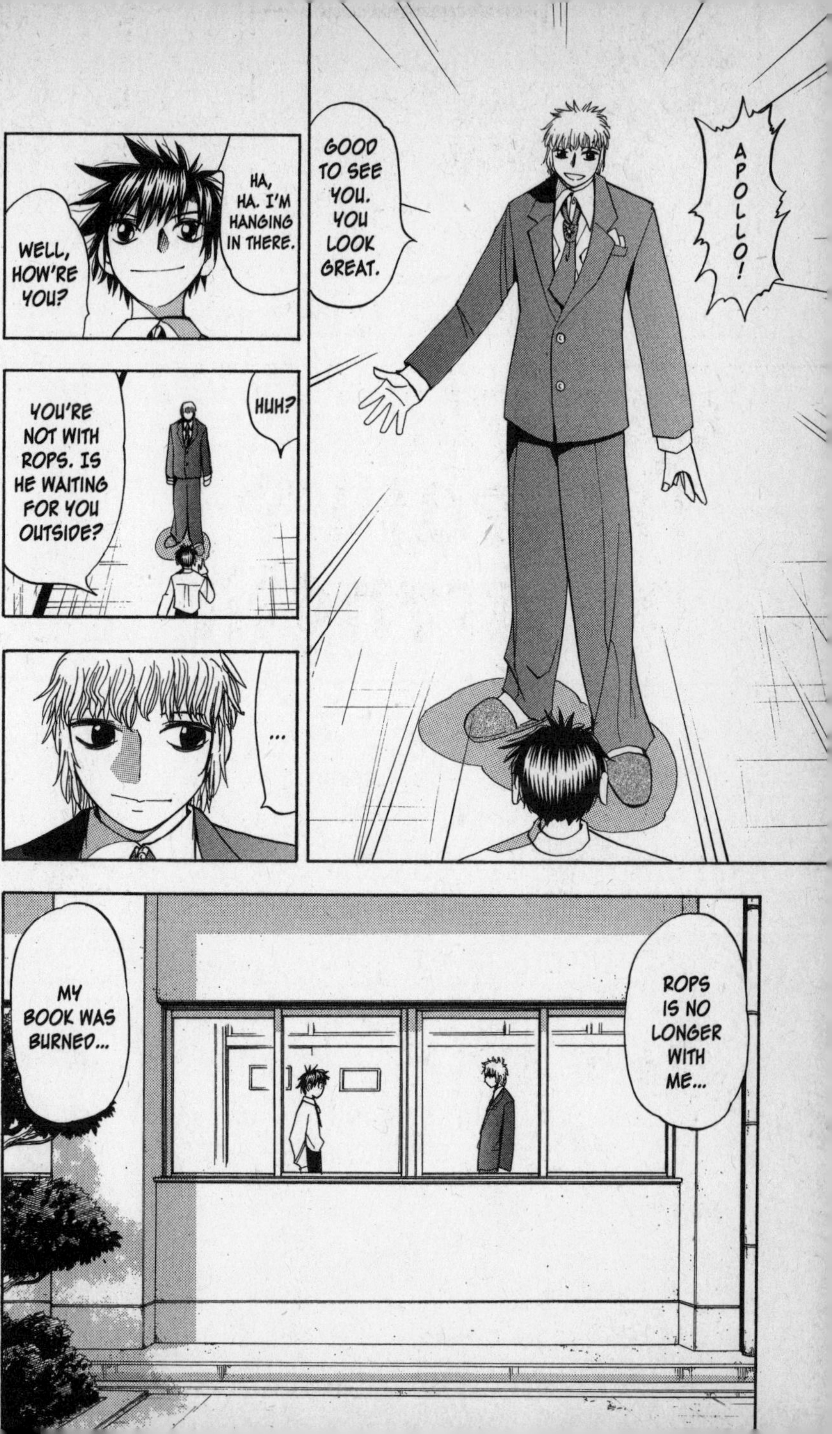
APOLLO!
GOOD TO SEE YOU. YOU LOOK GREAT.
HA, HA. I'M HANGING IN THERE.
WELL, HOW'RE YOU?
HUH?
YOU'RE NOT WITH ROPS. IS HE WAITING FOR YOU OUTSIDE?
...
ROPS IS NO LONGER WITH ME...
MY BOOK WAS BURNED...

LEVEL 76: A Measure of Strength

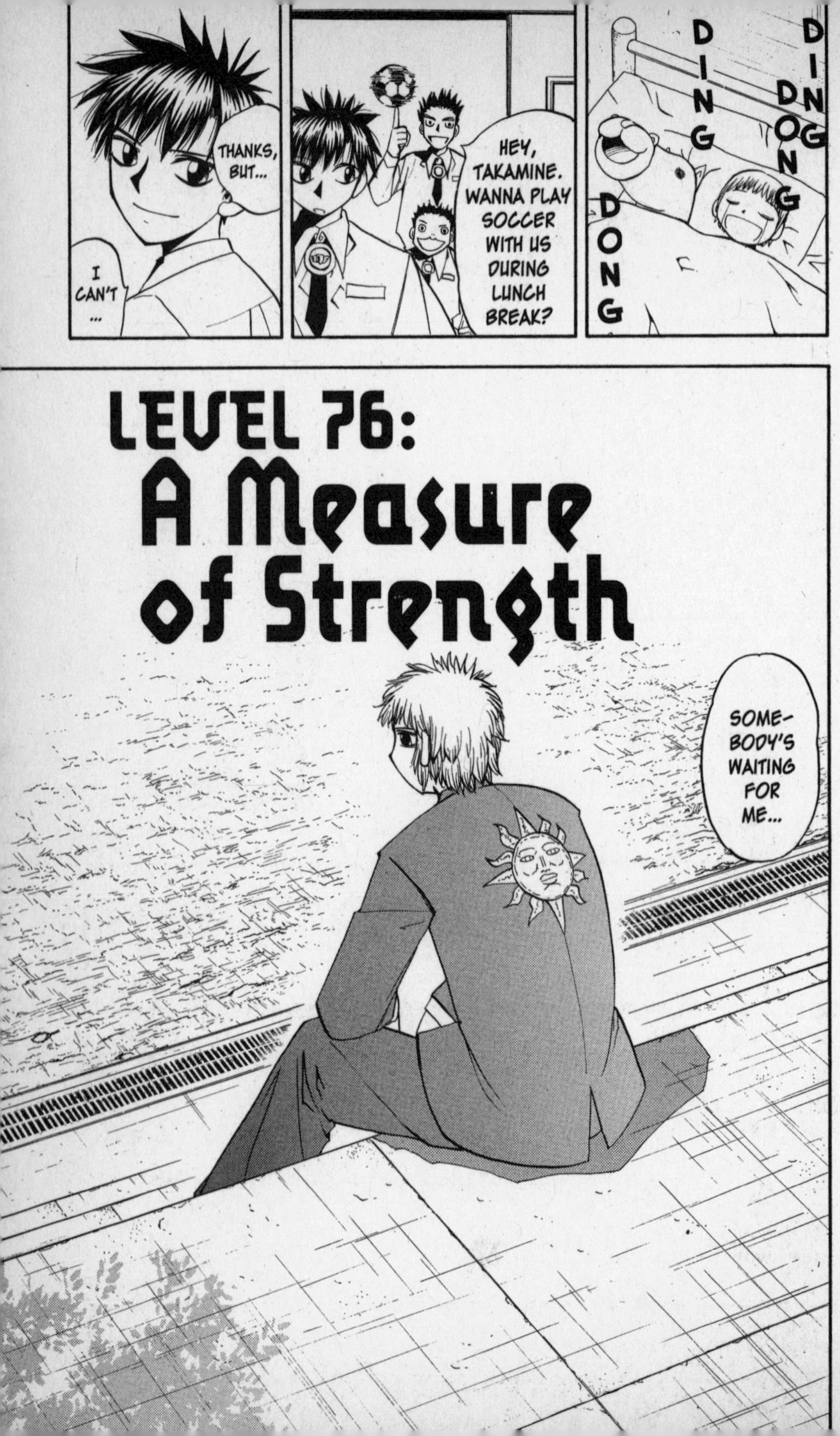
DING DONG
DING DONG
DONG
HEY, TAKAMINE. WANNA PLAY SOCCER WITH US DURING LUNCH BREAK?
THANKS, BUT...
I CAN'T ...
SOME-BODY'S WAITING FOR ME...

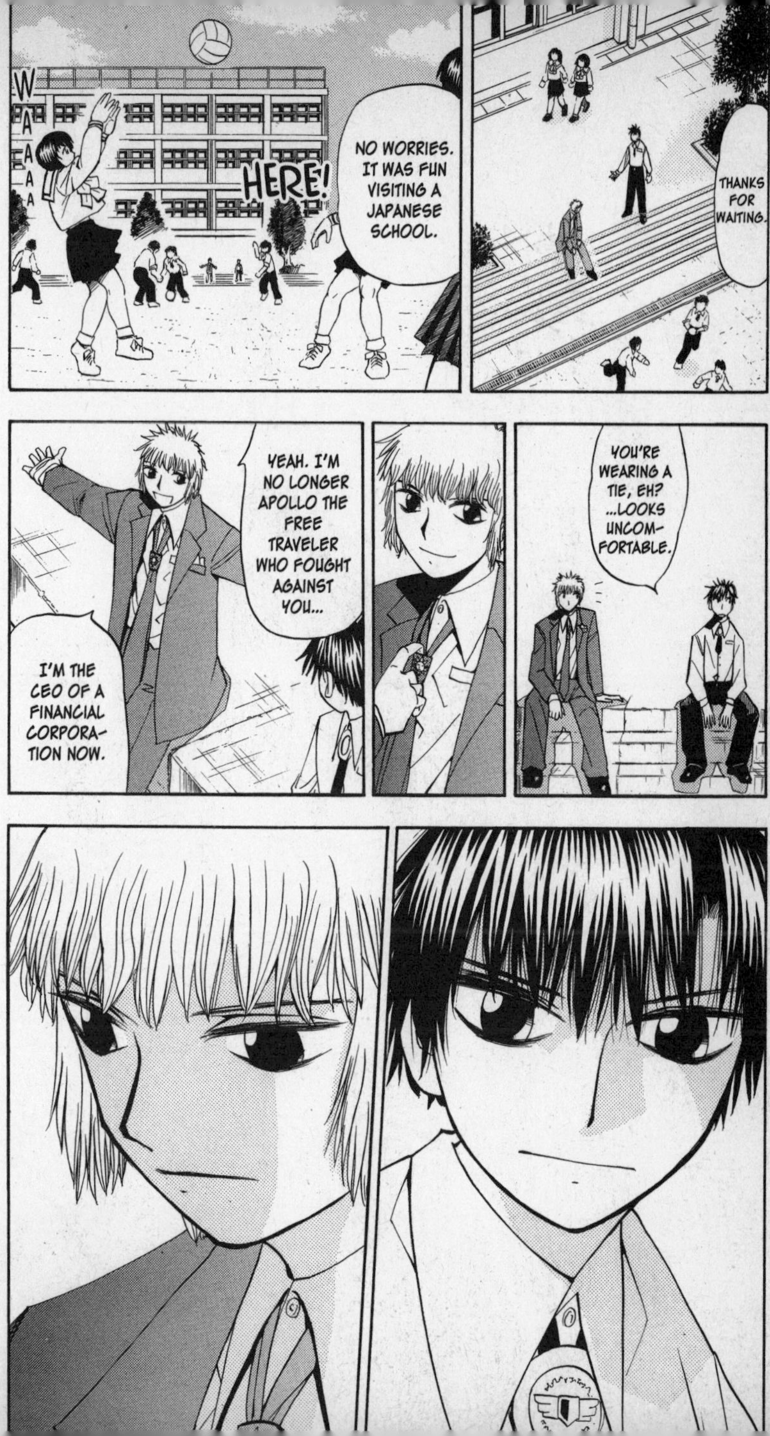
THANKS FOR WAITING.
NO WORRIES. IT WAS FUN VISITING A JAPANESE SCHOOL.
WAAAAA
HERE!
YOU'RE WEARING A TIE, EH? ...LOOKS UNCOM-FORTABLE.
YEAH. I'M NO LONGER APOLLO THE FREE TRAVELER WHO FOUGHT AGAINST YOU...
I'M THE CEO OF A FINANCIAL CORPORA-TION NOW.

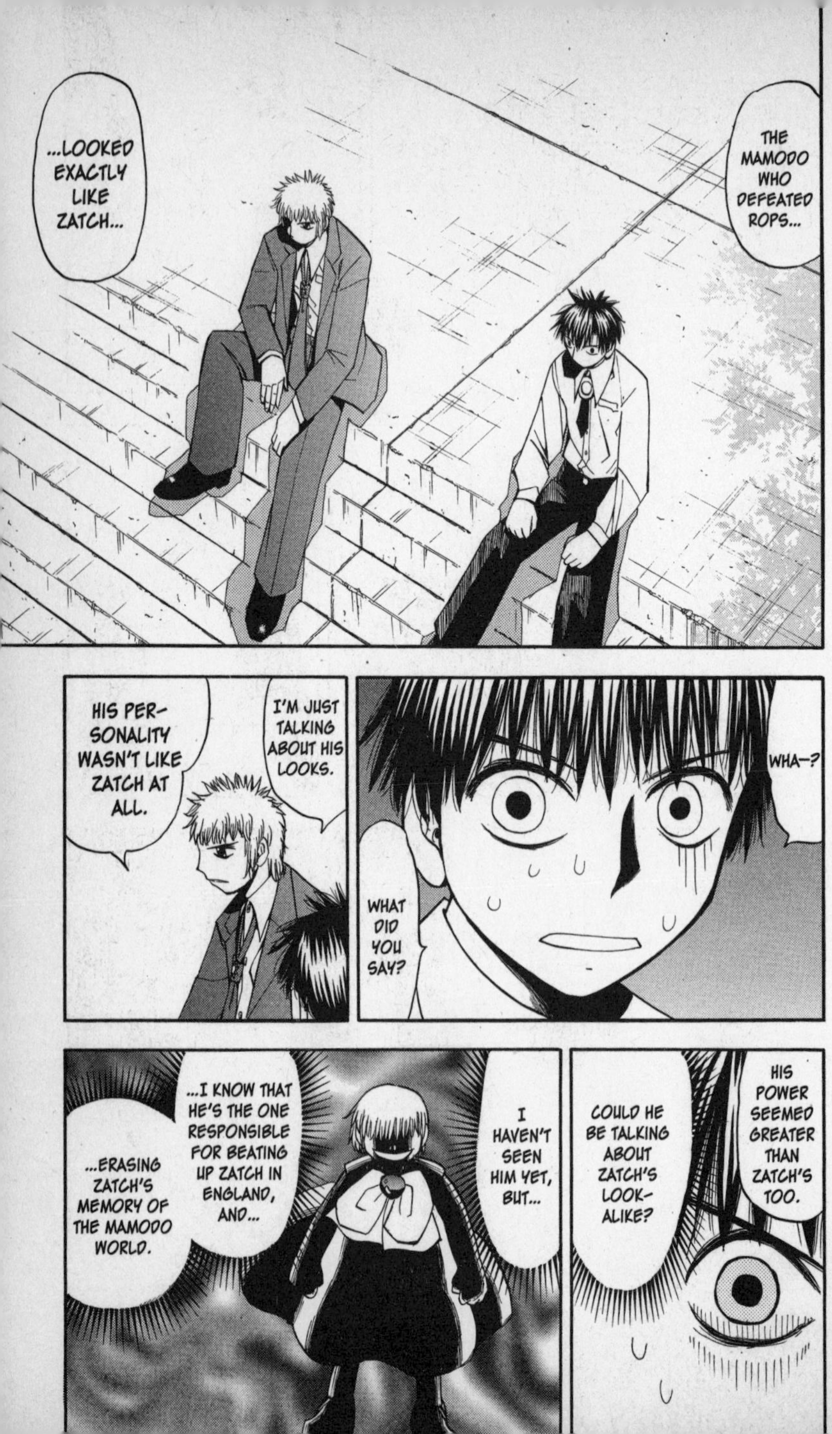
THE MAMODO WHO DEFEATED ROPS...
...LOOKED EXACTLY LIKE ZATCH...
WHA—?
WHAT DID YOU SAY?
I'M JUST TALKING ABOUT HIS LOOKS.
HIS PER-SONALITY WASN'T LIKE ZATCH AT ALL.
HIS POWER SEEMED GREATER THAN ZATCH'S TOO.
COULD HE BE TALKING ABOUT ZATCH'S LOOK-ALIKE?
I HAVEN'T SEEN HIM YET, BUT...
...I KNOW THAT HE'S THE ONE RESPONSIBLE FOR BEATING UP ZATCH IN ENGLAND, AND...
...ERASING ZATCH'S MEMORY OF THE MAMODO WORLD.

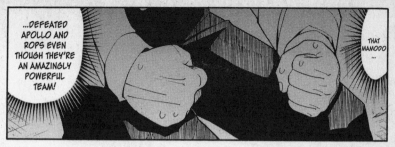

THAT MAMODO...
...DEFEATED APOLLO AND ROPS EVEN THOUGH THEY'RE AN AMAZINGLY POWERFUL TEAM!
UM... UH...
!
...COULD YOU TELL ME MORE ABOUT HIM?
I MET HIM THREE WEEKS AGO...
WE WERE TRAVELING IN HOLLAND.
HEY, ROPS. YOU WANNA GO THAT WAY NOW?
CAU!
CAU!
CAU!
!
CAU!
WHAT'S WRONG, ROPS?
!

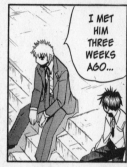

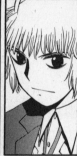

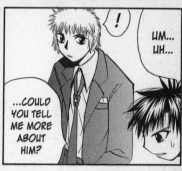

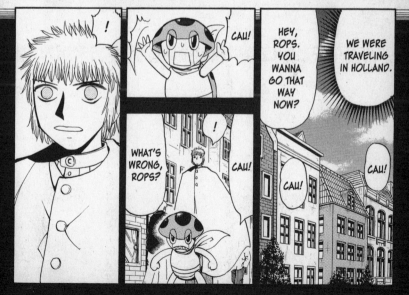

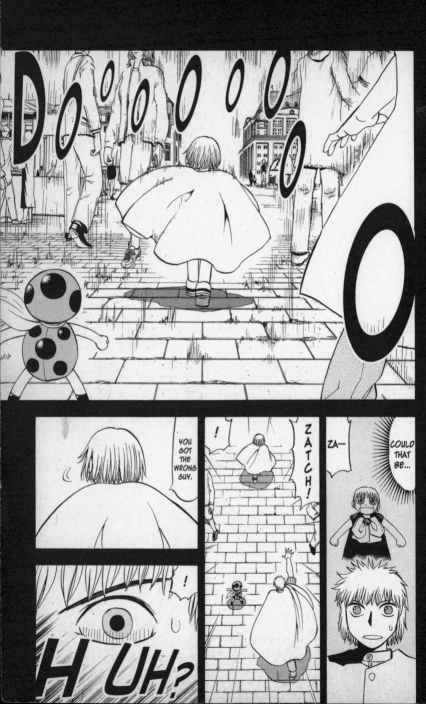

YOU GOT THE WRONG GUY.

!

ZATCH!

ZA—

COULD THAT BE...

H UH?

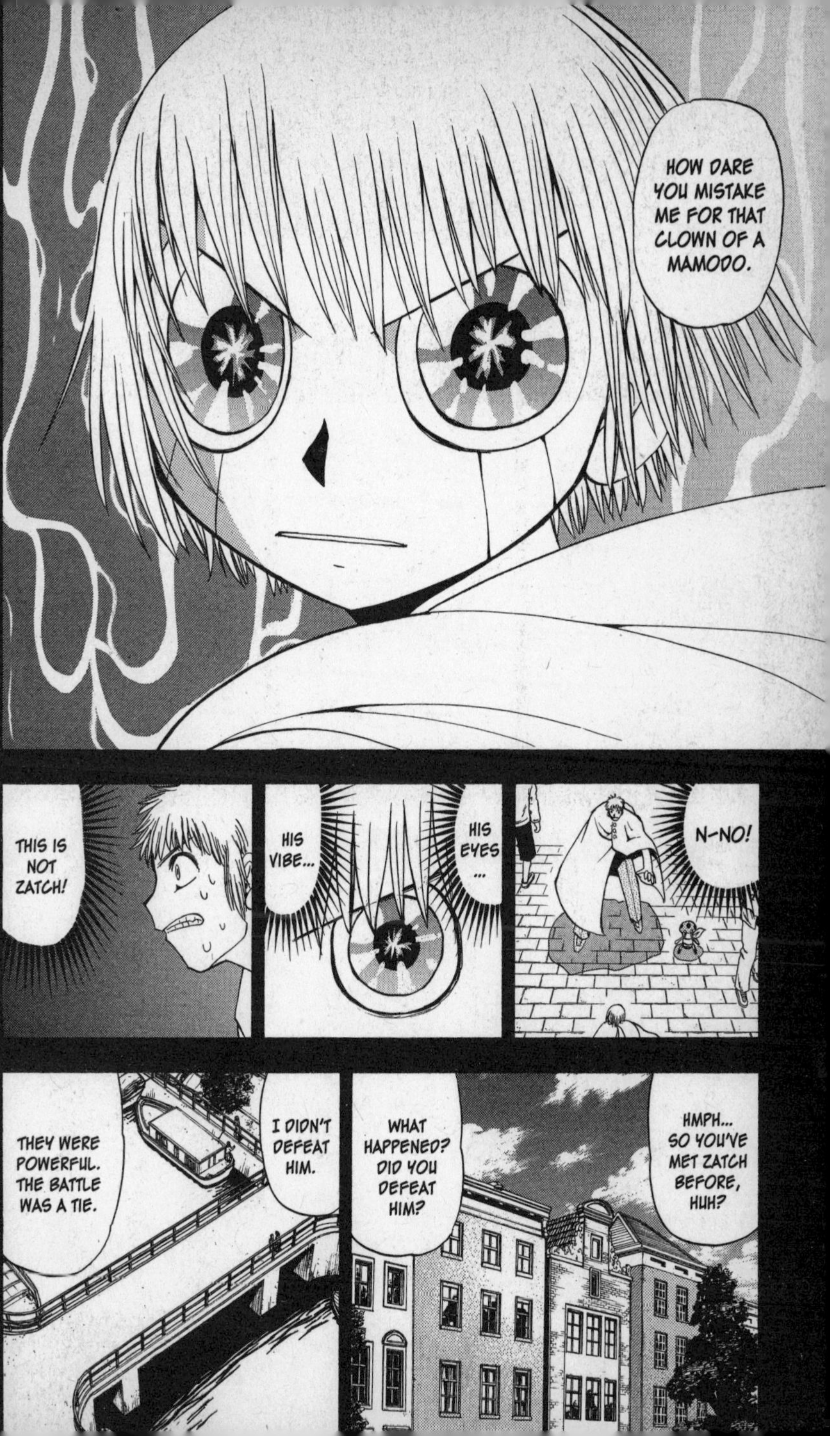
HOW DARE YOU MISTAKE ME FOR THAT CLOWN OF A MAMODO.
N-NO!
HIS EYES ...
HIS VIBE...
THIS IS NOT ZATCH!
HMPH... SO YOU'VE MET ZATCH BEFORE, HUH?
WHAT HAPPENED? DID YOU DEFEAT HIM?
I DIDN'T DEFEAT HIM.
THEY WERE POWERFUL. THE BATTLE WAS A TIE.

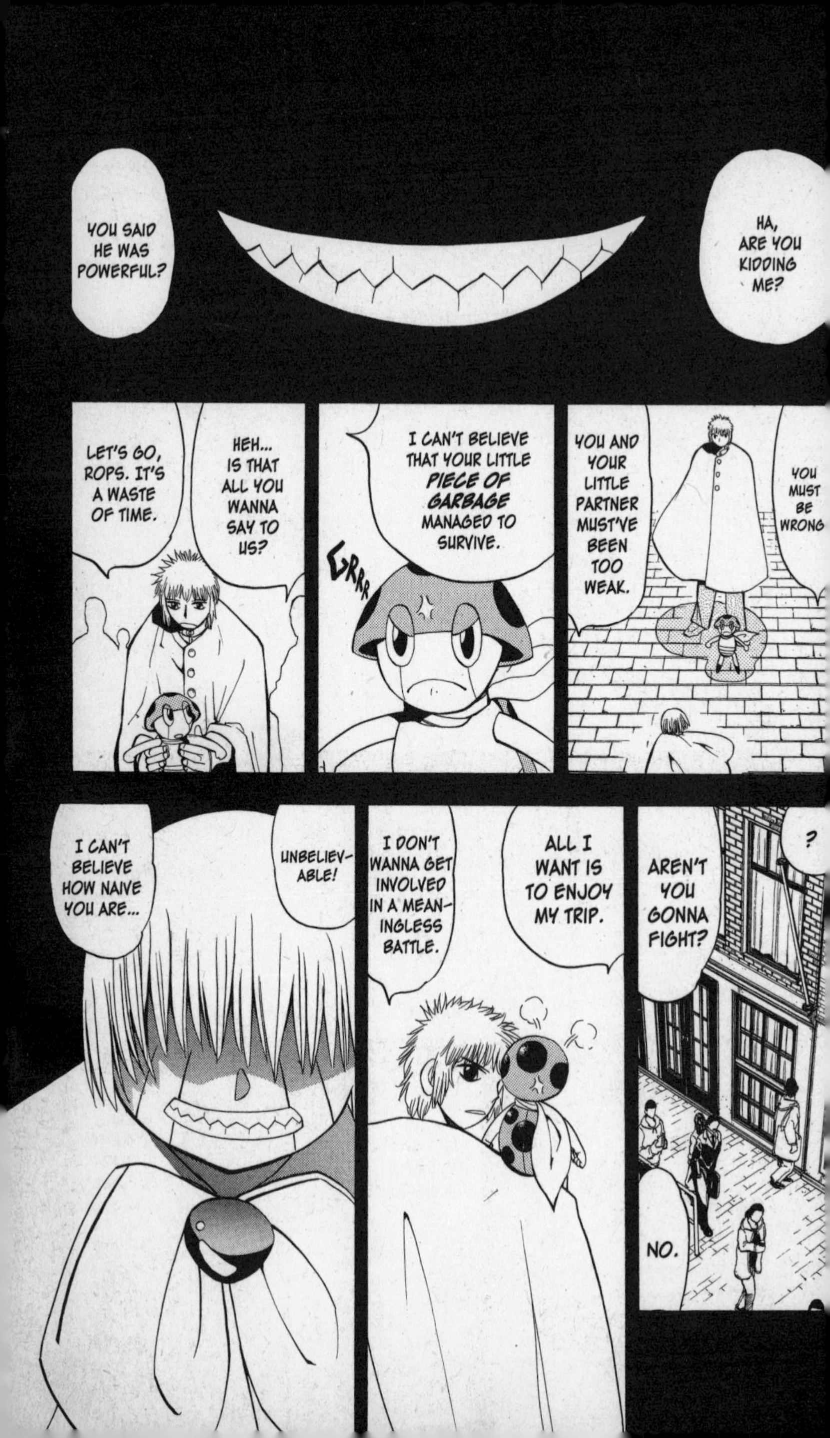
HA, ARE YOU KIDDING ME?
YOU SAID HE WAS POWERFUL?
YOU MUST BE WRONG
YOU AND YOUR LITTLE PARTNER MUST'VE BEEN TOO WEAK.
I CAN'T BELIEVE THAT YOUR LITTLE *PIECE OF GARBAGE* MANAGED TO SURVIVE.
GRRR
HEH... IS THAT ALL YOU WANNA SAY TO US?
LET'S GO, ROPS. IT'S A WASTE OF TIME.
?
AREN'T YOU GONNA FIGHT?
NO.
ALL I WANT IS TO ENJOY MY TRIP.
I DON'T WANNA GET INVOLVED IN A MEAN-INGLESS BATTLE.
UNBELIEV-ABLE!
I CAN'T BELIEVE HOW NAIVE YOU ARE...

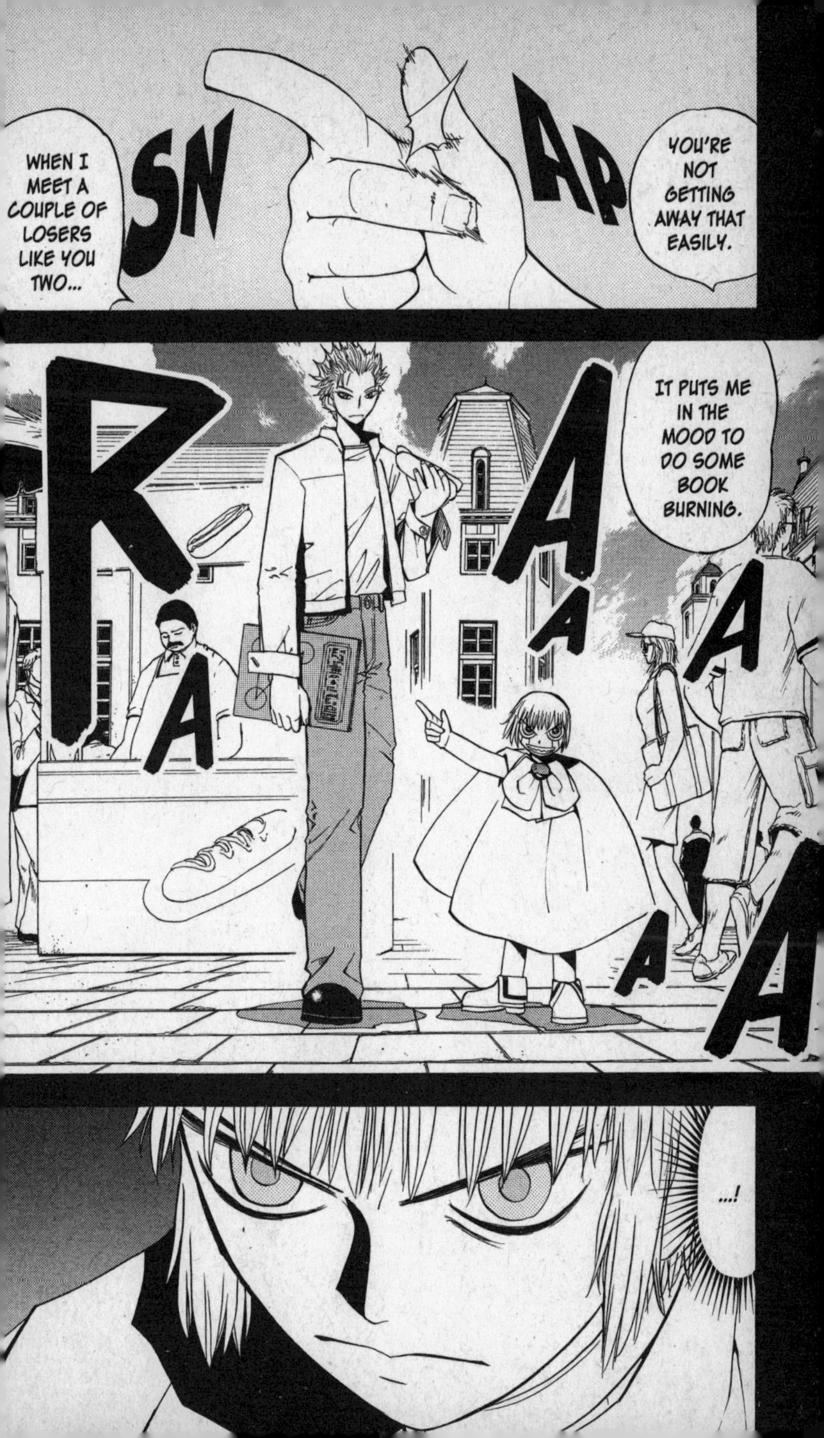
YOU'RE NOT GETTING AWAY THAT EASILY.
SNAP
WHEN I MEET A COUPLE OF LOSERS LIKE YOU TWO...
IT PUTS ME IN THE MOOD TO DO SOME BOOK BURNING.
RAAAAAA
...!

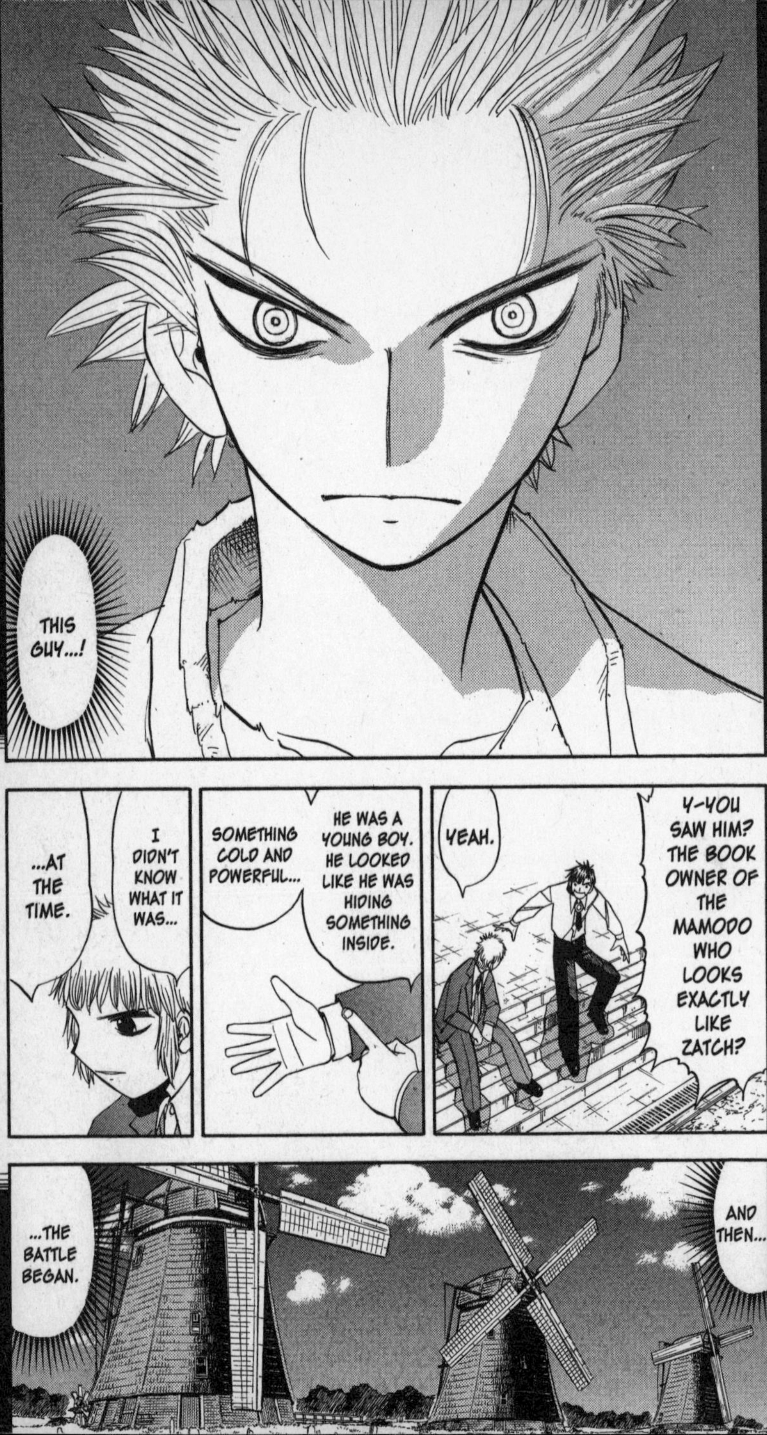
THIS GUY...!
Y-YOU SAW HIM? THE BOOK OWNER OF THE MAMODO WHO LOOKS EXACTLY LIKE ZATCH?
YEAH.
HE WAS A YOUNG BOY. HE LOOKED LIKE HE WAS HIDING SOMETHING INSIDE.
SOMETHING COLD AND POWERFUL...
I DIDN'T KNOW WHAT IT WAS...
...AT THE TIME.
AND THEN...
...THE BATTLE BEGAN.

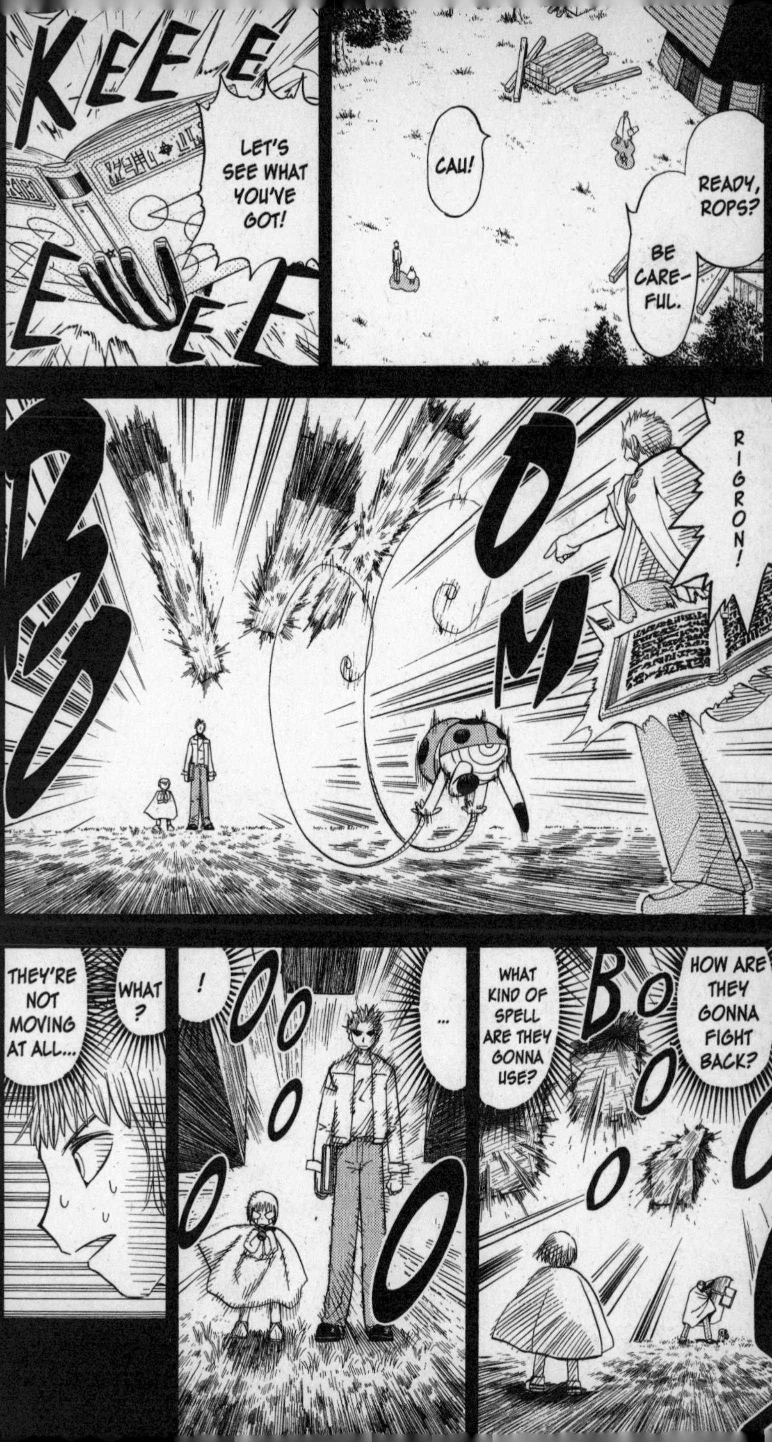
READY, ROPS?
BE CARE-FUL.
GAU!
LET'S SEE WHAT YOU'VE GOT!
RIGRON!
HOW ARE THEY GONNA FIGHT BACK?
WHAT KIND OF SPELL ARE THEY GONNA USE?
...
!
WHAT?
THEY'RE NOT MOVING AT ALL...

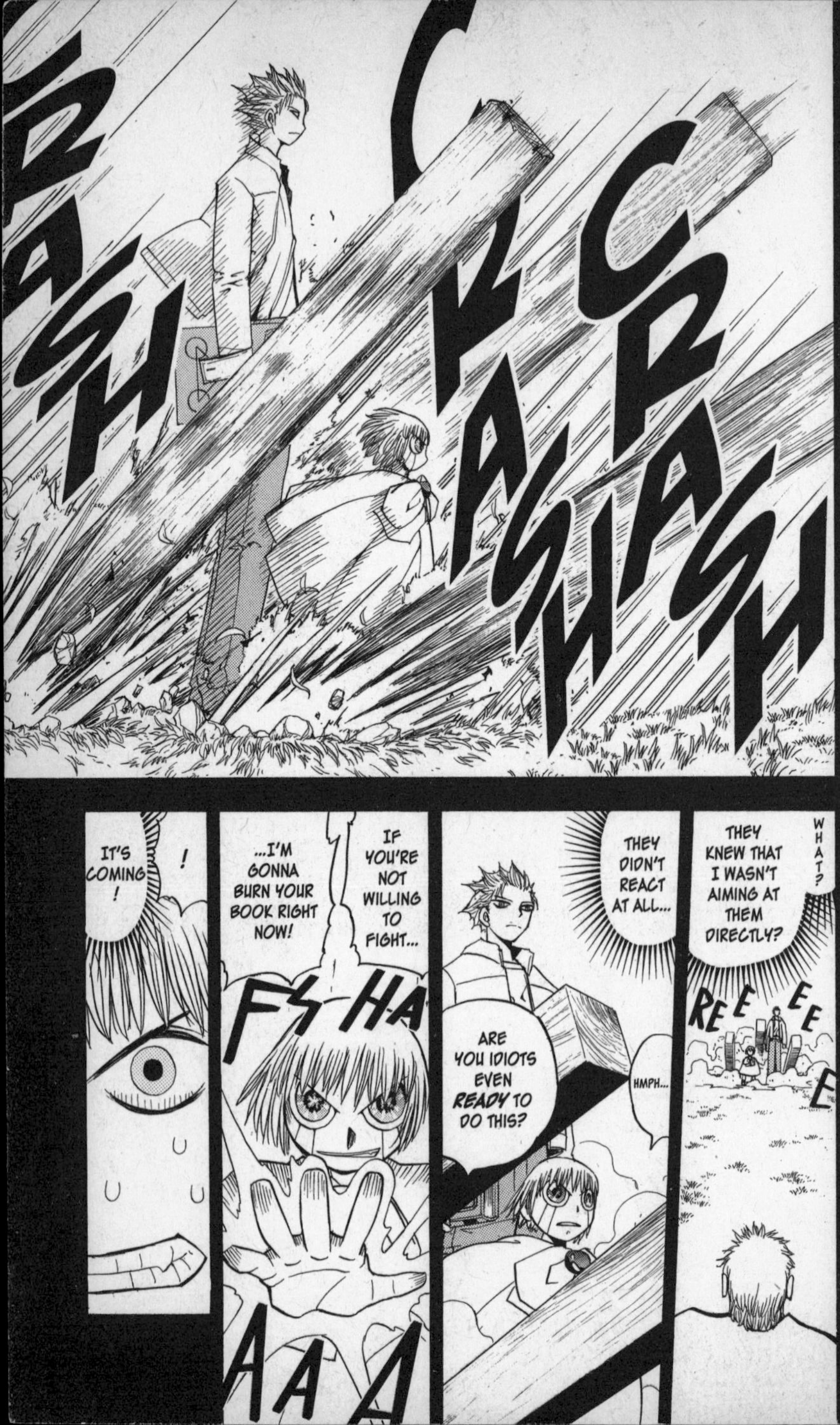

CRASH
CRASH
WHAT?
THEY KNEW THAT I WASN'T AIMING AT THEM DIRECTLY?
REEEEE
THEY DIDN'T REACT AT ALL...
HMPH...
ARE YOU IDIOTS EVEN *READY* TO DO THIS?
IF YOU'RE NOT WILLING TO FIGHT...
...I'M GONNA BURN YOUR BOOK RIGHT NOW!
FSHA-AAA
!
IT'S COMING!

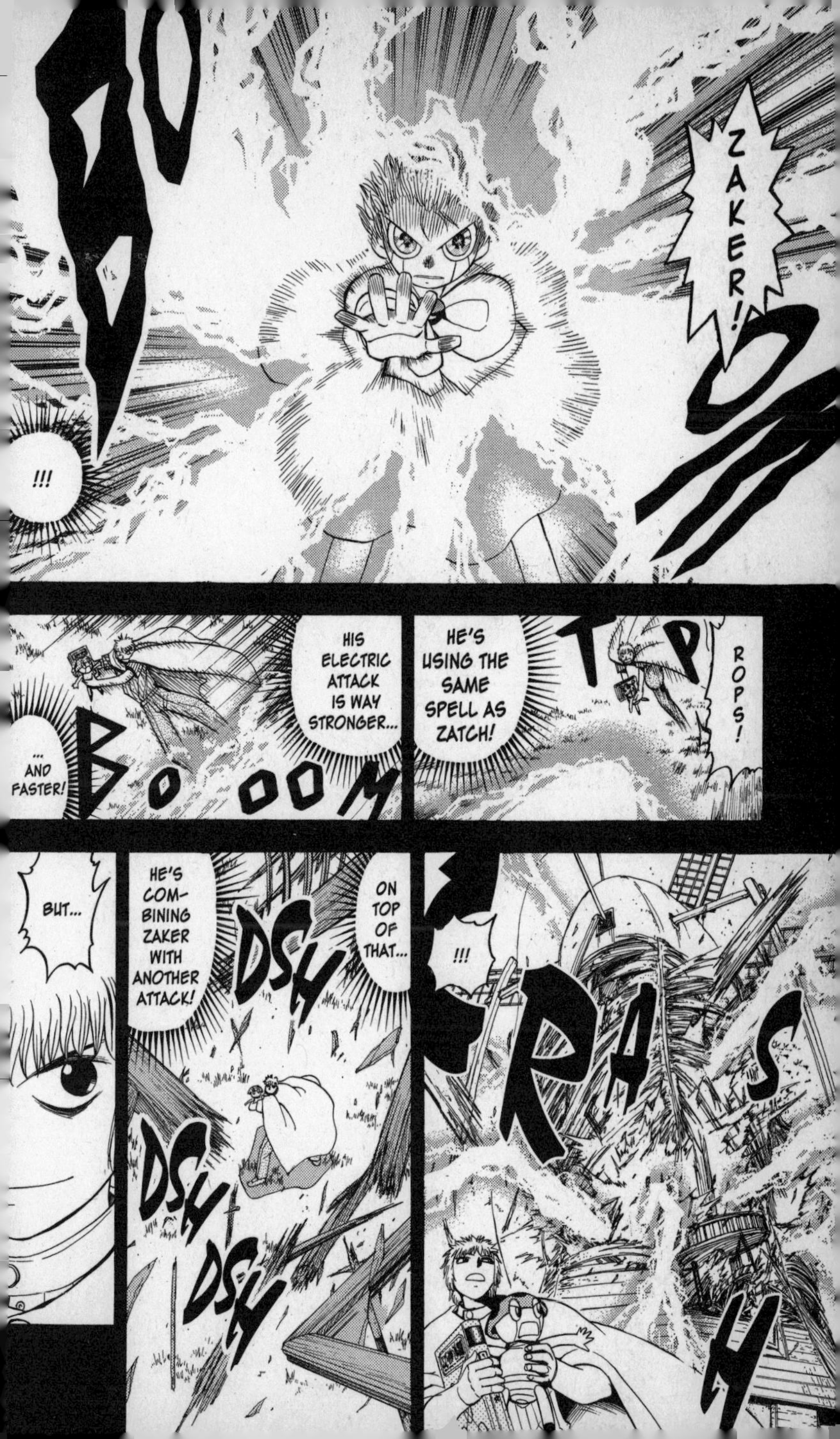
ZAKER!
!!!
ROPS!
HE'S USING THE SAME SPELL AS ZATCH!
HIS ELECTRIC ATTACK IS WAY STRONGER...
... AND FASTER!
BOOOM
!!!
ON TOP OF THAT...
DSH
HE'S COM-BINING ZAKER WITH ANOTHER ATTACK!
DSH
DSH
BUT...

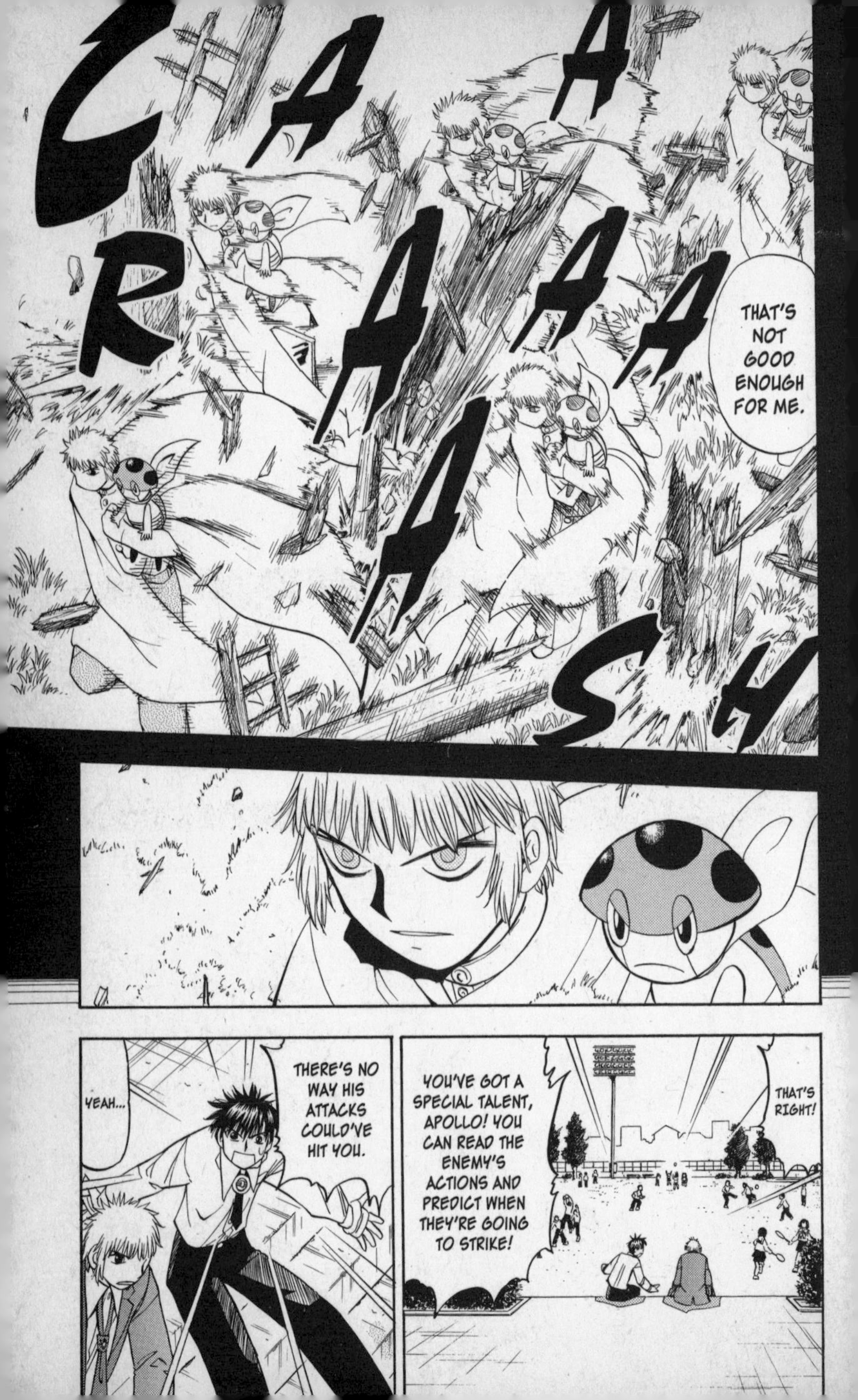
THAT'S NOT GOOD ENOUGH FOR ME.
THAT'S RIGHT!
YOU'VE GOT A SPECIAL TALENT, APOLLO! YOU CAN READ THE ENEMY'S ACTIONS AND PREDICT WHEN THEY'RE GOING TO STRIKE!
THERE'S NO WAY HIS ATTACKS COULD'VE HIT YOU.
YEAH...

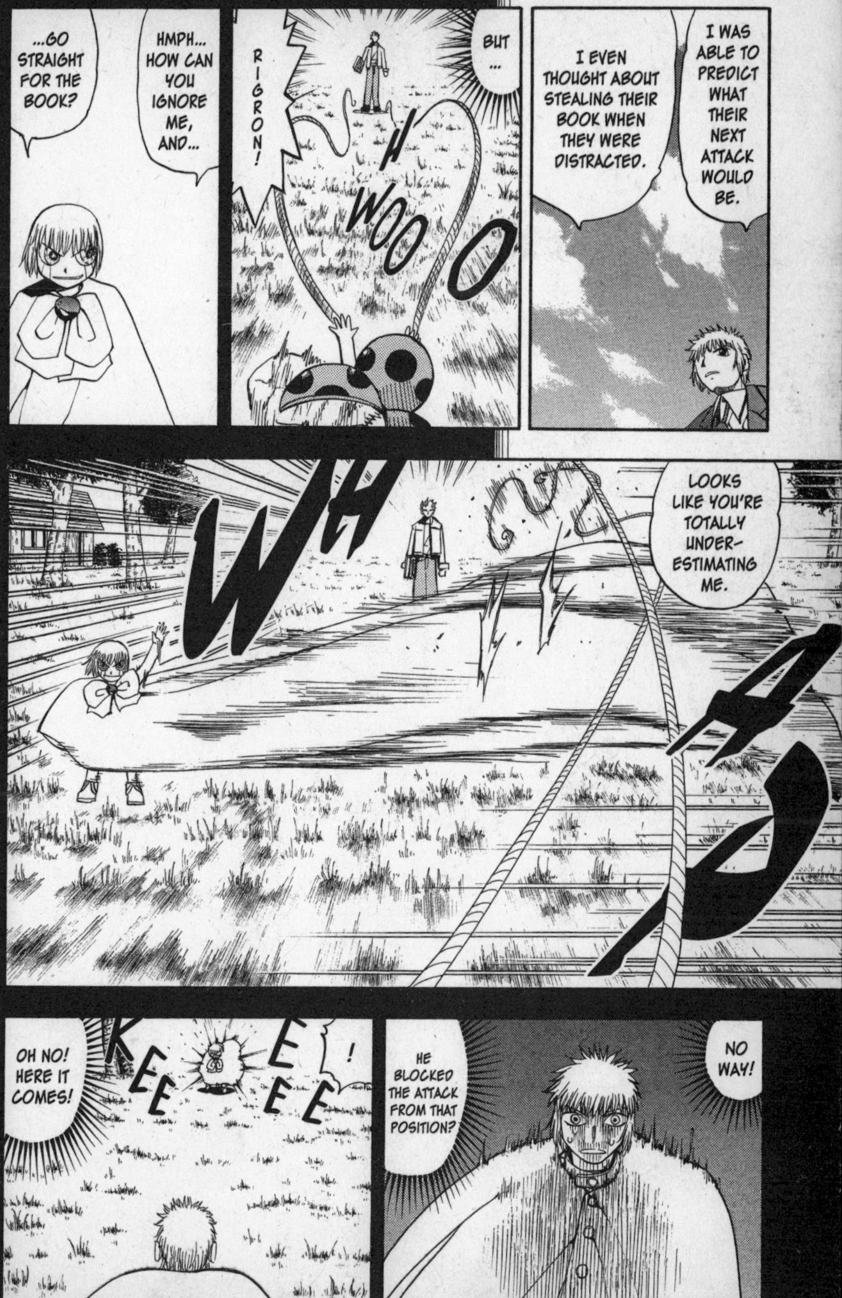
I WAS ABLE TO PREDICT WHAT THEIR NEXT ATTACK WOULD BE.
I EVEN THOUGHT ABOUT STEALING THEIR BOOK WHEN THEY WERE DISTRACTED.
BUT ...
RIGRON!
WHOOO
HMPH... HOW CAN YOU IGNORE ME, AND...
...GO STRAIGHT FOR THE BOOK?
LOOKS LIKE YOU'RE TOTALLY UNDER-ESTIMATING ME.
WHA
NO WAY!
HE BLOCKED THE ATTACK FROM THAT POSITION?
OH NO! HERE IT COMES!
KEEEEE!

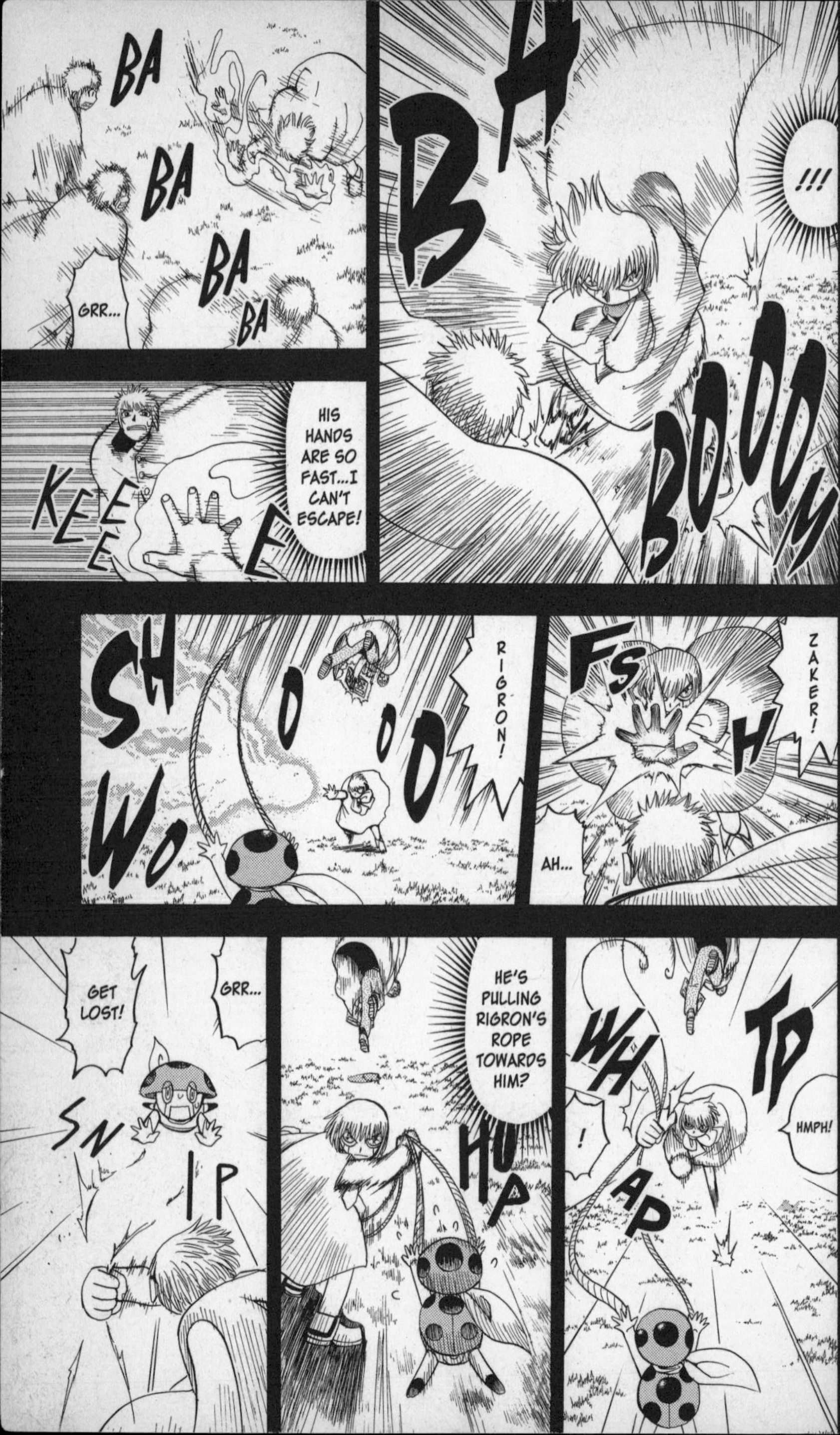
!!!
BAH
BOOOM
BA BA BA BA
GRR...
HIS HANDS ARE SO FAST...I CAN'T ESCAPE!
KEEEE
ZAKER!
FSSH
AH...
RIGRON!
SHWOOOD
HMPH!
TD
!
WHAP
HE'S PULLING RIGRON'S ROPE TOWARDS HIM?
HUP
GRR...
GET LOST!
SNIP

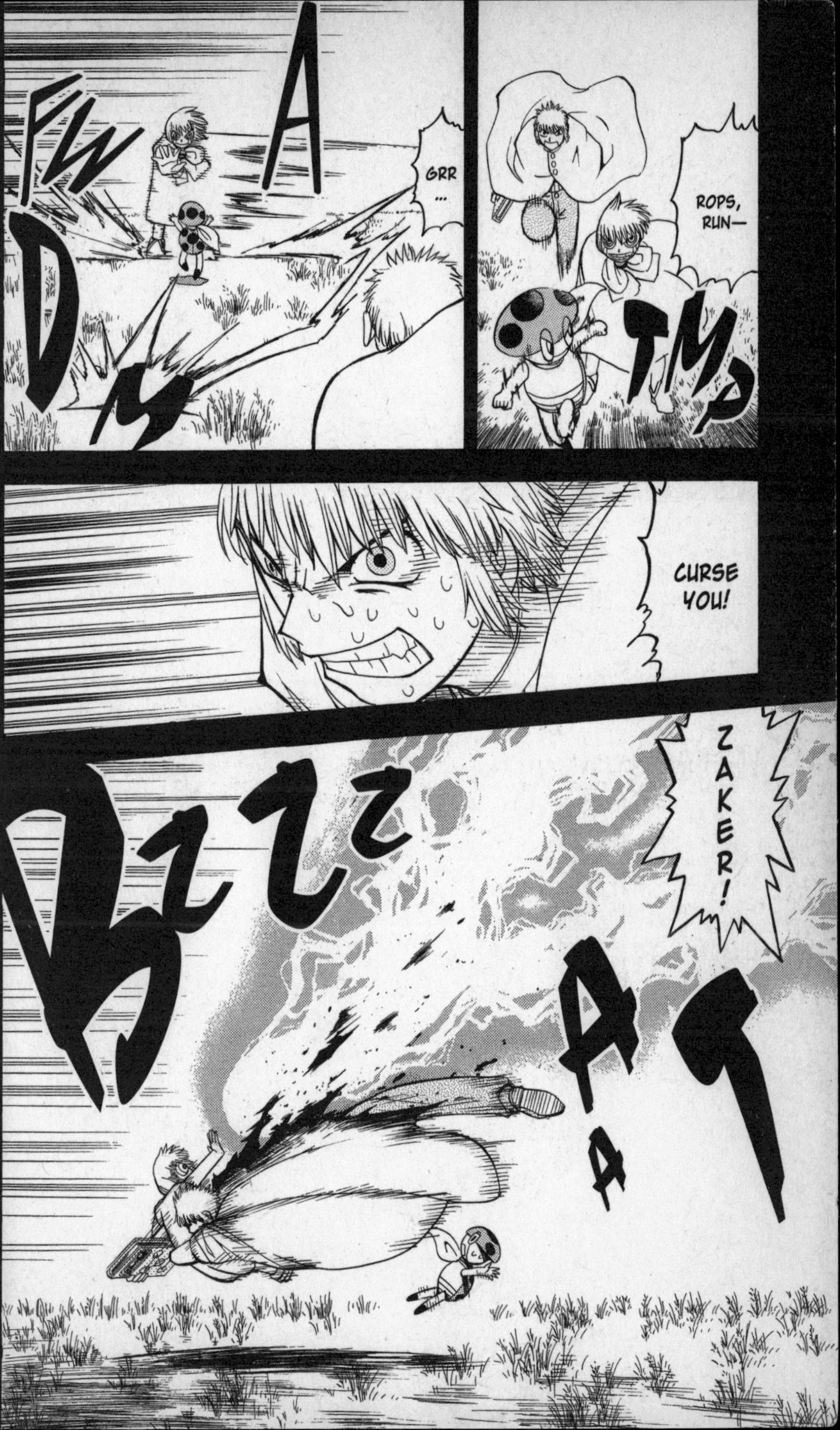
ROPS, RUN—
TMP
GRR ...
FWA
CURSE YOU!
ZAKER!

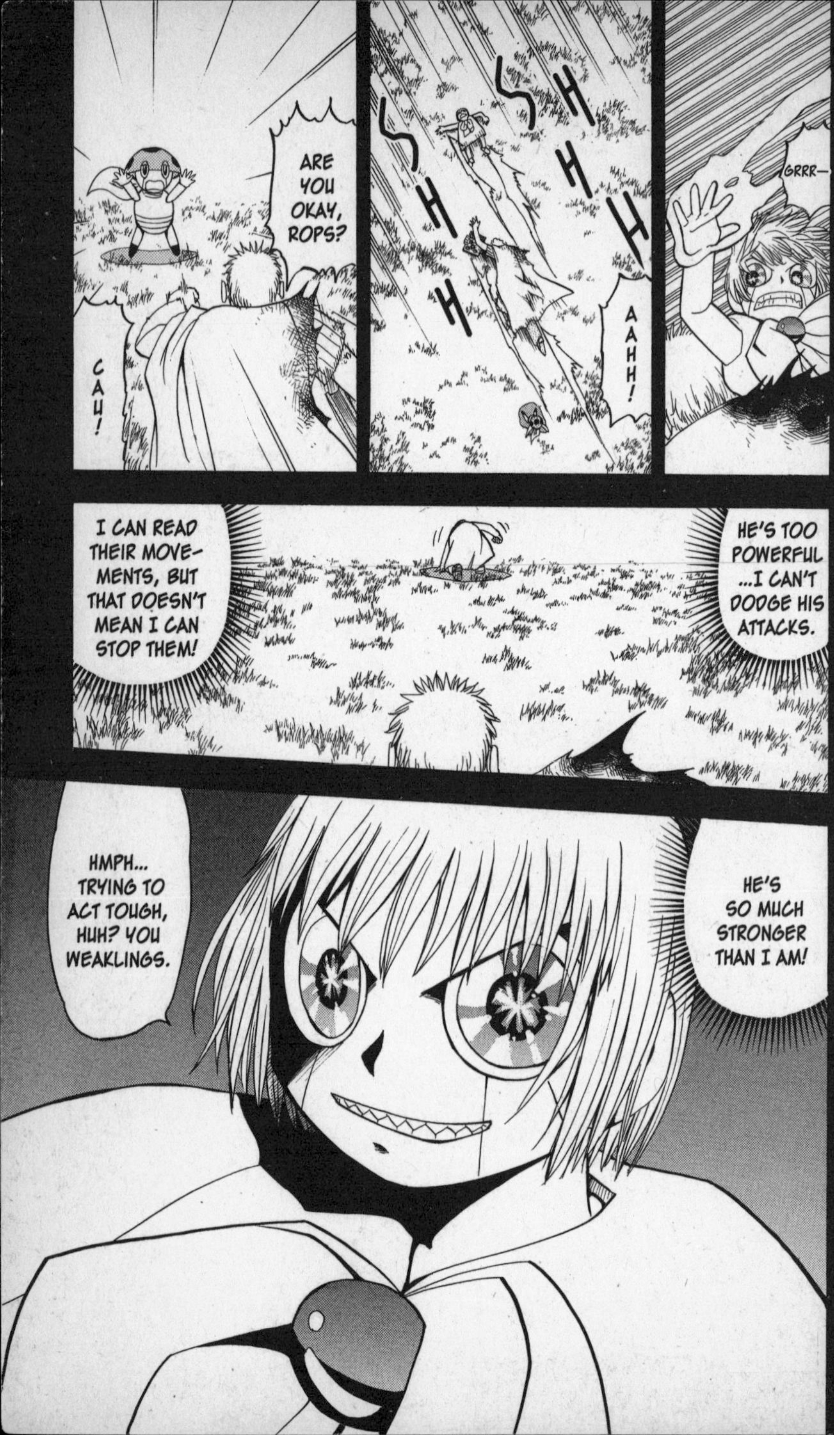
GRRR—
SHHH
SHH
AAHH!
ARE YOU OKAY, ROPS?
CAU!
HE'S TOO POWERFUL ...I CAN'T DODGE HIS ATTACKS.
I CAN READ THEIR MOVEMENTS, BUT THAT DOESN'T MEAN I CAN STOP THEM!
HE'S SO MUCH STRONGER THAN I AM!
HMPH... TRYING TO ACT TOUGH, HUH? YOU WEAKLINGS.

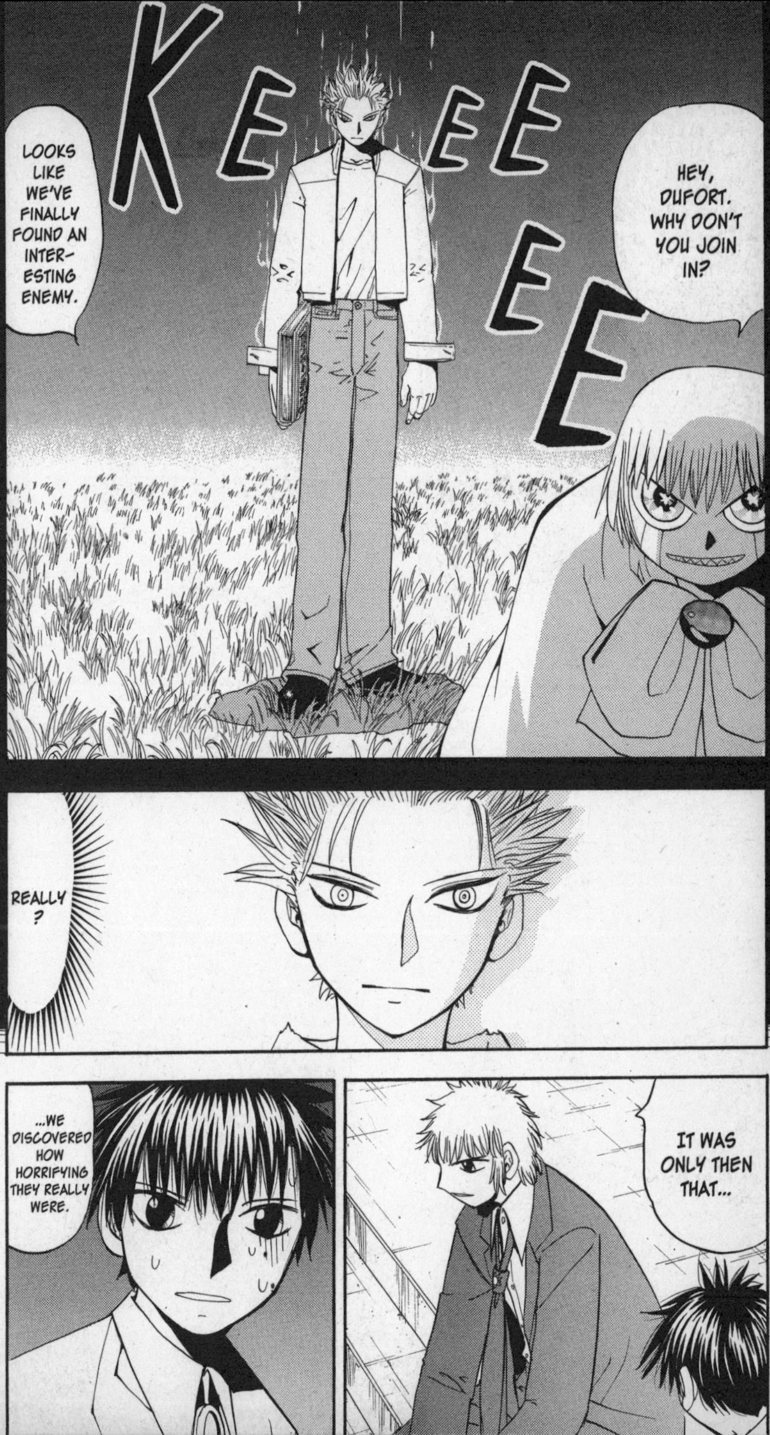
HEY, DUFORT. WHY DON'T YOU JOIN IN?
KEEEEE
LOOKS LIKE WE'VE FINALLY FOUND AN INTER-ESTING ENEMY.
REALLY?
IT WAS ONLY THEN THAT...
...WE DISCOVERED HOW HORRIFYING THEY REALLY WERE.

LEVEL 77:
Fearless Heart

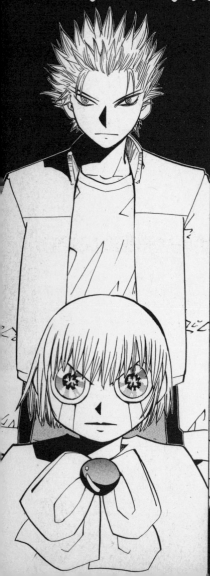
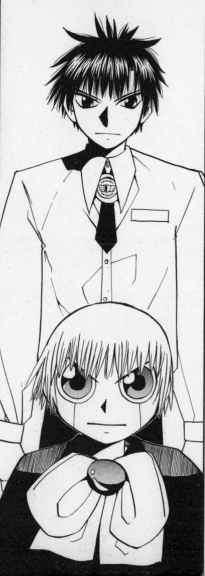

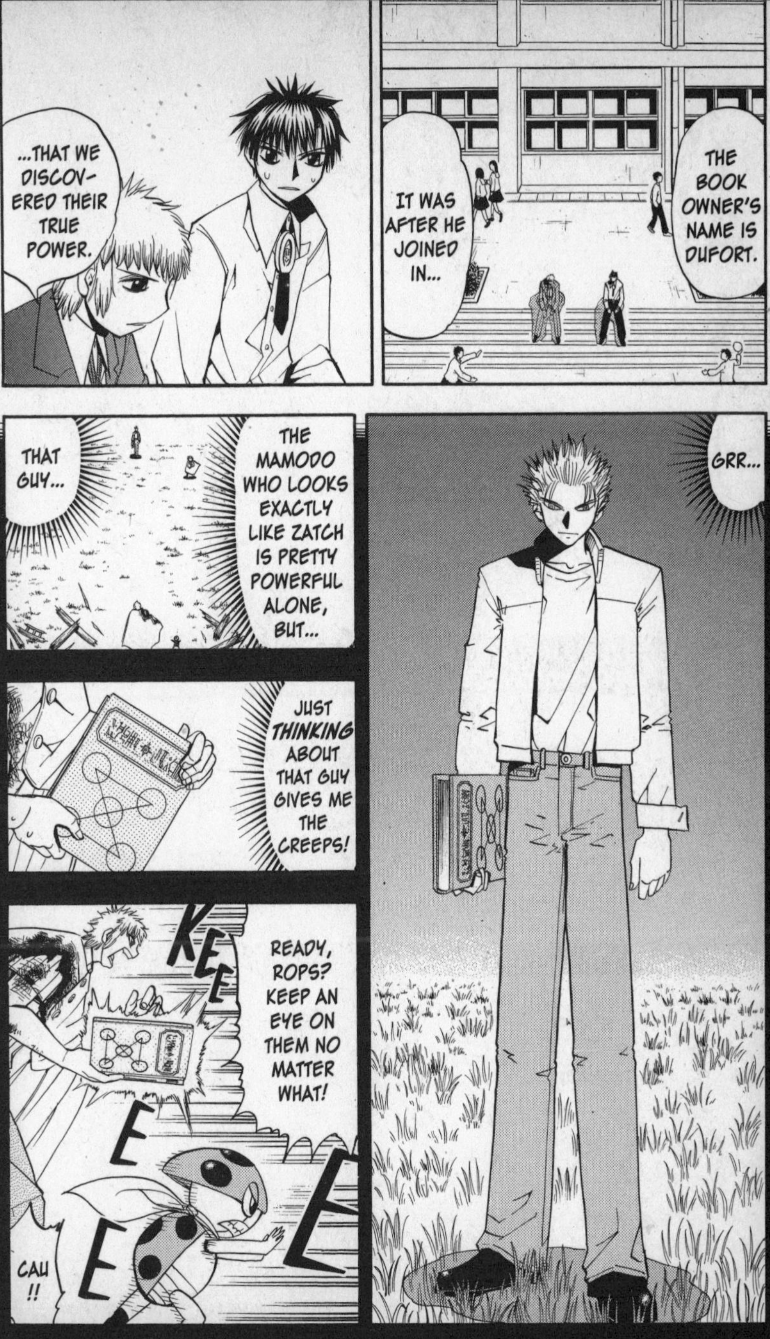
THE BOOK OWNER'S NAME IS DUFORT.
IT WAS AFTER HE JOINED IN...
...THAT WE DISCOVERED THEIR TRUE POWER.
GRR...
THE MAMODO WHO LOOKS EXACTLY LIKE ZATCH IS PRETTY POWERFUL ALONE, BUT...
THAT GUY...
JUST *THINKING* ABOUT THAT GUY GIVES ME THE CREEPS!
KEEEEE
READY, ROPS? KEEP AN EYE ON THEM NO MATTER WHAT!
CAU!!

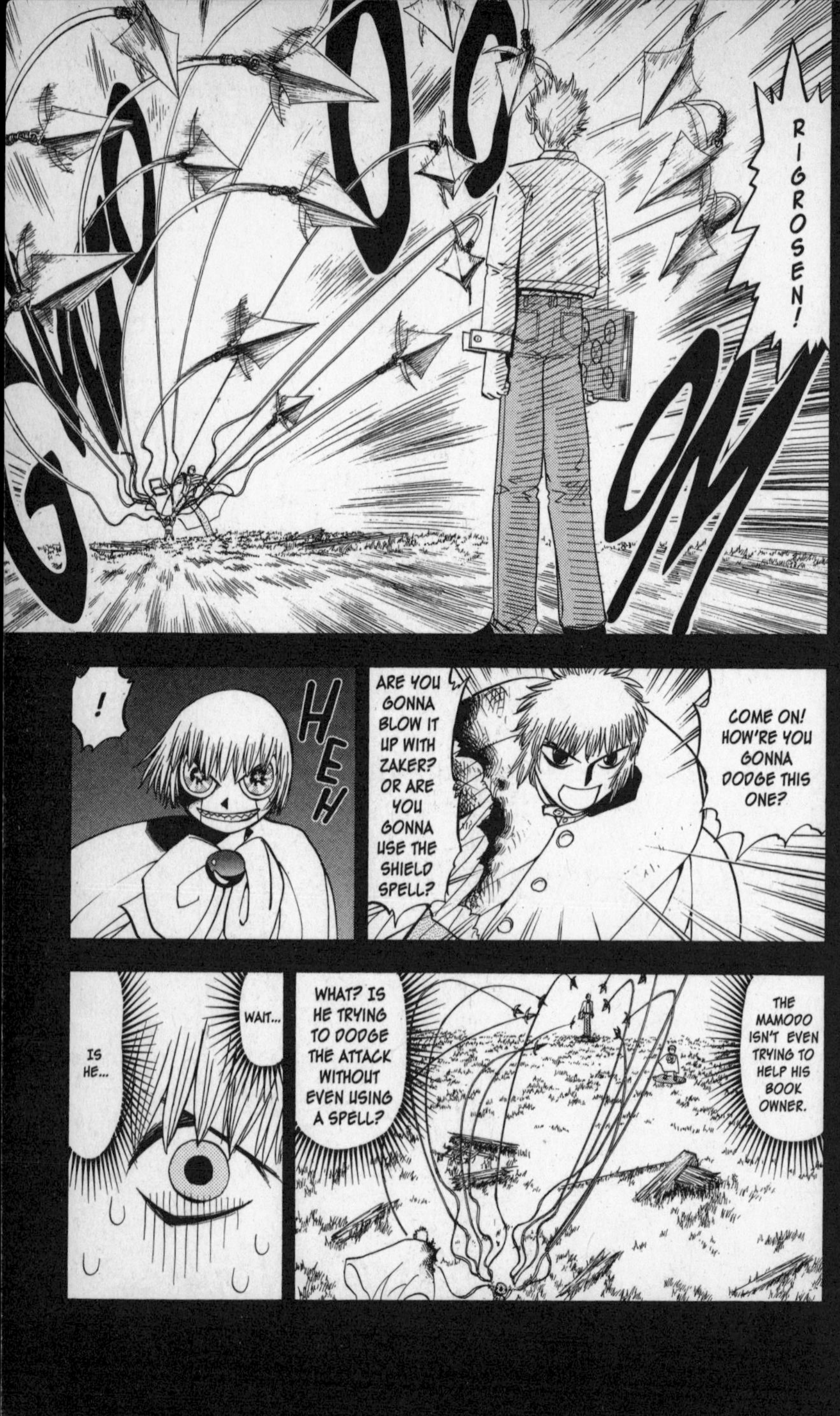
RIGROSEN!
COME ON! HOW'RE YOU GONNA DODGE THIS ONE?
ARE YOU GONNA BLOW IT UP WITH ZAKER? OR ARE YOU GONNA USE THE SHIELD SPELL?
HEH
!
THE MAMODO ISN'T EVEN TRYING TO HELP HIS BOOK OWNER.
WHAT? IS HE TRYING TO DODGE THE ATTACK WITHOUT EVEN USING A SPELL?
WAIT...
IS HE...

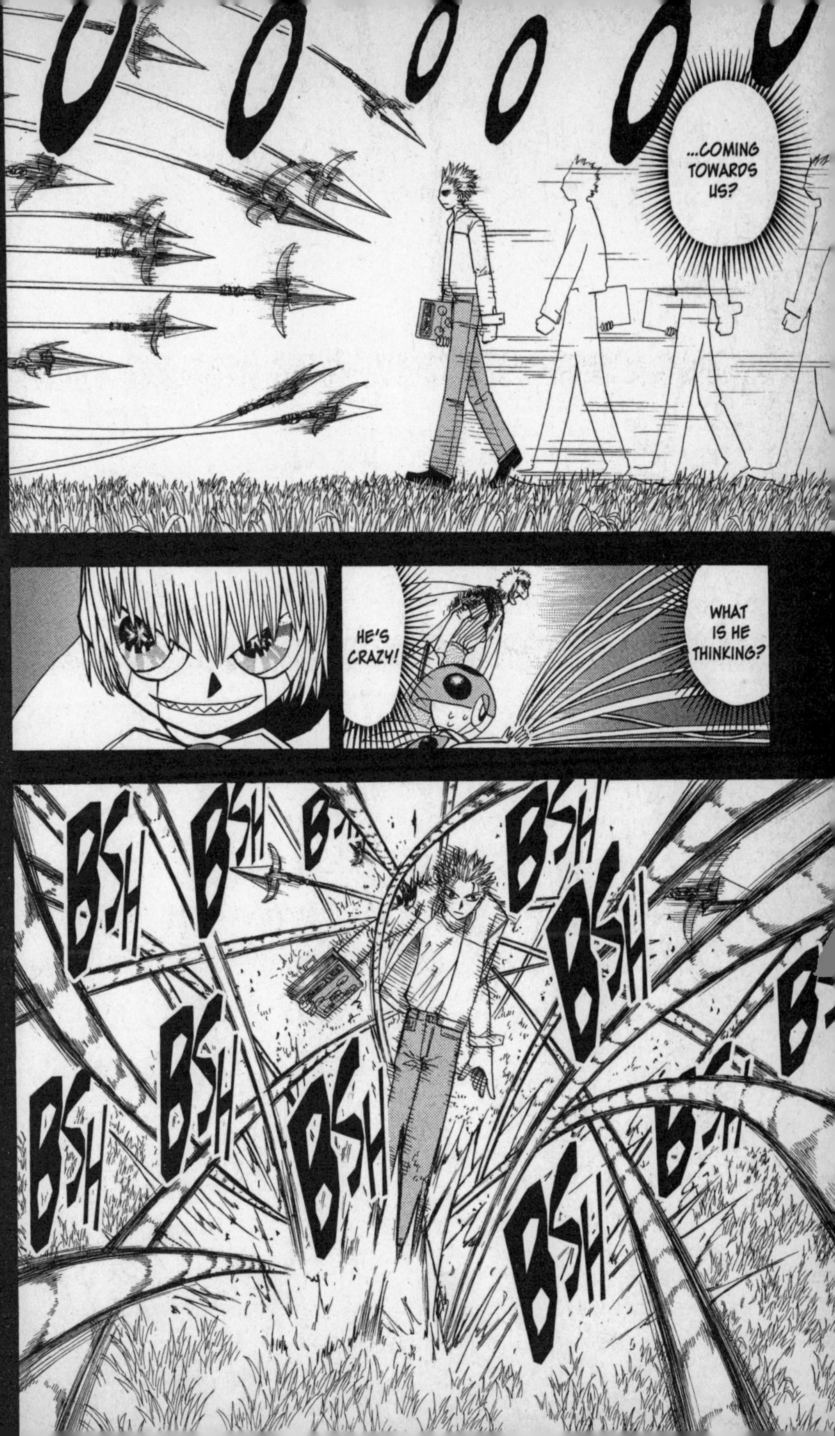

...COMING TOWARDS US?
WHAT IS HE THINKING?
HE'S CRAZY!
BSH
BSH
BSH
BSH
BSH
BSH
BSH
BSH

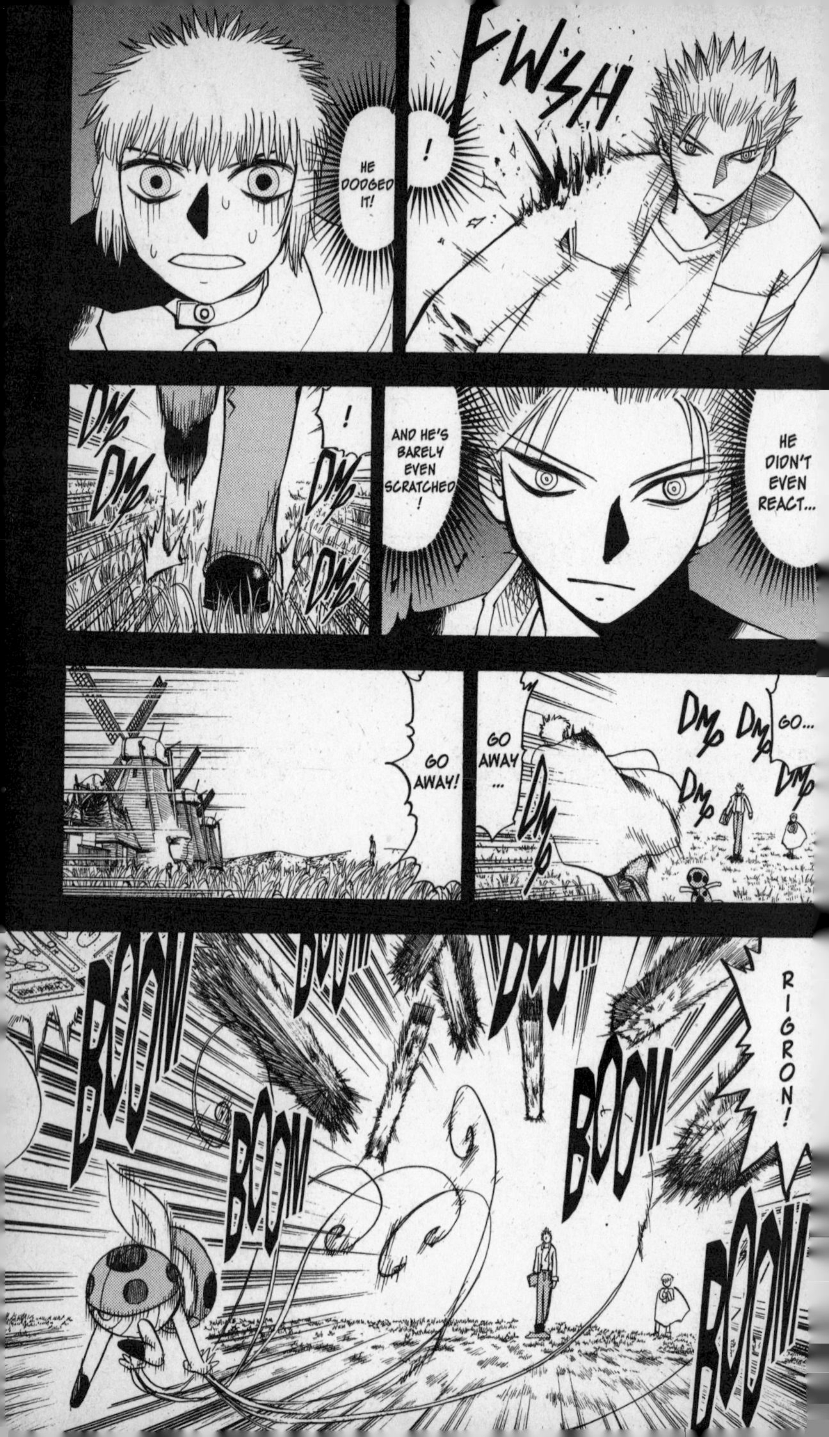
FWSH
!
HE DODGED IT!
HE DIDN'T EVEN REACT...
AND HE'S BARELY EVEN SCRATCHED!
DMP
DMP
!
DMP
DMP
GO...
DMP DMP
DMP
DMP
GO AWAY...
DMP
GO AWAY!
RIGRON!
BOOM
BOOM
BOOM
BOOM
BOOM
BOOM
BOOM

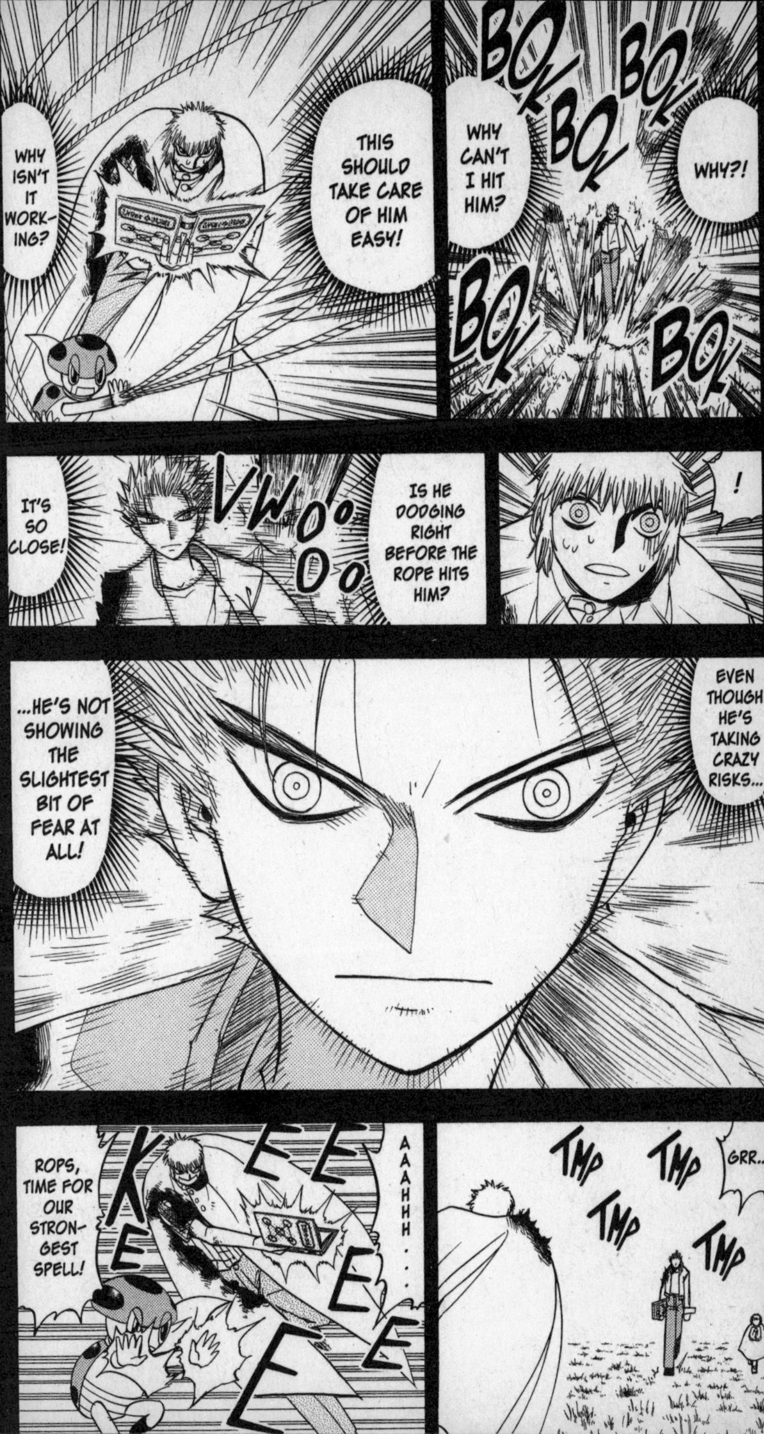

BOK BOK BOK
WHY?!
WHY CAN'T I HIT HIM?
BOK BOK
THIS SHOULD TAKE CARE OF HIM EASY!
WHY ISN'T IT WORKING?
!
IS HE DODGING RIGHT BEFORE THE ROPE HITS HIM?
VWOOOO
IT'S SO CLOSE!
EVEN THOUGH HE'S TAKING CRAZY RISKS...
...HE'S NOT SHOWING THE SLIGHTEST BIT OF FEAR AT ALL!
GRR...
TMP TMP TMP TMP TMP
AAAAHHH...
KEEEEEE
ROPS, TIME FOR OUR STRONGEST SPELL!

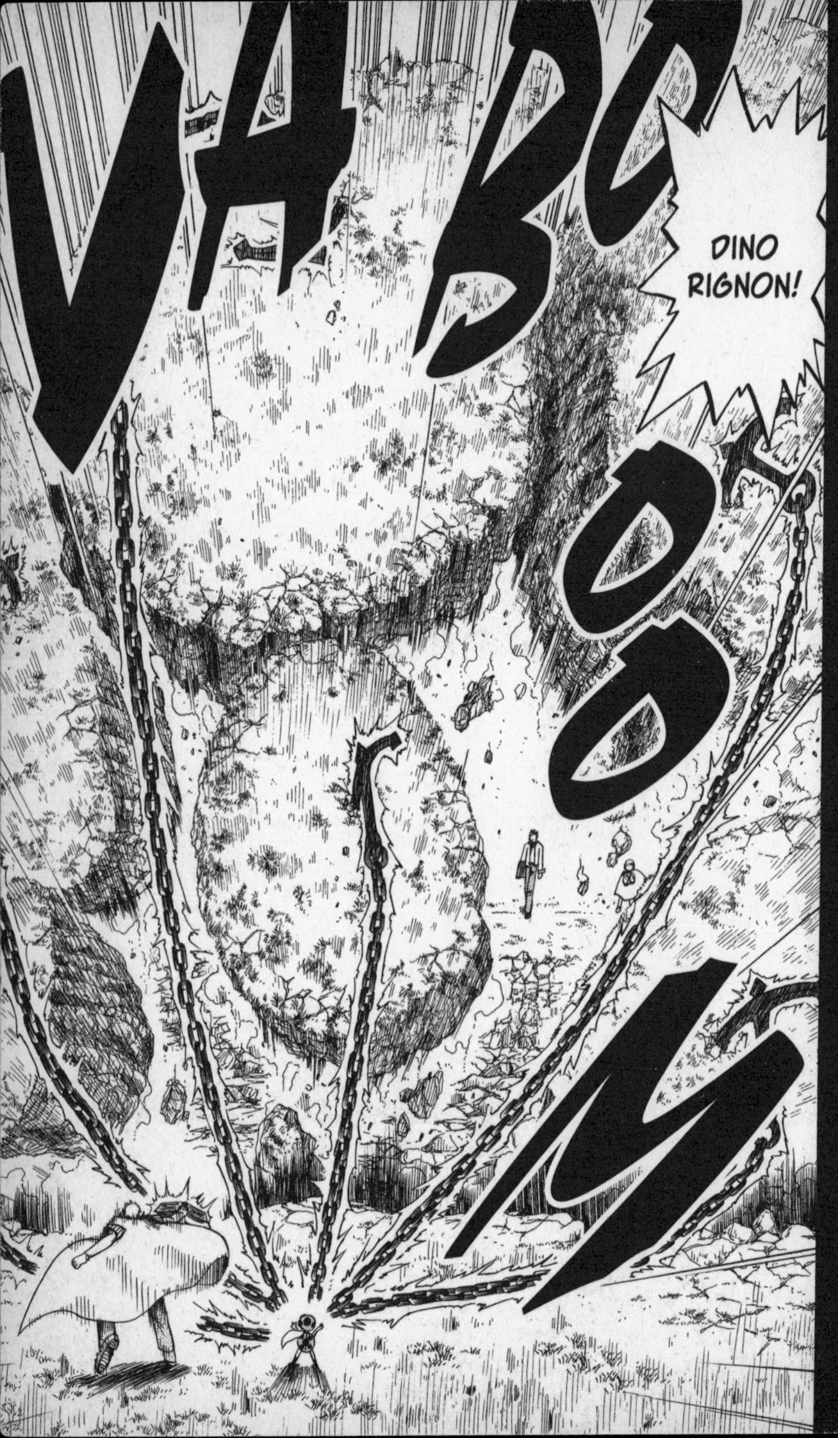
DINO
RIGNON!

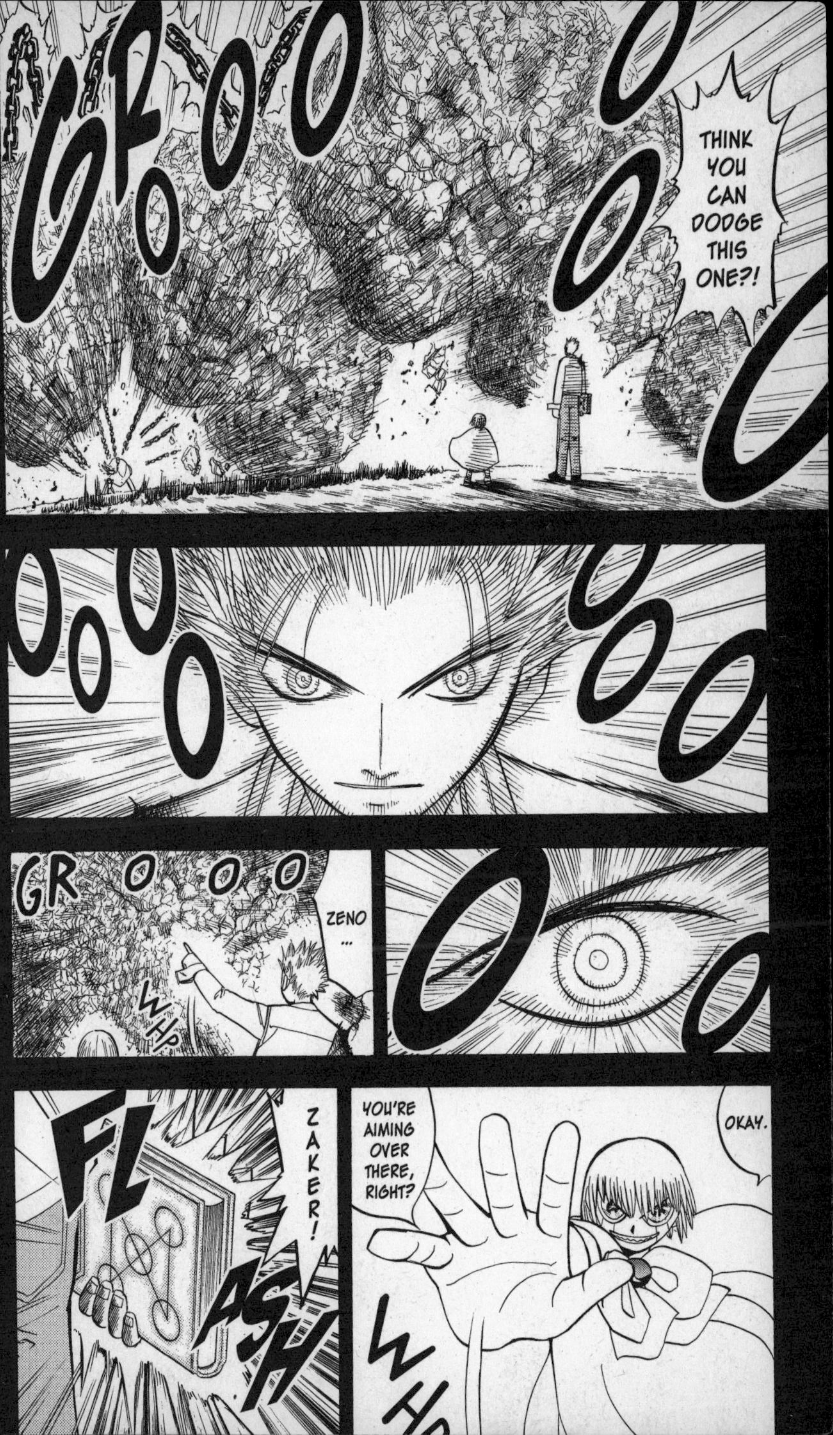
GROOOOOOO
THINK YOU CAN DODGE THIS ONE?!
GROOOO
ZENO ...
WHP
OKAY.
YOU'RE AIMING OVER THERE, RIGHT?
ZAKER!
FZASH

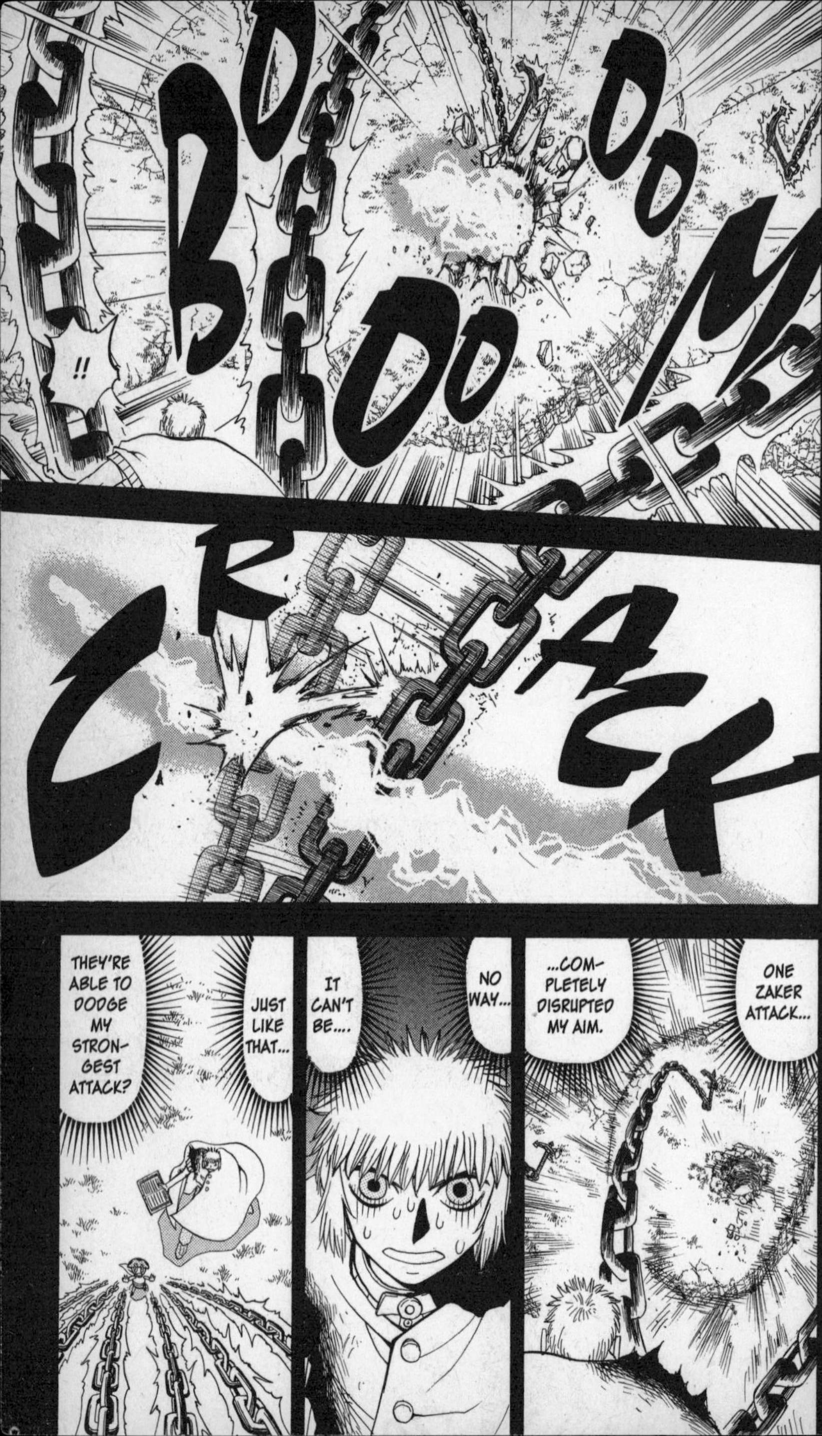
!!
CRACK
ONE ZAKER ATTACK...
...COMPLETELY DISRUPTED MY AIM.
NO WAY...
IT CAN'T BE....
JUST LIKE THAT...
THEY'RE ABLE TO DODGE MY STRONGEST ATTACK?

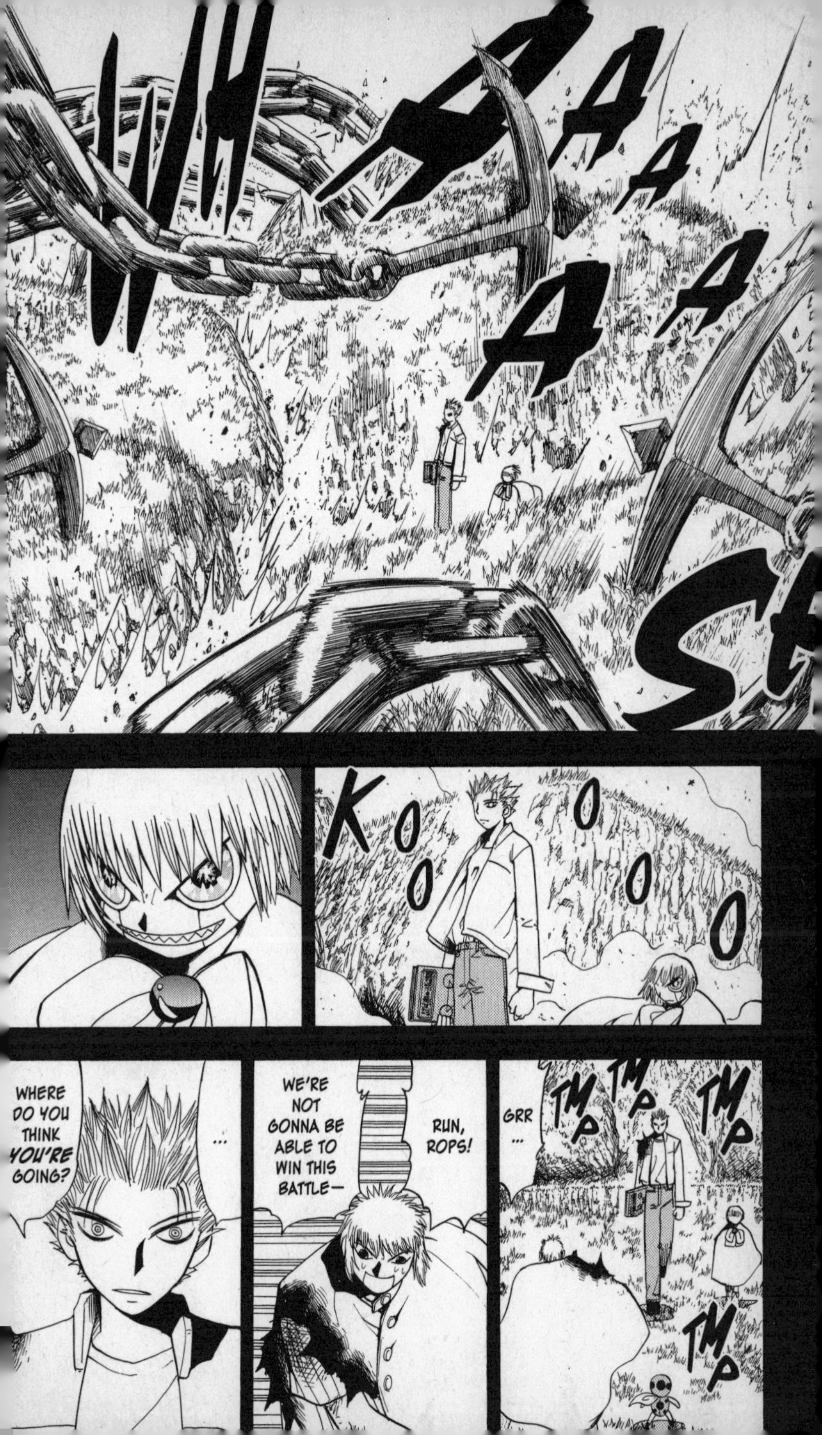
WHAAAAAA
ST
KOOOOOO
TMP
TMP
TMP
GRR...
TMP
RUN, ROPS!
WE'RE NOT GONNA BE ABLE TO WIN THIS BATTLE—
...
WHERE DO YOU THINK *YOU'RE* GOING?

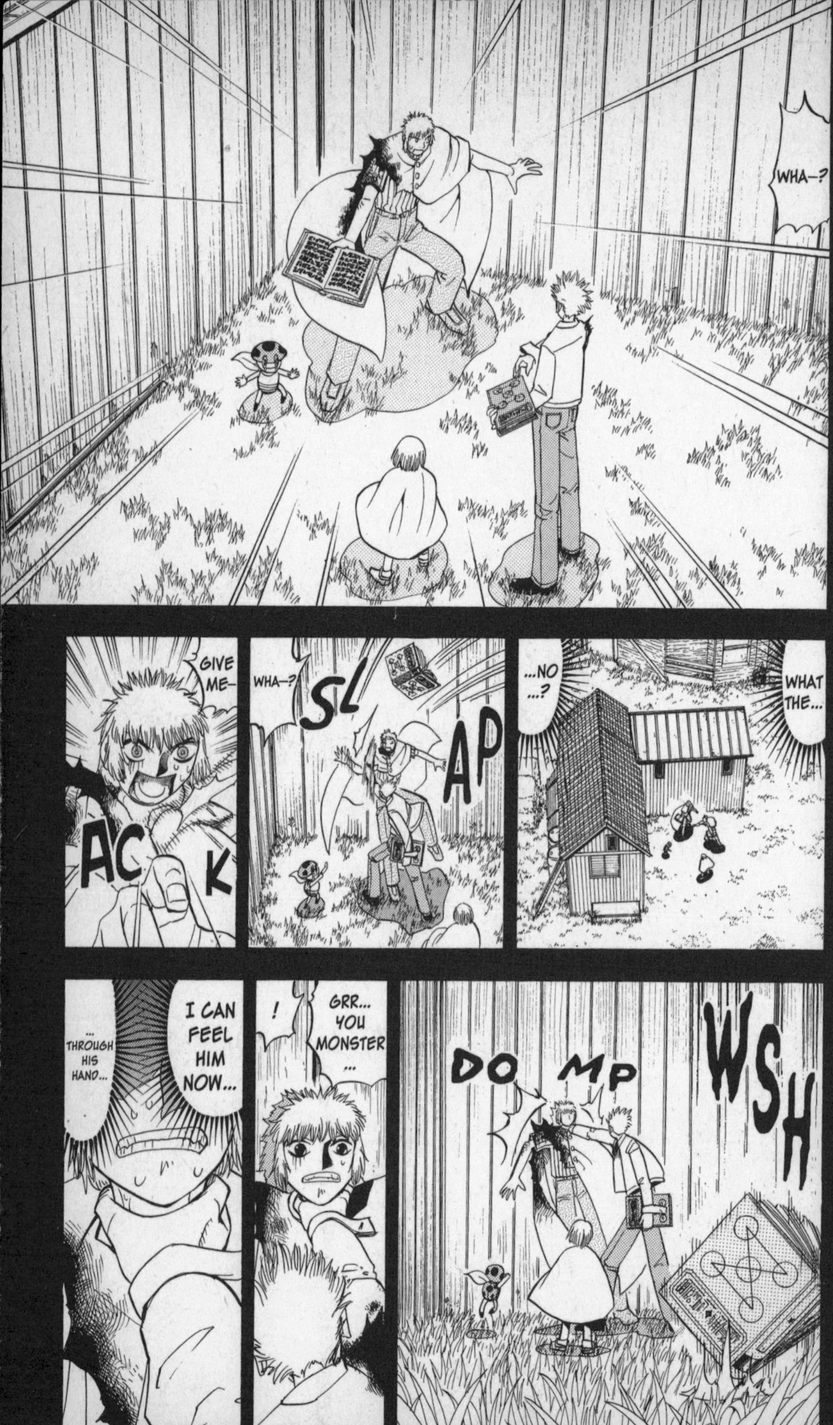
WHA–?
WHAT THE...
...NO ...?
WHA–?
SL AP
GIVE ME–
AC K
WSH
DO MP
!
GRR... YOU MONSTER ...
I CAN FEEL HIM NOW...
... THROUGH HIS HAND...

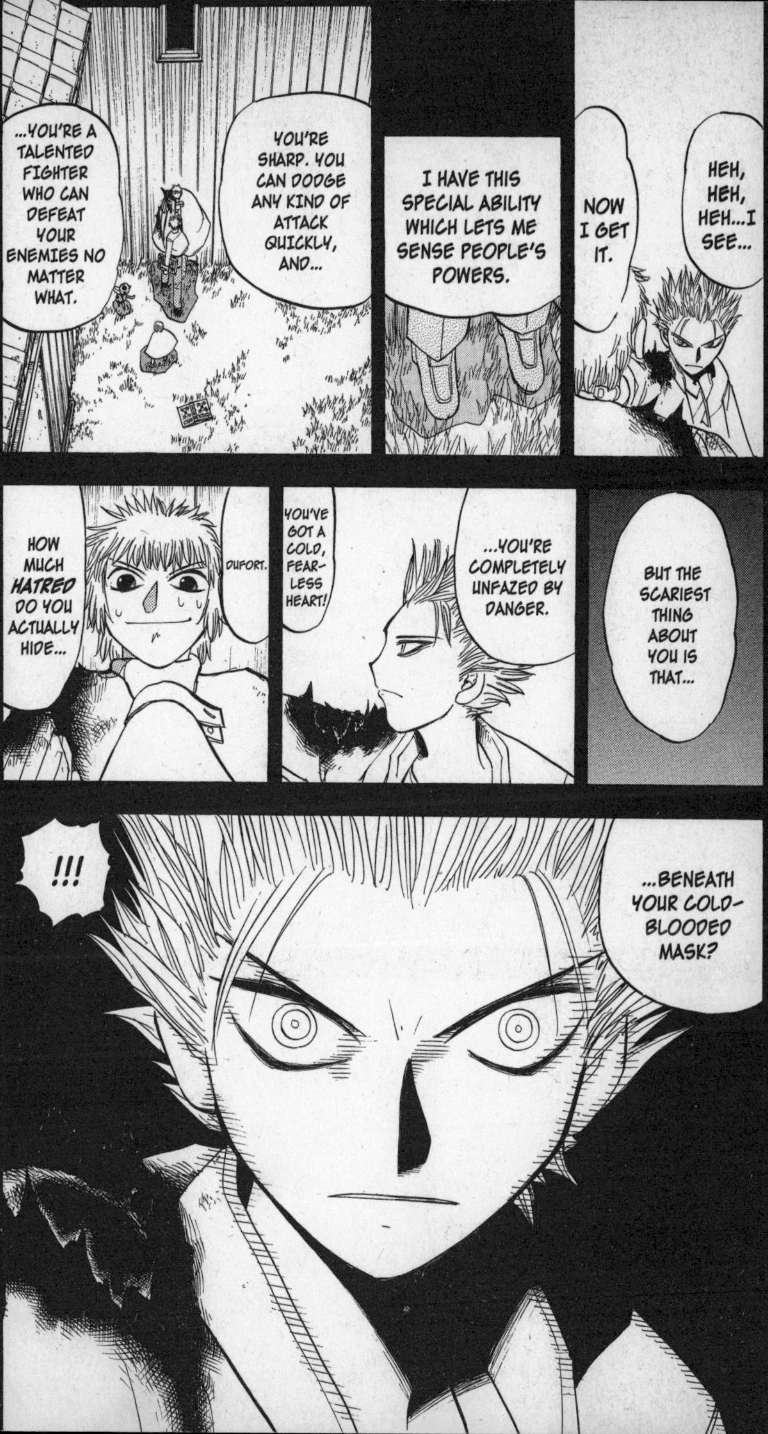

HEH, HEH, HEH...I SEE...
NOW I GET IT.
I HAVE THIS SPECIAL ABILITY WHICH LETS ME SENSE PEOPLE'S POWERS.
YOU'RE SHARP. YOU CAN DODGE ANY KIND OF ATTACK QUICKLY, AND...
...YOU'RE A TALENTED FIGHTER WHO CAN DEFEAT YOUR ENEMIES NO MATTER WHAT.
BUT THE SCARIEST THING ABOUT YOU IS THAT...
...YOU'RE COMPLETELY UNFAZED BY DANGER.
YOU'VE GOT A COLD, FEAR-LESS HEART!
DUFORT.
HOW MUCH *HATRED* DO YOU ACTUALLY HIDE...
...BENEATH YOUR COLD-BLOODED MASK?
!!!

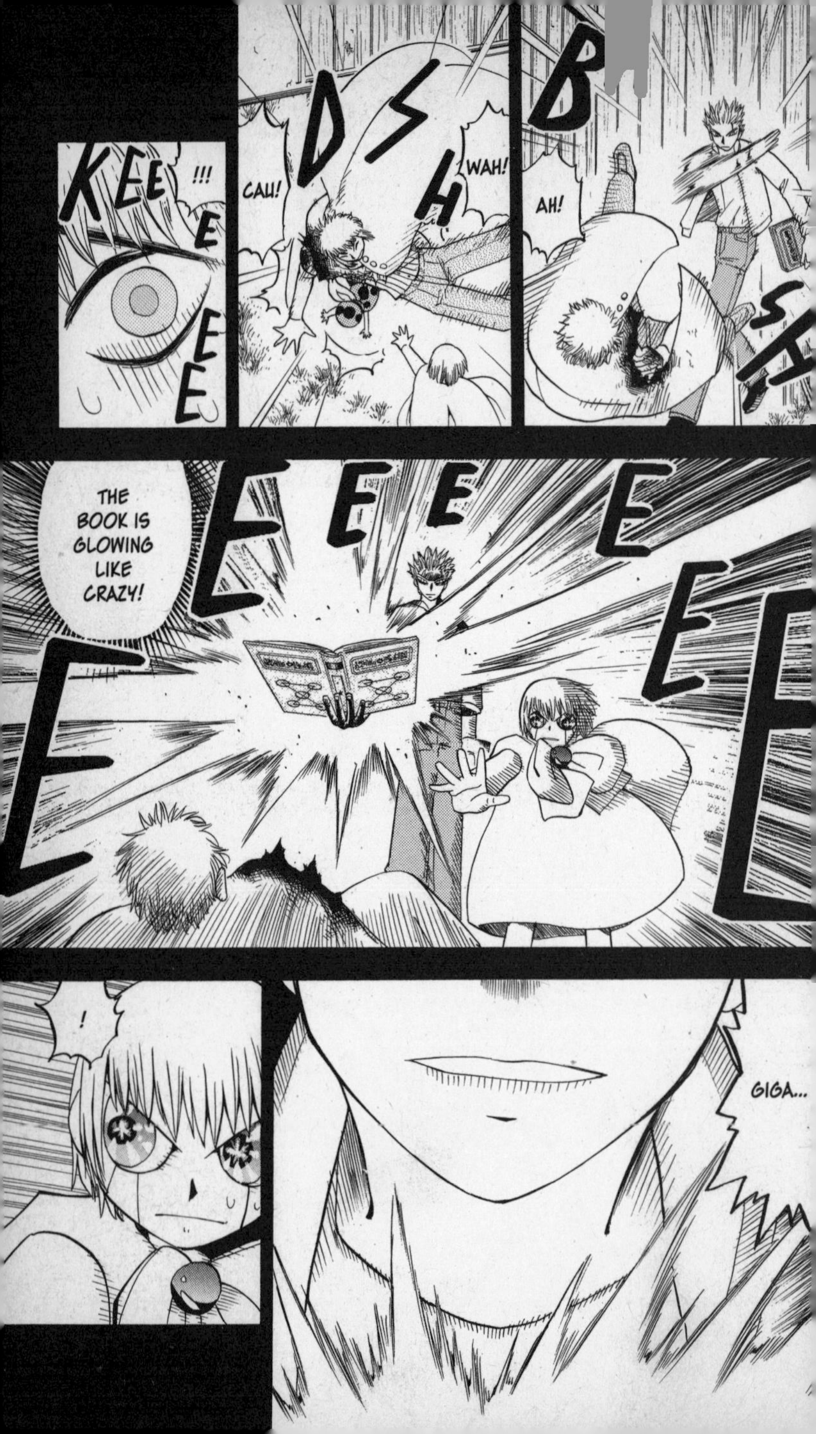
B
AH!
SH
DSH
WAH!
CAU!
KEEEEE
!!!
EEEEEEE
THE BOOK IS GLOWING LIKE CRAZY!
GIGA...
!

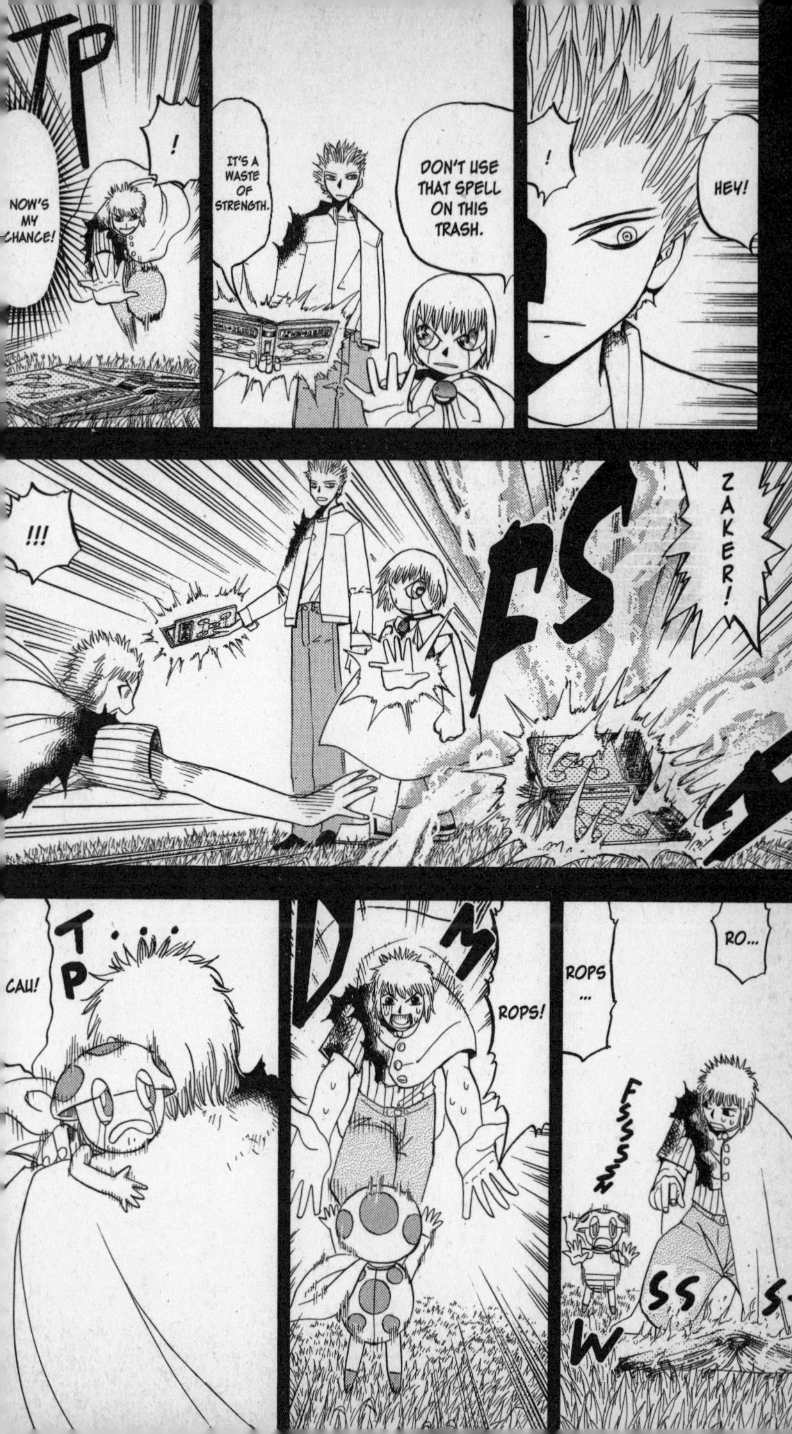
HEY!
!
DON'T USE THAT SPELL ON THIS TRASH.
IT'S A WASTE OF STRENGTH.
!
TP
NOW'S MY CHANCE!
ZAKER!
FS
H
!!!
RO...
ROPS ...
FSSSSS
SS
ST
W
ROPS!
D
M
TP
...
CAU!

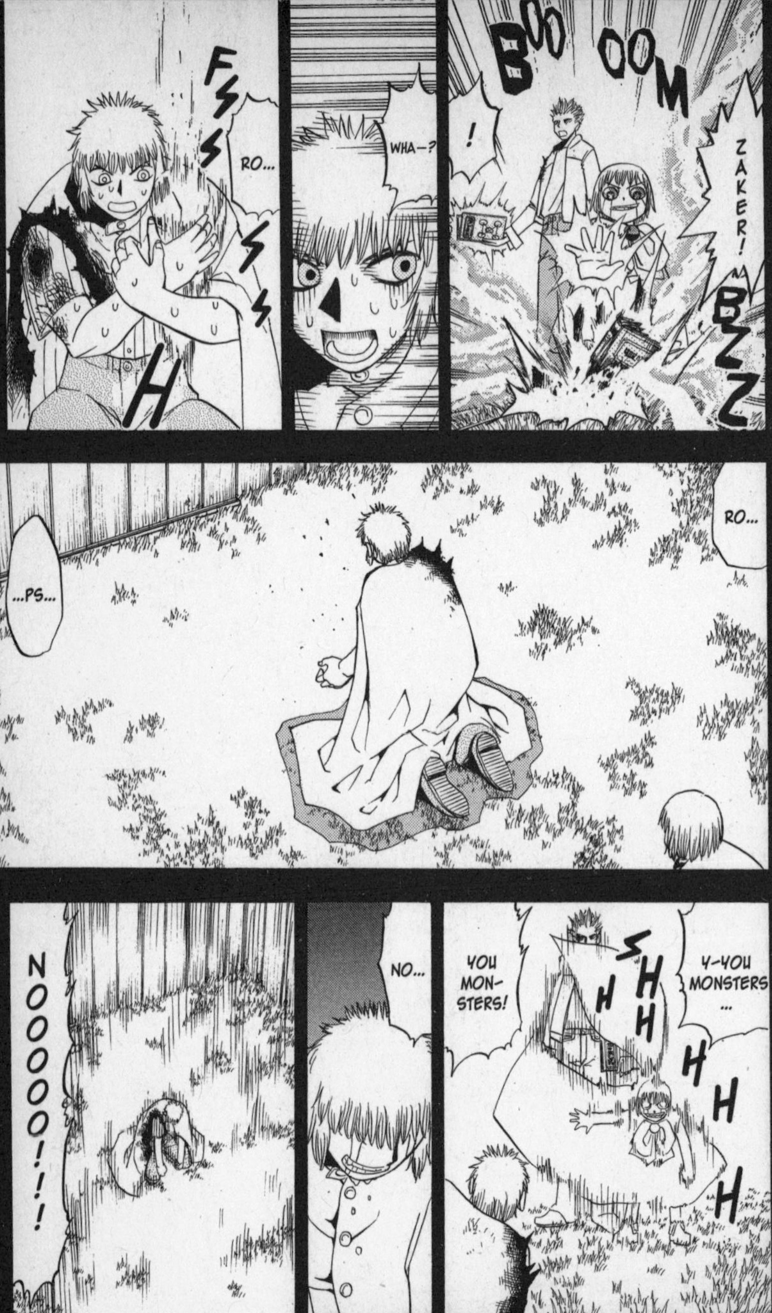

BOOOOM
!
ZAKER!
BZZZ
WHA-?
RO...
FSSSH
RO...
...PS...
Y-YOU MONSTERS ...
YOU MON-STERS!
SHHHHHHH
NO...
NOOOOOO!!!

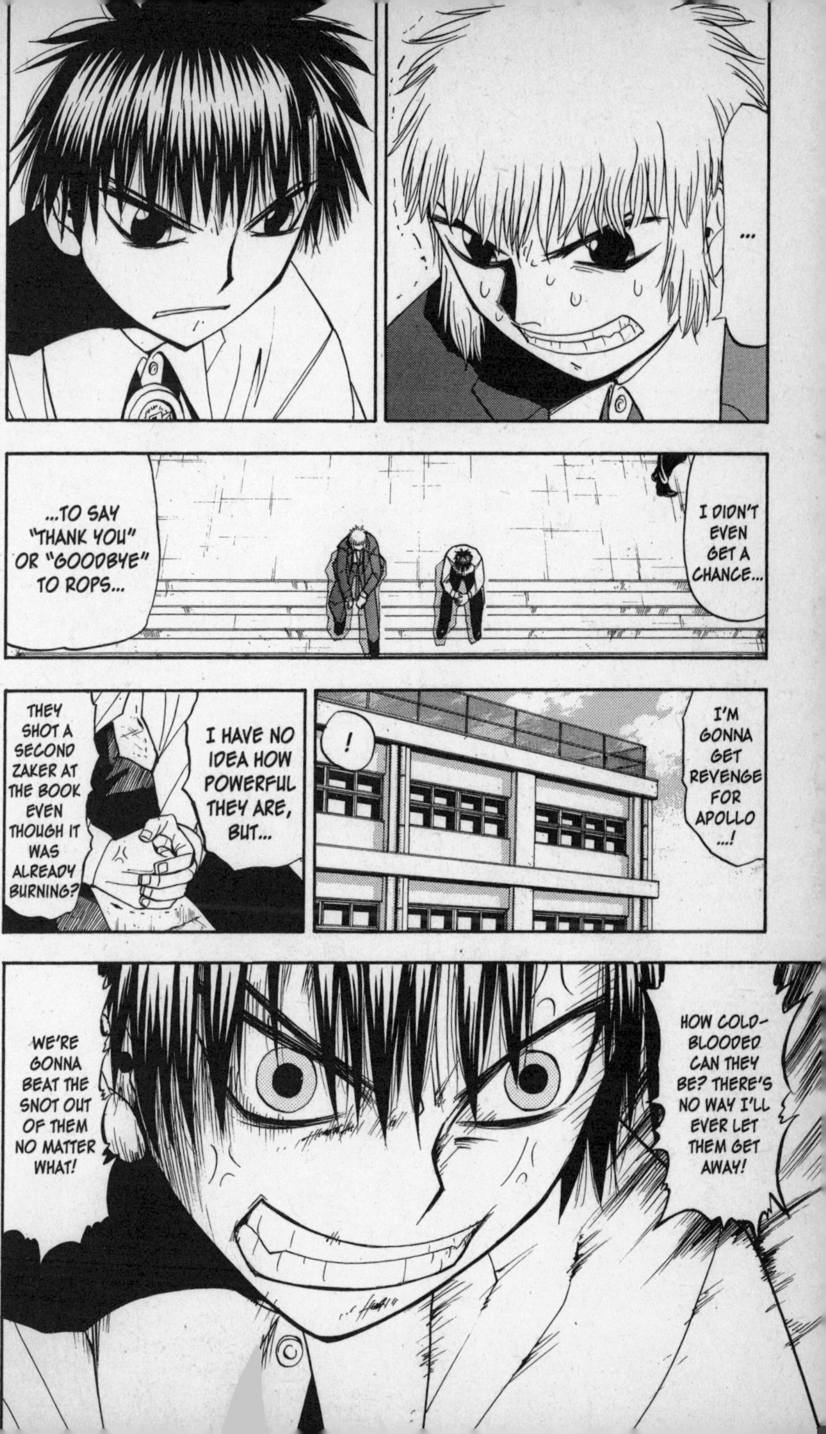
...
I DIDN'T EVEN GET A CHANCE...
...TO SAY "THANK YOU" OR "GOODBYE" TO ROPS...
I'M GONNA GET REVENGE FOR APOLLO ...!
!
I HAVE NO IDEA HOW POWERFUL THEY ARE, BUT...
THEY SHOT A SECOND ZAKER AT THE BOOK EVEN THOUGH IT WAS ALREADY BURNING?
HOW COLD-BLOODED CAN THEY BE? THERE'S NO WAY I'LL EVER LET THEM GET AWAY!
WE'RE GONNA BEAT THE SNOT OUT OF THEM NO MATTER WHAT!

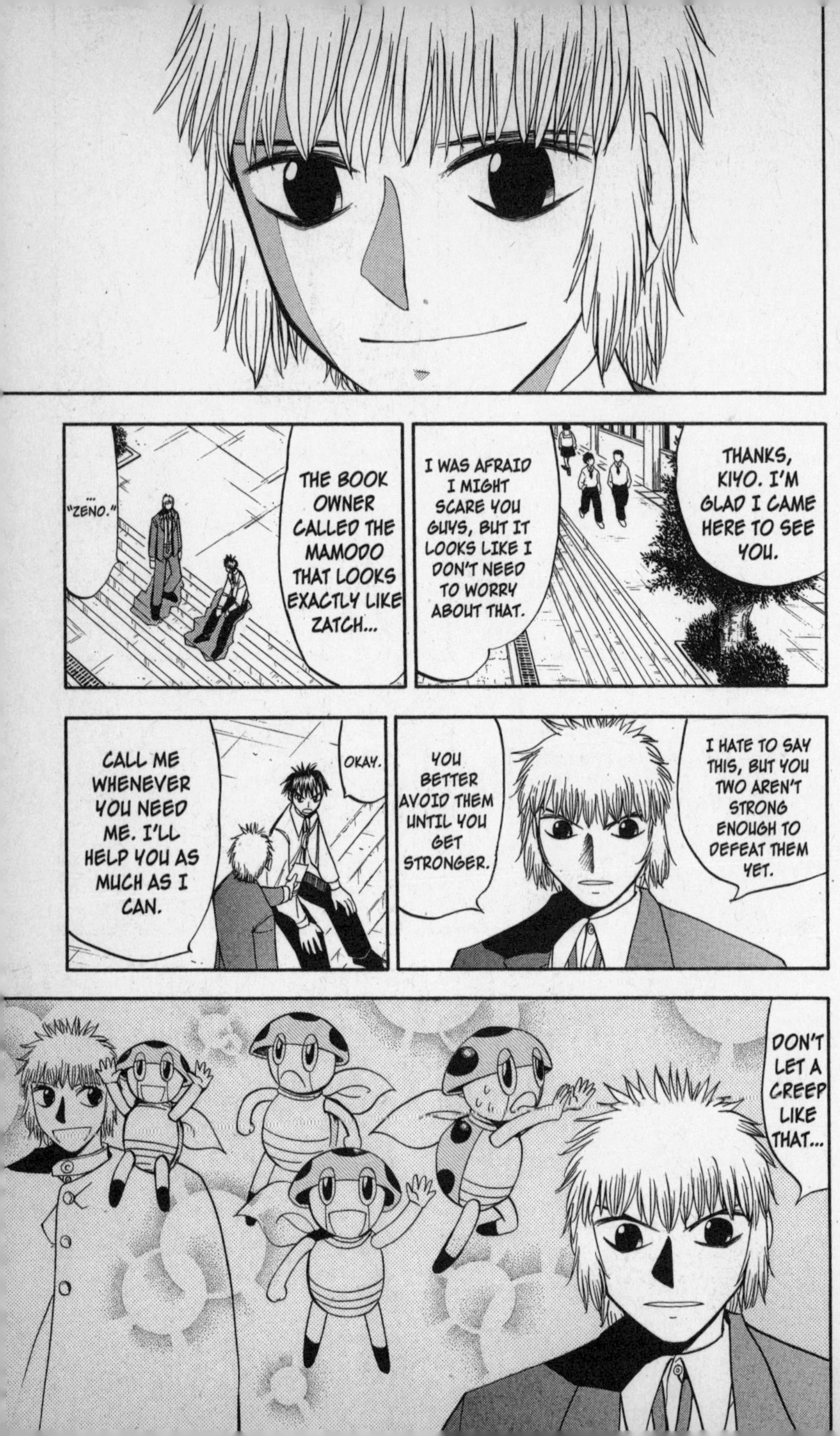
THANKS, KIYO. I'M GLAD I CAME HERE TO SEE YOU.
I WAS AFRAID I MIGHT SCARE YOU GUYS, BUT IT LOOKS LIKE I DON'T NEED TO WORRY ABOUT THAT.
THE BOOK OWNER CALLED THE MAMODO THAT LOOKS EXACTLY LIKE ZATCH...
... "ZENO."
I HATE TO SAY THIS, BUT YOU TWO AREN'T STRONG ENOUGH TO DEFEAT THEM YET.
YOU BETTER AVOID THEM UNTIL YOU GET STRONGER.
OKAY.
CALL ME WHENEVER YOU NEED ME. I'LL HELP YOU AS MUCH AS I CAN.
DON'T LET A CREEP LIKE THAT...

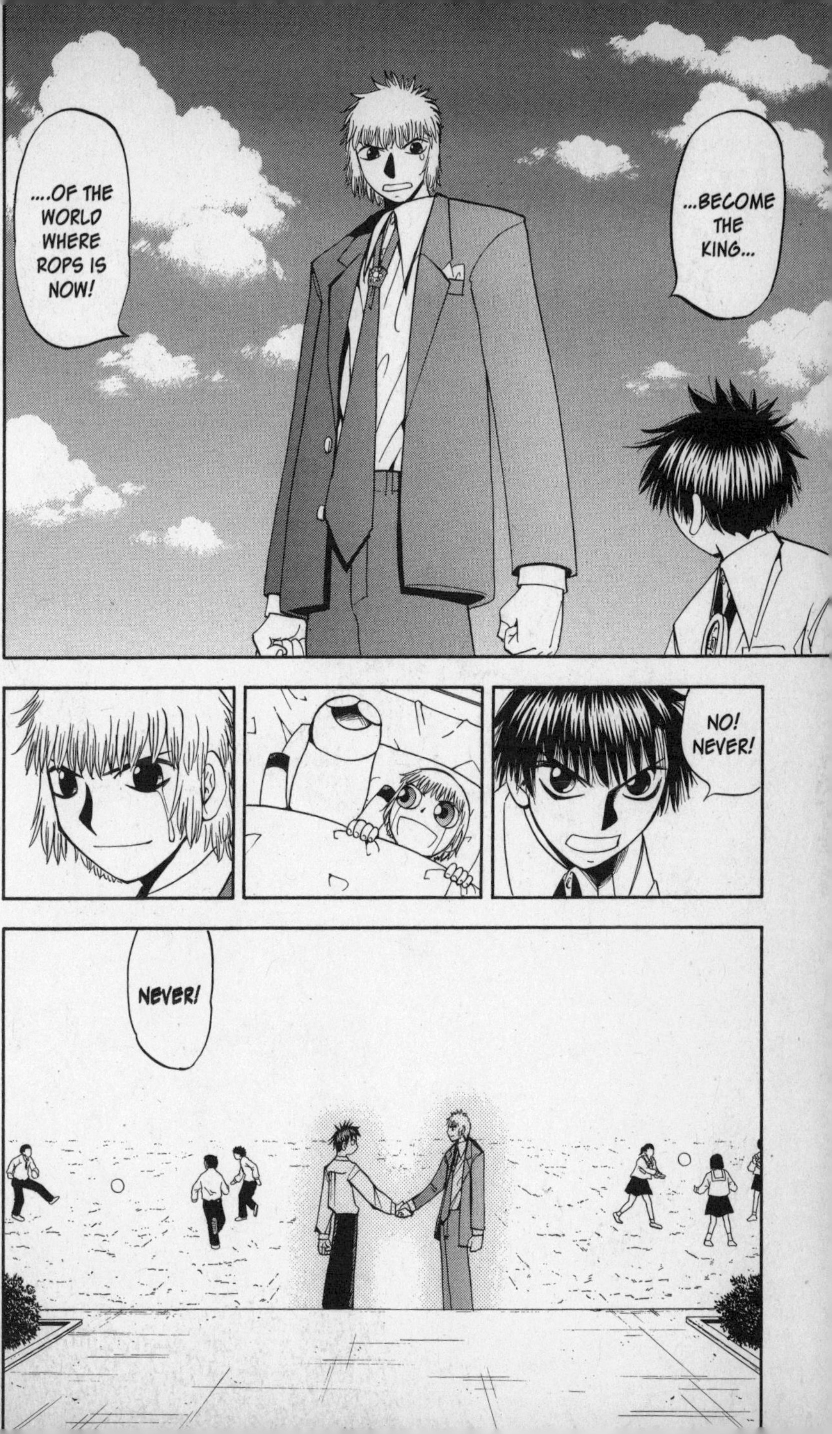
...BECOME THE KING...
....OF THE WORLD WHERE ROPS IS NOW!
NO! NEVER!
NEVER!

LEVEL 78: A Happy Day

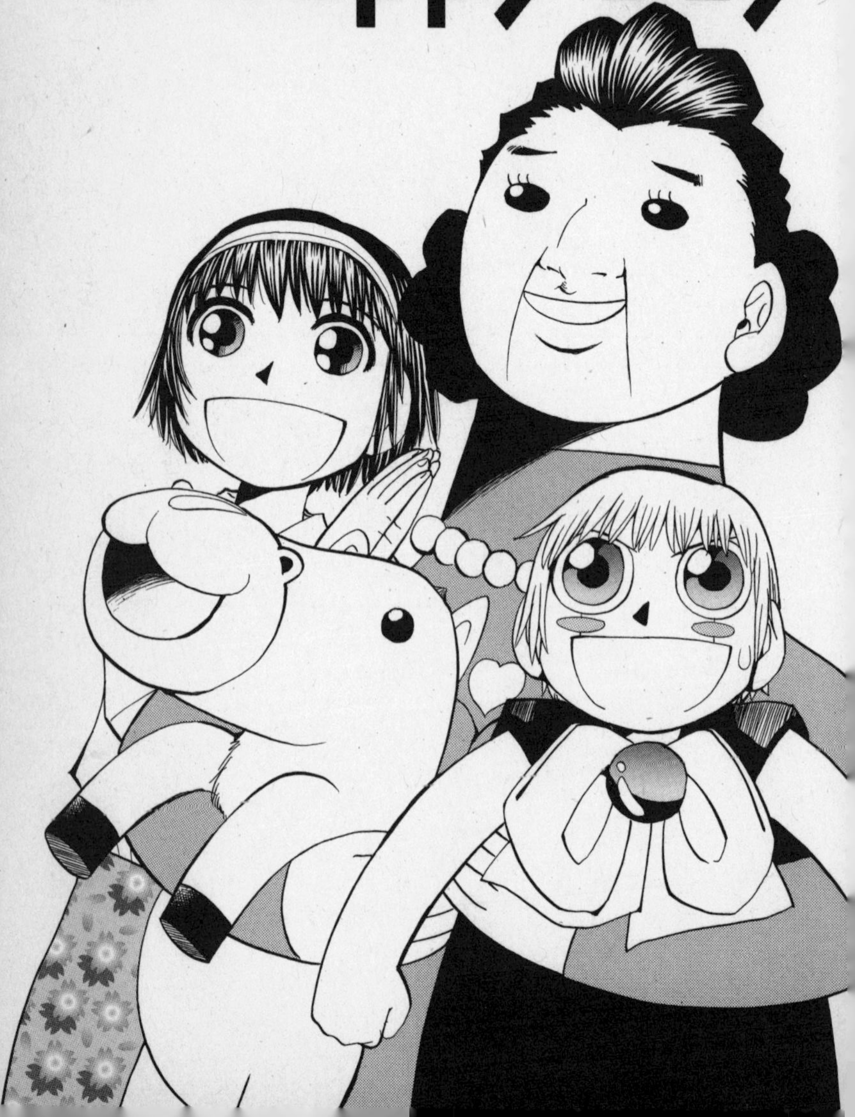

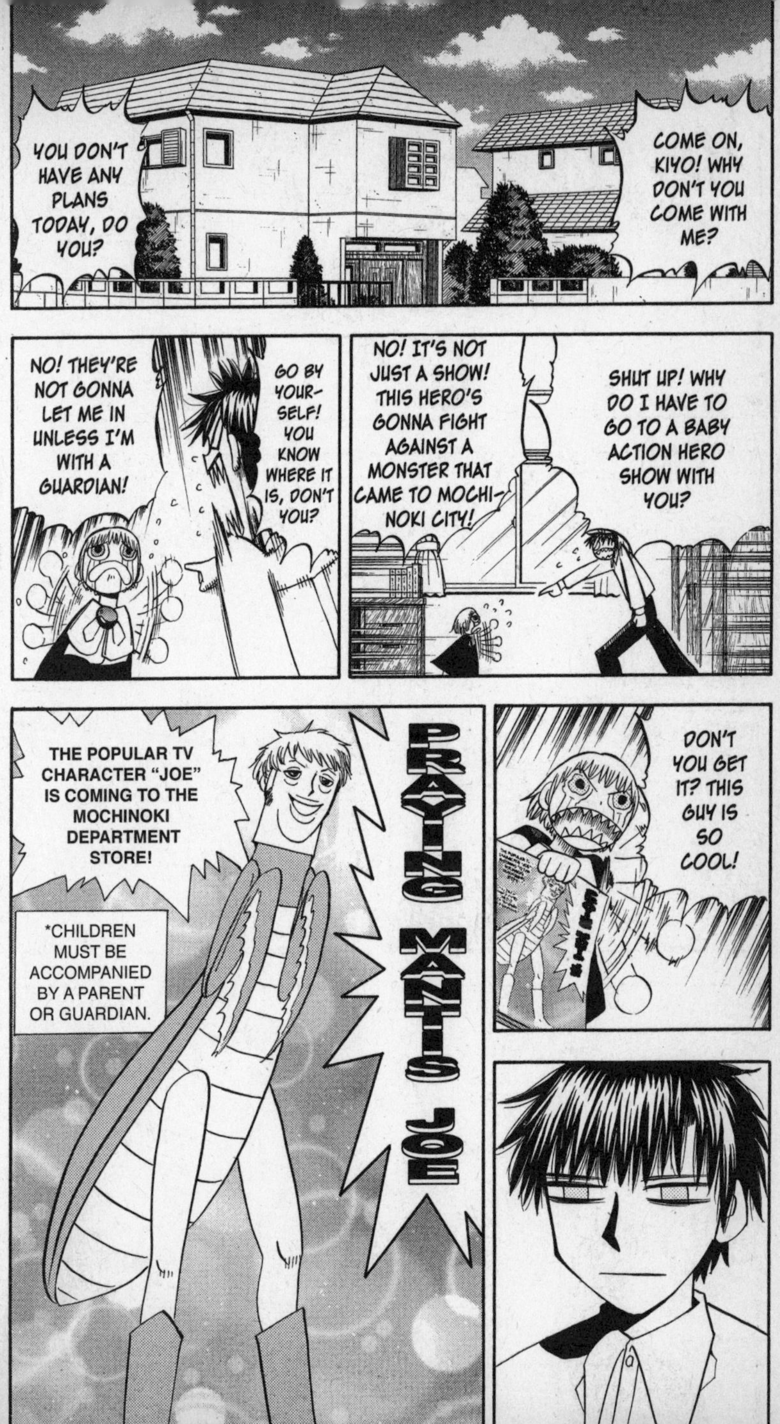
COME ON, KIYO! WHY DON'T YOU COME WITH ME?
YOU DON'T HAVE ANY PLANS TODAY, DO YOU?
SHUT UP! WHY DO I HAVE TO GO TO A BABY ACTION HERO SHOW WITH YOU?
NO! IT'S NOT JUST A SHOW! THIS HERO'S GONNA FIGHT AGAINST A MONSTER THAT CAME TO MOCHI-NOKI CITY!
GO BY YOUR-SELF! YOU KNOW WHERE IT IS, DON'T YOU?
NO! THEY'RE NOT GONNA LET ME IN UNLESS I'M WITH A GUARDIAN!
DON'T YOU GET IT? THIS GUY IS SO COOL!
PRAYING MANTIS JOE
THE POPULAR TV CHARACTER "JOE" IS COMING TO THE MOCHINOKI DEPARTMENT STORE!
*CHILDREN MUST BE ACCOMPANIED BY A PARENT OR GUARDIAN.

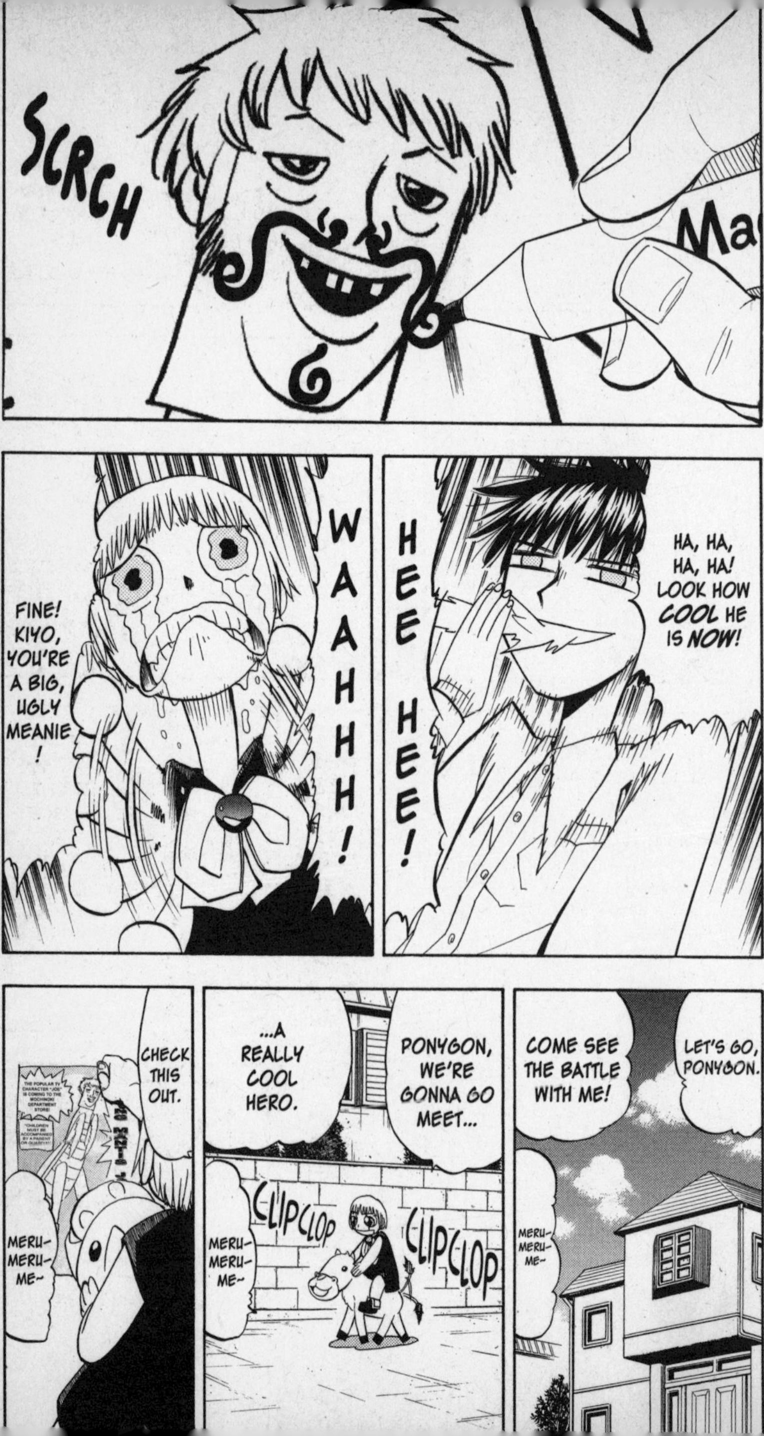
SCRCH
Ma
HA, HA, HA, HA! LOOK HOW ***COOL*** HE IS ***NOW!***
HEE HEE HEE!
WAAHHH!
FINE! KIYO, YOU'RE A BIG, UGLY MEANIE!
LET'S GO, PONYGON.
COME SEE THE BATTLE WITH ME!
MERU-MERU-ME~
PONYGON, WE'RE GONNA GO MEET...
...A REALLY COOL HERO.
CLIPCLOP
CLIPCLOP
MERU-MERU-ME~
CHECK THIS OUT.
THE POPULAR TV CHARACTER "JOE" IS COMING TO THE MOCHINOKI DEPARTMENT STORE!
*CHILDREN MUST BE ACCOMPANIED BY A PARENT OR GUARDIAN!
MERU-MERU-ME~

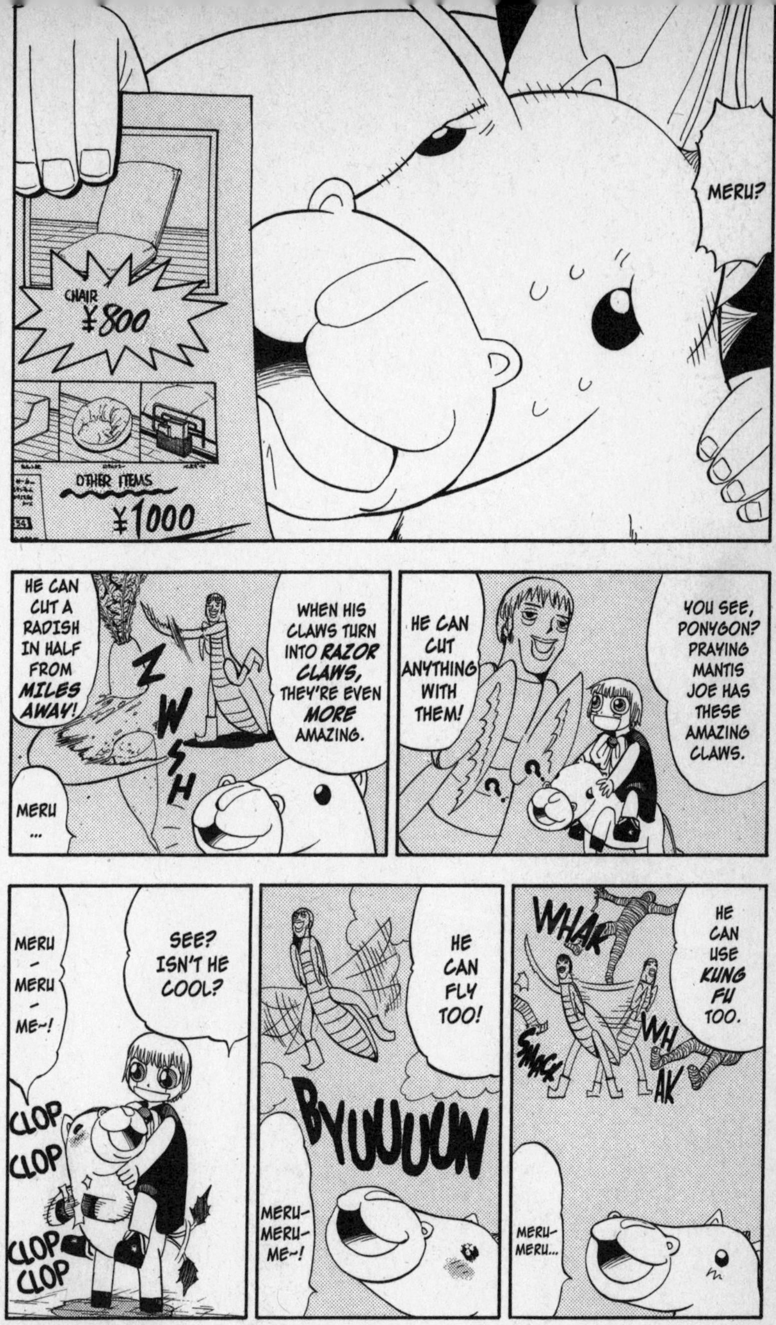
MERU?
CHAIR ¥800
OTHER ITEMS ¥1000
YOU SEE, PONYGON? PRAYING MANTIS JOE HAS THESE AMAZING CLAWS.
HE CAN CUT ANYTHING WITH THEM!
WHEN HIS CLAWS TURN INTO RAZOR CLAWS, THEY'RE EVEN MORE AMAZING.
HE CAN CUT A RADISH IN HALF FROM MILES AWAY!
ZWSH
MERU ...
HE CAN USE KUNG FU TOO.
WHAK
WHAK
SMACK
MERU-MERU...
HE CAN FLY TOO!
BYUUUUN
MERU-MERU-ME~!
SEE? ISN'T HE COOL?
MERU-MERU-ME~!
CLOP CLOP
CLOP CLOP

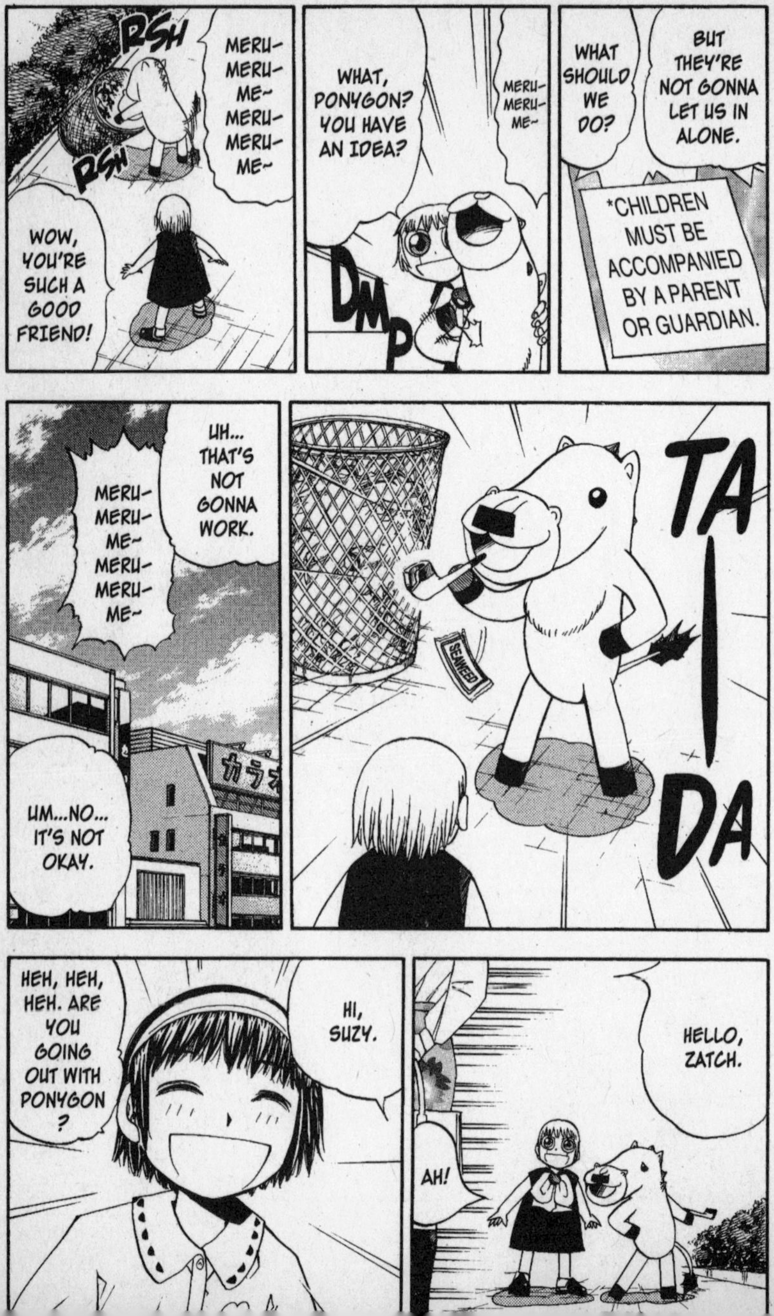
BUT THEY'RE NOT GONNA LET US IN ALONE.
WHAT SHOULD WE DO?
*CHILDREN MUST BE ACCOMPANIED BY A PARENT OR GUARDIAN.
MERU-MERU-ME~
WHAT, PONYGON? YOU HAVE AN IDEA?
DMP
MERU-MERU-ME~ MERU-MERU-ME~
RSH
RSH
WOW, YOU'RE SUCH A GOOD FRIEND!
TA-DA
SEAWEED
UH... THAT'S NOT GONNA WORK.
MERU-MERU-ME~ MERU-MERU-ME~
UM...NO... IT'S NOT OKAY.
HELLO, ZATCH.
AH!
HI, SUZY.
HEH, HEH, HEH. ARE YOU GOING OUT WITH PONYGON?

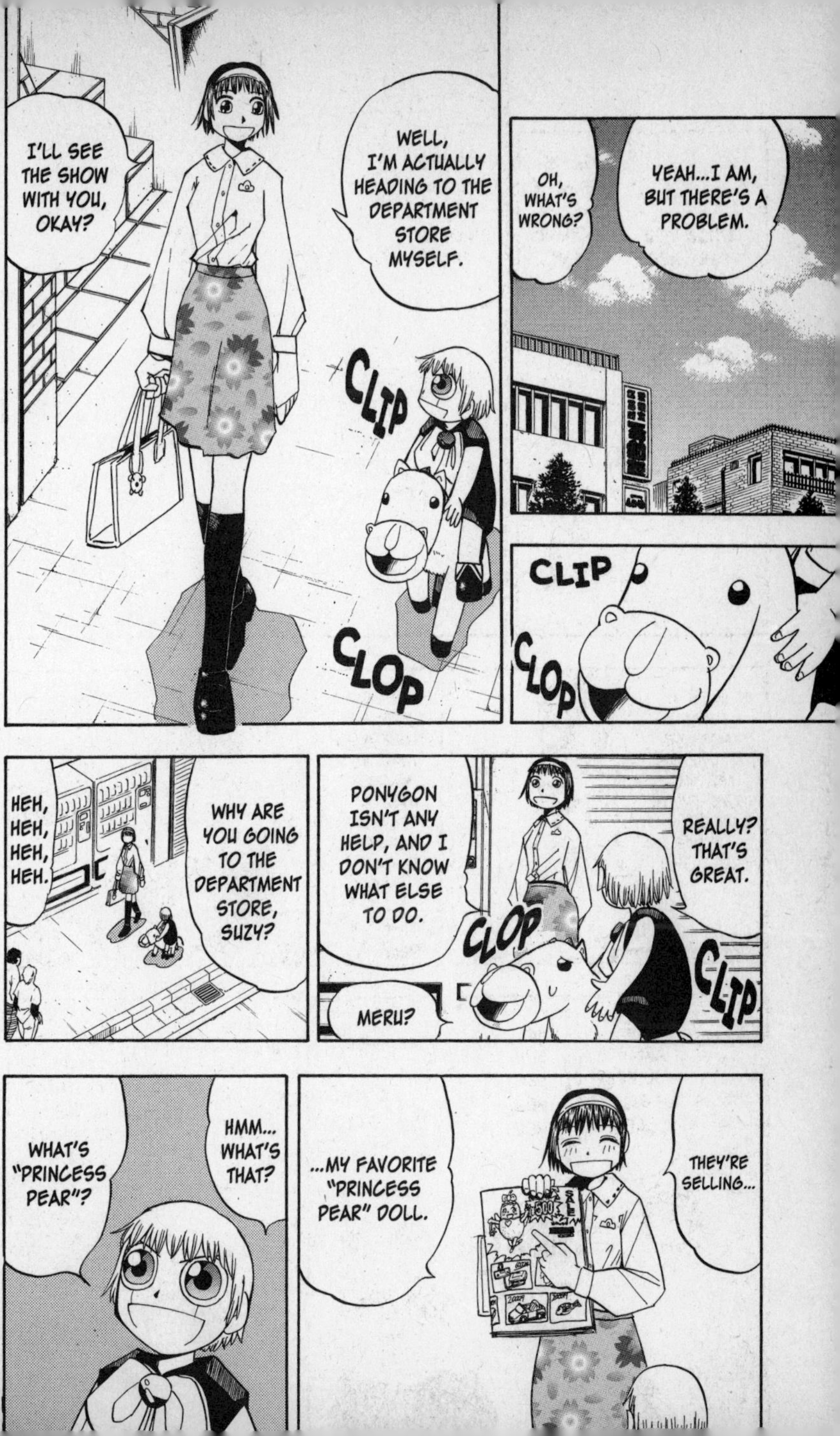
YEAH...I AM, BUT THERE'S A PROBLEM.
OH, WHAT'S WRONG?
CLIP
CLOP
WELL, I'M ACTUALLY HEADING TO THE DEPARTMENT STORE MYSELF.
CLIP
CLOP
I'LL SEE THE SHOW WITH YOU, OKAY?
REALLY? THAT'S GREAT.
CLIP
CLOP
PONYGON ISN'T ANY HELP, AND I DON'T KNOW WHAT ELSE TO DO.
MERU?
WHY ARE YOU GOING TO THE DEPARTMENT STORE, SUZY?
HEH, HEH, HEH, HEH.
THEY'RE SELLING...
...MY FAVORITE "PRINCESS PEAR" DOLL.
SALE
HMM... WHAT'S THAT?
WHAT'S "PRINCESS PEAR"?

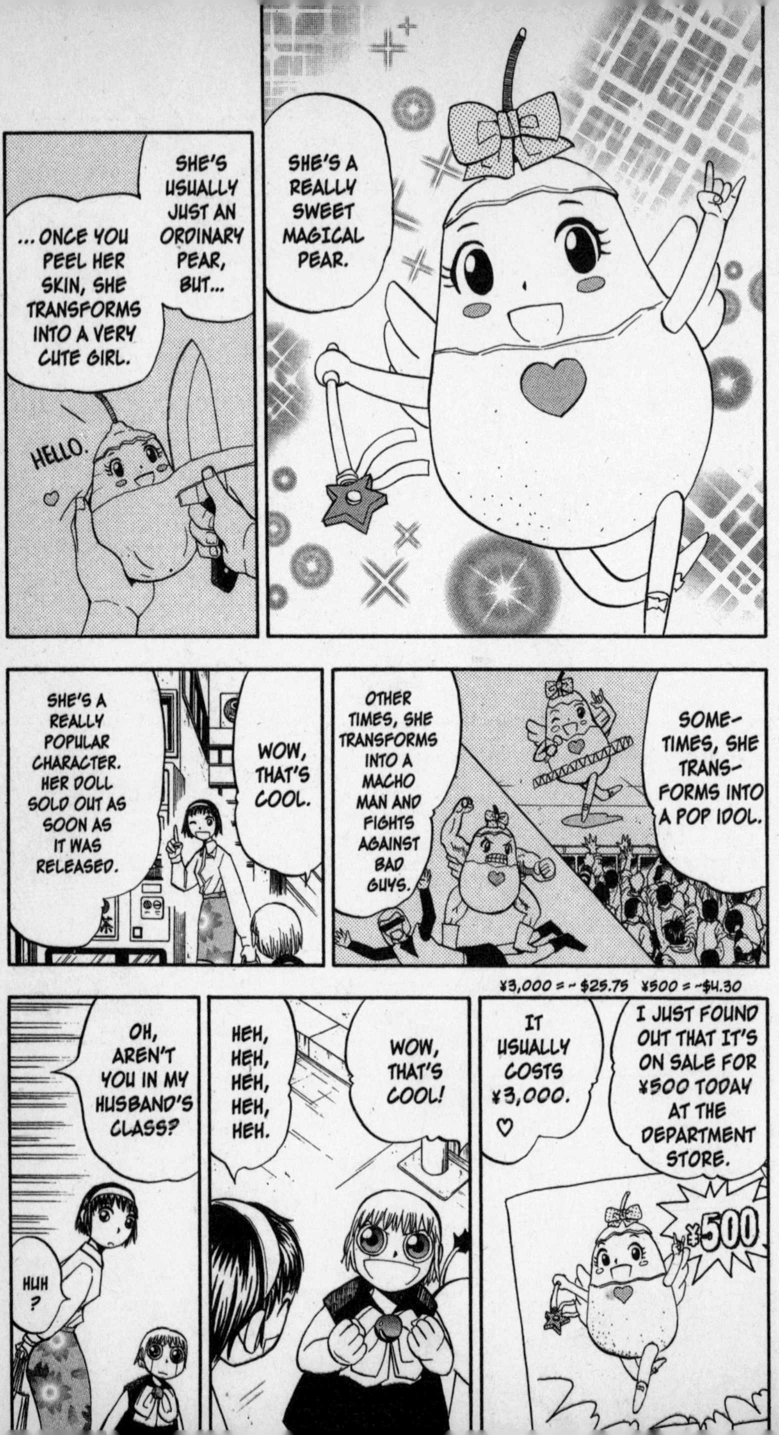
SHE'S A REALLY SWEET MAGICAL PEAR.
SHE'S USUALLY JUST AN ORDINARY PEAR, BUT...
...ONCE YOU PEEL HER SKIN, SHE TRANSFORMS INTO A VERY CUTE GIRL.
HELLO.
SOMETIMES, SHE TRANSFORMS INTO A POP IDOL.
OTHER TIMES, SHE TRANSFORMS INTO A MACHO MAN AND FIGHTS AGAINST BAD GUYS.
WOW, THAT'S COOL.
SHE'S A REALLY POPULAR CHARACTER. HER DOLL SOLD OUT AS SOON AS IT WAS RELEASED.
I JUST FOUND OUT THAT IT'S ON SALE FOR ¥500 TODAY AT THE DEPARTMENT STORE.
¥500
IT USUALLY COSTS ¥3,000. ♡
WOW, THAT'S COOL!
HEH, HEH, HEH, HEH, HEH.
OH, AREN'T YOU IN MY HUSBAND'S CLASS?
HUH?

¥3,000 = ~$25.75 ¥500 = ~$4.30

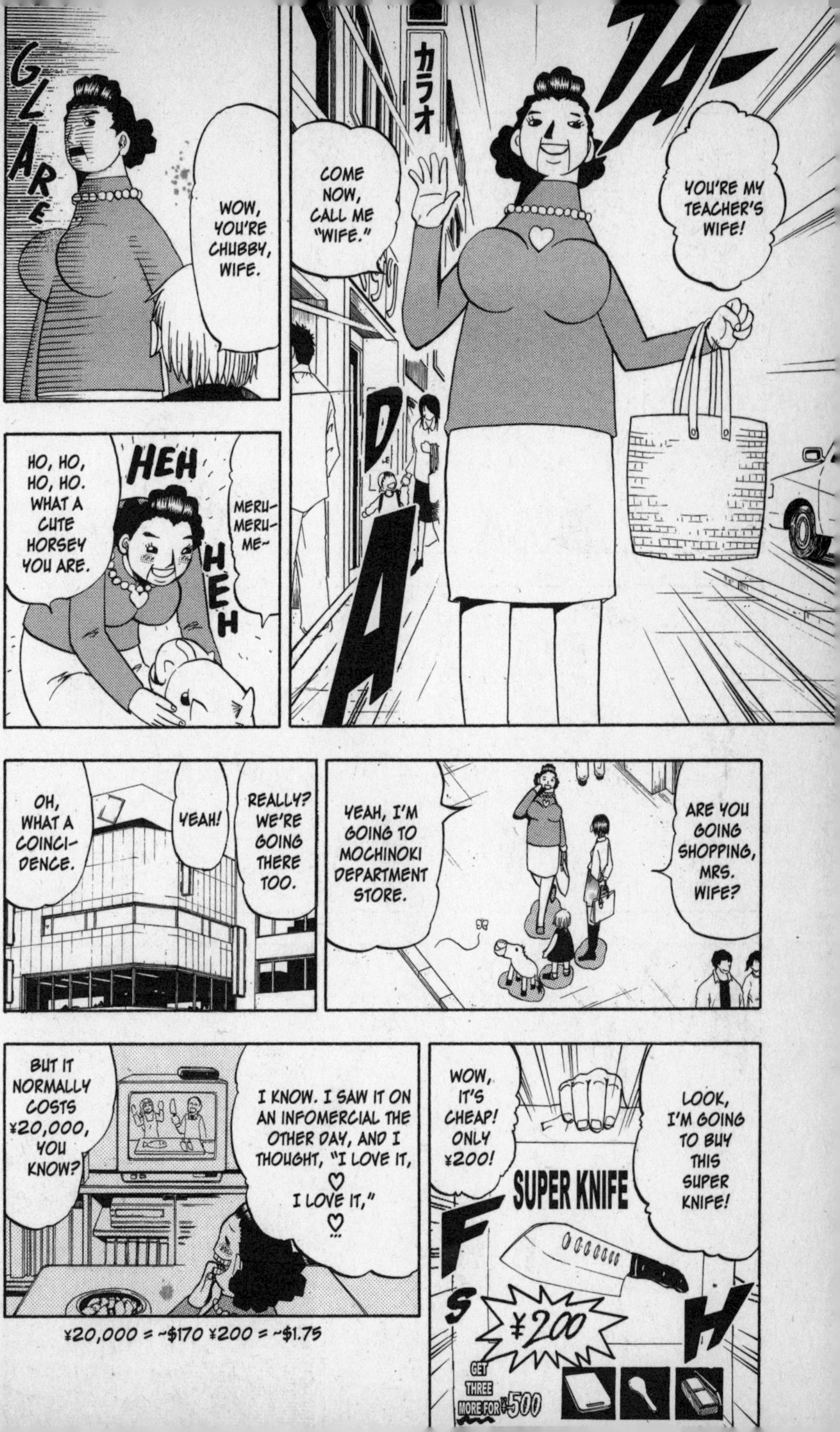
ZA-
YOU'RE MY TEACHER'S WIFE!
カラオ
COME NOW, CALL ME "WIFE."
DA
WOW, YOU'RE CHUBBY, WIFE.
GLARE
MERU-MERU-ME~
HEH HEH
HO, HO, HO, HO. WHAT A CUTE HORSEY YOU ARE.
ARE YOU GOING SHOPPING, MRS. WIFE?
YEAH, I'M GOING TO MOCHINOKI DEPARTMENT STORE.
REALLY? WE'RE GOING THERE TOO.
YEAH!
OH, WHAT A COINCIDENCE.
LOOK, I'M GOING TO BUY THIS SUPER KNIFE!
WOW, IT'S CHEAP! ONLY ¥200!
SUPER KNIFE
FSH
¥200
GET THREE MORE FOR ¥500
I KNOW. I SAW IT ON AN INFOMERCIAL THE OTHER DAY, AND I THOUGHT, "I LOVE IT, ♡ I LOVE IT," ♡...
BUT IT NORMALLY COSTS ¥20,000, YOU KNOW?
¥20,000 = ~$170 ¥200 = ~$1.75

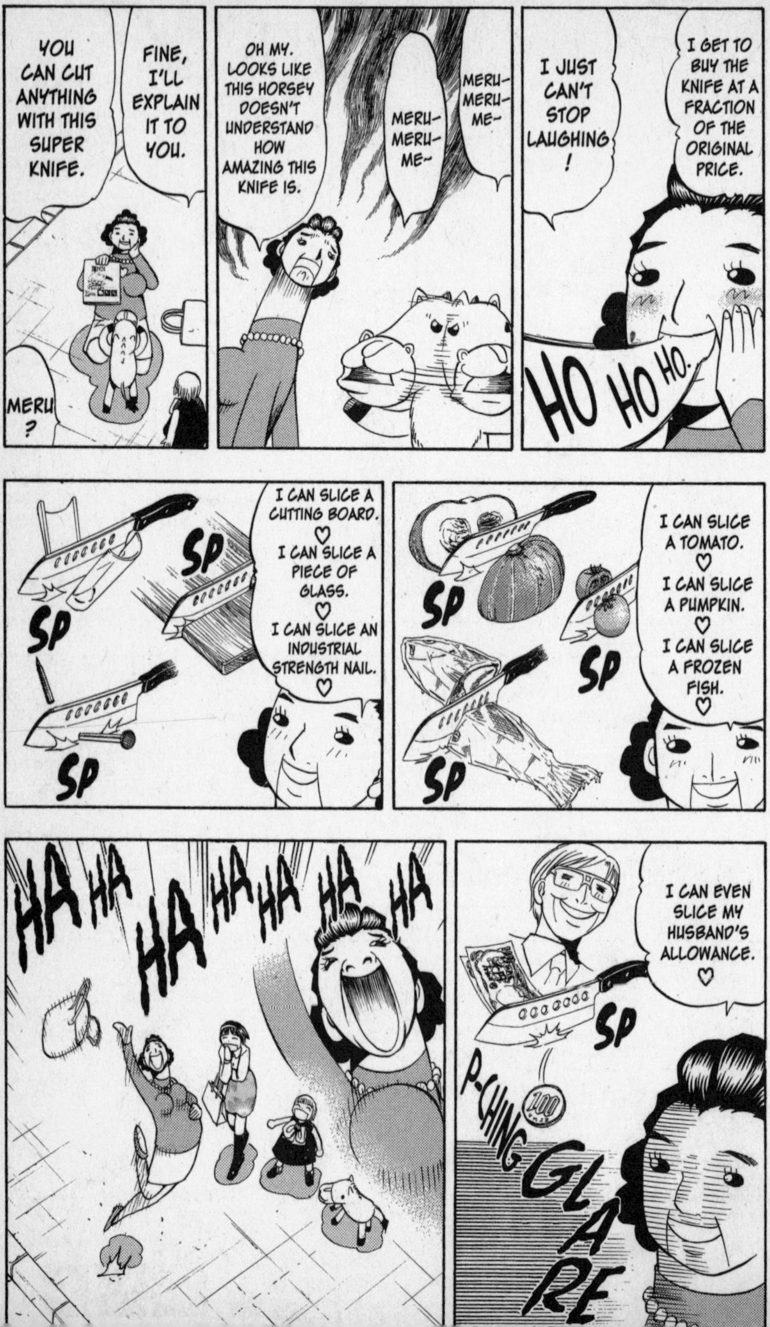
I GET TO BUY THE KNIFE AT A FRACTION OF THE ORIGINAL PRICE.
I JUST CAN'T STOP LAUGHING!
HO HO HO.
MERU-MERU-ME~
MERU-MERU-ME~
OH MY. LOOKS LIKE THIS HORSEY DOESN'T UNDERSTAND HOW AMAZING THIS KNIFE IS.
FINE, I'LL EXPLAIN IT TO YOU.
YOU CAN CUT ANYTHING WITH THIS SUPER KNIFE.
MERU?
I CAN SLICE A TOMATO. ♡ I CAN SLICE A PUMPKIN. ♡ I CAN SLICE A FROZEN FISH. ♡
SP
SP
SP
SP
I CAN SLICE A CUTTING BOARD. ♡ I CAN SLICE A PIECE OF GLASS. ♡ I CAN SLICE AN INDUSTRIAL STRENGTH NAIL. ♡
SP
SP
SP
I CAN EVEN SLICE MY HUSBAND'S ALLOWANCE. ♡
SP
P-CHING
GLARE
HA HA HA HA HA HA HA HA

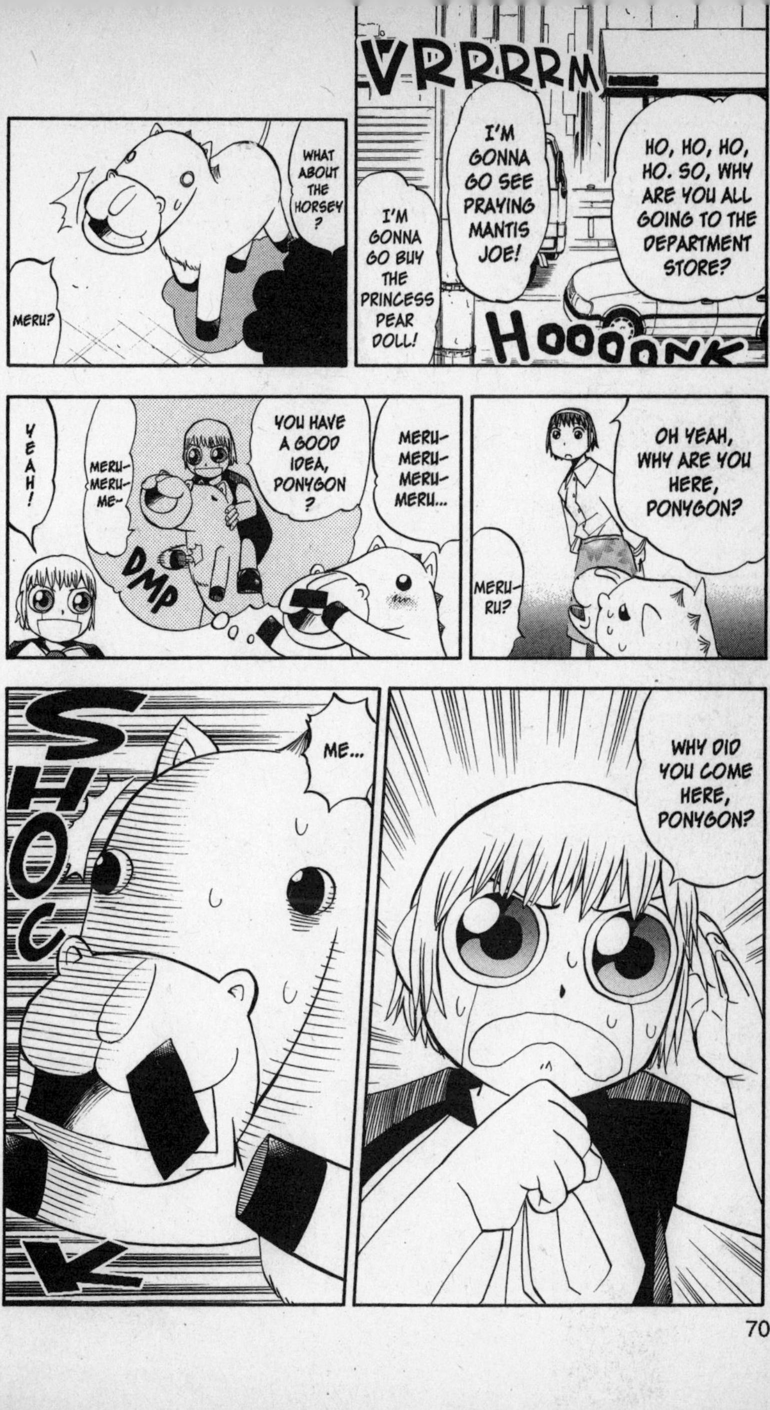
VRRRRM
HO, HO, HO, HO. SO, WHY ARE YOU ALL GOING TO THE DEPARTMENT STORE?
I'M GONNA GO SEE PRAYING MANTIS JOE!
I'M GONNA GO BUY THE PRINCESS PEAR DOLL!
HOOOOONK
WHAT ABOUT THE HORSEY?
MERU?
OH YEAH, WHY ARE YOU HERE, PONYGON?
MERURU?
MERU-MERU-MERU-MERU...
YOU HAVE A GOOD IDEA, PONYGON?
MERU-MERU-ME~
DMP
YEAH!
WHY DID YOU COME HERE, PONYGON?
ME...
SHOCK

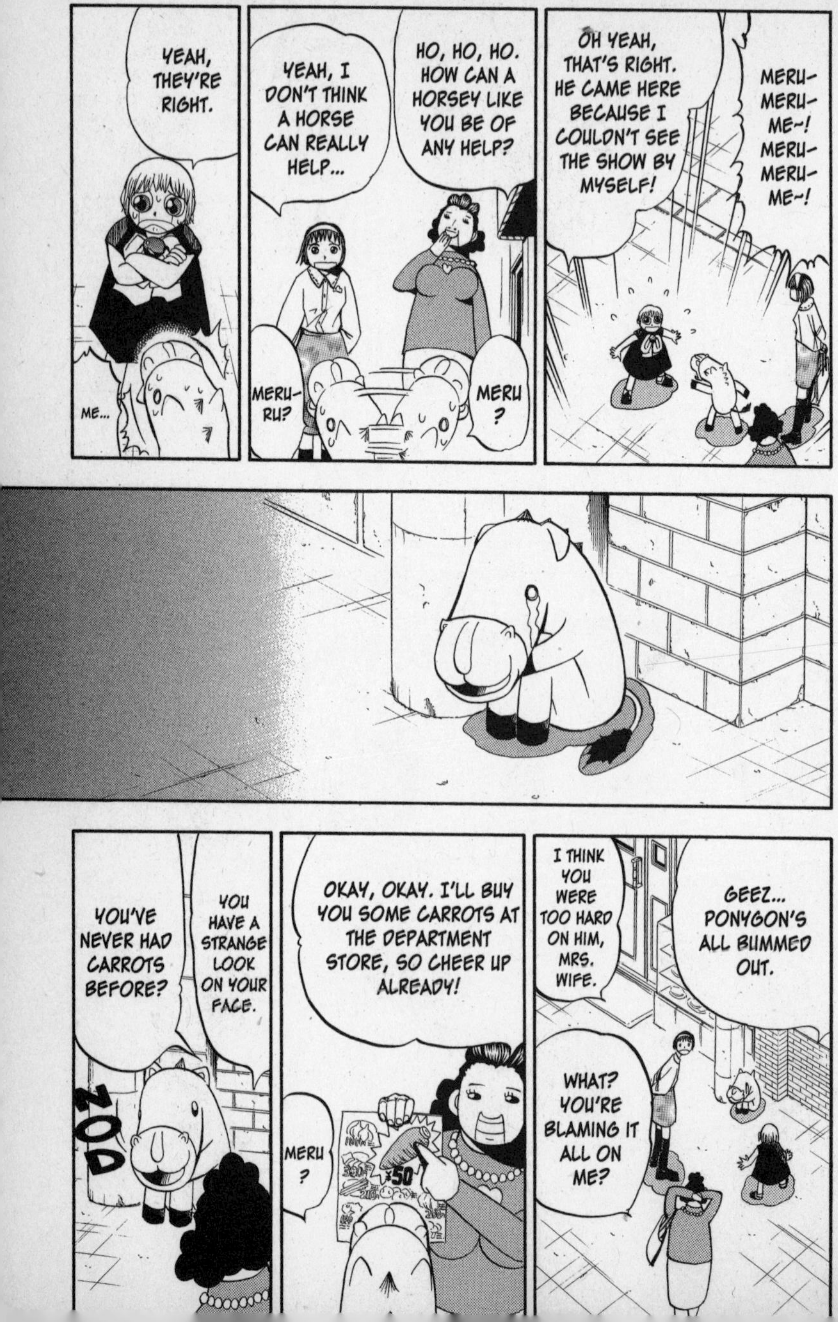
MERU-MERU-ME~! MERU-MERU-ME~!
OH YEAH, THAT'S RIGHT. HE CAME HERE BECAUSE I COULDN'T SEE THE SHOW BY MYSELF!
HO, HO, HO. HOW CAN A HORSEY LIKE YOU BE OF ANY HELP?
YEAH, I DON'T THINK A HORSE CAN REALLY HELP...
MERU ?
MERU-RU?
YEAH, THEY'RE RIGHT.
ME...
GEEZ... PONYGON'S ALL BUMMED OUT.
I THINK YOU WERE TOO HARD ON HIM, MRS. WIFE.
WHAT? YOU'RE BLAMING IT ALL ON ME?
OKAY, OKAY. I'LL BUY YOU SOME CARROTS AT THE DEPARTMENT STORE, SO CHEER UP ALREADY!
MERU ?
¥50
YOU HAVE A STRANGE LOOK ON YOUR FACE.
YOU'VE NEVER HAD CARROTS BEFORE?
ZOD

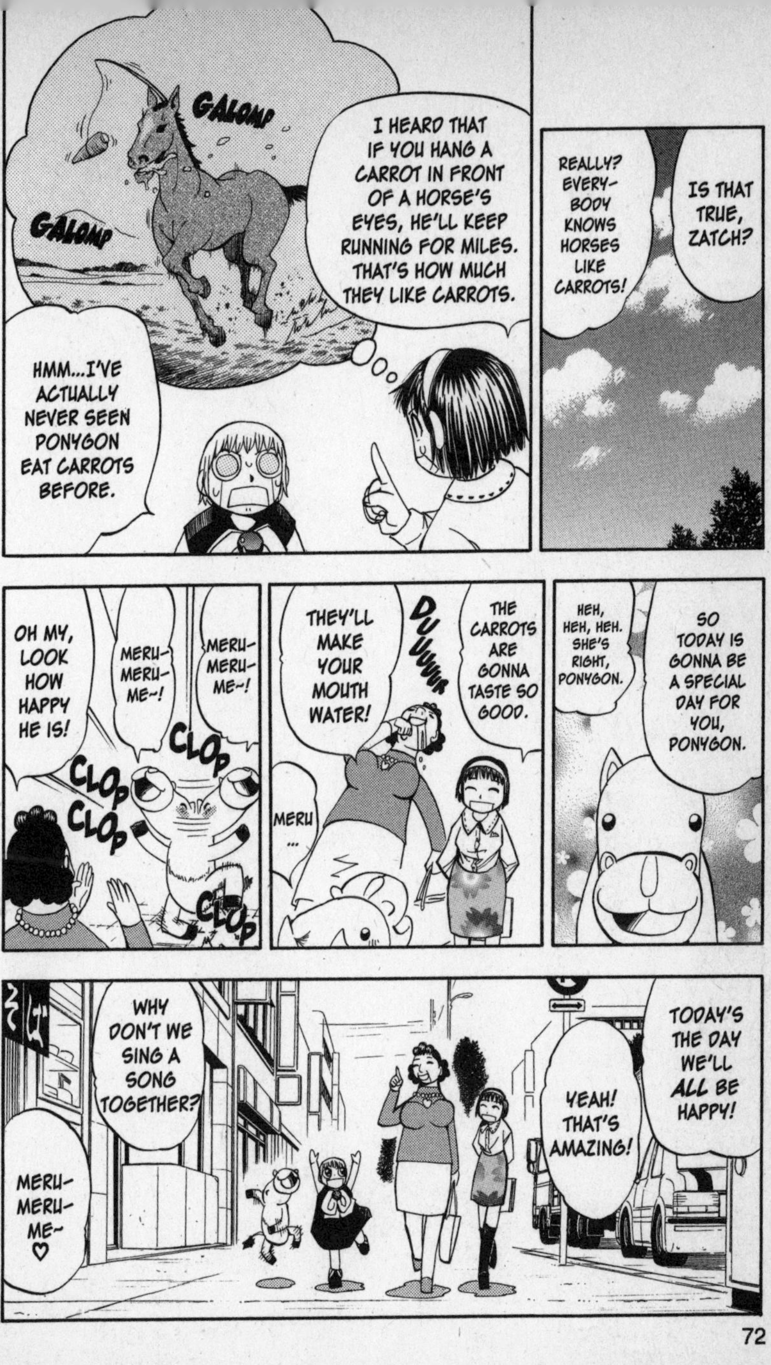
IS THAT TRUE, ZATCH?
REALLY? EVERYBODY KNOWS HORSES LIKE CARROTS!
I HEARD THAT IF YOU HANG A CARROT IN FRONT OF A HORSE'S EYES, HE'LL KEEP RUNNING FOR MILES. THAT'S HOW MUCH THEY LIKE CARROTS.
GALOMP
GALOMP
HMM...I'VE ACTUALLY NEVER SEEN PONYGON EAT CARROTS BEFORE.
SO TODAY IS GONNA BE A SPECIAL DAY FOR YOU, PONYGON.
HEH, HEH, HEH. SHE'S RIGHT, PONYGON.
THE CARROTS ARE GONNA TASTE SO GOOD.
DUUUUUR
THEY'LL MAKE YOUR MOUTH WATER!
MERU ...
MERU-MERU-ME~!
MERU-MERU-ME~!
CLOP
CLOP
CLOP
CLOP
OH MY, LOOK HOW HAPPY HE IS!
TODAY'S THE DAY WE'LL ALL BE HAPPY!
YEAH! THAT'S AMAZING!
WHY DON'T WE SING A SONG TOGETHER?
MERU-MERU-ME~ ♡

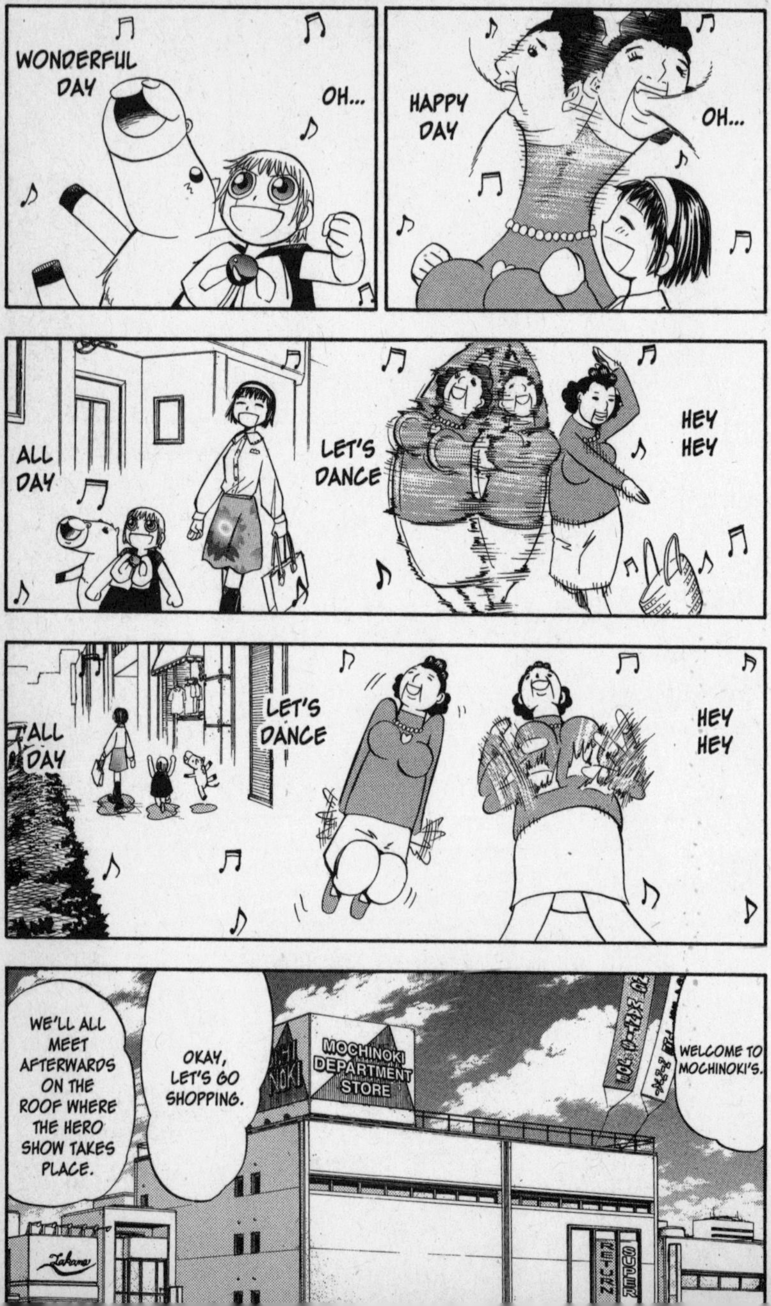
OH...
HAPPY DAY
OH...
WONDERFUL DAY
HEY HEY
LET'S DANCE
ALL DAY
HEY HEY
LET'S DANCE
ALL DAY
WELCOME TO MOCHINOKI'S.
MOCHINOKI DEPARTMENT STORE
OKAY, LET'S GO SHOPPING.
WE'LL ALL MEET AFTERWARDS ON THE ROOF WHERE THE HERO SHOW TAKES PLACE.
SUPER
RETURN

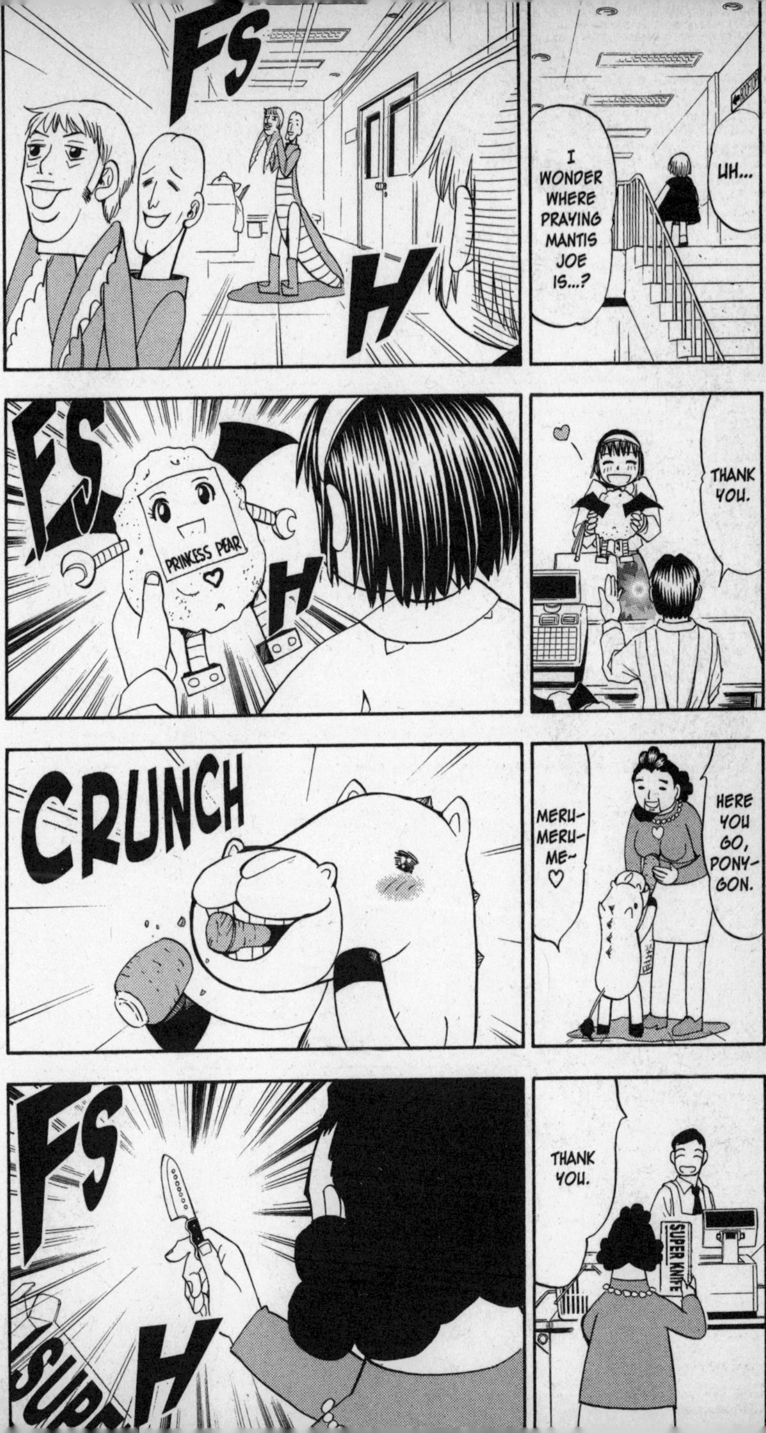
UH...
I WONDER WHERE PRAYING MANTIS JOE IS...?
FS
H
THANK YOU.
FS
PRINKESS PEAR
H
HERE YOU GO, PONY-GON.
MERU-MERU-ME~♡
CRUNCH
THANK YOU.
SUPER KNIFE
FS
H
SUPE

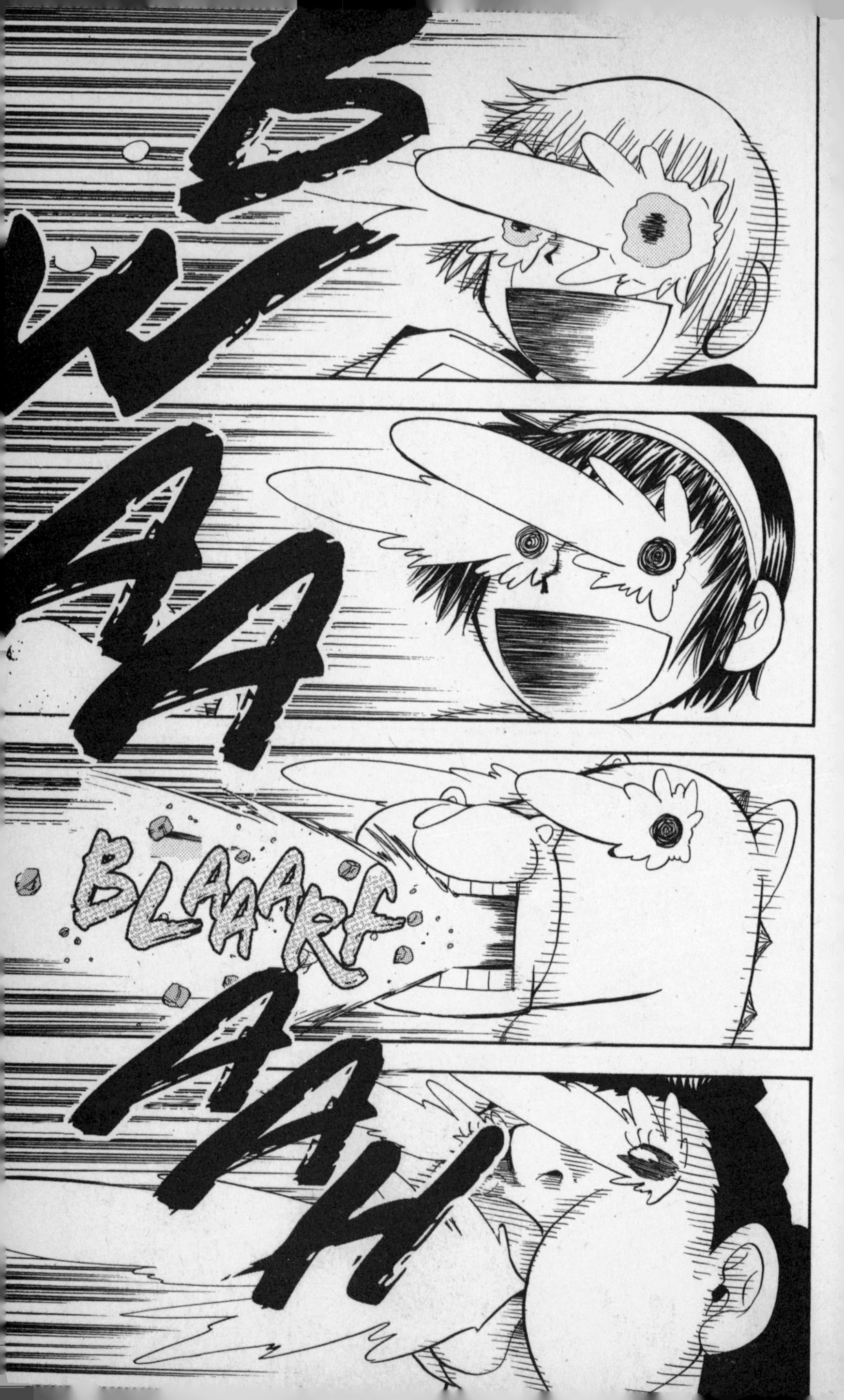
BLAAARF

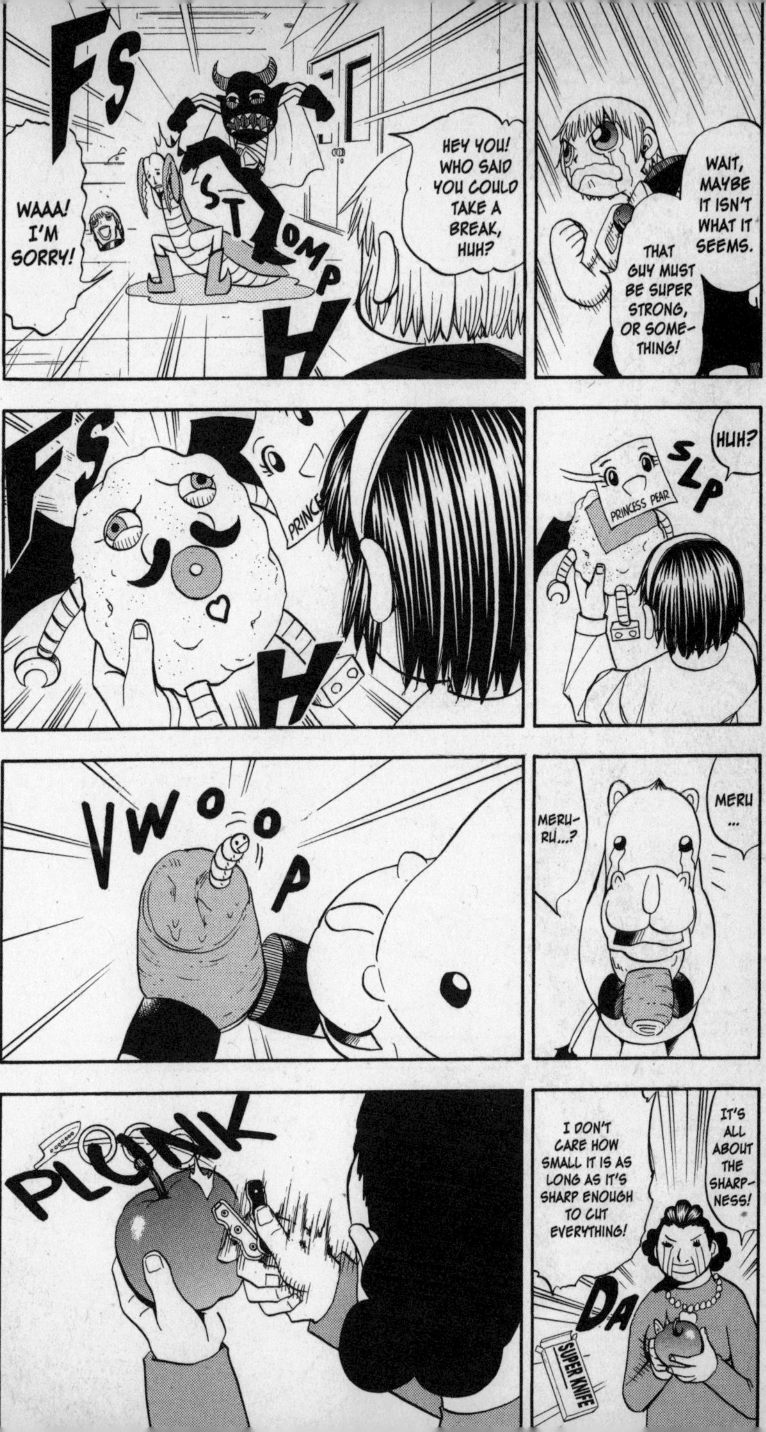
WAIT, MAYBE IT ISN'T WHAT IT SEEMS.
THAT GUY MUST BE SUPER STRONG, OR SOMETHING!
HEY YOU! WHO SAID YOU COULD TAKE A BREAK, HUH?
FS
STOMPH
WAAA! I'M SORRY!
HUH?
SLP
PRINCESS PEAR
FSH
PRINCE
MERU ...
MERU-RU...?
VWOOOP
IT'S ALL ABOUT THE SHARPNESS!
I DON'T CARE HOW SMALL IT IS AS LONG AS IT'S SHARP ENOUGH TO CUT EVERYTHING!
DA
SUPER KNIFE
PLUNK

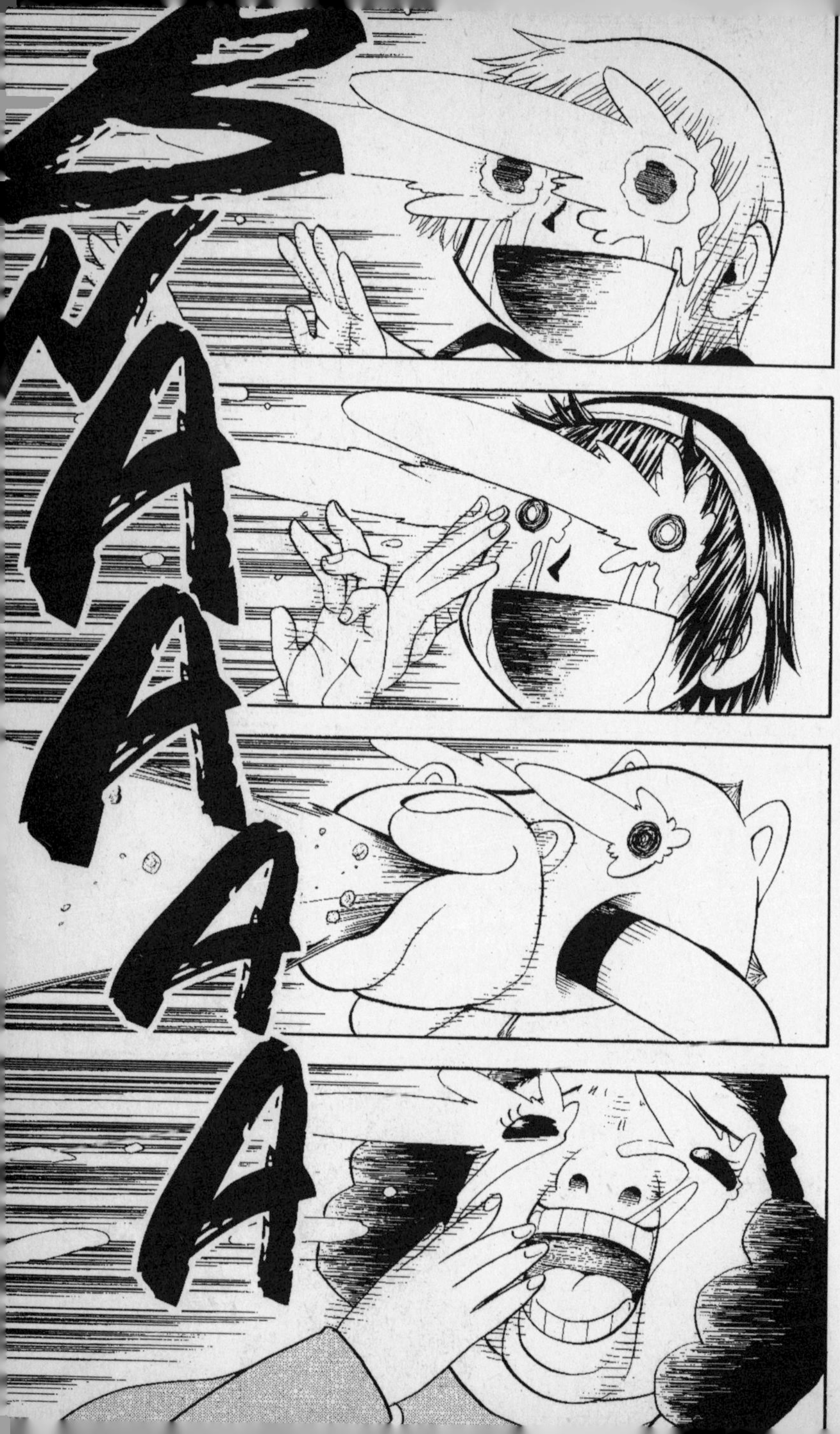
BHAAAA

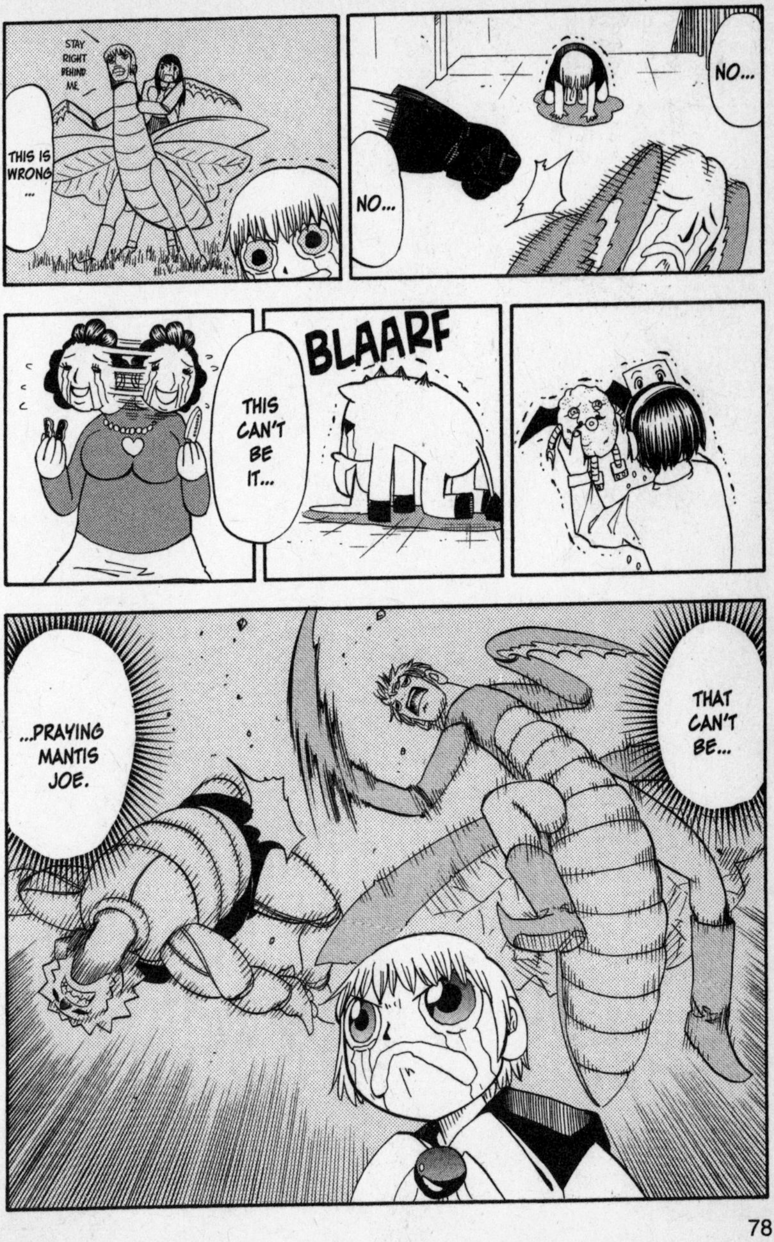
NO...
NO...
STAY RIGHT BEHIND ME.
THIS IS WRONG ...
BLAARF
THIS CAN'T BE IT...
THAT CAN'T BE...
...PRAYING MANTIS JOE.

LEVEL 79: The True Hero

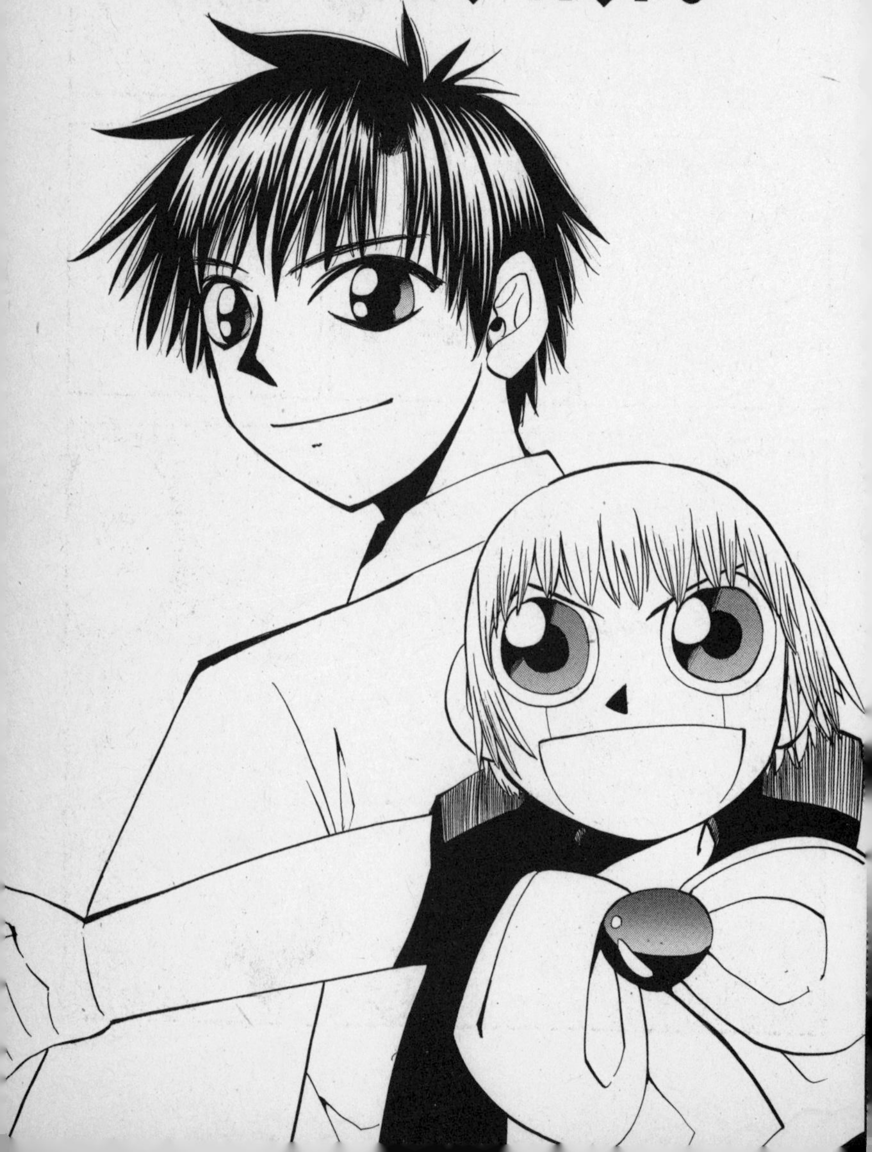

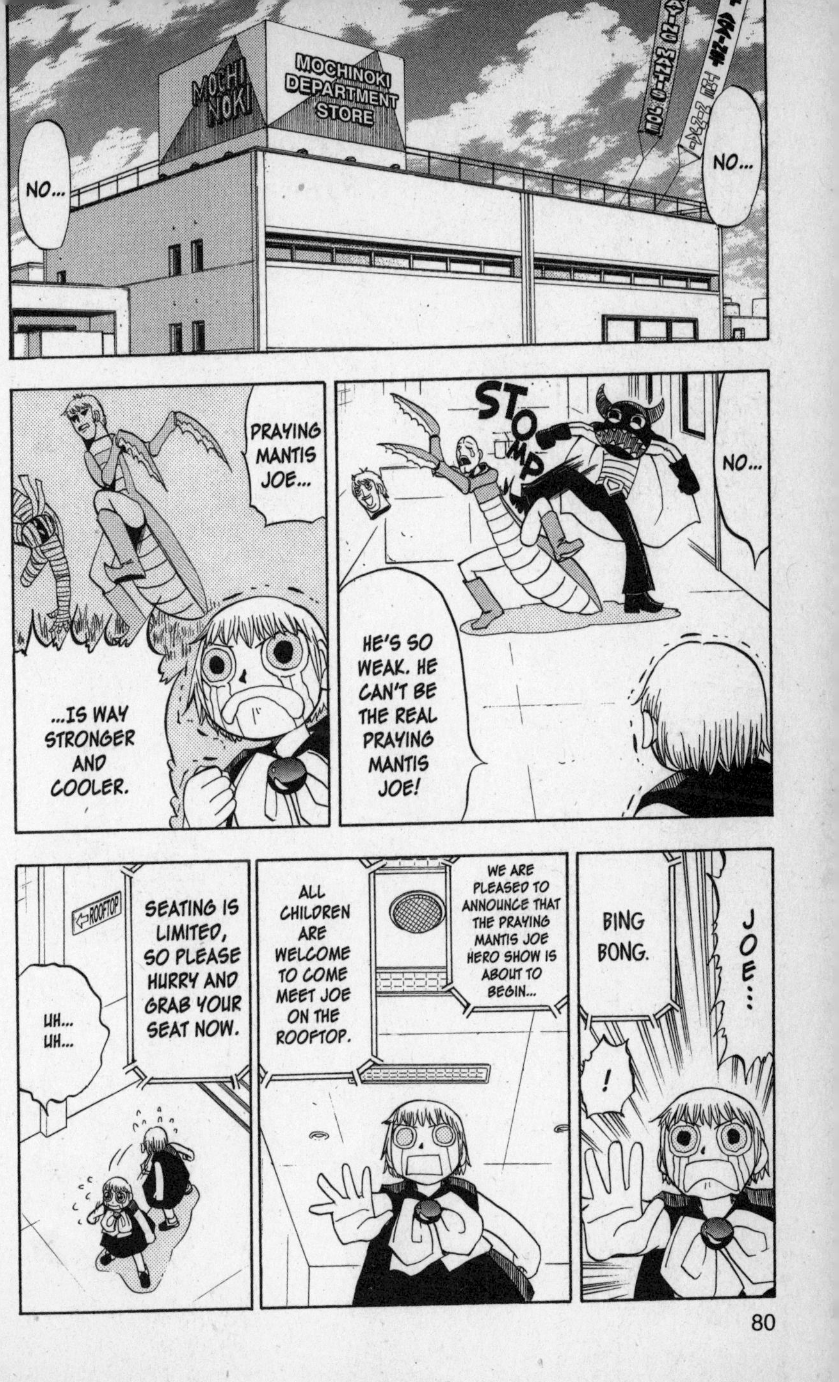
MOCHINOKI DEPARTMENT STORE
MOCHI NOKI
NO...
NO...
NO...
STOMP
HE'S SO WEAK. HE CAN'T BE THE REAL PRAYING MANTIS JOE!
PRAYING MANTIS JOE...
...IS WAY STRONGER AND COOLER.
JOE...
BING BONG.
!
WE ARE PLEASED TO ANNOUNCE THAT THE PRAYING MANTIS JOE HERO SHOW IS ABOUT TO BEGIN...
ALL CHILDREN ARE WELCOME TO COME MEET JOE ON THE ROOFTOP.
SEATING IS LIMITED, SO PLEASE HURRY AND GRAB YOUR SEAT NOW.
ROOFTOP
UH... UH...

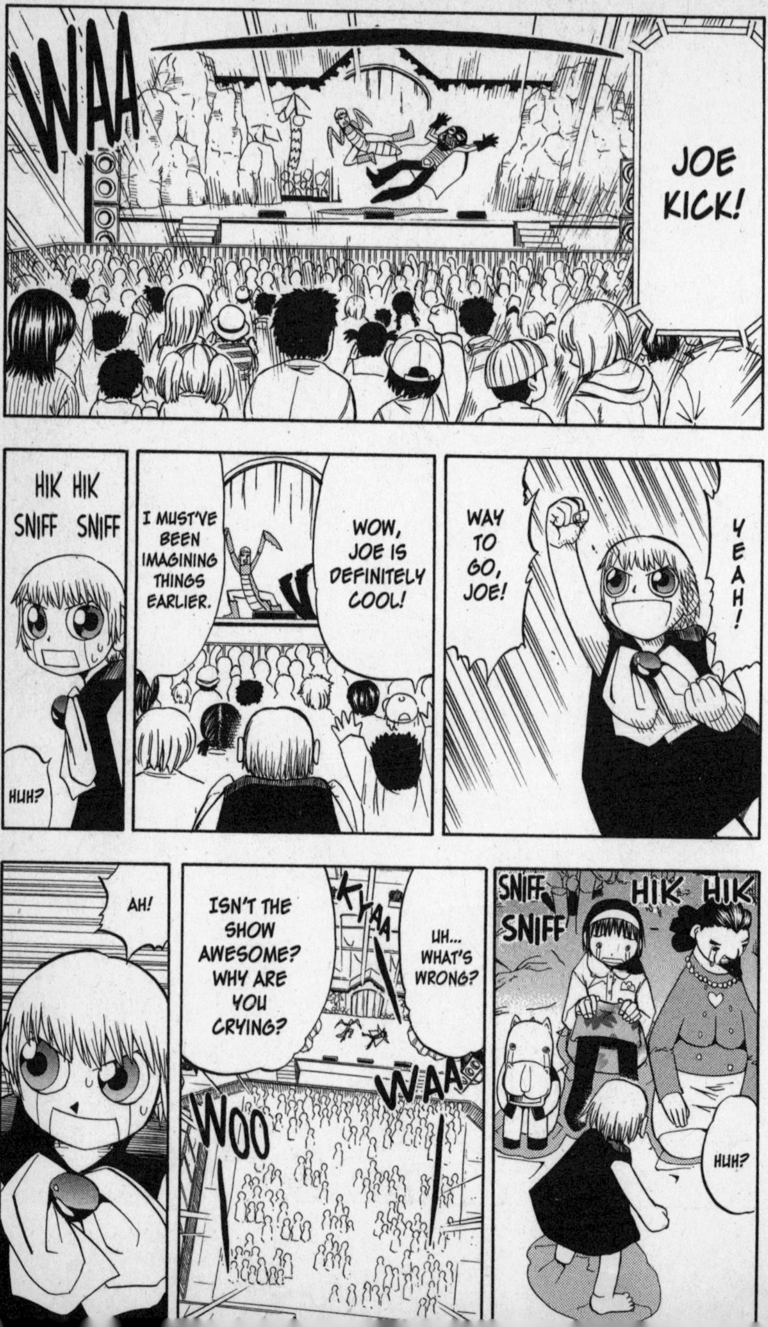
JOE KICK!
WAA
YEAH!
WAY TO GO, JOE!
WOW, JOE IS DEFINITELY COOL!
I MUST'VE BEEN IMAGINING THINGS EARLIER.
HIK HIK
SNIFF SNIFF
HUH?
HIK HIK
SNIFF SNIFF
HUH?
UH... WHAT'S WRONG?
KYAA
ISN'T THE SHOW AWESOME? WHY ARE YOU CRYING?
WAA
WOO
AH!

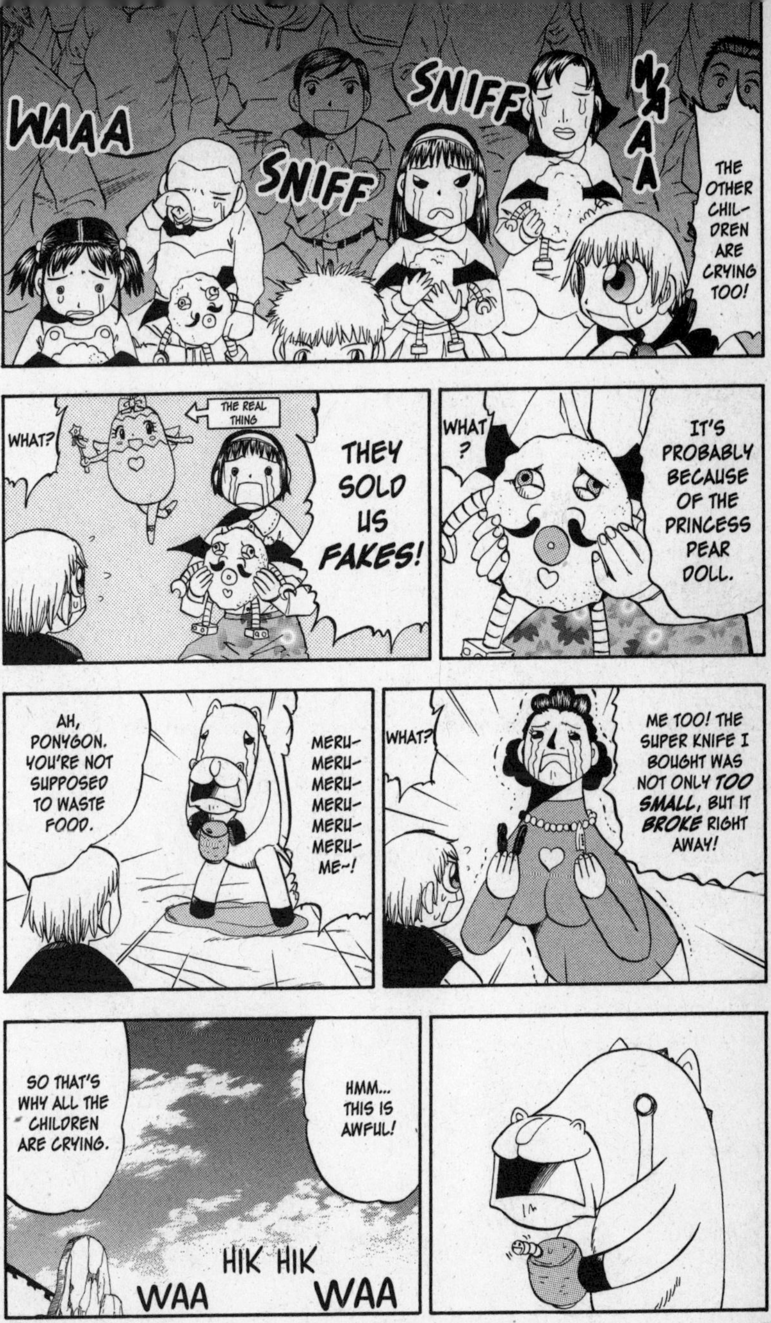
THE OTHER CHILDREN ARE CRYING TOO!
WAAA
SNIFF
SNIFF
WAAA
IT'S PROBABLY BECAUSE OF THE PRINCESS PEAR DOLL.
WHAT?
THEY SOLD US FAKES!
THE REAL THING
WHAT?
ME TOO! THE SUPER KNIFE I BOUGHT WAS NOT ONLY *TOO SMALL*, BUT IT *BROKE* RIGHT AWAY!
WHAT?
MERU-MERU-MERU-MERU-MERU-MERU-MERUME~!
AH, PONYGON. YOU'RE NOT SUPPOSED TO WASTE FOOD.
HMM... THIS IS AWFUL!
SO THAT'S WHY ALL THE CHILDREN ARE CRYING.
HIK HIK
WAA
WAA

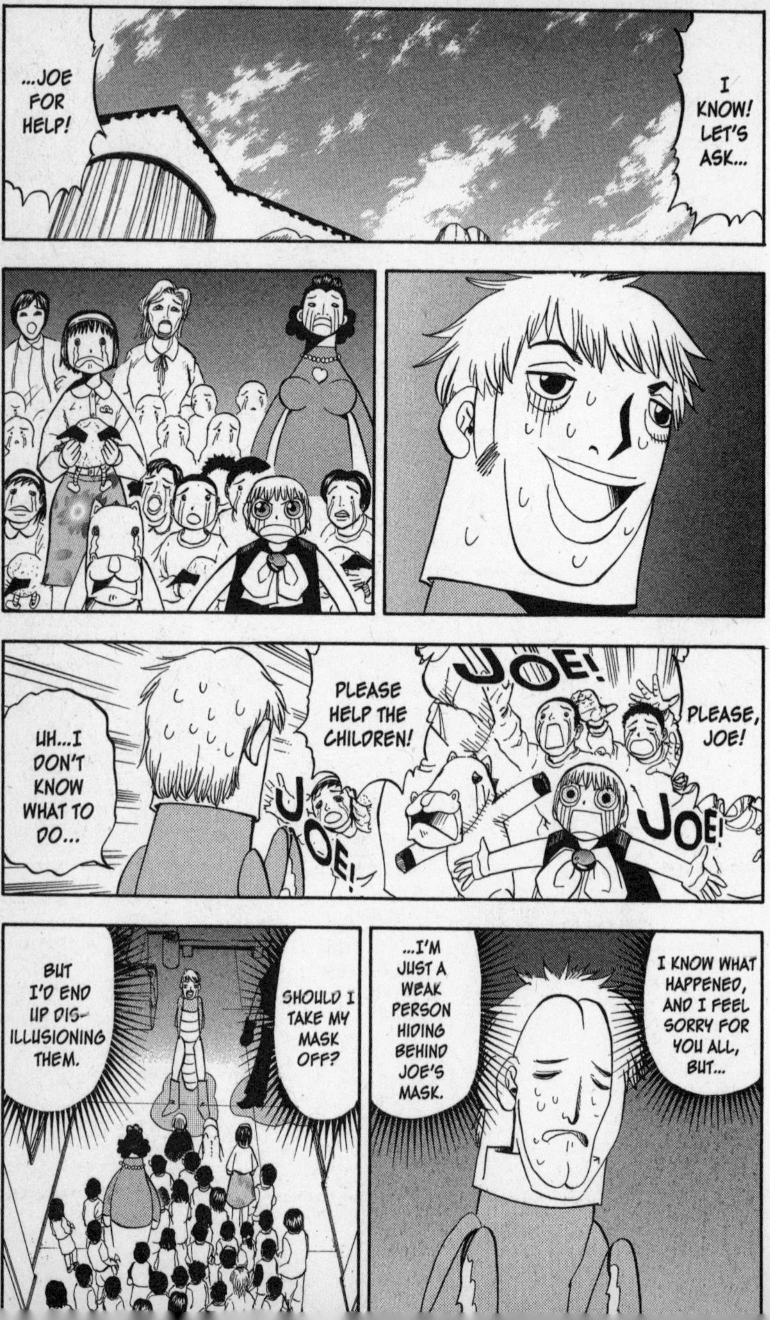
I KNOW! LET'S ASK...
...JOE FOR HELP!
JOE!
PLEASE, JOE!
PLEASE HELP THE CHILDREN!
JOE!
JOE!
UH...I DON'T KNOW WHAT TO DO...
I KNOW WHAT HAPPENED, AND I FEEL SORRY FOR YOU ALL, BUT...
...I'M JUST A WEAK PERSON HIDING BEHIND JOE'S MASK.
SHOULD I TAKE MY MASK OFF?
BUT I'D END UP DIS-ILLUSIONING THEM.

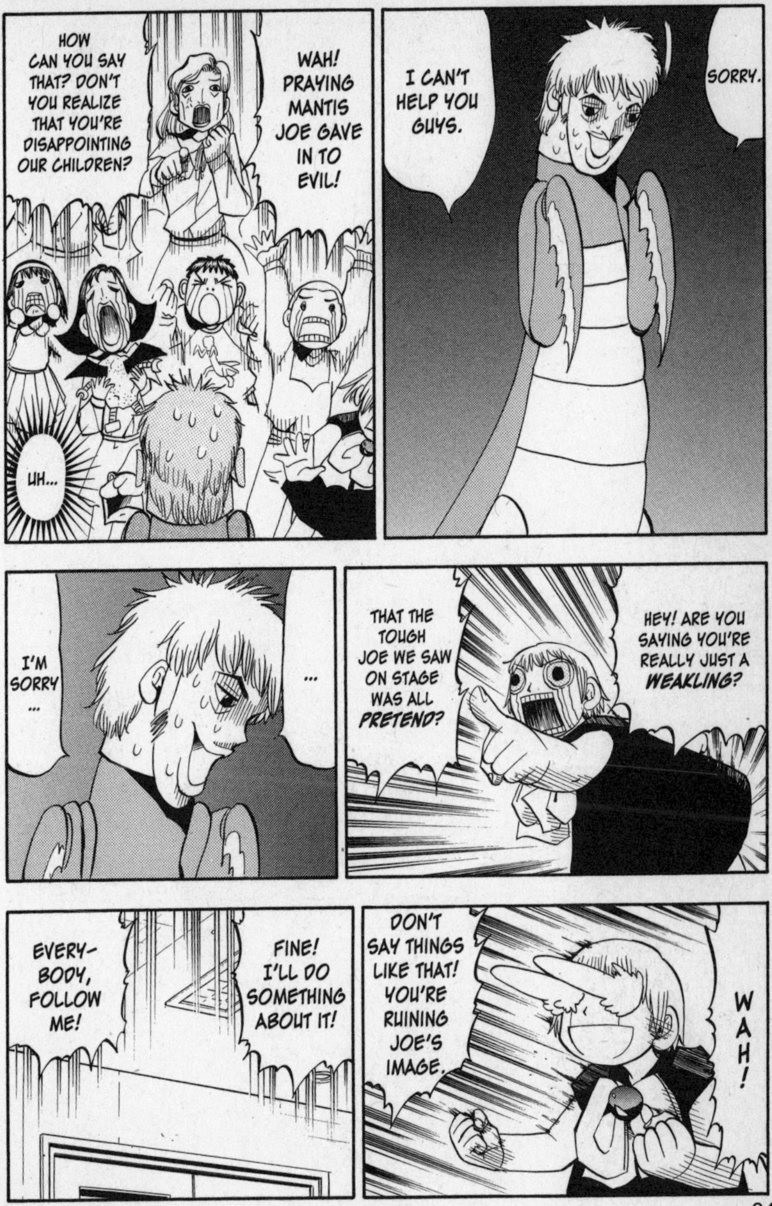
SORRY.
I CAN'T HELP YOU GUYS.
WAH! PRAYING MANTIS JOE GAVE IN TO EVIL!
HOW CAN YOU SAY THAT? DON'T YOU REALIZE THAT YOU'RE DISAPPOINTING OUR CHILDREN?
UH...
HEY! ARE YOU SAYING YOU'RE REALLY JUST A *WEAKLING?*
THAT THE TOUGH JOE WE SAW ON STAGE WAS ALL *PRETEND?*
...
I'M SORRY ...
WAH!
DON'T SAY THINGS LIKE THAT! YOU'RE RUINING JOE'S IMAGE.
FINE! I'LL DO SOMETHING ABOUT IT!
EVERY-BODY, FOLLOW ME!

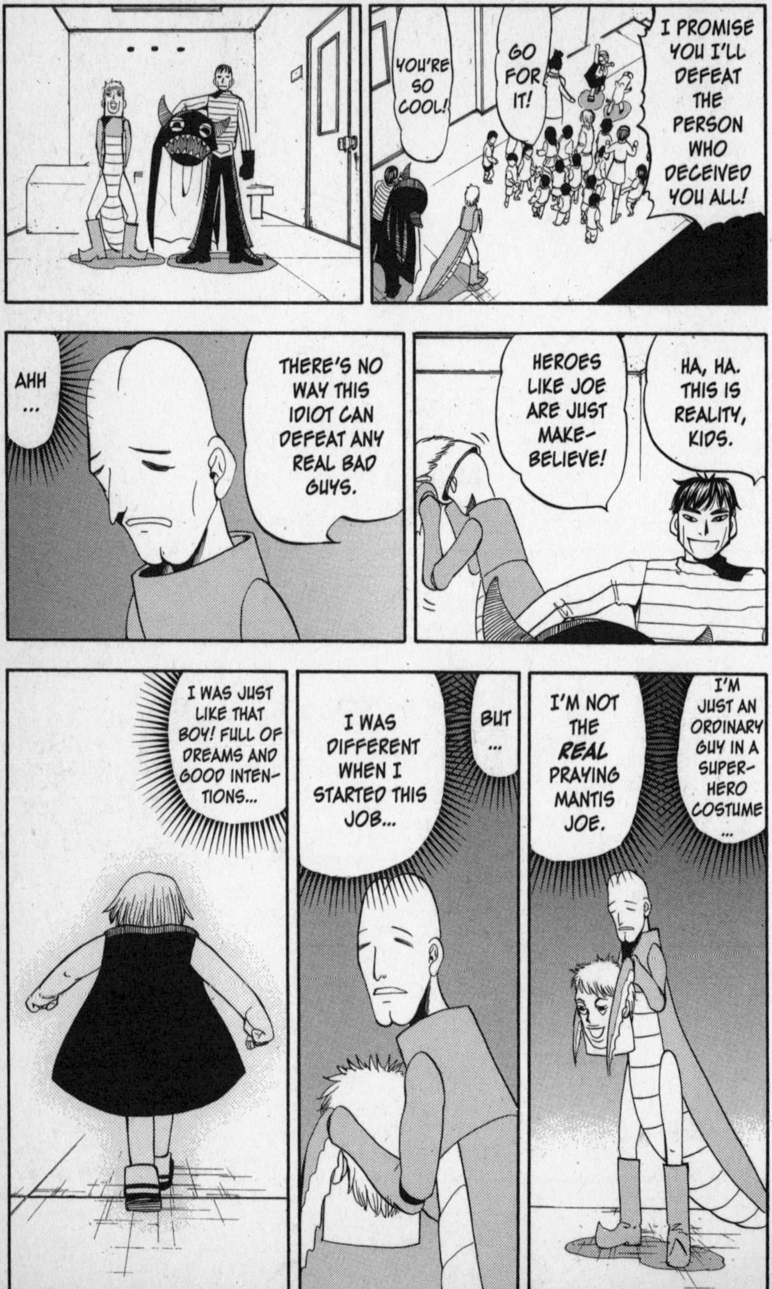
I PROMISE YOU I'LL DEFEAT THE PERSON WHO DECEIVED YOU ALL!
GO FOR IT!
YOU'RE SO COOL!
HA, HA. THIS IS REALITY, KIDS.
HEROES LIKE JOE ARE JUST MAKE-BELIEVE!
THERE'S NO WAY THIS IDIOT CAN DEFEAT ANY REAL BAD GUYS.
AHH...
I'M JUST AN ORDINARY GUY IN A SUPER-HERO COSTUME...
I'M NOT THE *REAL* PRAYING MANTIS JOE.
BUT...
I WAS DIFFERENT WHEN I STARTED THIS JOB...
I WAS JUST LIKE THAT BOY! FULL OF DREAMS AND GOOD INTENTIONS...

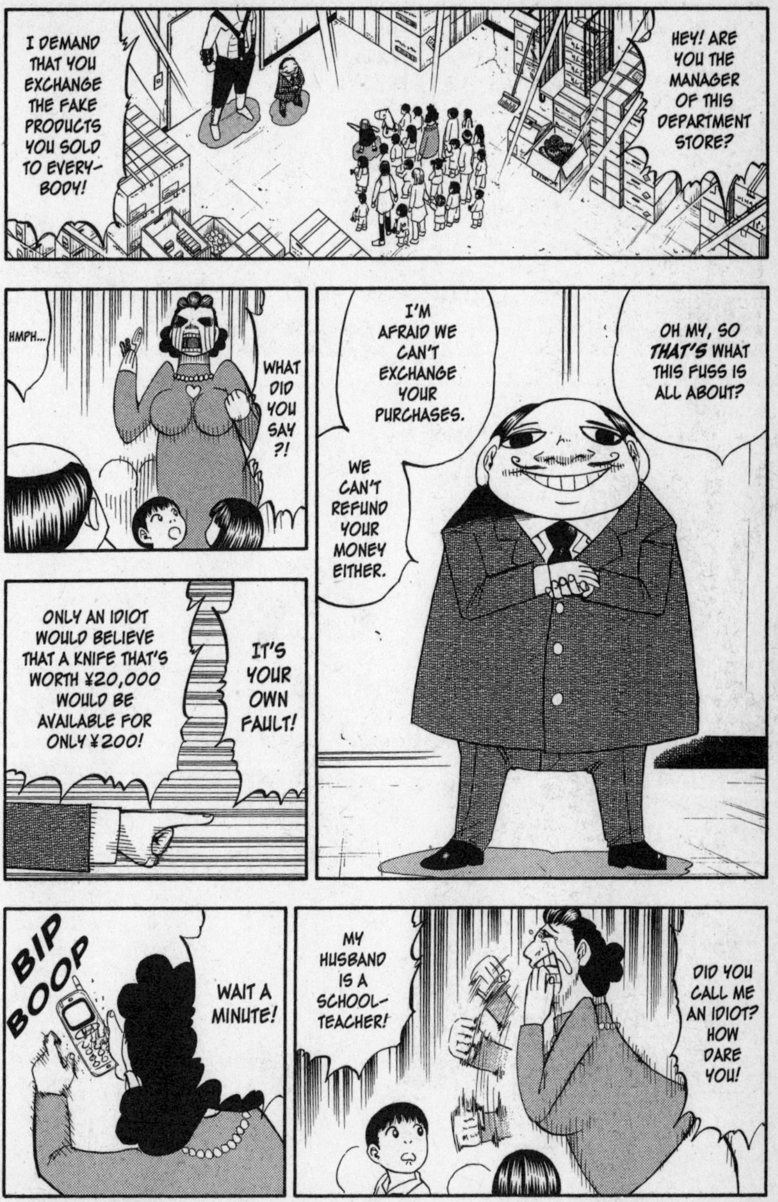
HEY! ARE YOU THE MANAGER OF THIS DEPARTMENT STORE?
I DEMAND THAT YOU EXCHANGE THE FAKE PRODUCTS YOU SOLD TO EVERY-BODY!
OH MY, SO THAT'S WHAT THIS FUSS IS ALL ABOUT?
I'M AFRAID WE CAN'T EXCHANGE YOUR PURCHASES.
WE CAN'T REFUND YOUR MONEY EITHER.
WHAT DID YOU SAY?!
HMPH...
IT'S YOUR OWN FAULT!
ONLY AN IDIOT WOULD BELIEVE THAT A KNIFE THAT'S WORTH ¥20,000 WOULD BE AVAILABLE FOR ONLY ¥200!
DID YOU CALL ME AN IDIOT? HOW DARE YOU!
MY HUSBAND IS A SCHOOL-TEACHER!
WAIT A MINUTE!
BIP BOOP

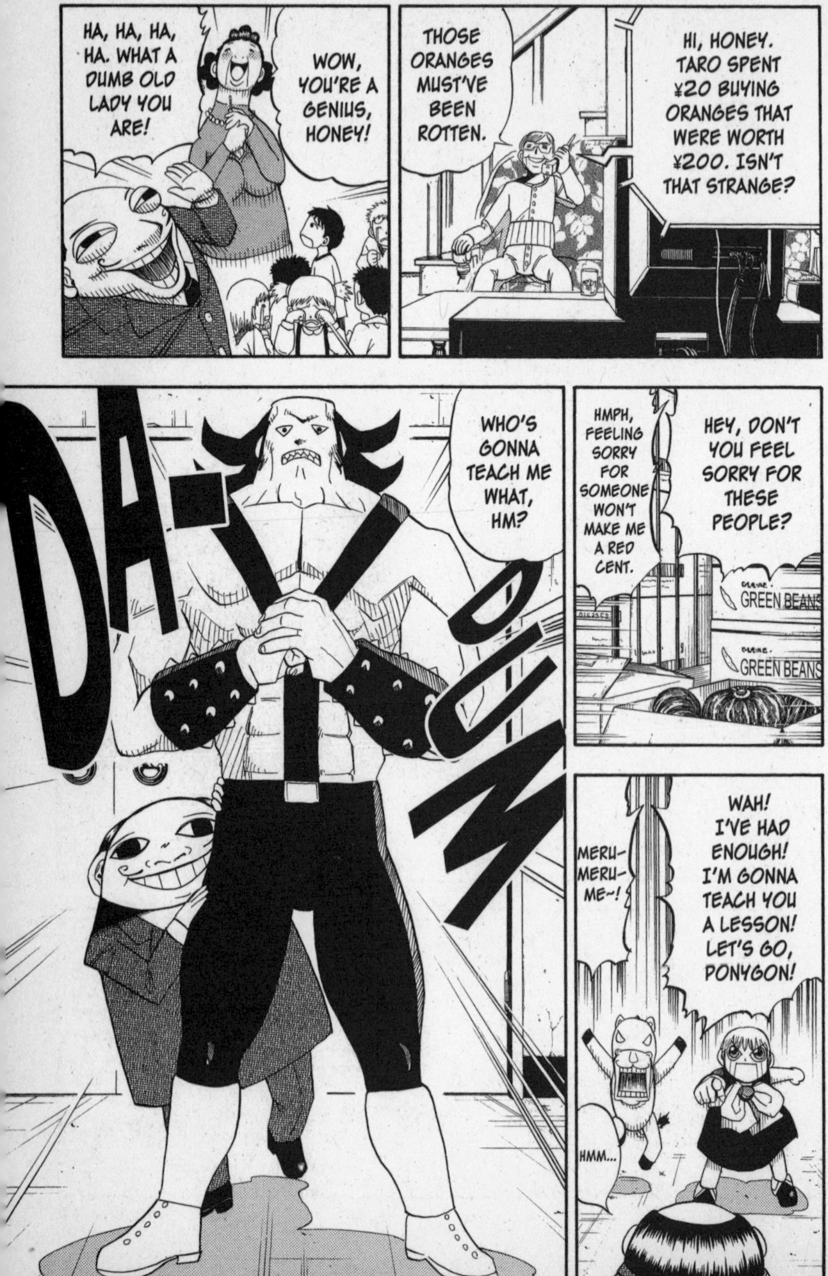
HI, HONEY. TARO SPENT ¥20 BUYING ORANGES THAT WERE WORTH ¥200. ISN'T THAT STRANGE?
THOSE ORANGES MUST'VE BEEN ROTTEN.
WOW, YOU'RE A GENIUS, HONEY!
HA, HA, HA, HA. WHAT A DUMB OLD LADY YOU ARE!
HEY, DON'T YOU FEEL SORRY FOR THESE PEOPLE?
HMPH, FEELING SORRY FOR SOMEONE WON'T MAKE ME A RED CENT.
GREEN BEANS
GREEN BEANS
WAH! I'VE HAD ENOUGH! I'M GONNA TEACH YOU A LESSON! LET'S GO, PONYGON!
MERU-MERU-ME~!
HMM...
WHO'S GONNA TEACH ME WHAT, HM?
DA-
DUN

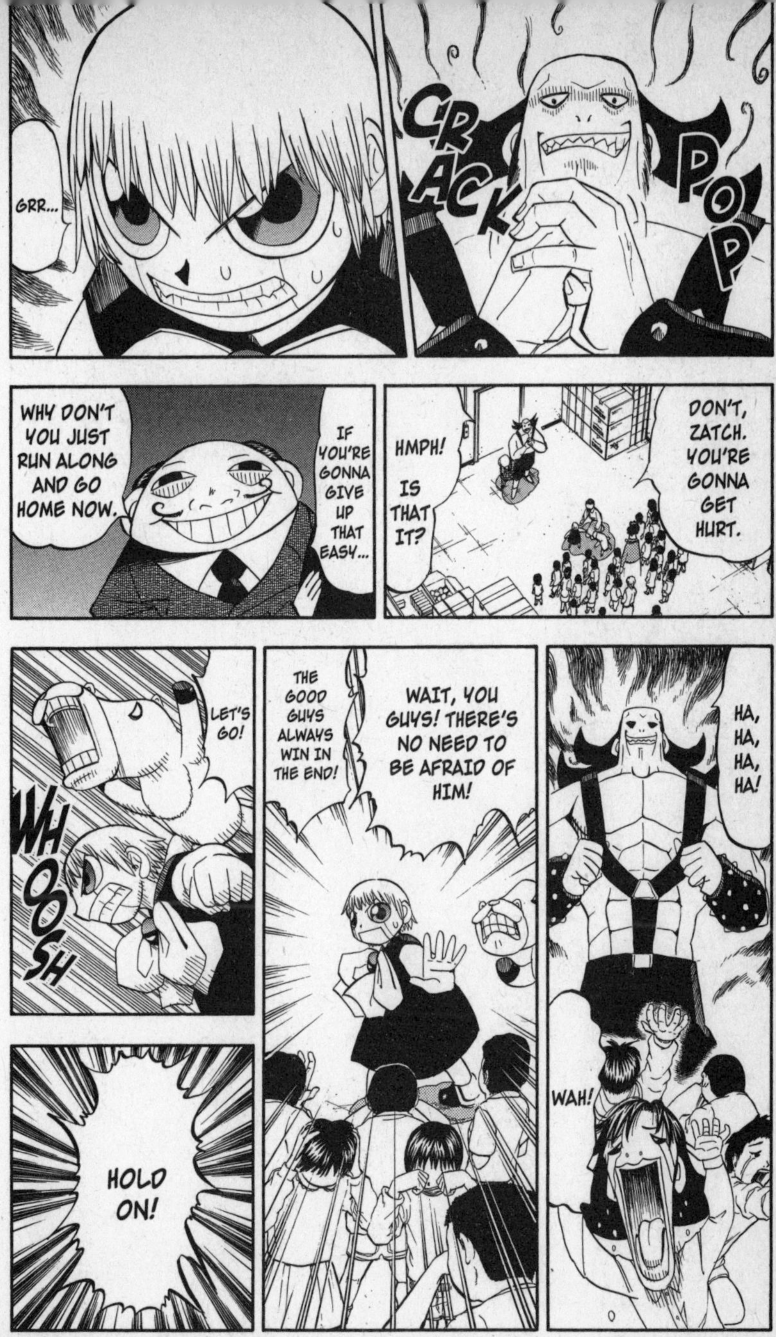
CRACK
POP
GRR...
DON'T, ZATCH. YOU'RE GONNA GET HURT.
HMPH! IS THAT IT?
IF YOU'RE GONNA GIVE UP THAT EASY...
WHY DON'T YOU JUST RUN ALONG AND GO HOME NOW.
HA, HA, HA, HA!
WAH!
WAIT, YOU GUYS! THERE'S NO NEED TO BE AFRAID OF HIM!
THE GOOD GUYS ALWAYS WIN IN THE END!
LET'S GO!
WHOOSH
HOLD ON!

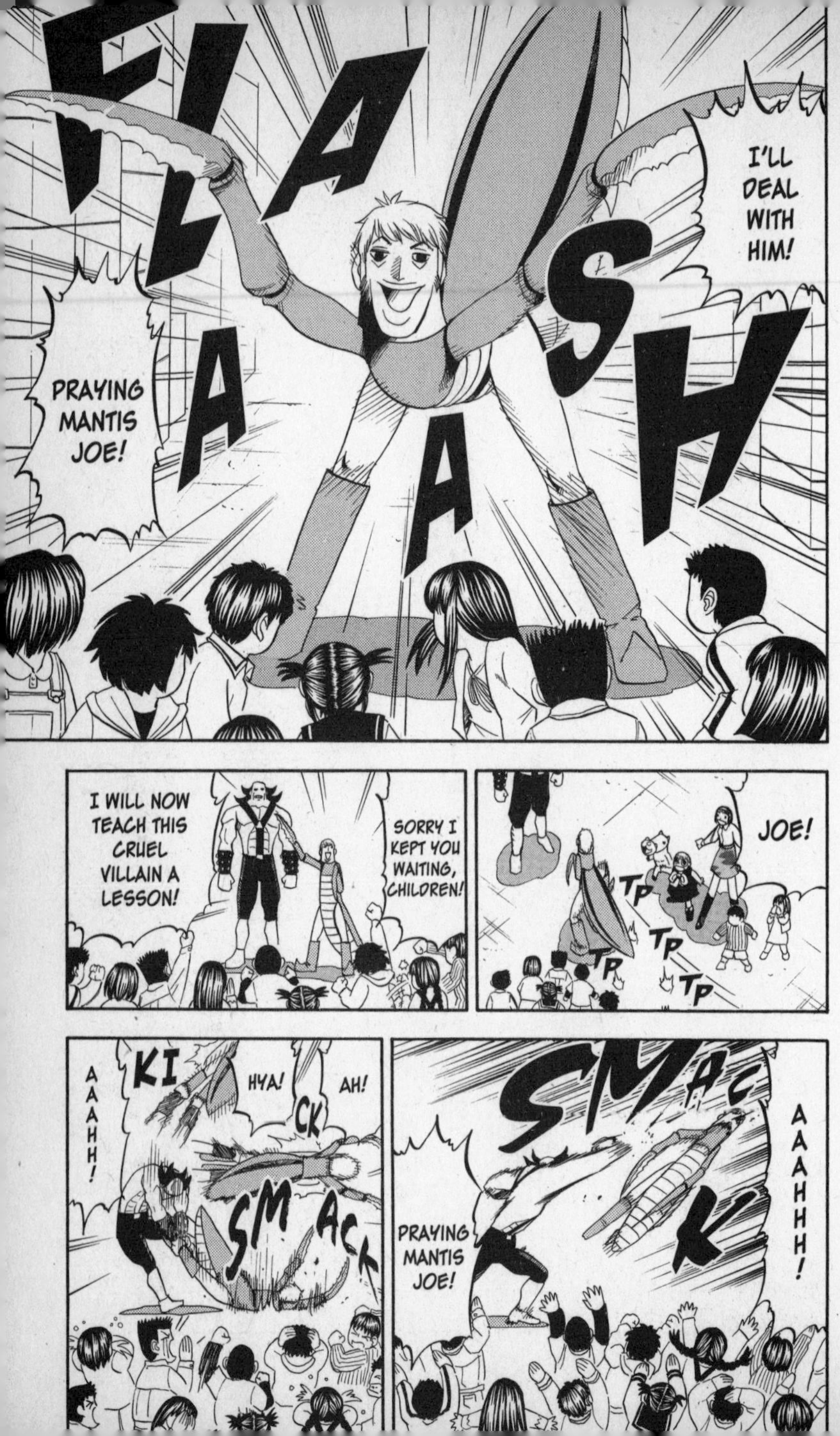
I'LL DEAL WITH HIM!
FLAAASH
PRAYING MANTIS JOE!
JOE!
TP TP TP TP
SORRY I KEPT YOU WAITING, CHILDREN!
I WILL NOW TEACH THIS CRUEL VILLAIN A LESSON!
SMACK
AAAHHHH!
PRAYING MANTIS JOE!
AH!
HYA!
KICK
AAAHH!
SMACK

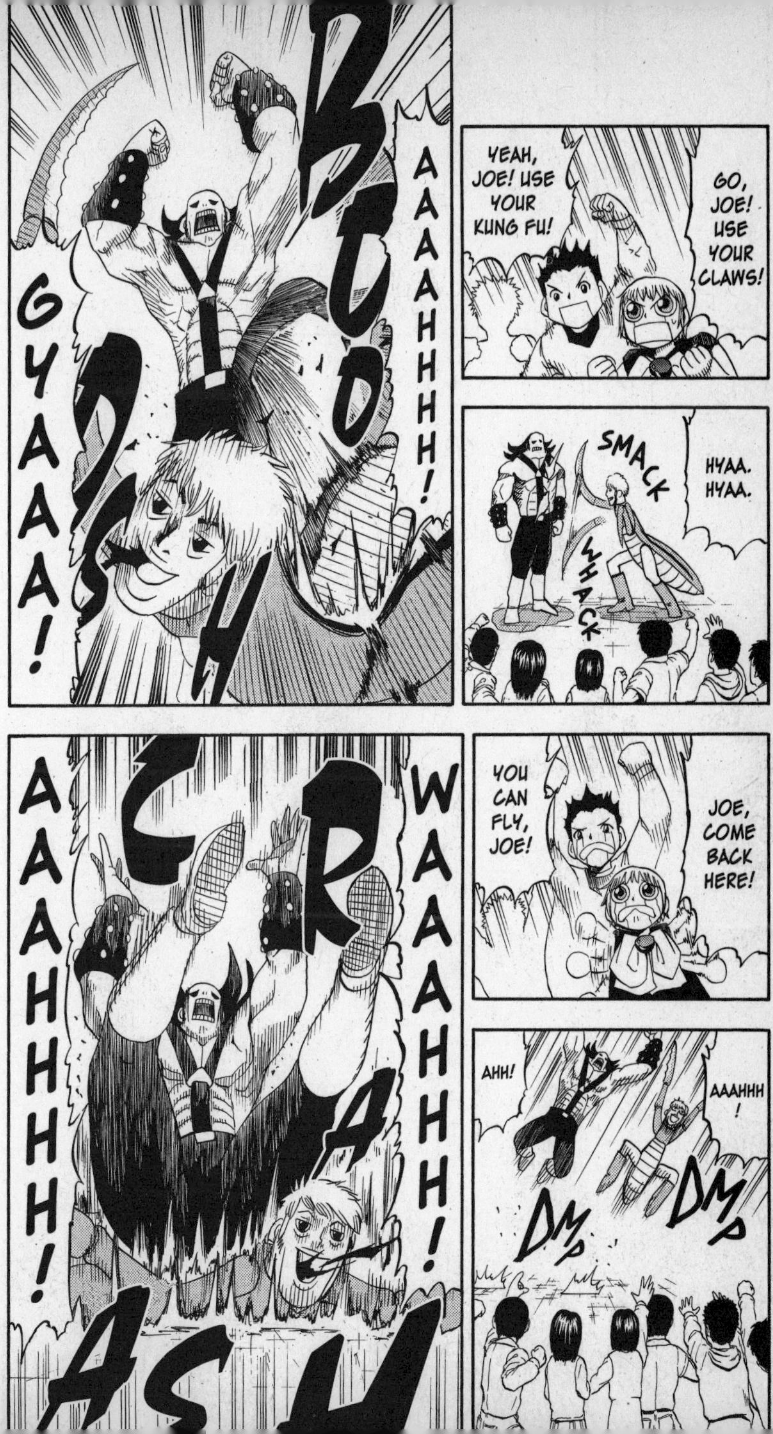
GO, JOE! USE YOUR CLAWS!
YEAH, JOE! USE YOUR KUNG FU!
HYAA. HYAA.
SMACK
WHACK
AAAAAHHHHH!
GYAAAA!
JOE, COME BACK HERE!
YOU CAN FLY, JOE!
AAAHHH!
AHH!
DMP
DMP
WAAAAAHHHH!
CRASH
AAAAHHHHH!

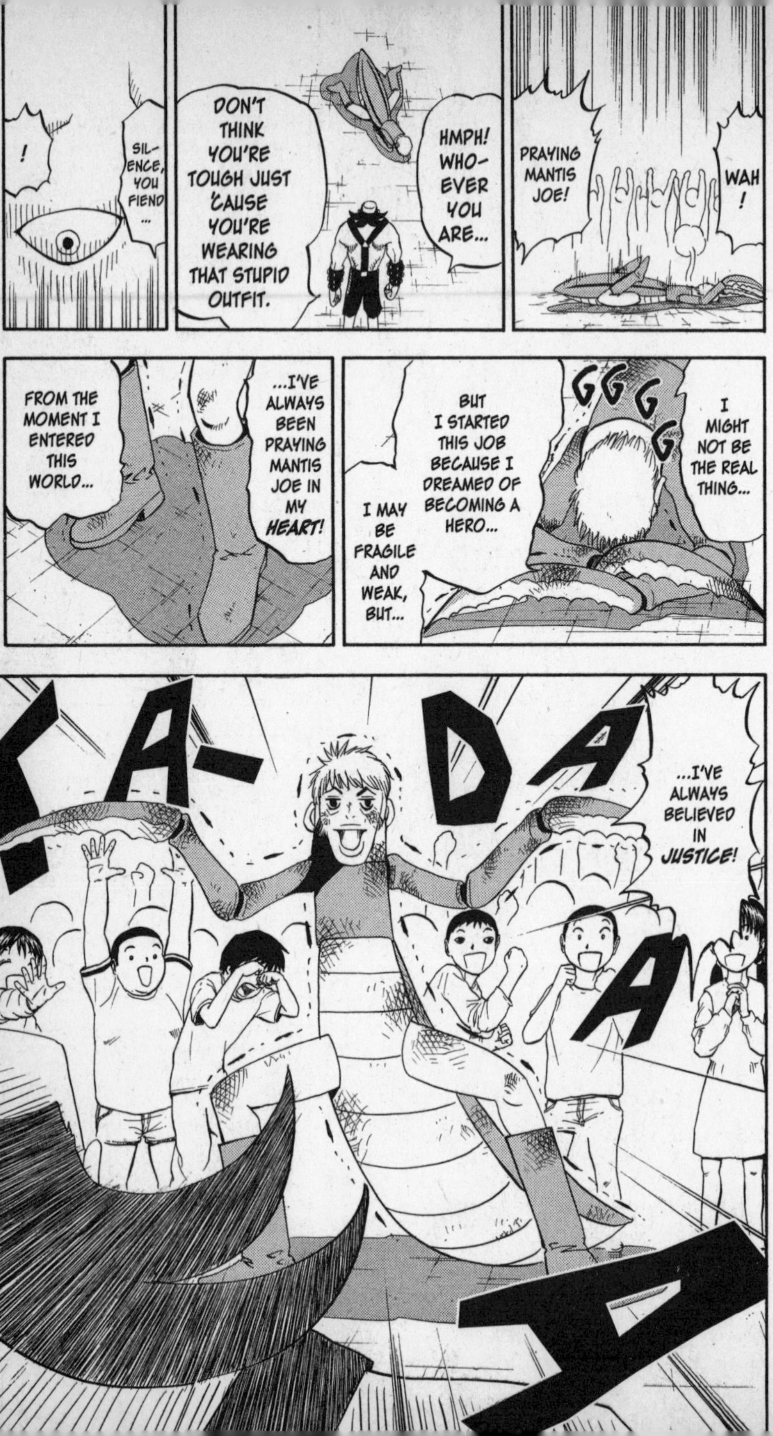
WAH!
PRAYING MANTIS JOE!
HMPH! WHOEVER YOU ARE...
DON'T THINK YOU'RE TOUGH JUST 'CAUSE YOU'RE WEARING THAT STUPID OUTFIT.
SILENCE, YOU FIEND...
!
I MIGHT NOT BE THE REAL THING...
GGGG
BUT I STARTED THIS JOB BECAUSE I DREAMED OF BECOMING A HERO...
I MAY BE FRAGILE AND WEAK, BUT...
...I'VE ALWAYS BEEN PRAYING MANTIS JOE IN MY *HEART!*
FROM THE MOMENT I ENTERED THIS WORLD...
...I'VE ALWAYS BELIEVED IN *JUSTICE!*
TA-DAAA

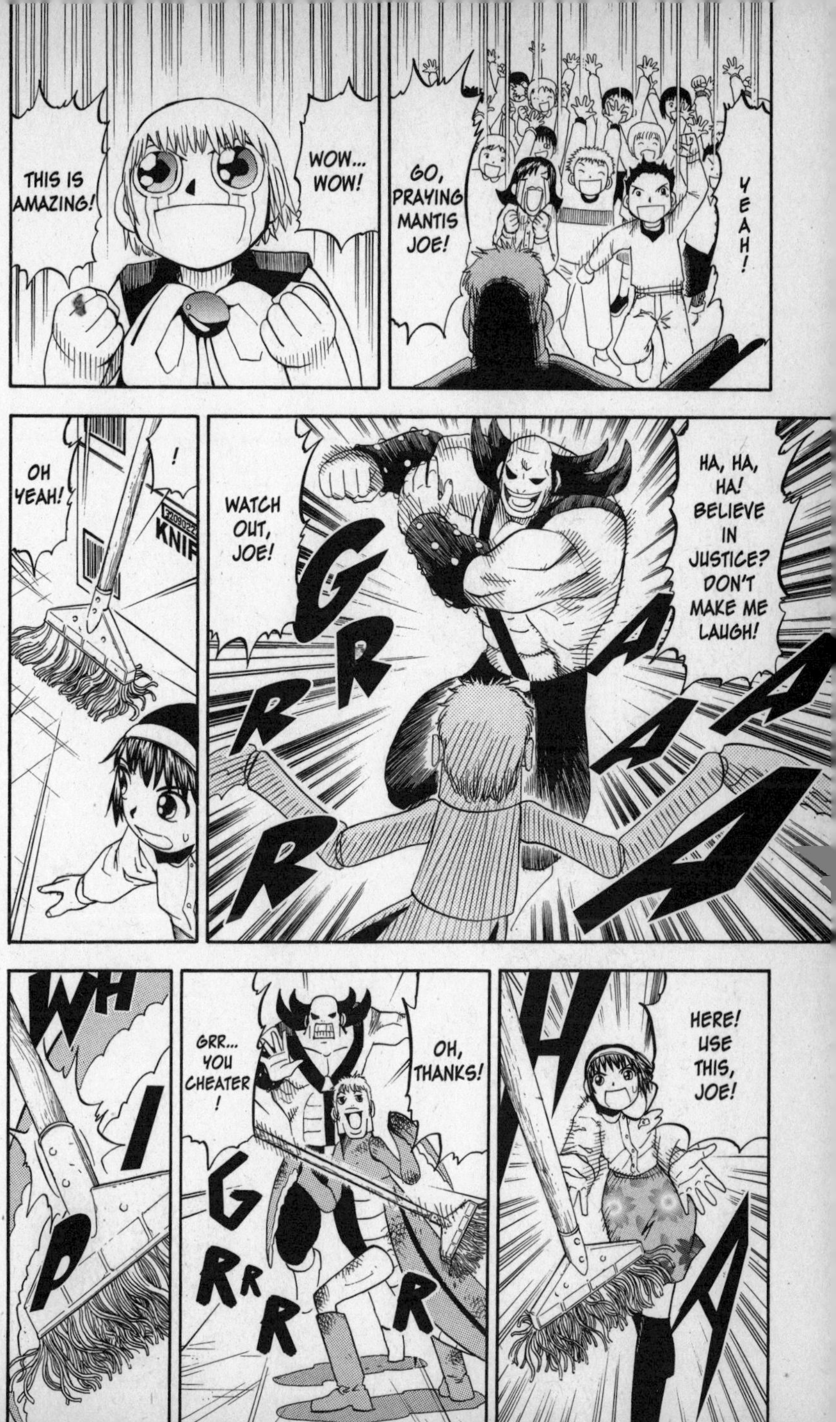
YEAH!
GO, PRAYING MANTIS JOE!
WOW... WOW!
THIS IS AMAZING!
HA, HA, HA! BELIEVE IN JUSTICE? DON'T MAKE ME LAUGH!
GRRRRAAAA
WATCH OUT, JOE!
!
OH YEAH!
HERE! USE THIS, JOE!
OH, THANKS!
GRR... YOU CHEATER!
GRRRR
WHIP

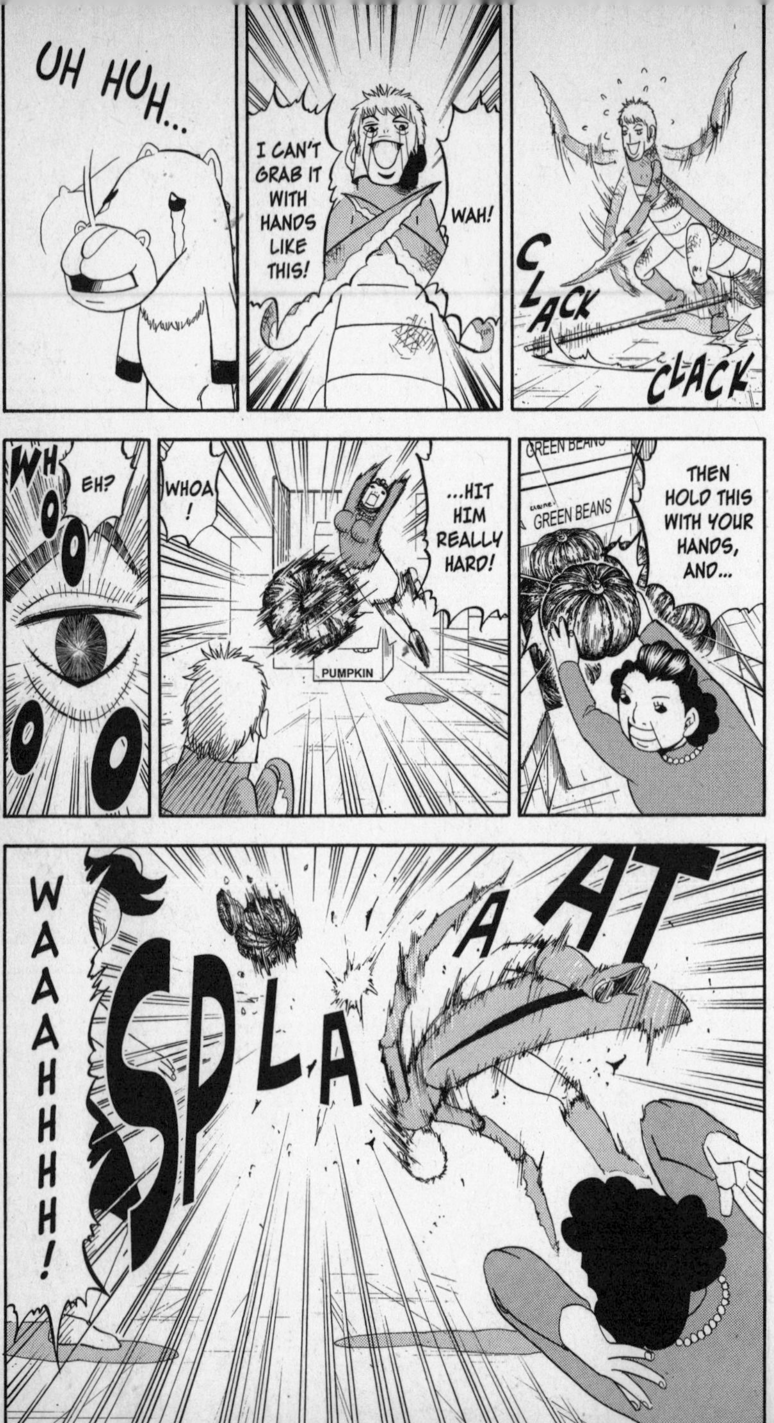
CLACK
CLACK
I CAN'T GRAB IT WITH HANDS LIKE THIS!
WAH!
UH HUH...
GREEN BEANS
GREEN BEANS
THEN HOLD THIS WITH YOUR HANDS, AND...
...HIT HIM REALLY HARD!
WHOA!
PUMPKIN
EH?
WHOOOOO
SPLAAAT
WAAAAHHHHH!

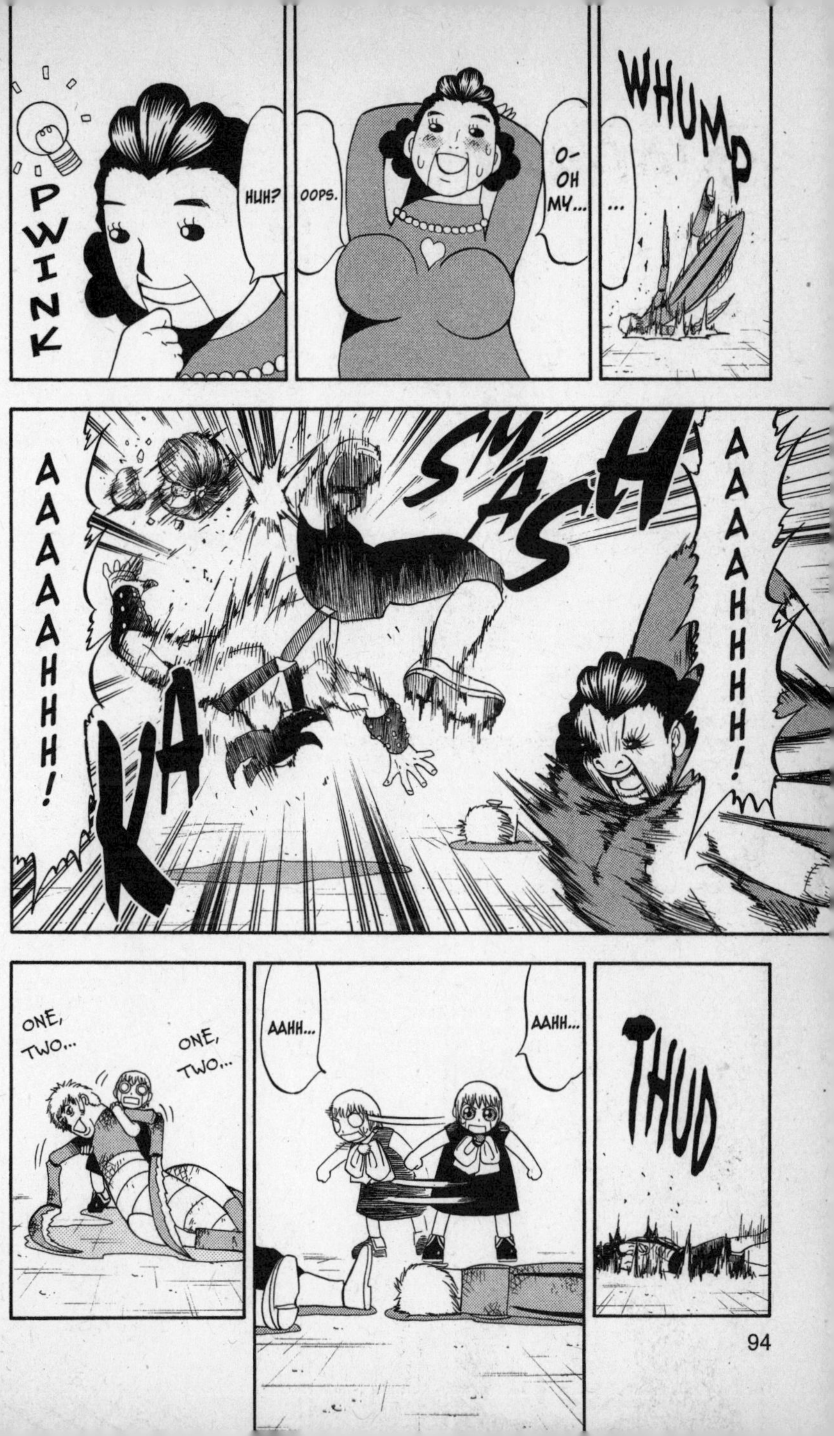
WHUMP
...
O-OH MY...
OOPS.
HUH?
PWINK
AAAAAHHHHH!
SMASH
AAAAAAHHHH!
KA
THUD
AAHH...
AAHH...
ONE, TWO...
ONE, TWO...

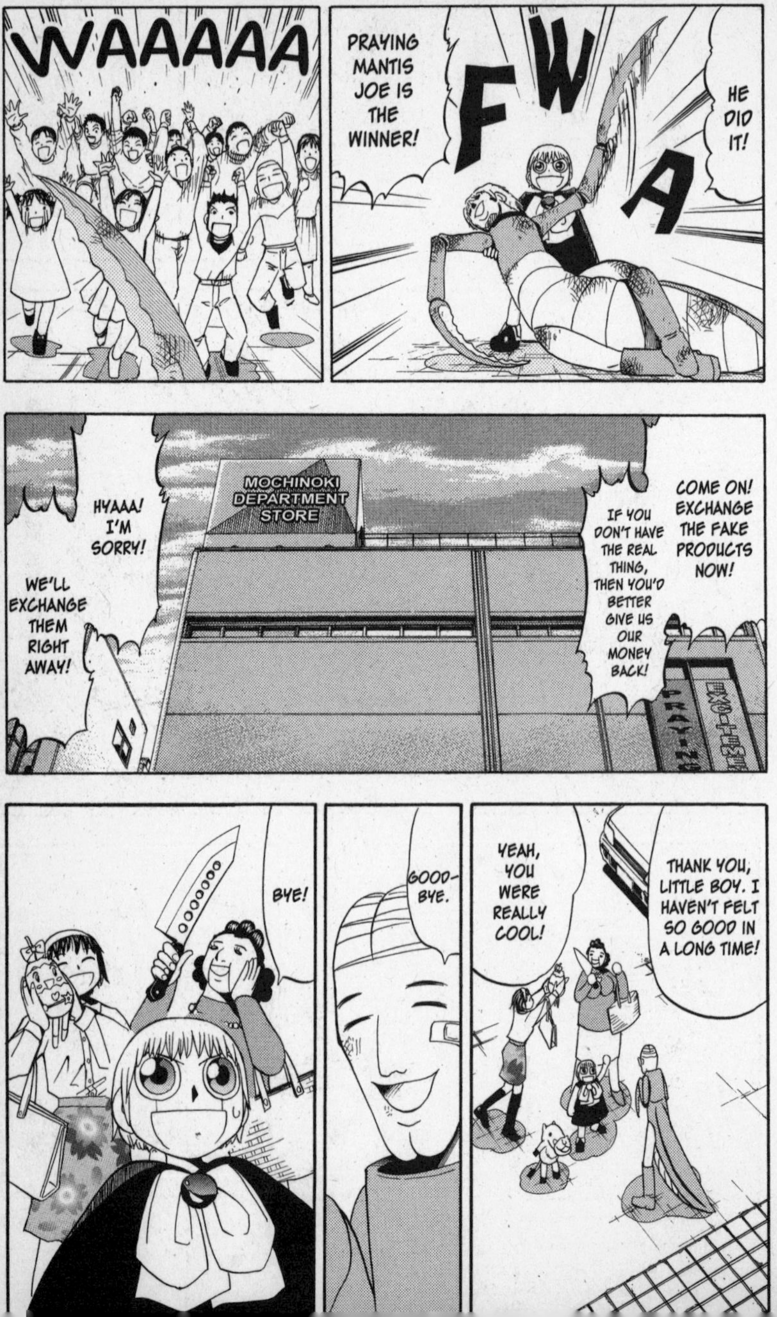
HE DID IT!
FWA
PRAYING MANTIS JOE IS THE WINNER!
WAAAAA
COME ON! EXCHANGE THE FAKE PRODUCTS NOW!
IF YOU DON'T HAVE THE REAL THING, THEN YOU'D BETTER GIVE US OUR MONEY BACK!
PRAYING
MOCHINOKI DEPARTMENT STORE
HYAAA! I'M SORRY!
WE'LL EXCHANGE THEM RIGHT AWAY!
THANK YOU, LITTLE BOY. I HAVEN'T FELT SO GOOD IN A LONG TIME!
YEAH, YOU WERE REALLY COOL!
GOOD-BYE.
BYE!

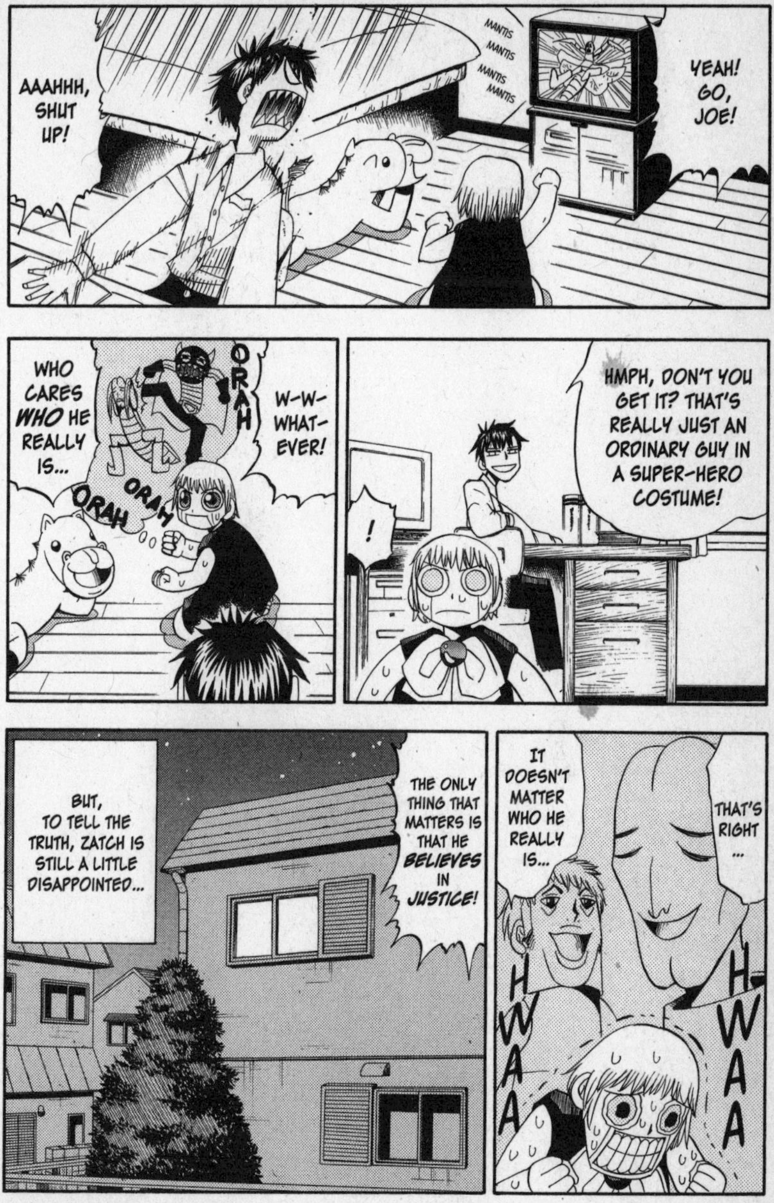
YEAH! GO, JOE!
MANTIS MANTIS MANTIS MANTIS
AAAHHH, SHUT UP!
HMPH, DON'T YOU GET IT? THAT'S REALLY JUST AN ORDINARY GUY IN A SUPER-HERO COSTUME!
!
W-W-WHAT-EVER!
ORAH
WHO CARES WHO HE REALLY IS...
ORAH ORAH
THAT'S RIGHT ...
IT DOESN'T MATTER WHO HE REALLY IS...
HWAA
HWAA
THE ONLY THING THAT MATTERS IS THAT HE BELIEVES IN JUSTICE!
BUT, TO TELL THE TRUTH, ZATCH IS STILL A LITTLE DISAPPOINTED...

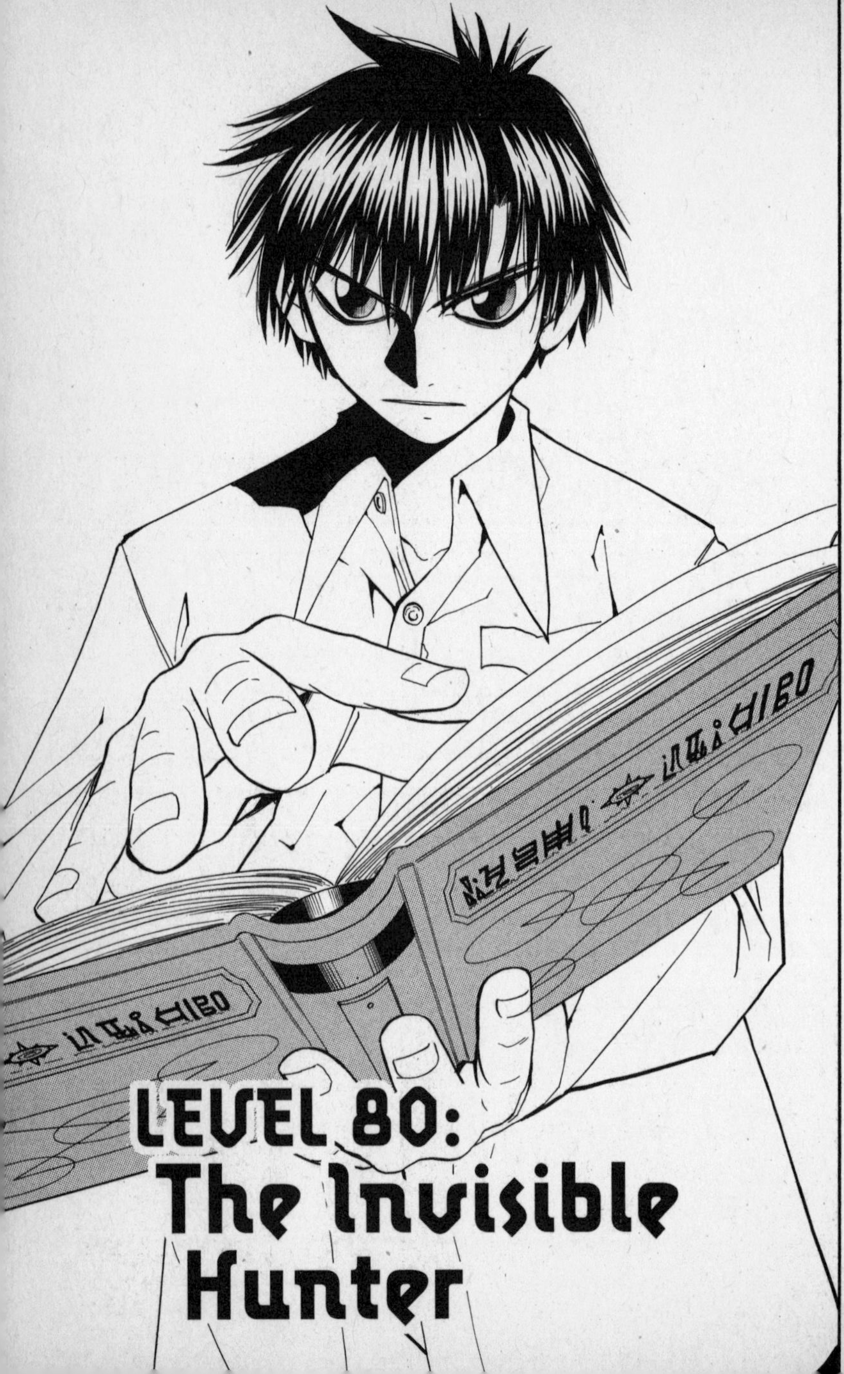
LEVEL 80:
The Invisible
Hunter

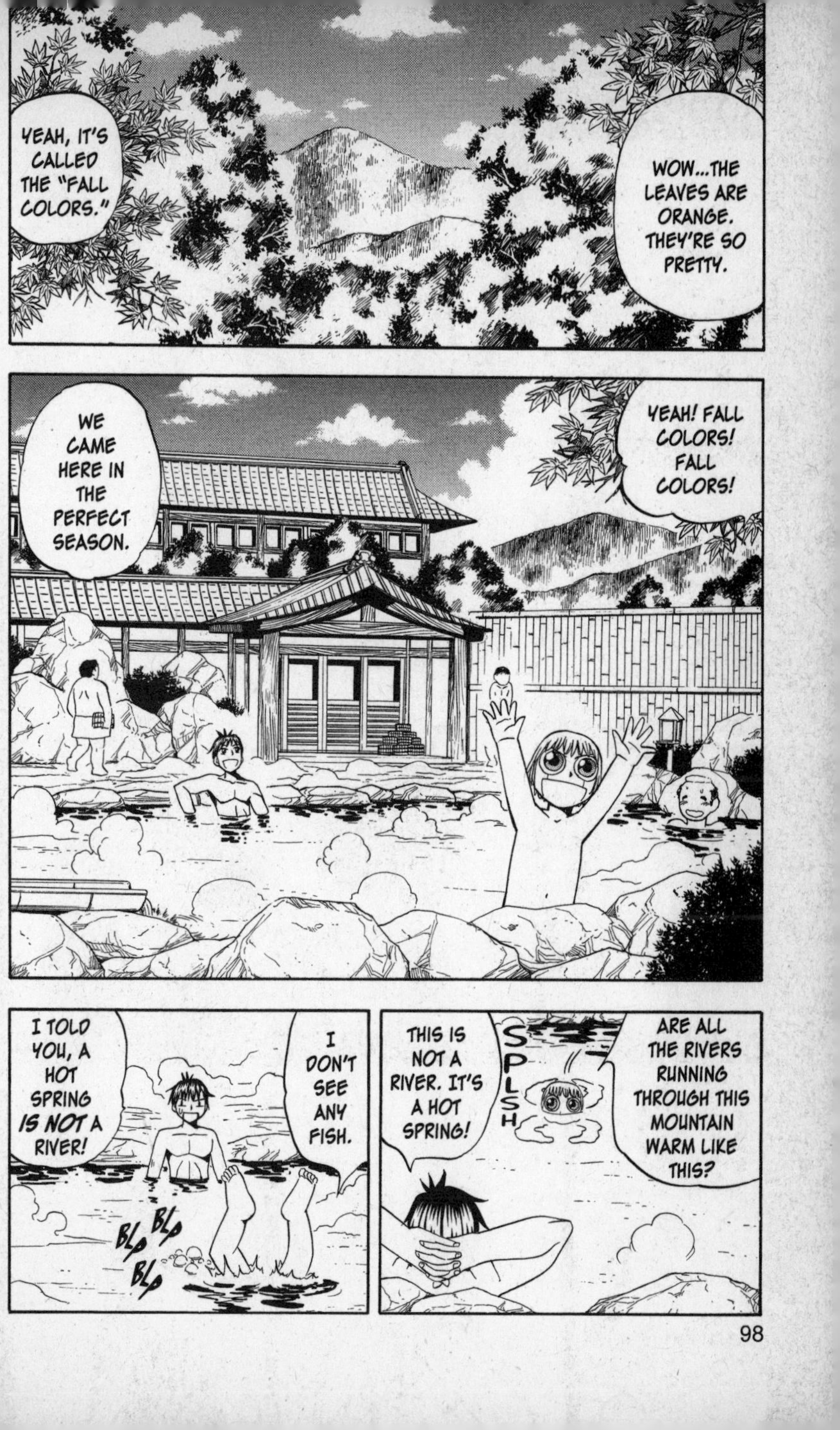
WOW...THE LEAVES ARE ORANGE. THEY'RE SO PRETTY.
YEAH, IT'S CALLED THE "FALL COLORS."
YEAH! FALL COLORS! FALL COLORS!
WE CAME HERE IN THE PERFECT SEASON.
ARE ALL THE RIVERS RUNNING THROUGH THIS MOUNTAIN WARM LIKE THIS?
SPLSH
THIS IS NOT A RIVER. IT'S A HOT SPRING!
I DON'T SEE ANY FISH.
I TOLD YOU, A HOT SPRING *IS NOT* A RIVER!
BLP BLP BLP

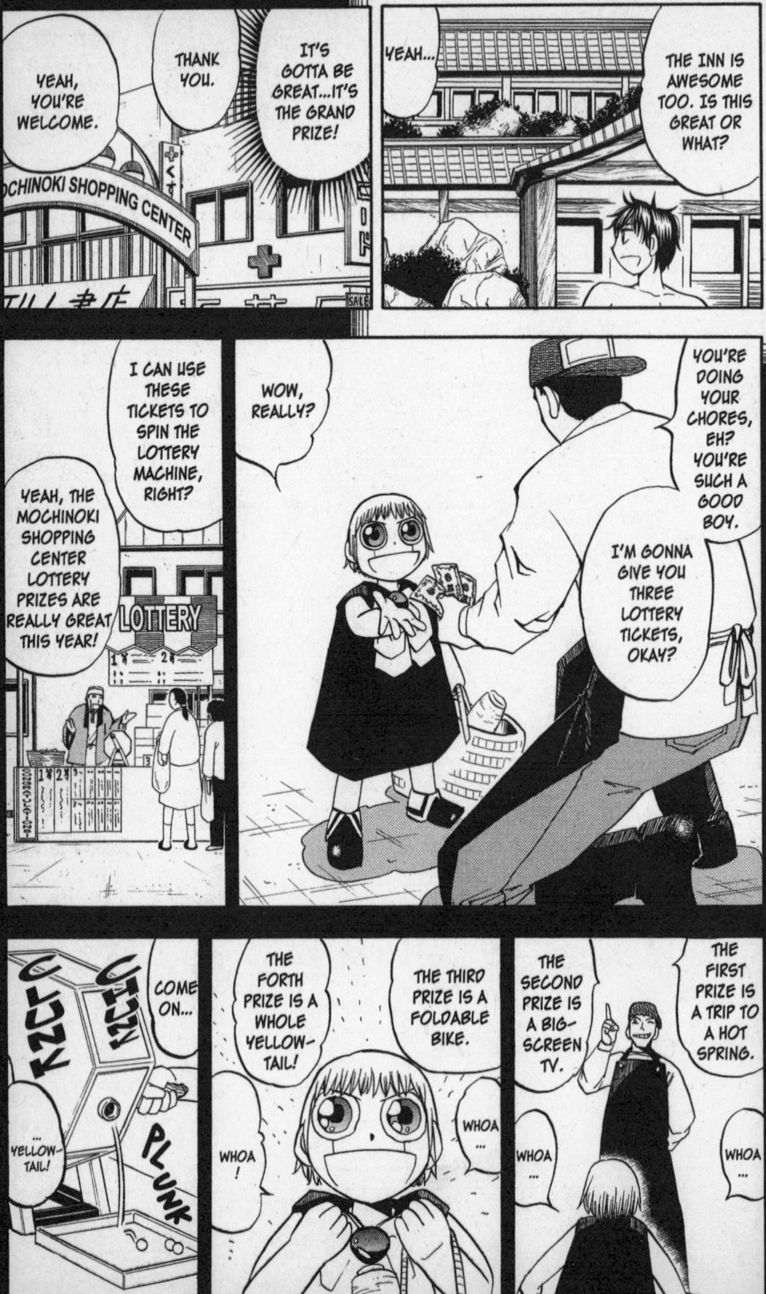
THE INN IS AWESOME TOO. IS THIS GREAT OR WHAT?
YEAH...
IT'S GOTTA BE GREAT...IT'S THE GRAND PRIZE!
THANK YOU.
YEAH, YOU'RE WELCOME.
OCHINOKI SHOPPING CENTER
YOU'RE DOING YOUR CHORES, EH? YOU'RE SUCH A GOOD BOY.
I'M GONNA GIVE YOU THREE LOTTERY TICKETS, OKAY?
WOW, REALLY?
I CAN USE THESE TICKETS TO SPIN THE LOTTERY MACHINE, RIGHT?
YEAH, THE MOCHINOKI SHOPPING CENTER LOTTERY PRIZES ARE REALLY GREAT THIS YEAR!
LOTTERY
THE FIRST PRIZE IS A TRIP TO A HOT SPRING.
WHOA...
THE SECOND PRIZE IS A BIG-SCREEN TV.
WHOA...
THE THIRD PRIZE IS A FOLDABLE BIKE.
WHOA...
THE FORTH PRIZE IS A WHOLE YELLOW-TAIL!
WHOA!
COME ON...
CHUNK
CHUNK
...YELLOW-TAIL!
PLUNK

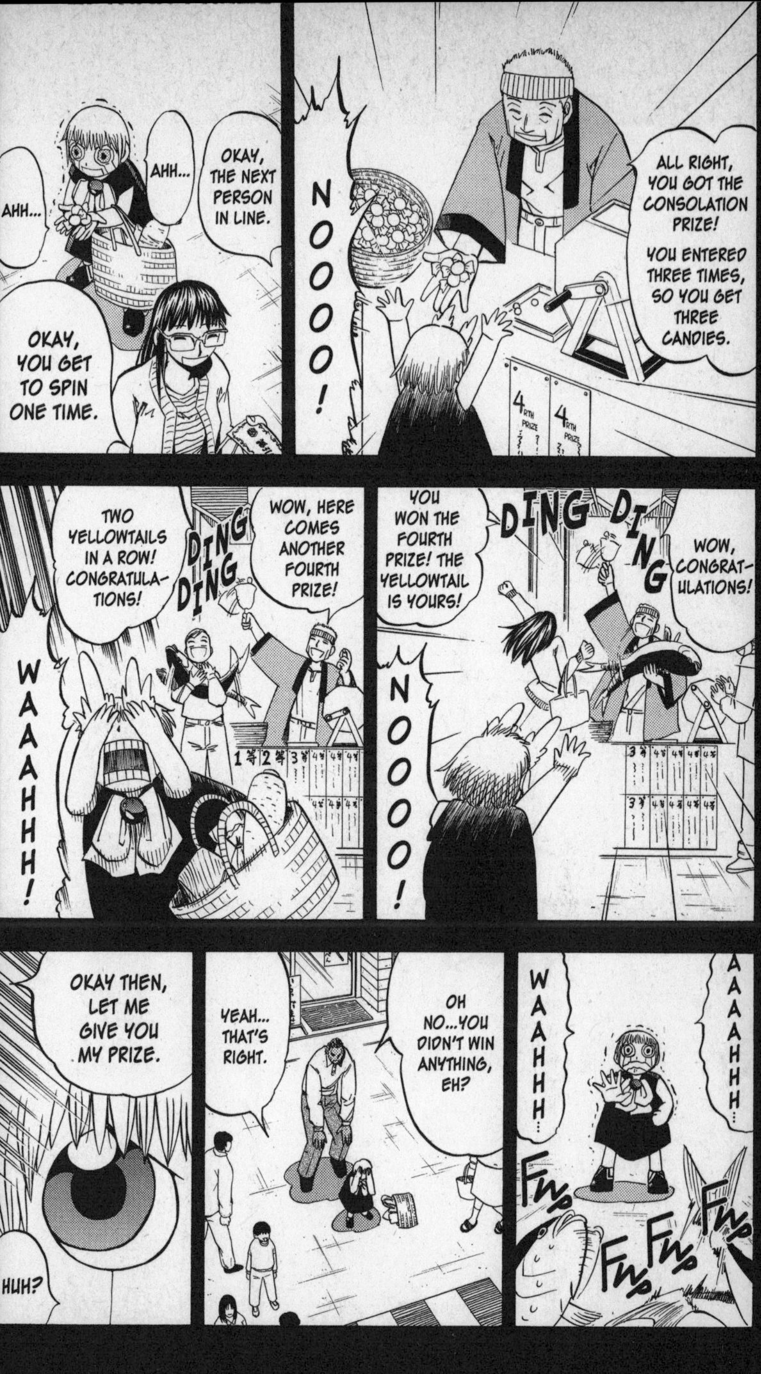
ALL RIGHT, YOU GOT THE CONSOLATION PRIZE!
YOU ENTERED THREE TIMES, SO YOU GET THREE CANDIES.
NOOOOO!
OKAY, THE NEXT PERSON IN LINE.
AHH...
AHH...
OKAY, YOU GET TO SPIN ONE TIME.
WOW, CONGRATULATIONS!
DING DING
YOU WON THE FOURTH PRIZE! THE YELLOWTAIL IS YOURS!
NOOOOO!
WOW, HERE COMES ANOTHER FOURTH PRIZE!
DING DING
TWO YELLOWTAILS IN A ROW! CONGRATULATIONS!
WAAAAHHH!
AAAAAHHH...
WAAHHH...
FWP FWP FWP FWP
OH NO...YOU DIDN'T WIN ANYTHING, EH?
YEAH... THAT'S RIGHT.
OKAY THEN, LET ME GIVE YOU MY PRIZE.
HUH?

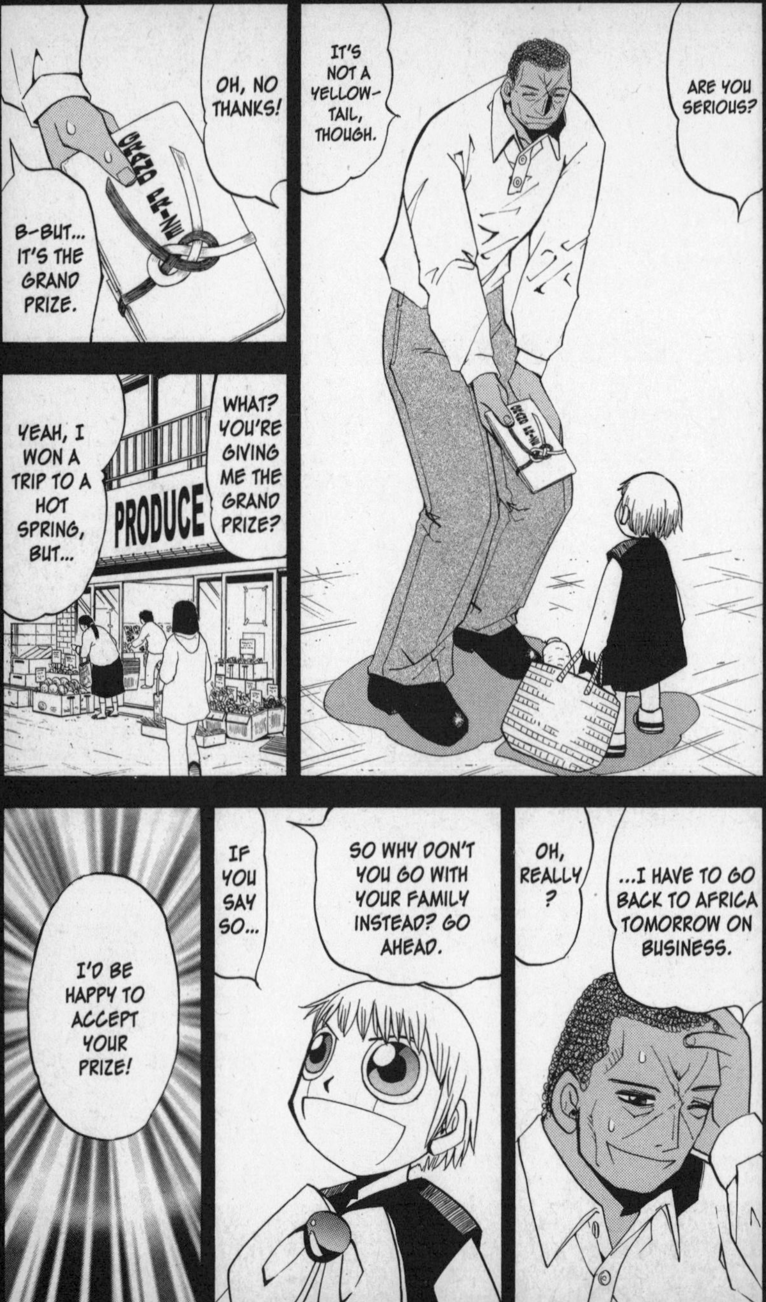
ARE YOU SERIOUS?
IT'S NOT A YELLOW-TAIL, THOUGH.
OH, NO THANKS!
GRAND PRIZE
B-BUT... IT'S THE GRAND PRIZE.
WHAT? YOU'RE GIVING ME THE GRAND PRIZE?
YEAH, I WON A TRIP TO A HOT SPRING, BUT...
PRODUCE
...I HAVE TO GO BACK TO AFRICA TOMORROW ON BUSINESS.
OH, REALLY?
SO WHY DON'T YOU GO WITH YOUR FAMILY INSTEAD? GO AHEAD.
IF YOU SAY SO...
I'D BE HAPPY TO ACCEPT YOUR PRIZE!

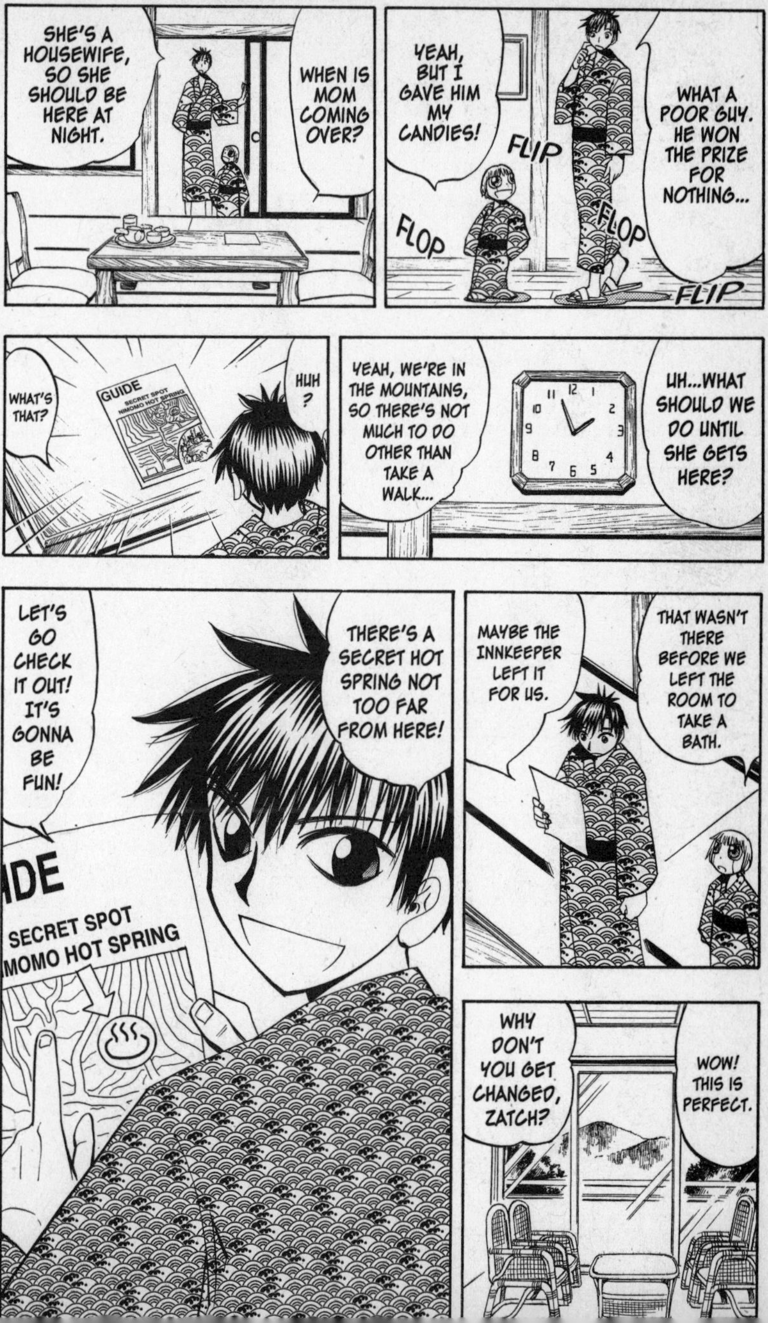
WHAT A POOR GUY. HE WON THE PRIZE FOR NOTHING...
YEAH, BUT I GAVE HIM MY CANDIES!
FLIP
FLOP
FLOP
FLIP
WHEN IS MOM COMING OVER?
SHE'S A HOUSEWIFE, SO SHE SHOULD BE HERE AT NIGHT.
UH...WHAT SHOULD WE DO UNTIL SHE GETS HERE?
YEAH, WE'RE IN THE MOUNTAINS, SO THERE'S NOT MUCH TO DO OTHER THAN TAKE A WALK...
HUH?
WHAT'S THAT?
GUIDE
SECRET SPOT NIMOMO HOT SPRING
THAT WASN'T THERE BEFORE WE LEFT THE ROOM TO TAKE A BATH.
MAYBE THE INNKEEPER LEFT IT FOR US.
WOW! THIS IS PERFECT.
WHY DON'T YOU GET CHANGED, ZATCH?
THERE'S A SECRET HOT SPRING NOT TOO FAR FROM HERE!
LET'S GO CHECK IT OUT! IT'S GONNA BE FUN!
DE
SECRET SPOT
IMOMO HOT SPRING

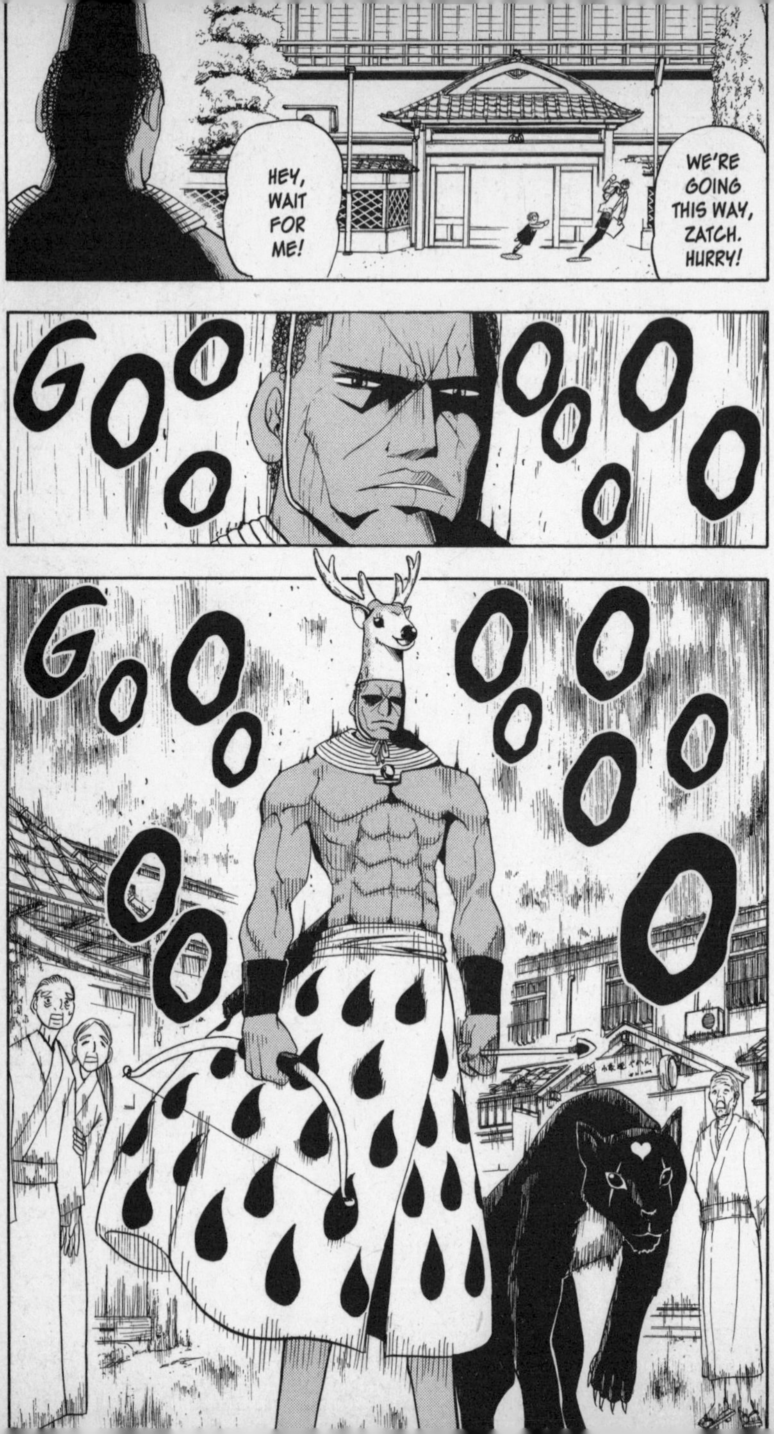
WE'RE GOING THIS WAY, ZATCH. HURRY!
HEY, WAIT FOR ME!
GOOOOOOOOO
GOOOOOOOOOOOOO

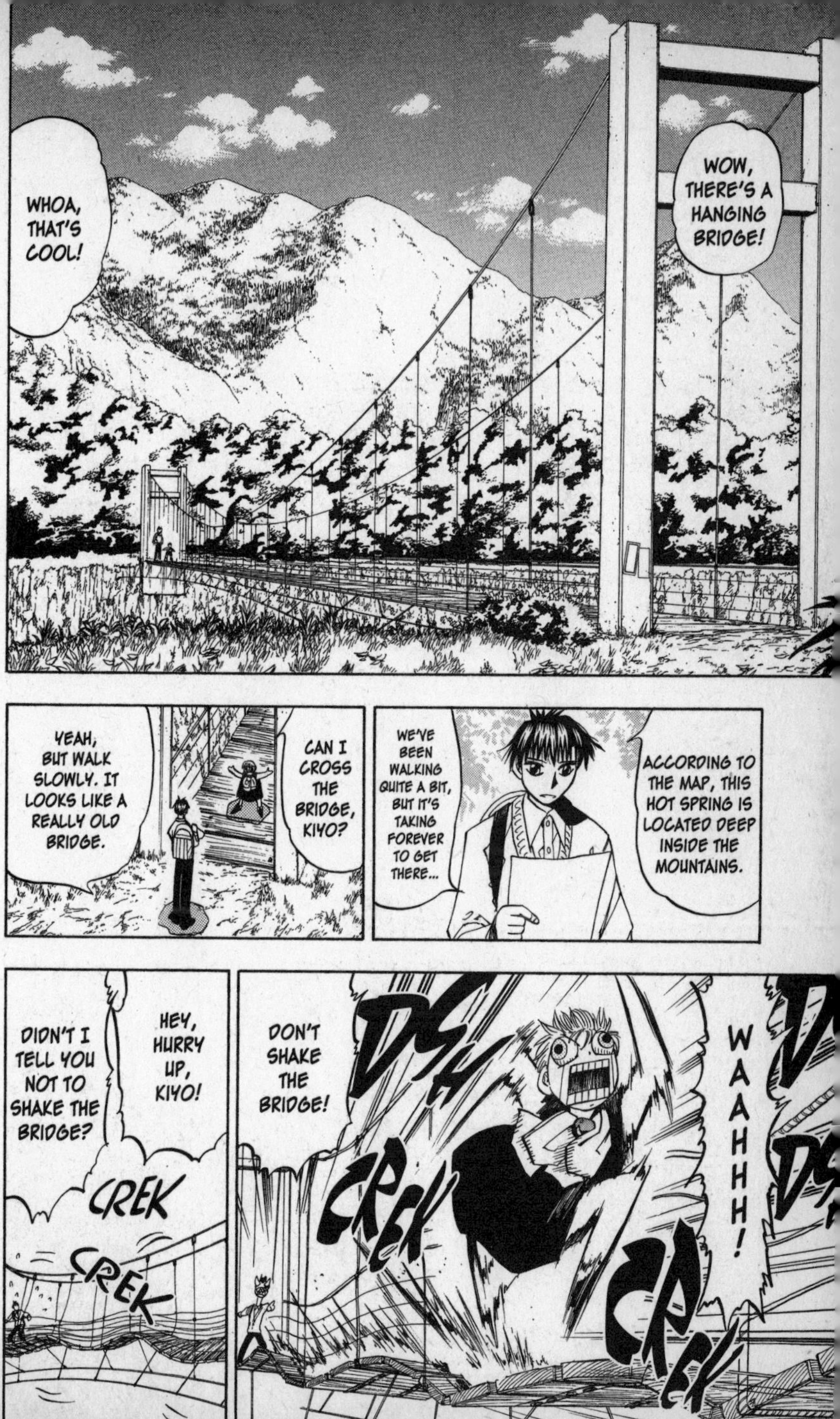
WOW, THERE'S A HANGING BRIDGE!
WHOA, THAT'S COOL!
ACCORDING TO THE MAP, THIS HOT SPRING IS LOCATED DEEP INSIDE THE MOUNTAINS.
WE'VE BEEN WALKING QUITE A BIT, BUT IT'S TAKING FOREVER TO GET THERE...
CAN I CROSS THE BRIDGE, KIYO?
YEAH, BUT WALK SLOWLY. IT LOOKS LIKE A REALLY OLD BRIDGE.
WAAHHH!
DSH
DON'T SHAKE THE BRIDGE!
CREK
CREK
HEY, HURRY UP, KIYO!
DIDN'T I TELL YOU NOT TO SHAKE THE BRIDGE?
CREK
CREK

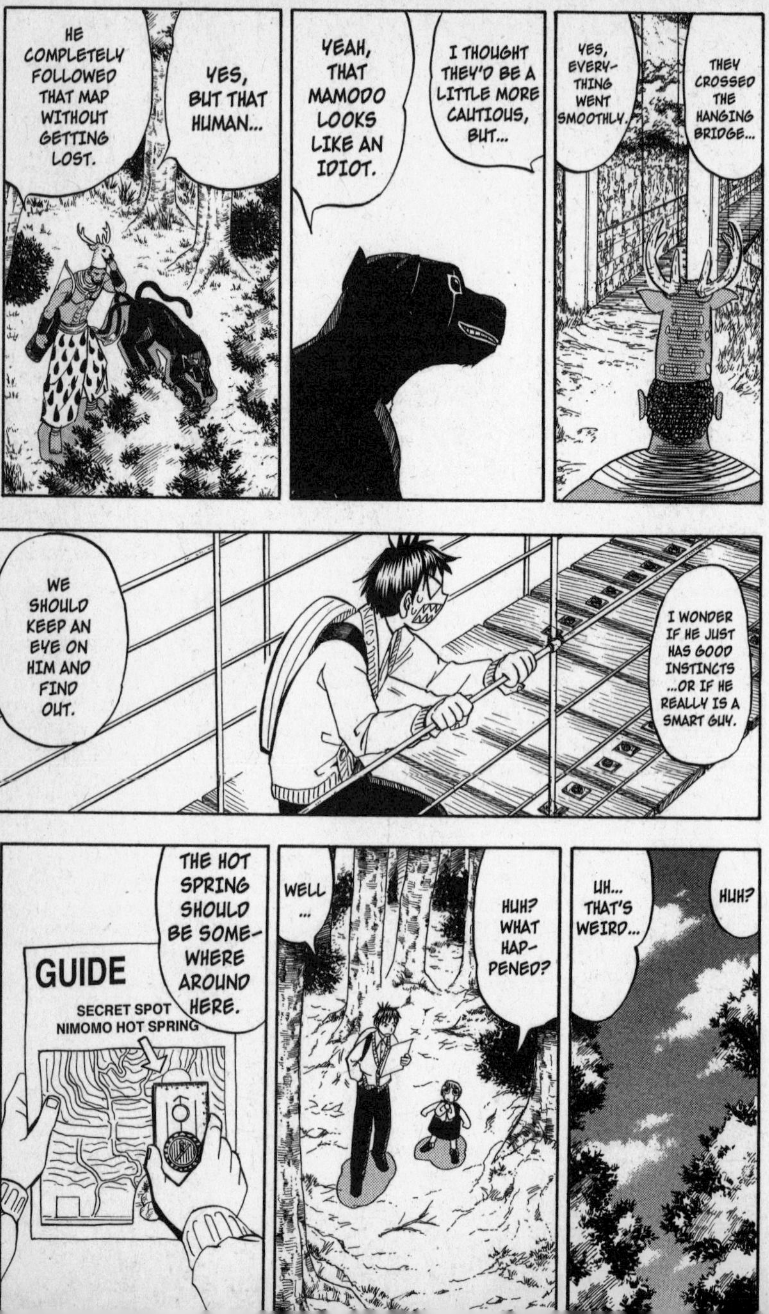
THEY CROSSED THE HANGING BRIDGE...
YES, EVERY-THING WENT SMOOTHLY.
I THOUGHT THEY'D BE A LITTLE MORE CAUTIOUS, BUT...
YEAH, THAT MAMODO LOOKS LIKE AN IDIOT.
YES, BUT THAT HUMAN...
HE COMPLETELY FOLLOWED THAT MAP WITHOUT GETTING LOST.
I WONDER IF HE JUST HAS GOOD INSTINCTS ...OR IF HE REALLY IS A SMART GUY.
WE SHOULD KEEP AN EYE ON HIM AND FIND OUT.
HUH?
UH... THAT'S WEIRD...
HUH? WHAT HAP-PENED?
WELL ...
THE HOT SPRING SHOULD BE SOME-WHERE AROUND HERE.
GUIDE
SECRET SPOT NIMOMO HOT SPRING

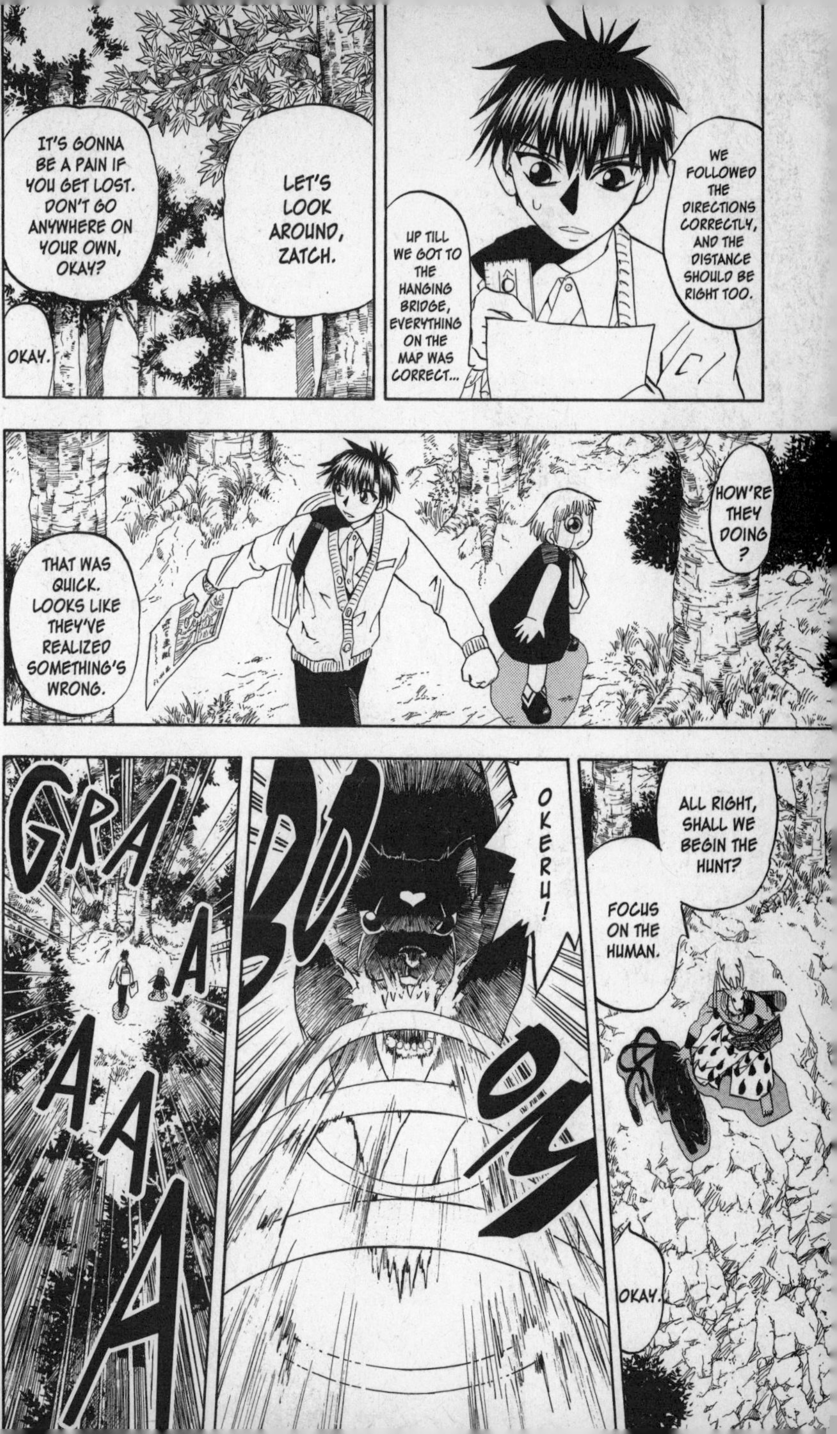
WE FOLLOWED THE DIRECTIONS CORRECTLY, AND THE DISTANCE SHOULD BE RIGHT TOO.
UP TILL WE GOT TO THE HANGING BRIDGE, EVERYTHING ON THE MAP WAS CORRECT...
LET'S LOOK AROUND, ZATCH.
IT'S GONNA BE A PAIN IF YOU GET LOST. DON'T GO ANYWHERE ON YOUR OWN, OKAY?
OKAY.
HOW'RE THEY DOING?
THAT WAS QUICK. LOOKS LIKE THEY'VE REALIZED SOMETHING'S WRONG.
ALL RIGHT, SHALL WE BEGIN THE HUNT?
FOCUS ON THE HUMAN.
OKAY.
OKERU!
DOOM
GRAAAAA

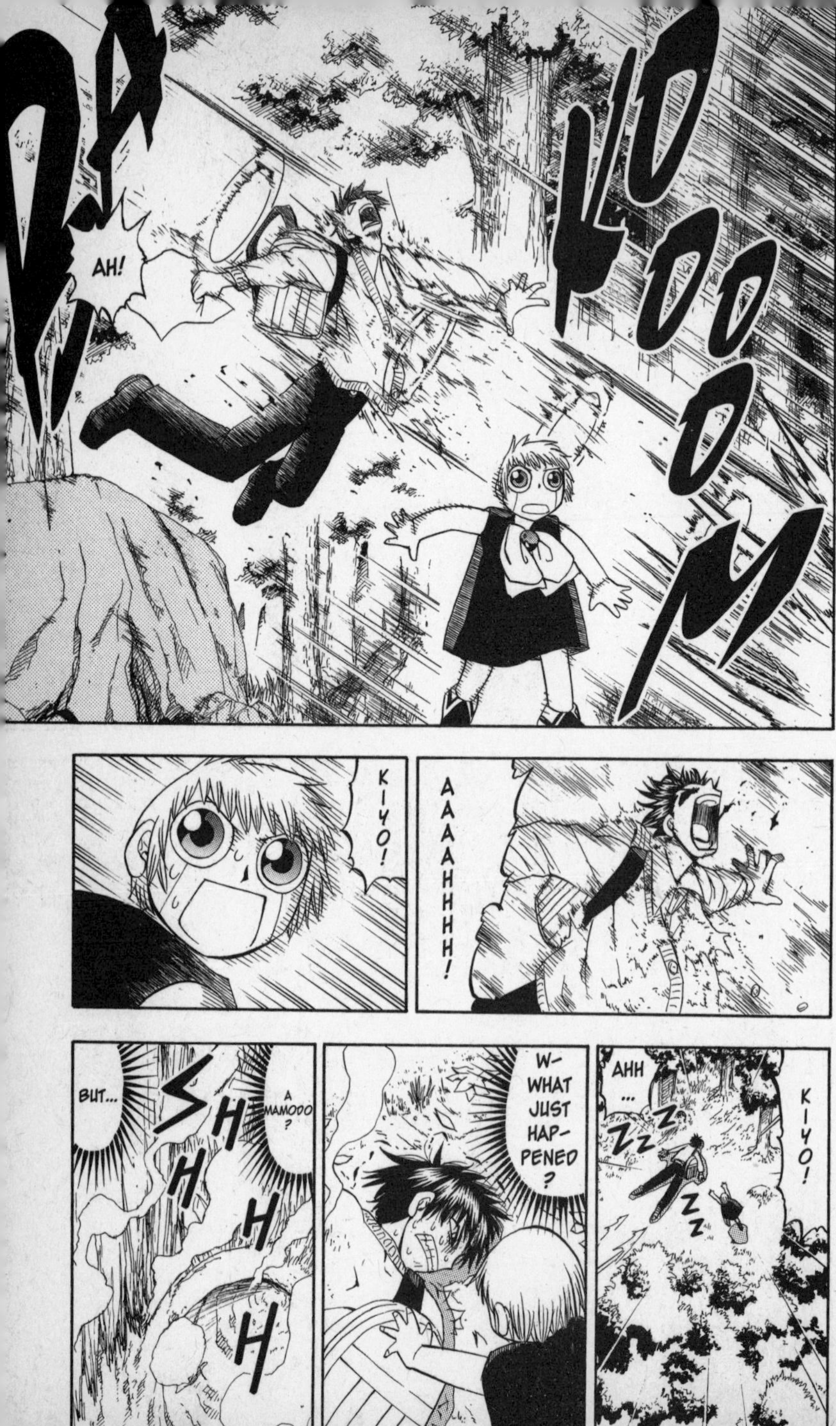
AH!
AAAAHHHHH!
KIYO!
KIYO!
AHH ...
W-WHAT JUST HAPPENED?
A MAMODO?
SHHHH
BUT...

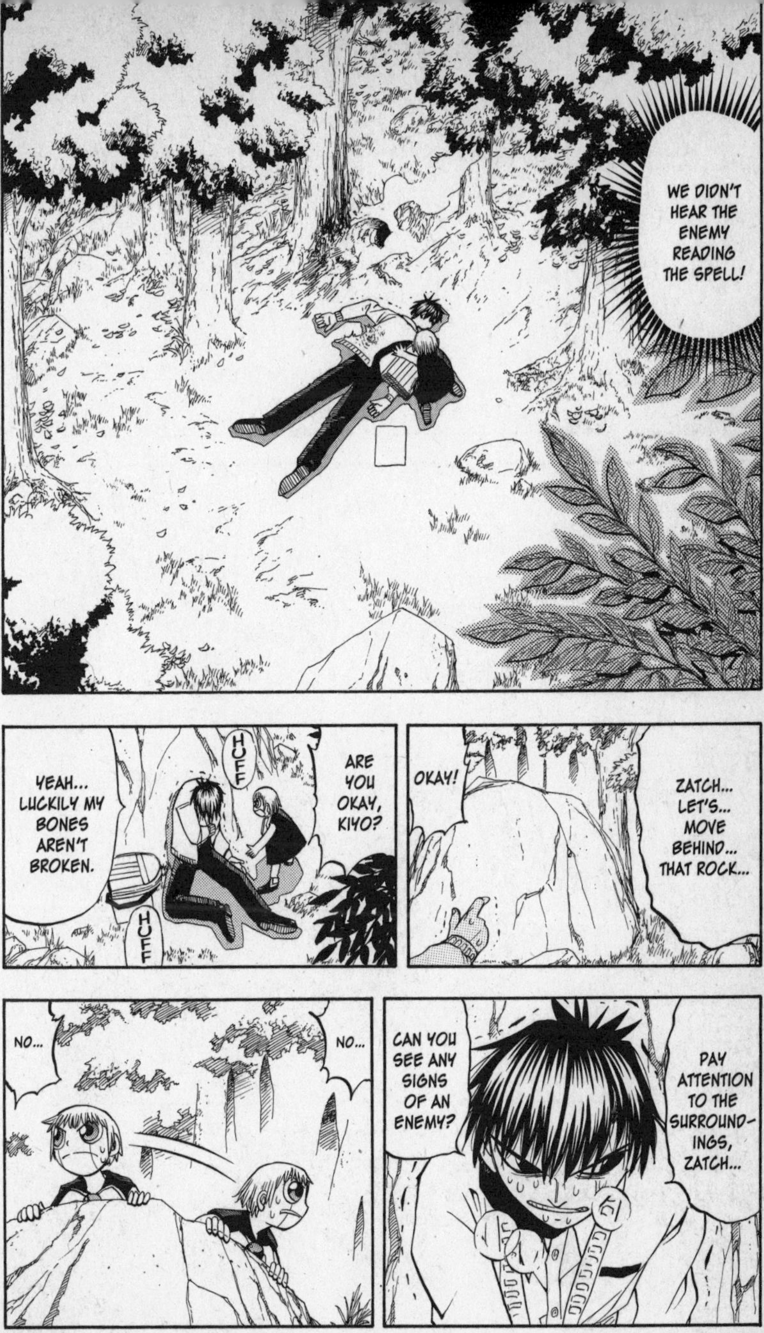

WE DIDN'T HEAR THE ENEMY READING THE SPELL!
ZATCH... LET'S... MOVE BEHIND... THAT ROCK...
OKAY!
ARE YOU OKAY, KIYO?
HUFF
YEAH... LUCKILY MY BONES AREN'T BROKEN.
HUFF
PAY ATTENTION TO THE SURROUND-INGS, ZATCH...
CAN YOU SEE ANY SIGNS OF AN ENEMY?
NO...
NO...

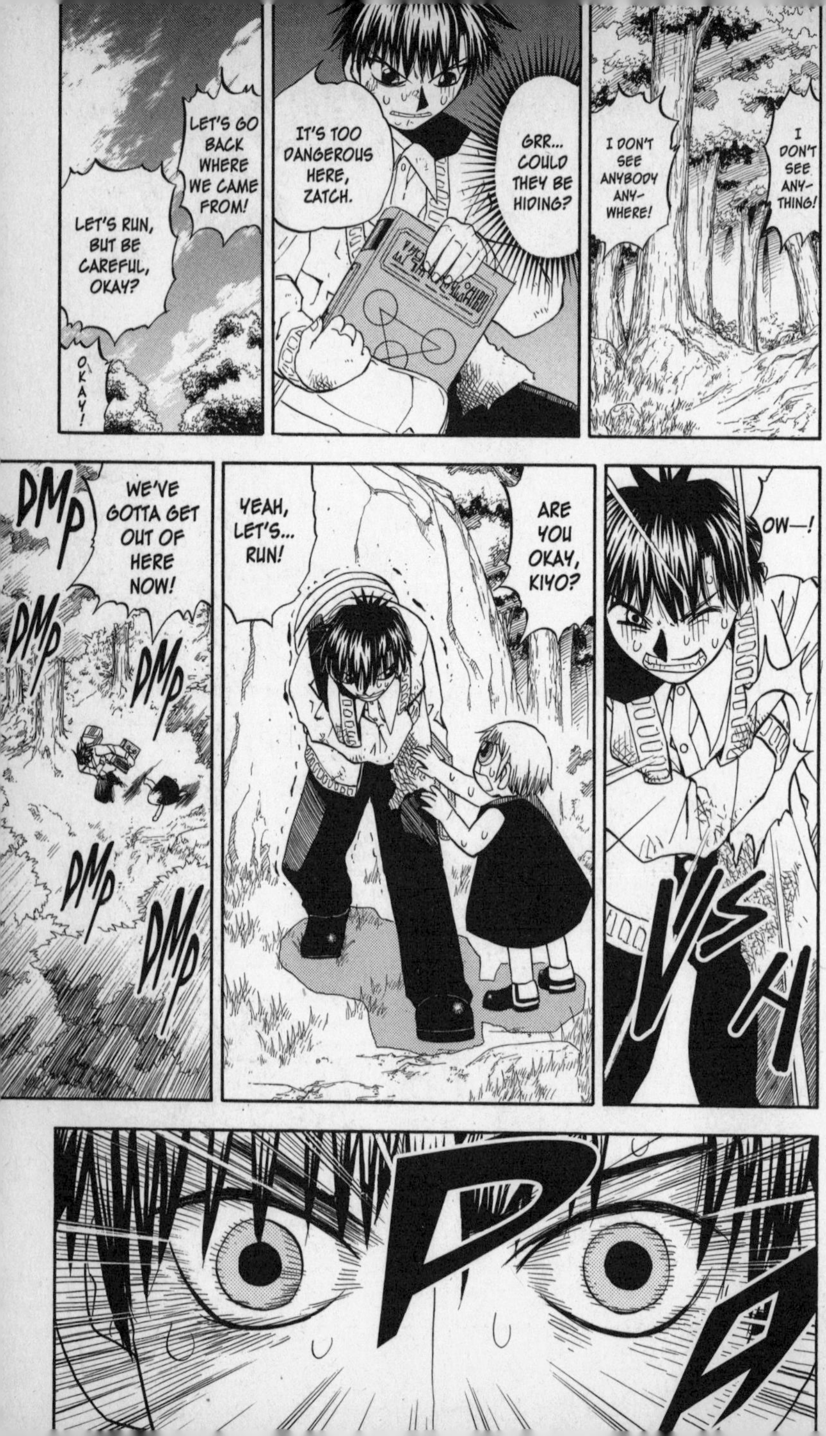
I DON'T SEE ANYTHING!
I DON'T SEE ANYBODY ANYWHERE!
GRR... COULD THEY BE HIDING?
IT'S TOO DANGEROUS HERE, ZATCH.
LET'S GO BACK WHERE WE CAME FROM!
LET'S RUN, BUT BE CAREFUL, OKAY?
OKAY!
OW—!
VSSH
ARE YOU OKAY, KIYO?
YEAH, LET'S... RUN!
WE'VE GOTTA GET OUT OF HERE NOW!
DMP
DMP
DMP
DMP
DMP

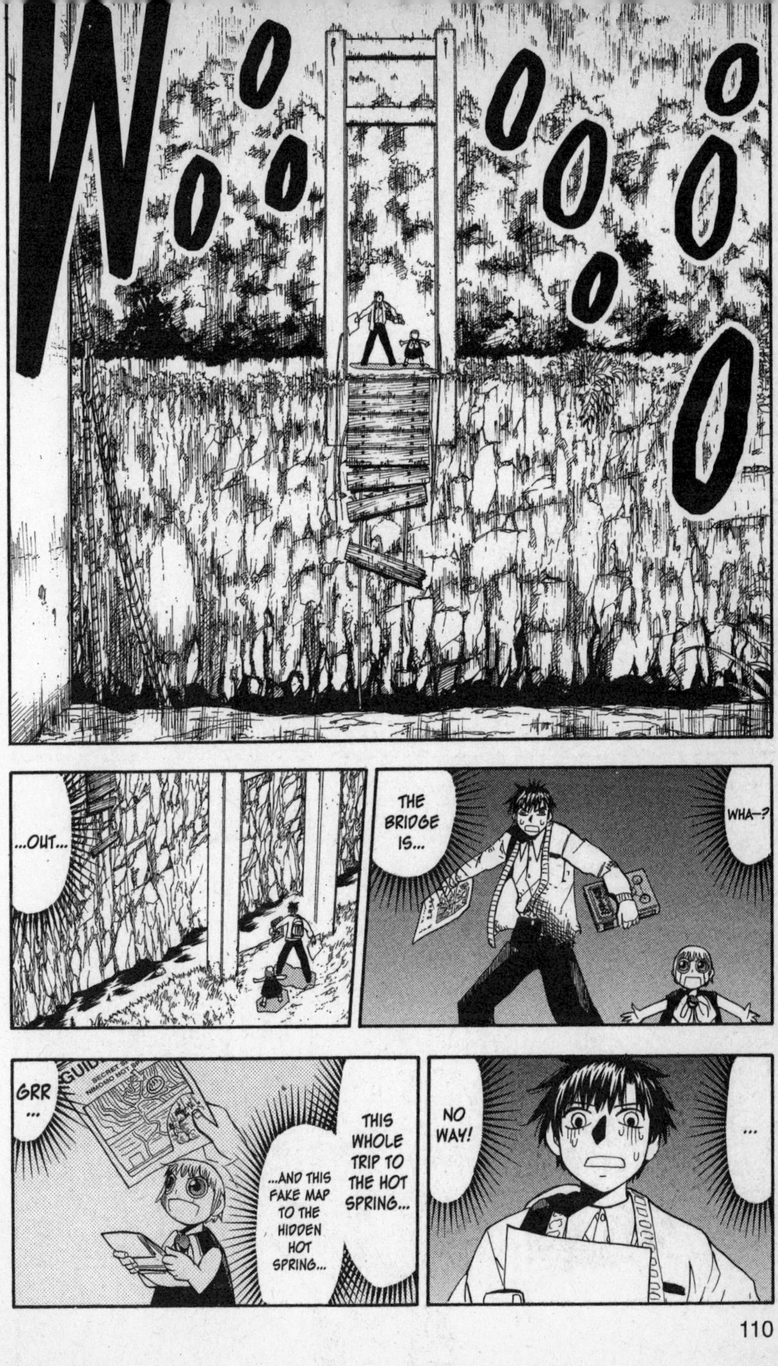
WOOOOOOOOO
WHA—?
THE BRIDGE IS...
...OUT...
...
NO WAY!
THIS WHOLE TRIP TO THE HOT SPRING...
...AND THIS FAKE MAP TO THE HIDDEN HOT SPRING...
GRR ...

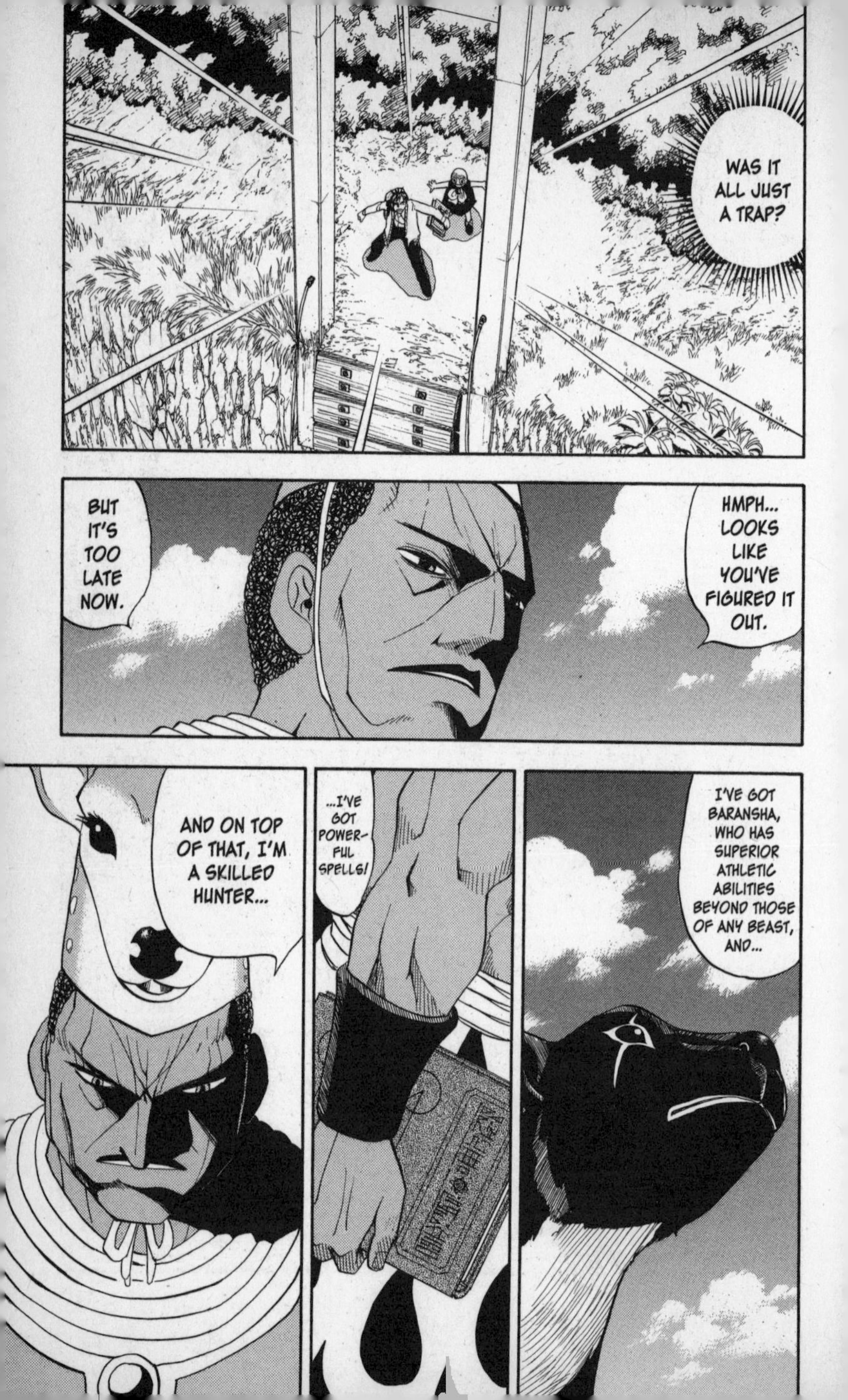
WAS IT ALL JUST A TRAP?
HMPH... LOOKS LIKE YOU'VE FIGURED IT OUT.
BUT IT'S TOO LATE NOW.
I'VE GOT BARANSHA, WHO HAS SUPERIOR ATHLETIC ABILITIES BEYOND THOSE OF ANY BEAST, AND...
...I'VE GOT POWER-FUL SPELLS!
AND ON TOP OF THAT, I'M A SKILLED HUNTER...

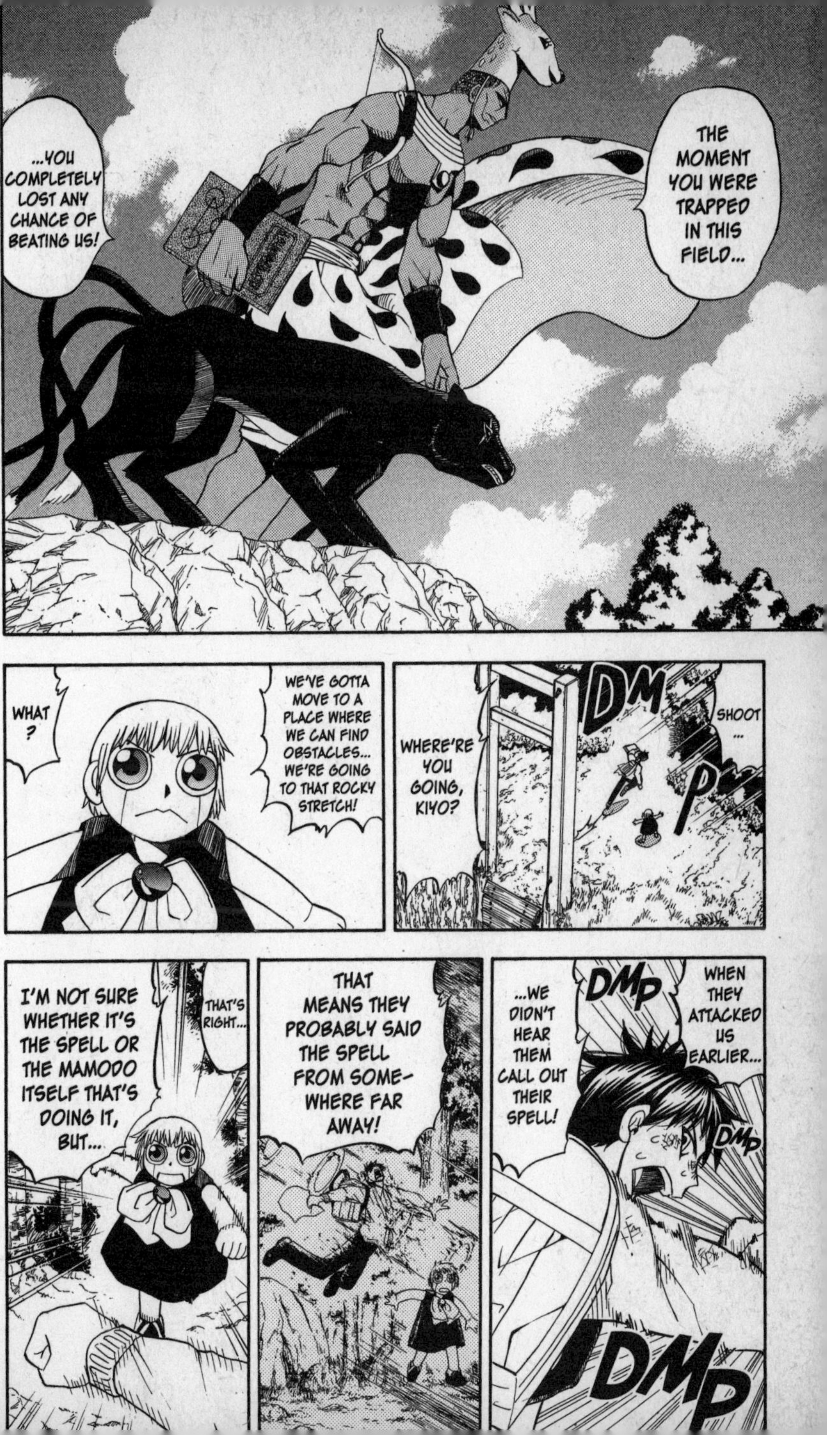
THE MOMENT YOU WERE TRAPPED IN THIS FIELD...
...YOU COMPLETELY LOST ANY CHANCE OF BEATING US!
DM
SHOOT...
P
WHERE'RE YOU GOING, KIYO?
WE'VE GOTTA MOVE TO A PLACE WHERE WE CAN FIND OBSTACLES... WE'RE GOING TO THAT ROCKY STRETCH!
WHAT?
WHEN THEY ATTACKED US EARLIER...
DMP
...WE DIDN'T HEAR THEM CALL OUT THEIR SPELL!
DMP
DMP
THAT MEANS THEY PROBABLY SAID THE SPELL FROM SOME-WHERE FAR AWAY!
THAT'S RIGHT...
I'M NOT SURE WHETHER IT'S THE SPELL OR THE MAMODO ITSELF THAT'S DOING IT, BUT...

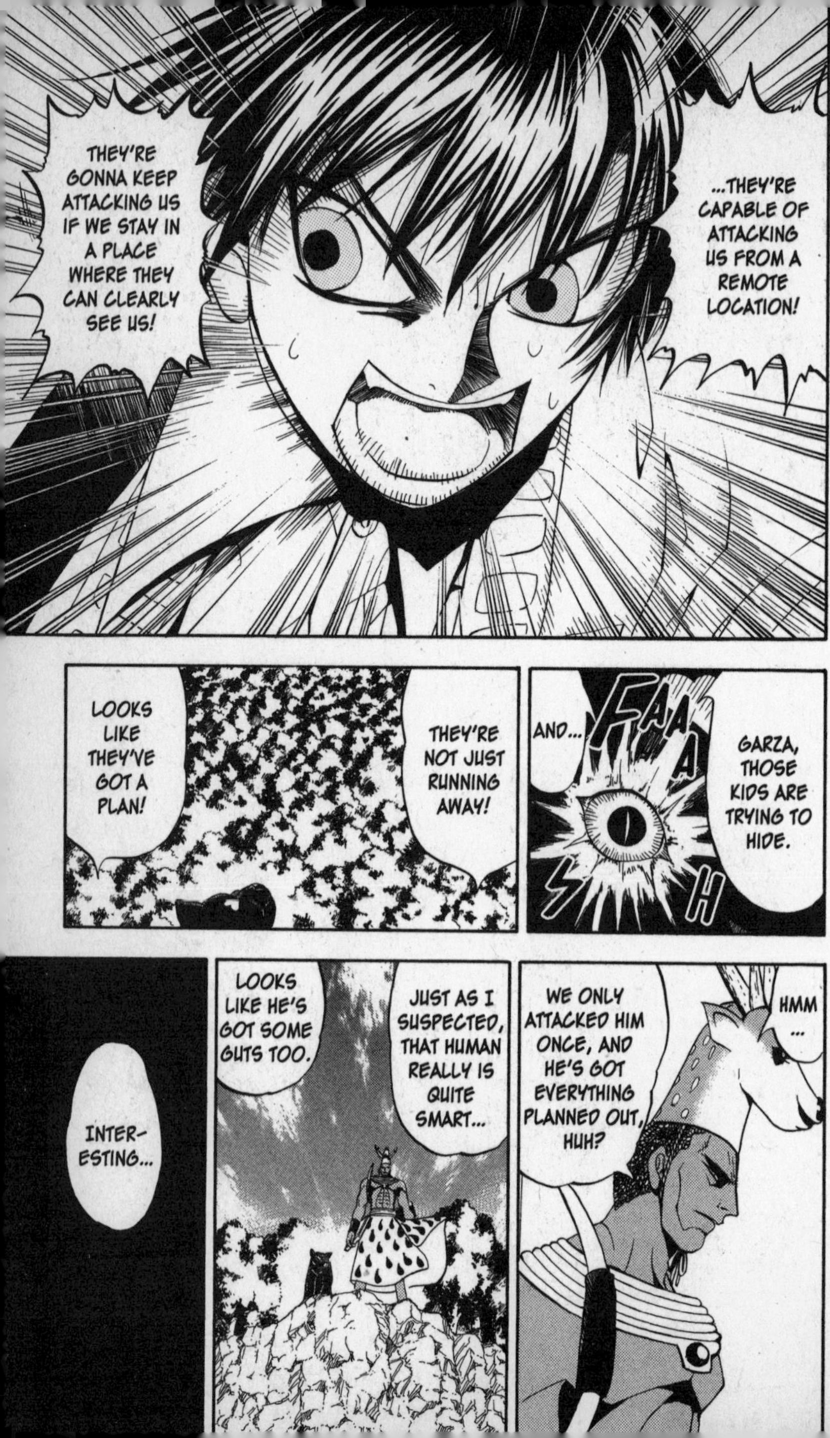
...THEY'RE CAPABLE OF ATTACKING US FROM A REMOTE LOCATION!
THEY'RE GONNA KEEP ATTACKING US IF WE STAY IN A PLACE WHERE THEY CAN CLEARLY SEE US!
GARZA, THOSE KIDS ARE TRYING TO HIDE.
FAAAASH
AND...
THEY'RE NOT JUST RUNNING AWAY!
LOOKS LIKE THEY'VE GOT A PLAN!
HMM ...
WE ONLY ATTACKED HIM ONCE, AND HE'S GOT EVERYTHING PLANNED OUT, HUH?
JUST AS I SUSPECTED, THAT HUMAN REALLY IS QUITE SMART...
LOOKS LIKE HE'S GOT SOME GUTS TOO.
INTER-ESTING...

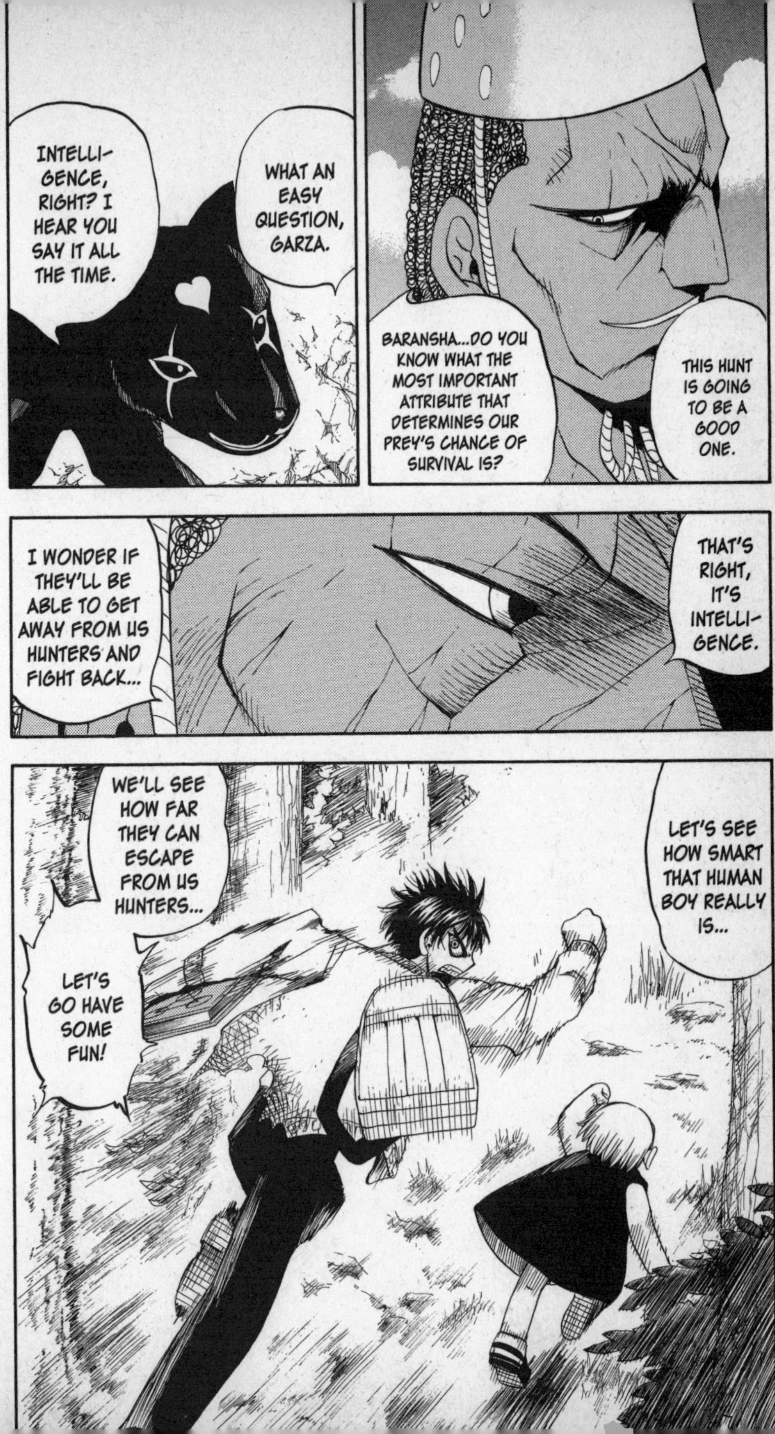
THIS HUNT IS GOING TO BE A GOOD ONE.
BARANSHA...DO YOU KNOW WHAT THE MOST IMPORTANT ATTRIBUTE THAT DETERMINES OUR PREY'S CHANCE OF SURVIVAL IS?
WHAT AN EASY QUESTION, GARZA.
INTELLIGENCE, RIGHT? I HEAR YOU SAY IT ALL THE TIME.
THAT'S RIGHT, IT'S INTELLIGENCE.
I WONDER IF THEY'LL BE ABLE TO GET AWAY FROM US HUNTERS AND FIGHT BACK...
LET'S SEE HOW SMART THAT HUMAN BOY REALLY IS...
WE'LL SEE HOW FAR THEY CAN ESCAPE FROM US HUNTERS...
LET'S GO HAVE SOME FUN!

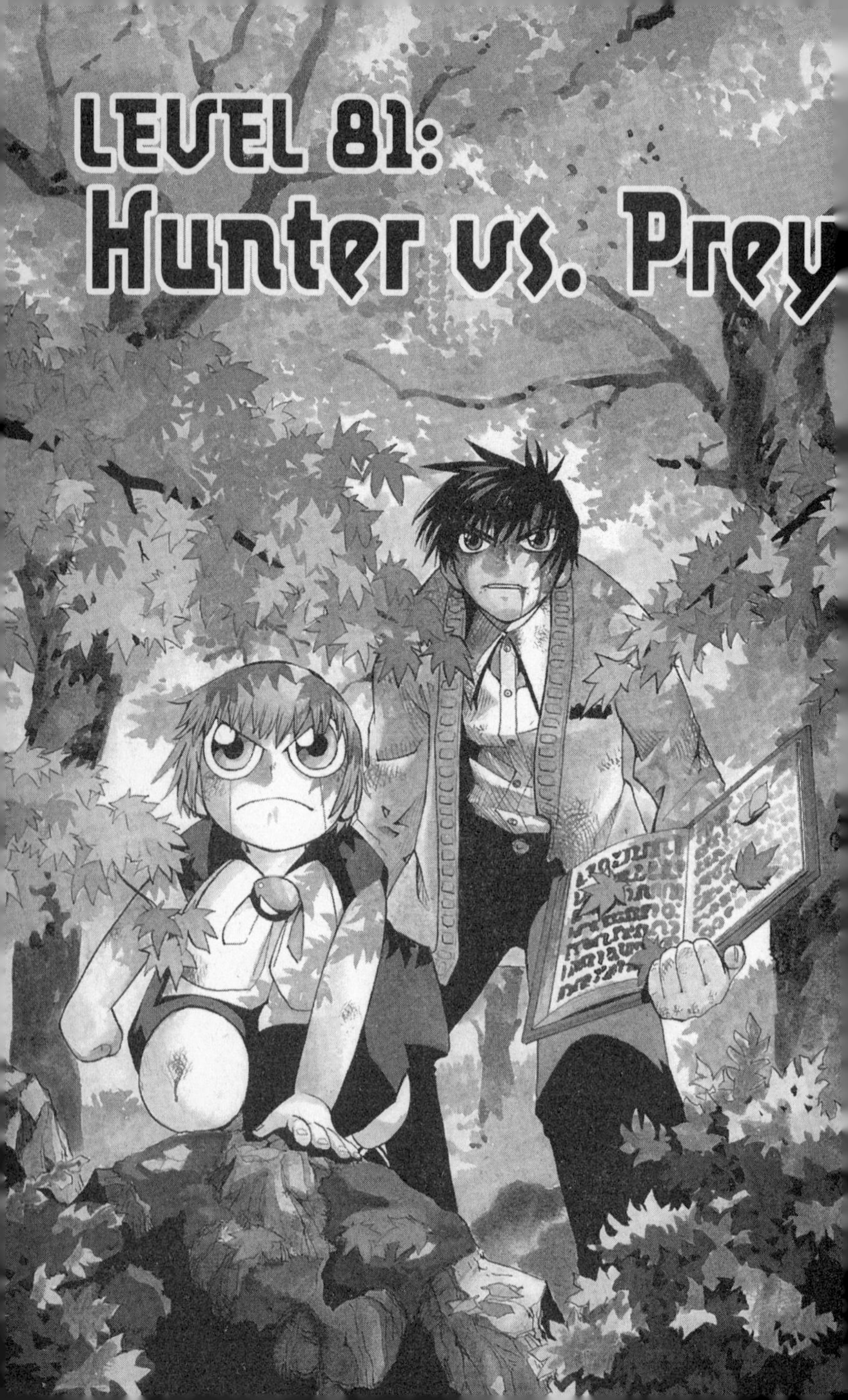
LEVEL 81:
Hunter vs. Prey

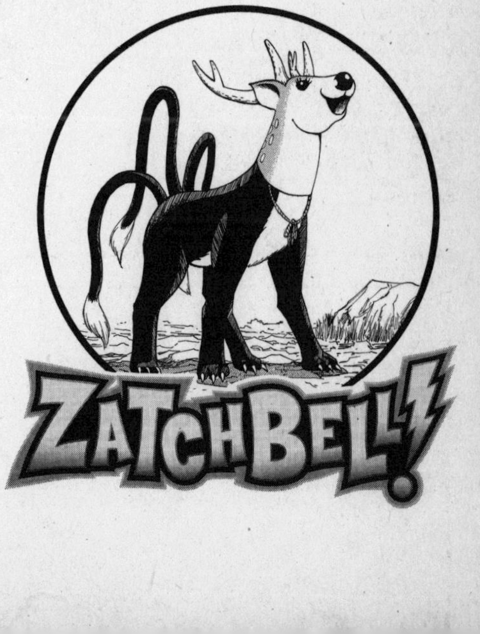

ZATCHBELL!

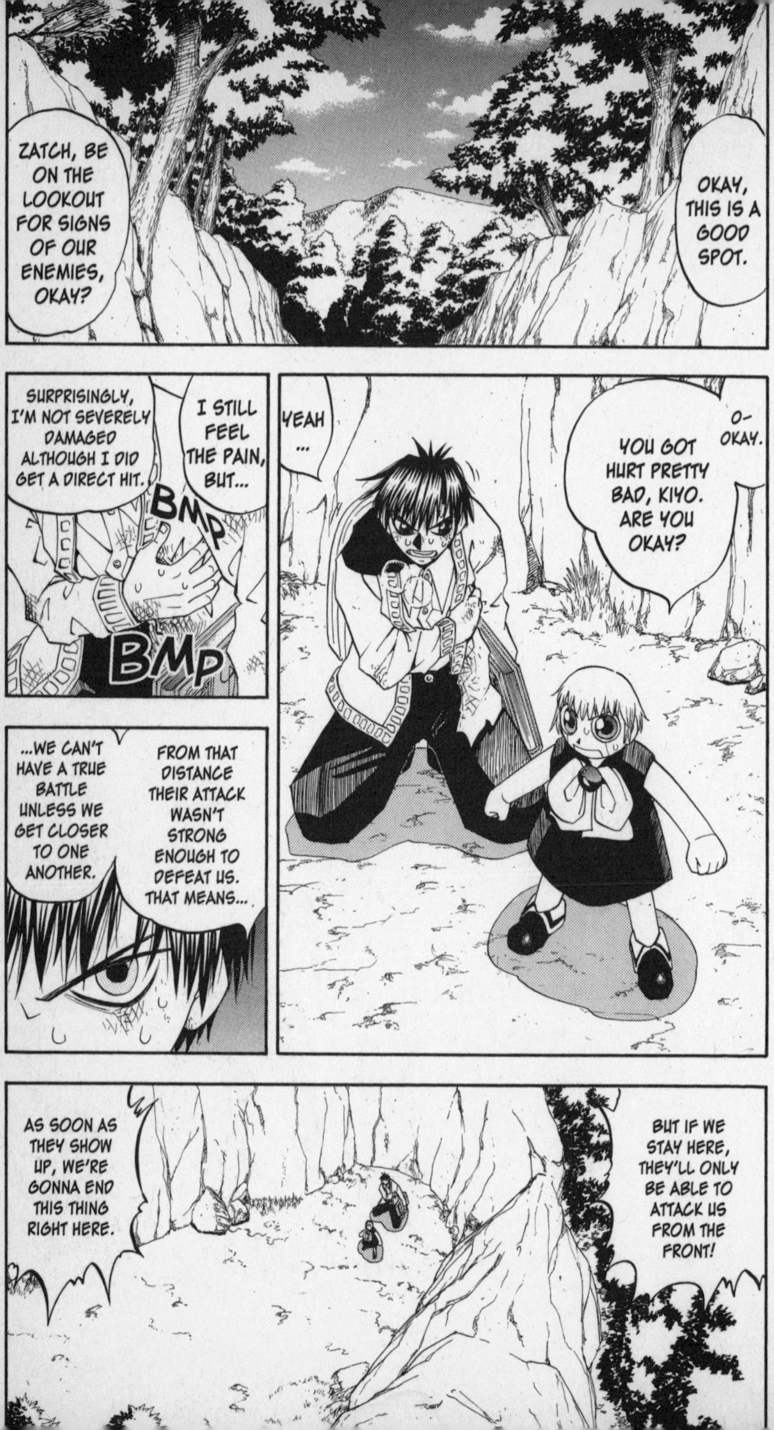
OKAY, THIS IS A GOOD SPOT.
ZATCH, BE ON THE LOOKOUT FOR SIGNS OF OUR ENEMIES, OKAY?
O-OKAY.
YOU GOT HURT PRETTY BAD, KIYO. ARE YOU OKAY?
YEAH ...
I STILL FEEL THE PAIN, BUT...
SURPRISINGLY, I'M NOT SEVERELY DAMAGED ALTHOUGH I DID GET A DIRECT HIT.
BMP
BMP
FROM THAT DISTANCE THEIR ATTACK WASN'T STRONG ENOUGH TO DEFEAT US. THAT MEANS...
...WE CAN'T HAVE A TRUE BATTLE UNLESS WE GET CLOSER TO ONE ANOTHER.
BUT IF WE STAY HERE, THEY'LL ONLY BE ABLE TO ATTACK US FROM THE FRONT!
AS SOON AS THEY SHOW UP, WE'RE GONNA END THIS THING RIGHT HERE.

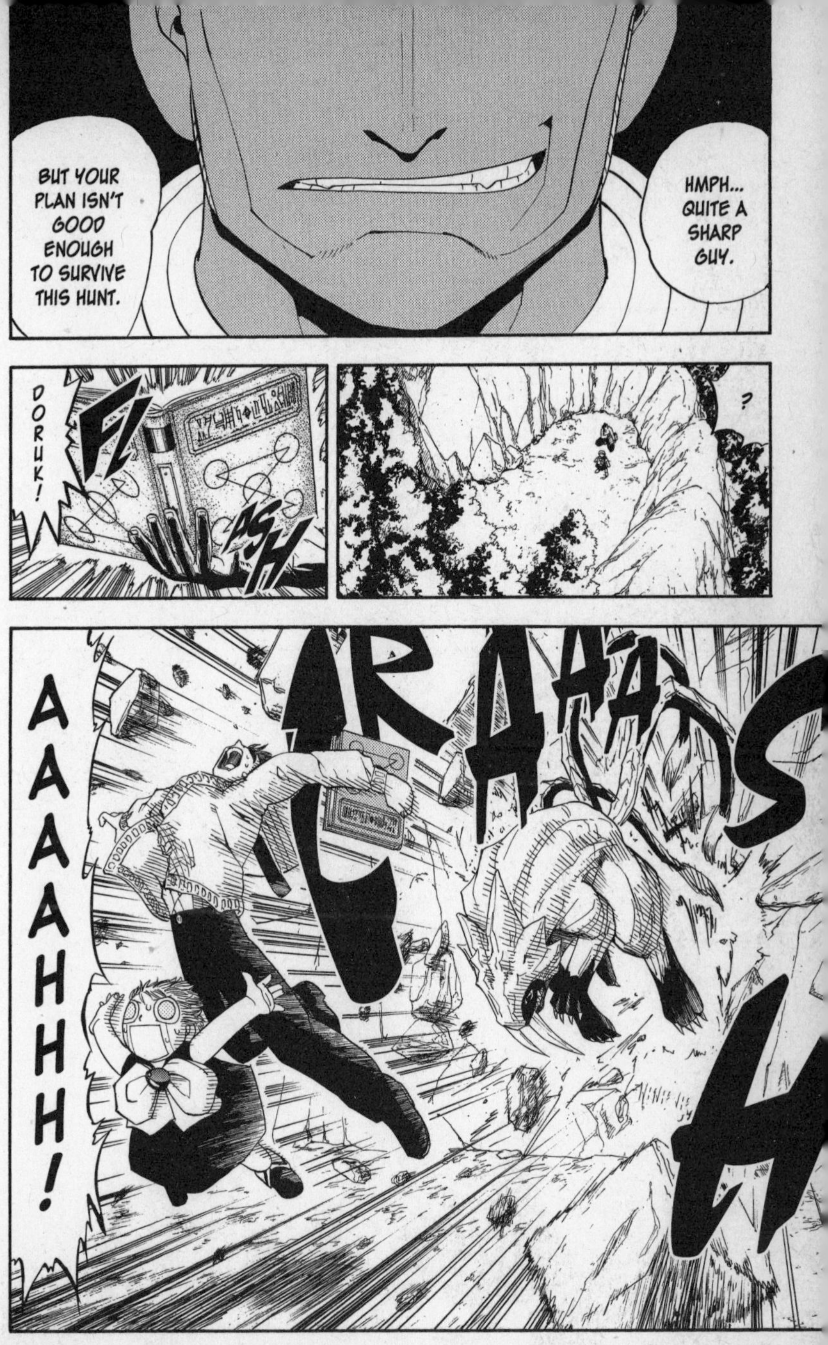
HMPH... QUITE A SHARP GUY.
BUT YOUR PLAN ISN'T GOOD ENOUGH TO SURVIVE THIS HUNT.
?
DORUK!
FLASH
RAAASH
AAAAHH!

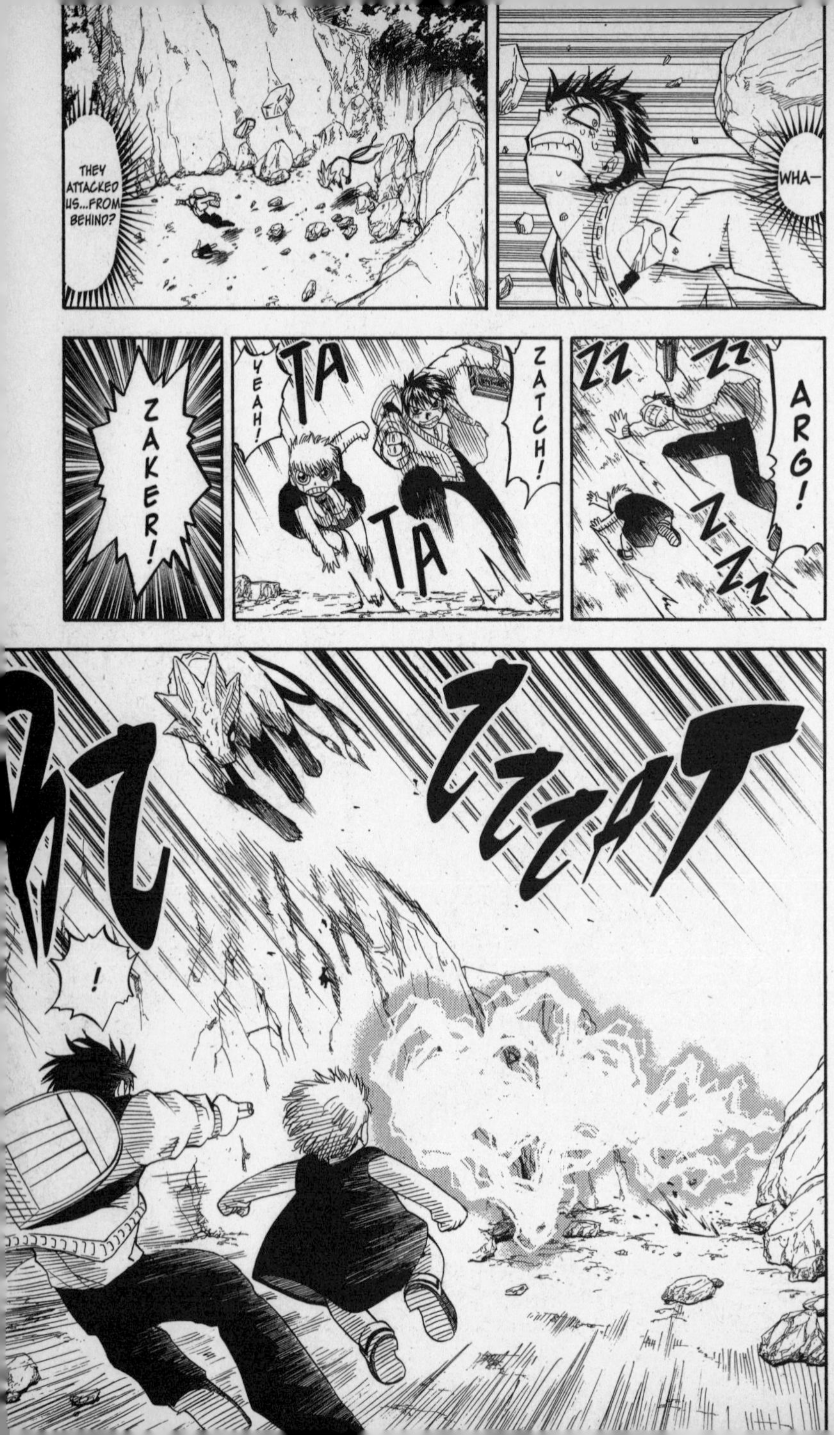

WHA—
THEY ATTACKED US...FROM BEHIND?
ZZ
ZZ
ARG!
Z
ZZ
ZATCH!
YEAH!
TA
TA
ZAKER!
ZZZAT
!

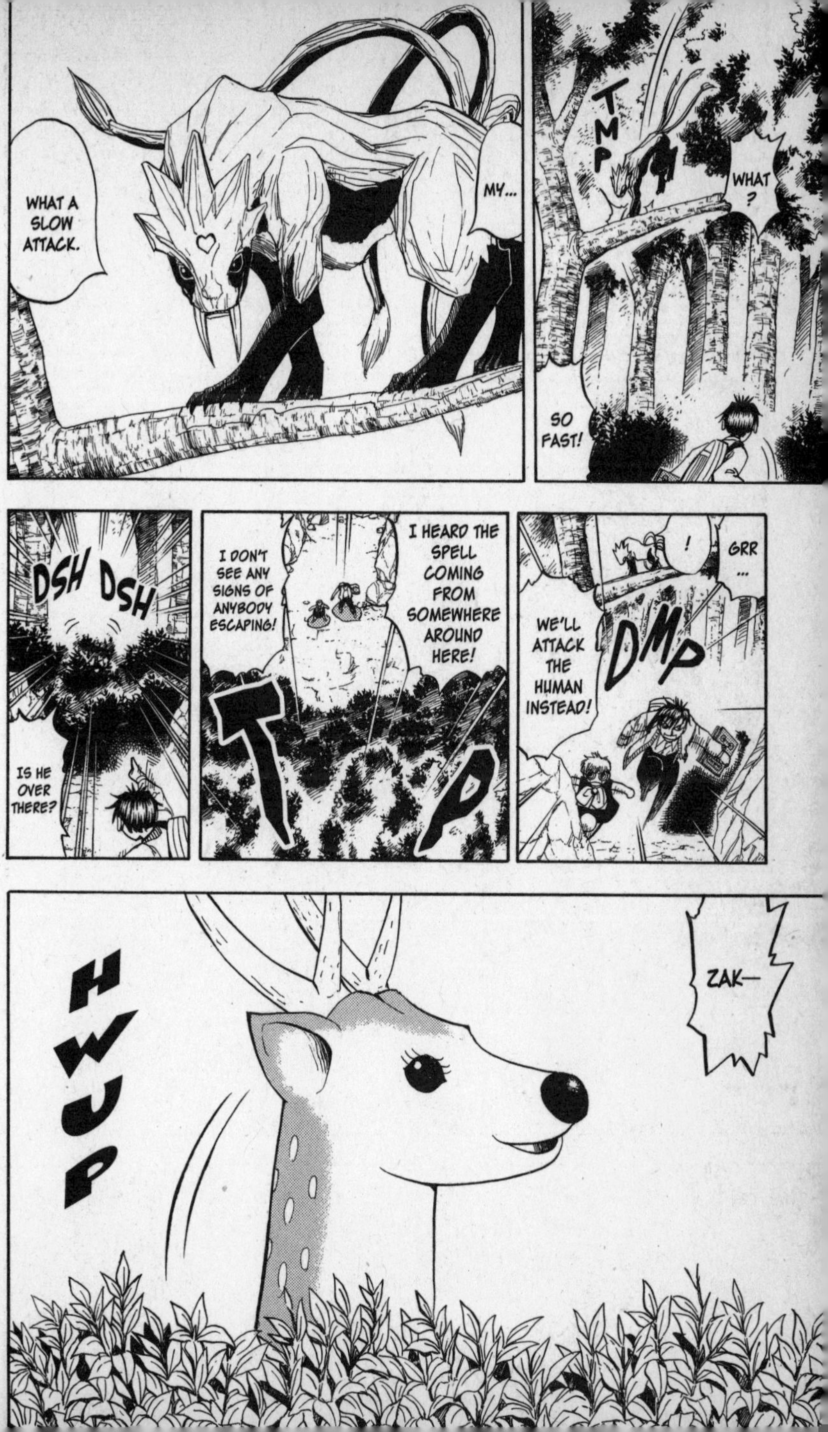
WHAT ?
TMP
SO FAST!
MY...
WHAT A SLOW ATTACK.
GRR ...
!
DMP
WE'LL ATTACK THE HUMAN INSTEAD!
I HEARD THE SPELL COMING FROM SOMEWHERE AROUND HERE!
I DON'T SEE ANY SIGNS OF ANYBODY ESCAPING!
TP
DSH DSH
IS HE OVER THERE?
ZAK—
HWUP

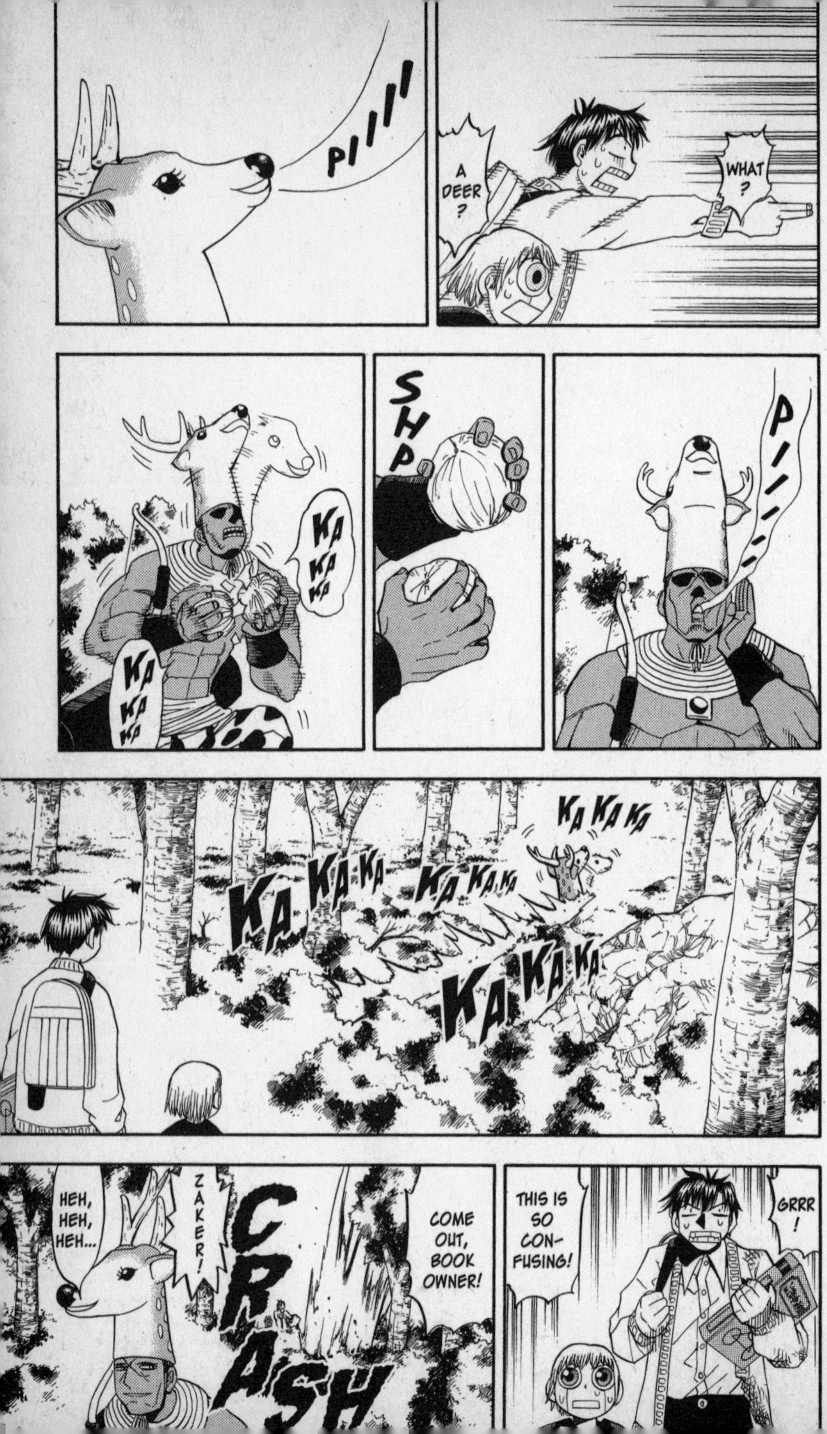
WHAT?
A DEER?
PIIII
PI----
SHP
KA KA KA KA
KA KA KA KA
KA KA KA
KA KA KA KA
KA KA KA KA
KA KA KA KA
GRRR!
THIS IS SO CON-FUSING!
COME OUT, BOOK OWNER!
CRASH
ZAKER!
HEH, HEH, HEH...

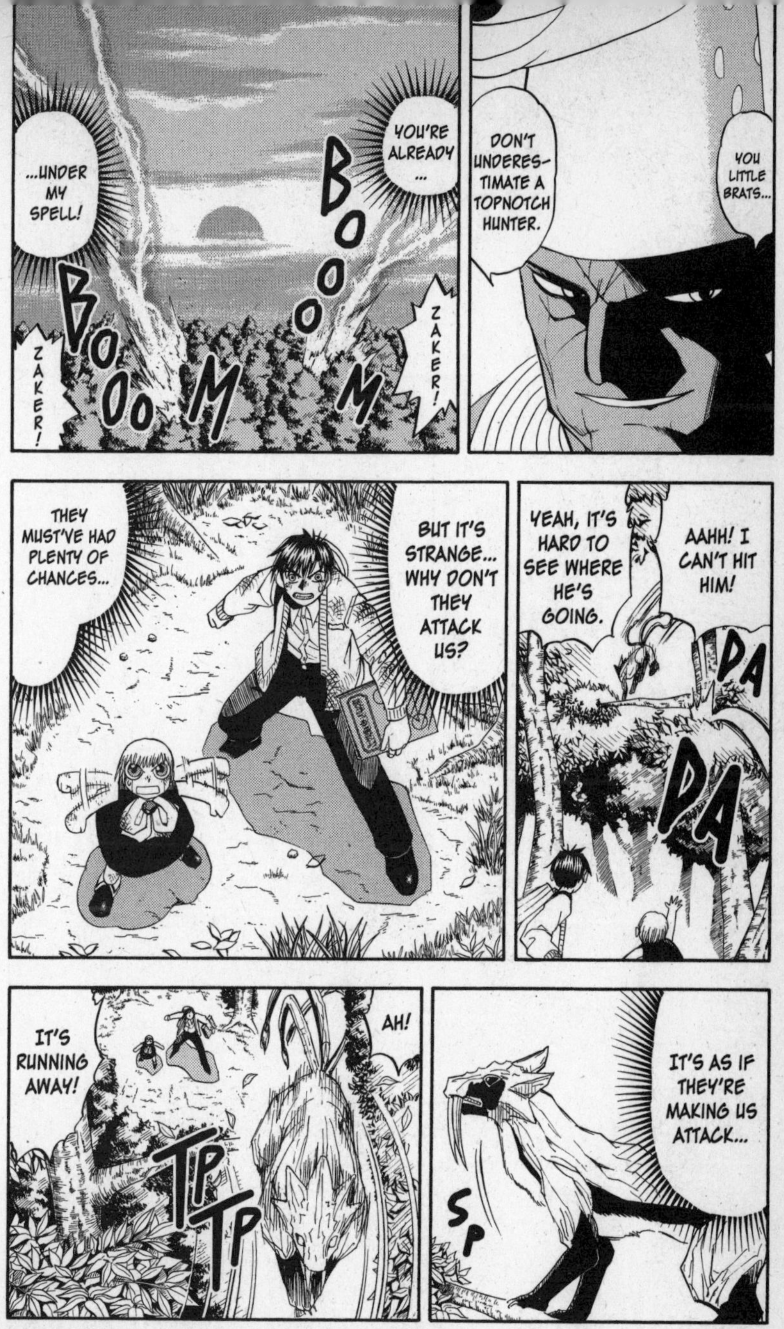
YOU LITTLE BRATS...
DON'T UNDERES-TIMATE A TOPNOTCH HUNTER.
ZAKER!
YOU'RE ALREADY ...
BOOOM
...UNDER MY SPELL!
ZAKER!
BOOOM
AAHH! I CAN'T HIT HIM!
YEAH, IT'S HARD TO SEE WHERE HE'S GOING.
DA
DA
BUT IT'S STRANGE... WHY DON'T THEY ATTACK US?
THEY MUST'VE HAD PLENTY OF CHANCES...
IT'S AS IF THEY'RE MAKING US ATTACK...
SP
AH!
IT'S RUNNING AWAY!
TP TP

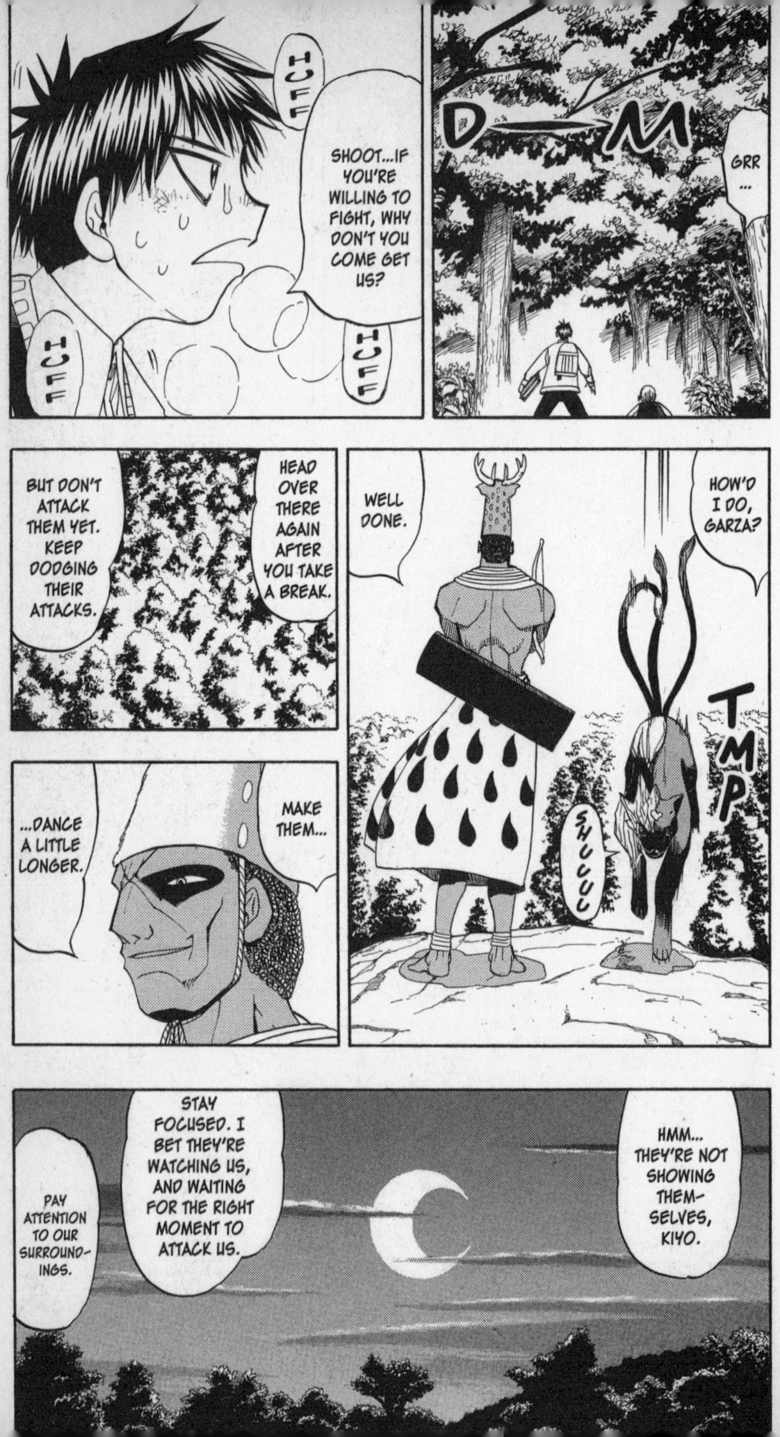
D—M
GRR...
HUFF
SHOOT...IF YOU'RE WILLING TO FIGHT, WHY DON'T YOU COME GET US?
HUFF
HUFF
HOW'D I DO, GARZA?
WELL DONE.
TMP
SHUUUU
HEAD OVER THERE AGAIN AFTER YOU TAKE A BREAK.
BUT DON'T ATTACK THEM YET. KEEP DODGING THEIR ATTACKS.
MAKE THEM...
...DANCE A LITTLE LONGER.
HMM... THEY'RE NOT SHOWING THEM-SELVES, KIYO.
STAY FOCUSED. I BET THEY'RE WATCHING US, AND WAITING FOR THE RIGHT MOMENT TO ATTACK US.
PAY ATTENTION TO OUR SURROUND-INGS.

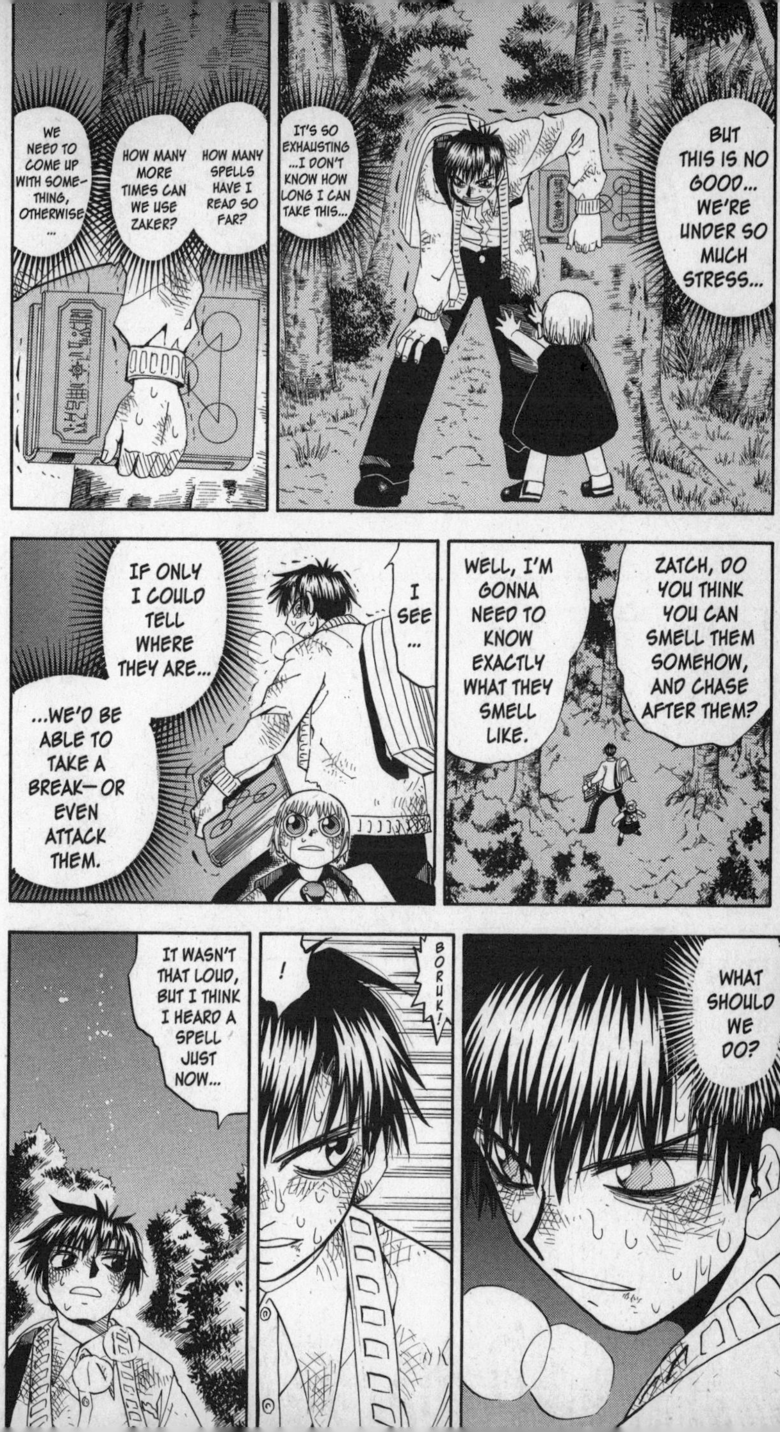
BUT THIS IS NO GOOD... WE'RE UNDER SO MUCH STRESS...
IT'S SO EXHAUSTING ...I DON'T KNOW HOW LONG I CAN TAKE THIS...
HOW MANY SPELLS HAVE I READ SO FAR?
HOW MANY MORE TIMES CAN WE USE ZAKER?
WE NEED TO COME UP WITH SOME-THING, OTHERWISE...
ZATCH, DO YOU THINK YOU CAN SMELL THEM SOMEHOW, AND CHASE AFTER THEM?
WELL, I'M GONNA NEED TO KNOW EXACTLY WHAT THEY SMELL LIKE.
I SEE...
IF ONLY I COULD TELL WHERE THEY ARE...
...WE'D BE ABLE TO TAKE A BREAK—OR EVEN ATTACK THEM.
WHAT SHOULD WE DO?
BORUK!
!
IT WASN'T THAT LOUD, BUT I THINK I HEARD A SPELL JUST NOW...

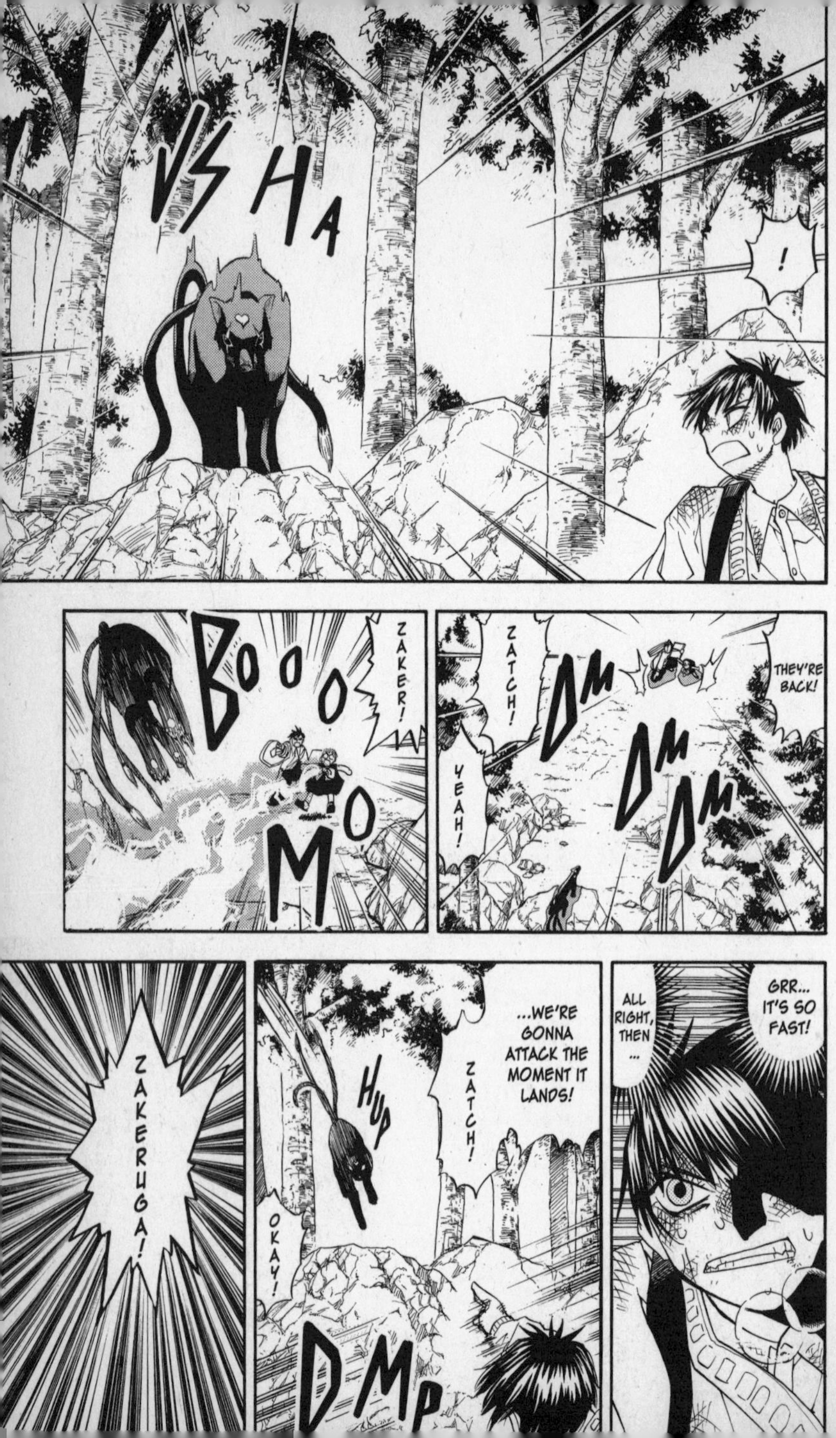
!
VSHA
THEY'RE BACK!
ZATCH!
DM DM DM
YEAH!
ZAKER!
BOOOOM
GRR... IT'S SO FAST!
ALL RIGHT, THEN ...
...WE'RE GONNA ATTACK THE MOMENT IT LANDS!
ZATCH!
HUP
OKAY!
DMP
ZAKERUGA!

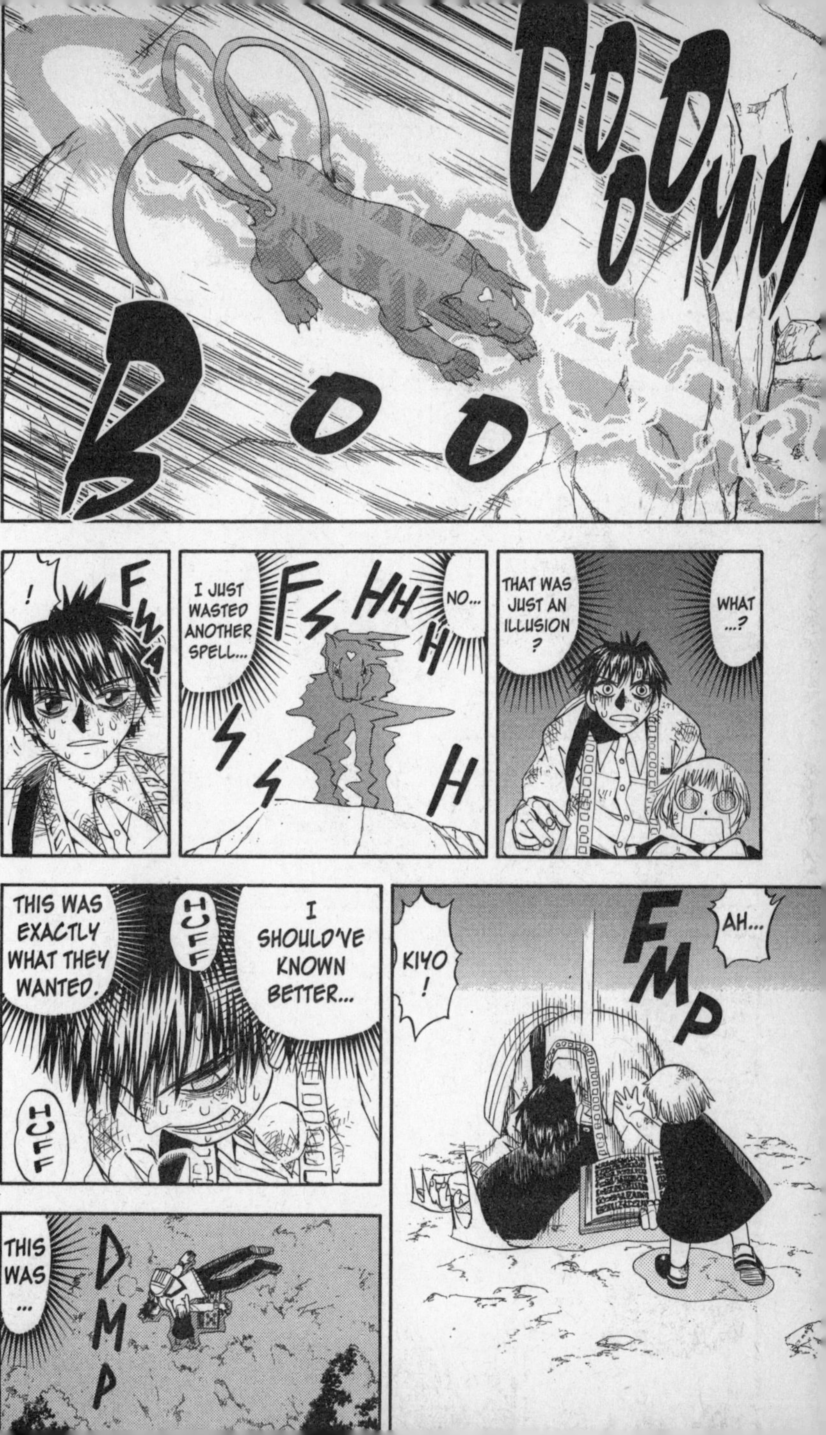
DOOOMM
BOOD
WHAT ...?
THAT WAS JUST AN ILLUSION ?
NO...
FSHHHH
I JUST WASTED ANOTHER SPELL...
!
FWA
AH...
FMP
KIYO !
I SHOULD'VE KNOWN BETTER...
HUFF
THIS WAS EXACTLY WHAT THEY WANTED.
HUFF
THIS WAS ...
DMP

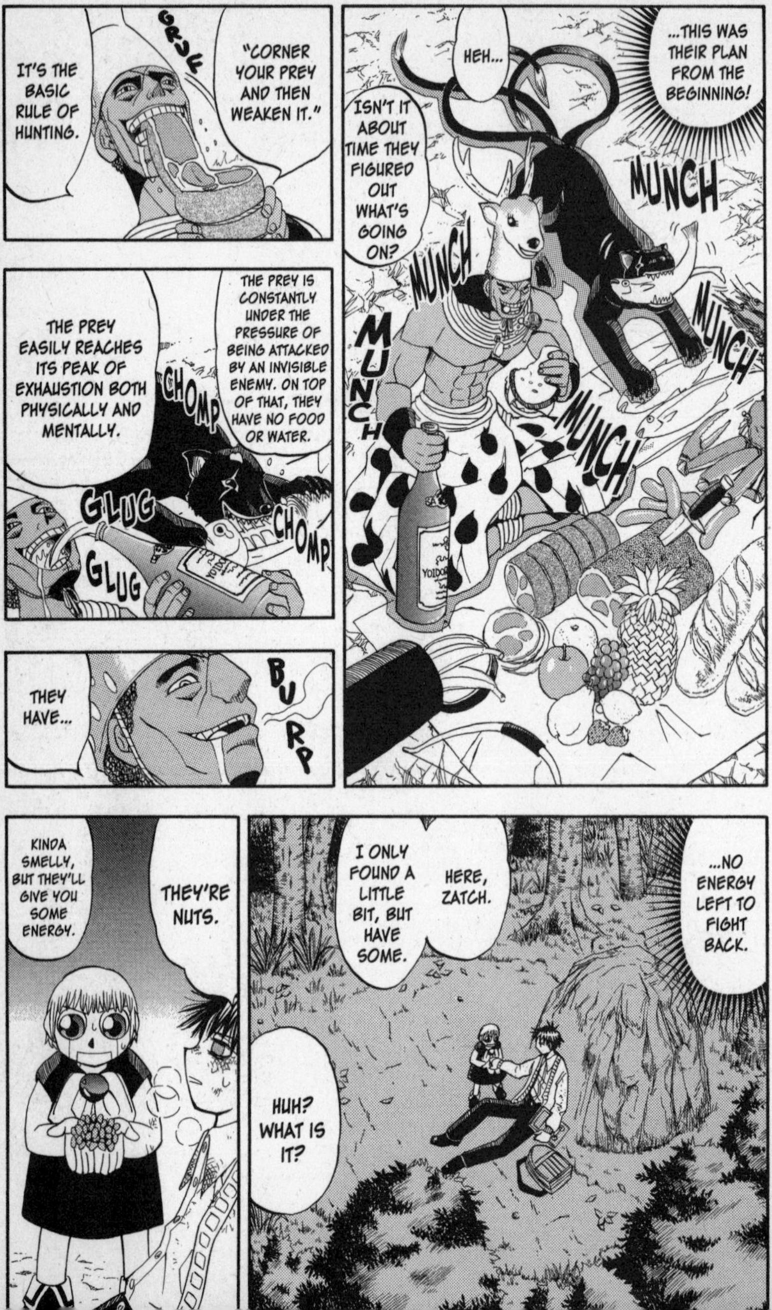
...THIS WAS THEIR PLAN FROM THE BEGINNING!
HEH...
ISN'T IT ABOUT TIME THEY FIGURED OUT WHAT'S GOING ON?
MUNCH
MUNCH
MUNCH
MUNCH
MUNCH
"CORNER YOUR PREY AND THEN WEAKEN IT."
GRUF
IT'S THE BASIC RULE OF HUNTING.
THE PREY IS CONSTANTLY UNDER THE PRESSURE OF BEING ATTACKED BY AN INVISIBLE ENEMY. ON TOP OF THAT, THEY HAVE NO FOOD OR WATER.
CHOMP
THE PREY EASILY REACHES ITS PEAK OF EXHAUSTION BOTH PHYSICALLY AND MENTALLY.
CHOMP
GLUG
GLUG
BURP
THEY HAVE...
...NO ENERGY LEFT TO FIGHT BACK.
HERE, ZATCH.
I ONLY FOUND A LITTLE BIT, BUT HAVE SOME.
HUH? WHAT IS IT?
THEY'RE NUTS.
KINDA SMELLY, BUT THEY'LL GIVE YOU SOME ENERGY.

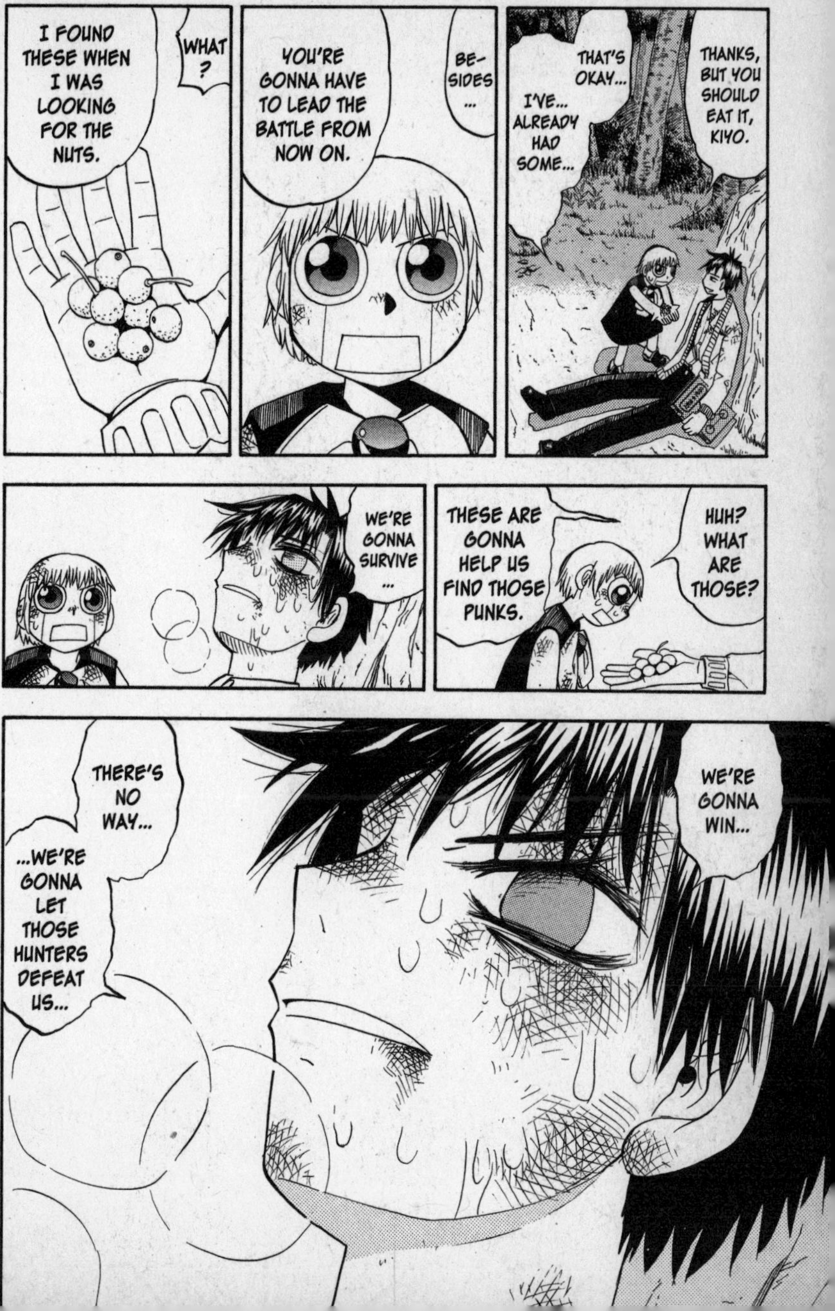
THANKS, BUT YOU SHOULD EAT IT, KIYO.
THAT'S OKAY...
I'VE... ALREADY HAD SOME...
BE-SIDES...
YOU'RE GONNA HAVE TO LEAD THE BATTLE FROM NOW ON.
WHAT?
I FOUND THESE WHEN I WAS LOOKING FOR THE NUTS.
HUH? WHAT ARE THOSE?
THESE ARE GONNA HELP US FIND THOSE PUNKS.
WE'RE GONNA SURVIVE...
WE'RE GONNA WIN...
THERE'S NO WAY...
...WE'RE GONNA LET THOSE HUNTERS DEFEAT US...

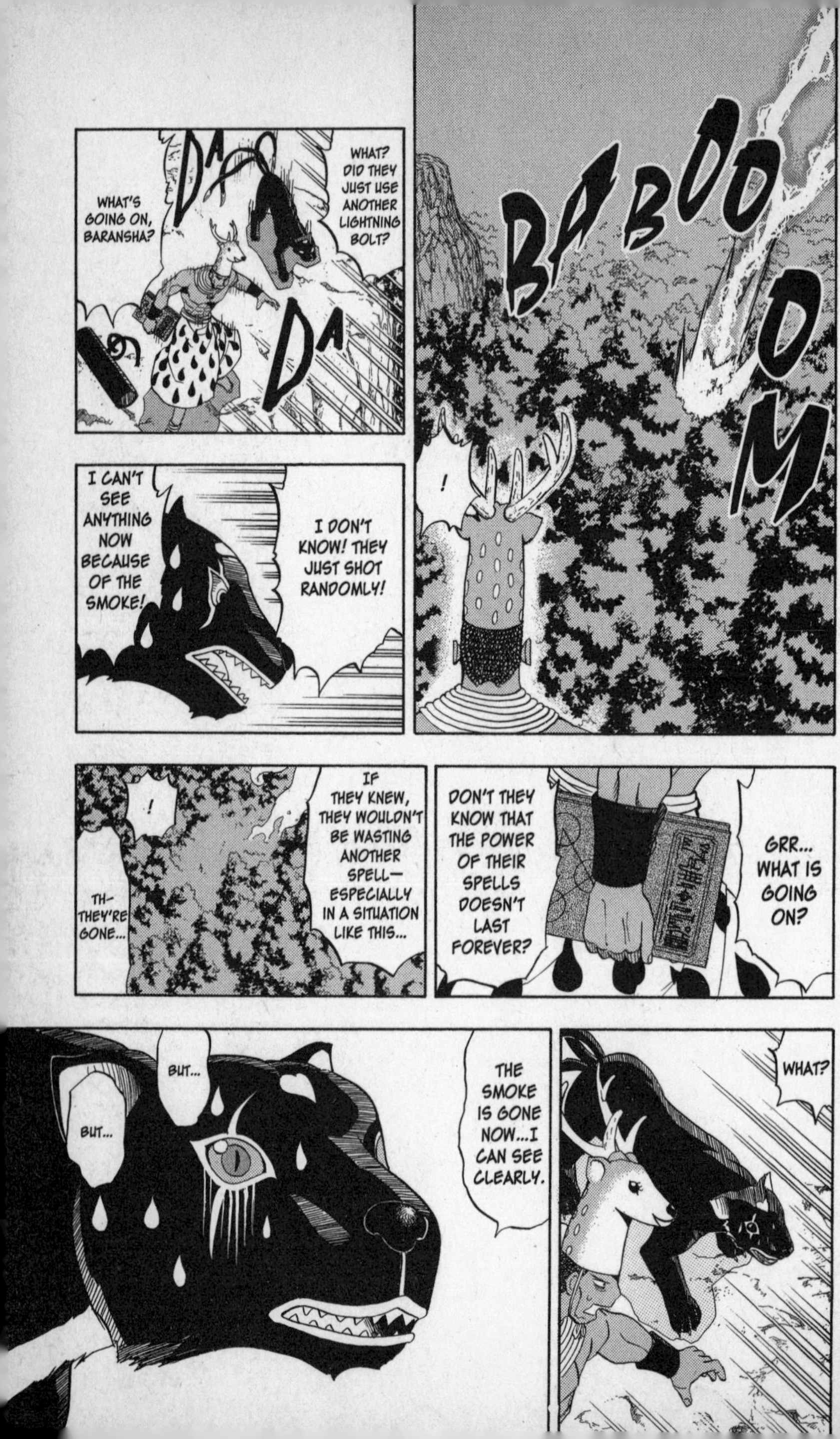
BABOOOM
!
WHAT? DID THEY JUST USE ANOTHER LIGHTNING BOLT?
DA
WHAT'S GOING ON, BARANSHA?
DA
I DON'T KNOW! THEY JUST SHOT RANDOMLY!
I CAN'T SEE ANYTHING NOW BECAUSE OF THE SMOKE!
GRR... WHAT IS GOING ON?
DON'T THEY KNOW THAT THE POWER OF THEIR SPELLS DOESN'T LAST FOREVER?
IF THEY KNEW, THEY WOULDN'T BE WASTING ANOTHER SPELL—ESPECIALLY IN A SITUATION LIKE THIS...
!
TH- THEY'RE GONE...
WHAT?
THE SMOKE IS GONE NOW...I CAN SEE CLEARLY.
BUT...
BUT...

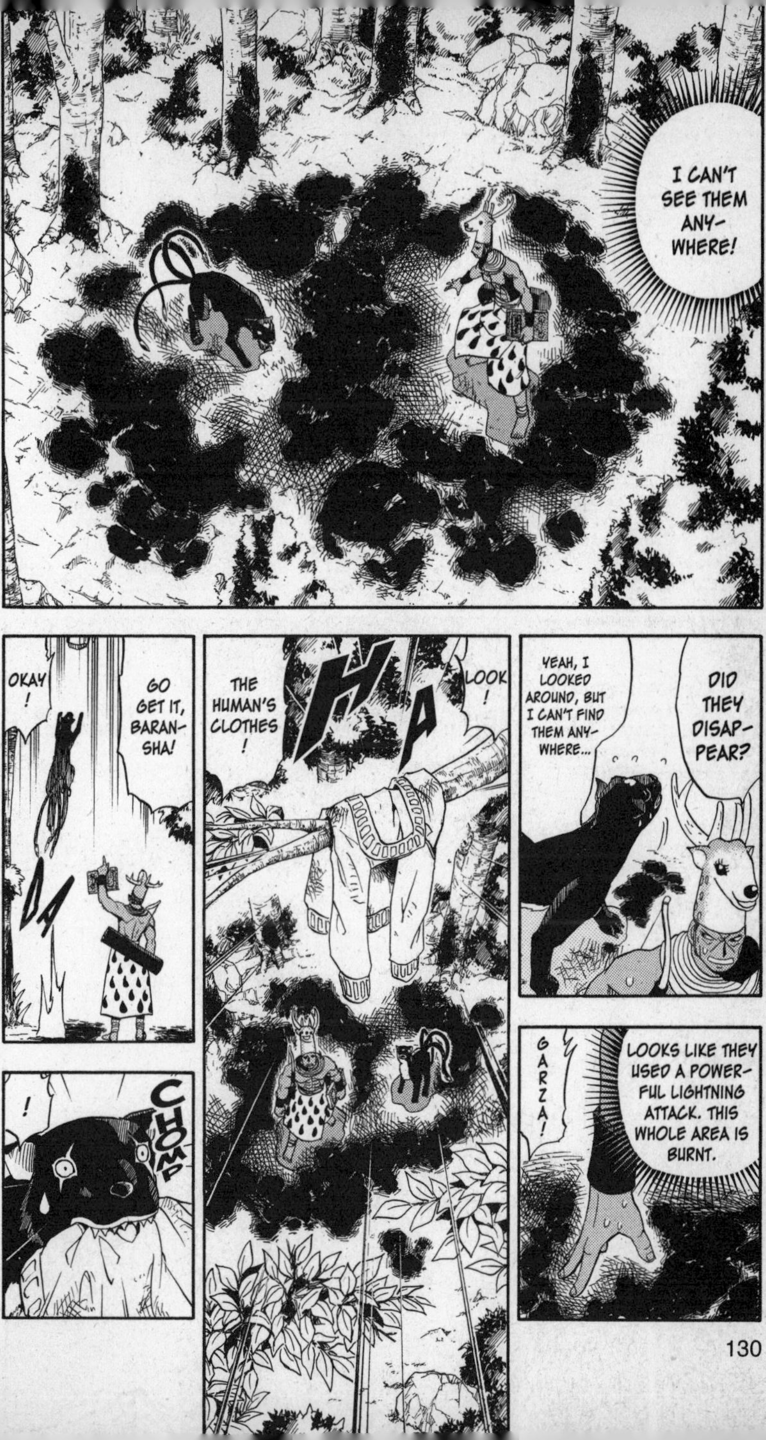
I CAN'T SEE THEM ANY-WHERE!
DID THEY DISAP-PEAR?
YEAH, I LOOKED AROUND, BUT I CAN'T FIND THEM ANY-WHERE...
LOOKS LIKE THEY USED A POWER-FUL LIGHTNING ATTACK. THIS WHOLE AREA IS BURNT.
GARZA!
LOOK!
HA
THE HUMAN'S CLOTHES!
GO GET IT, BARAN-SHA!
OKAY!
DA
CHOMP
!

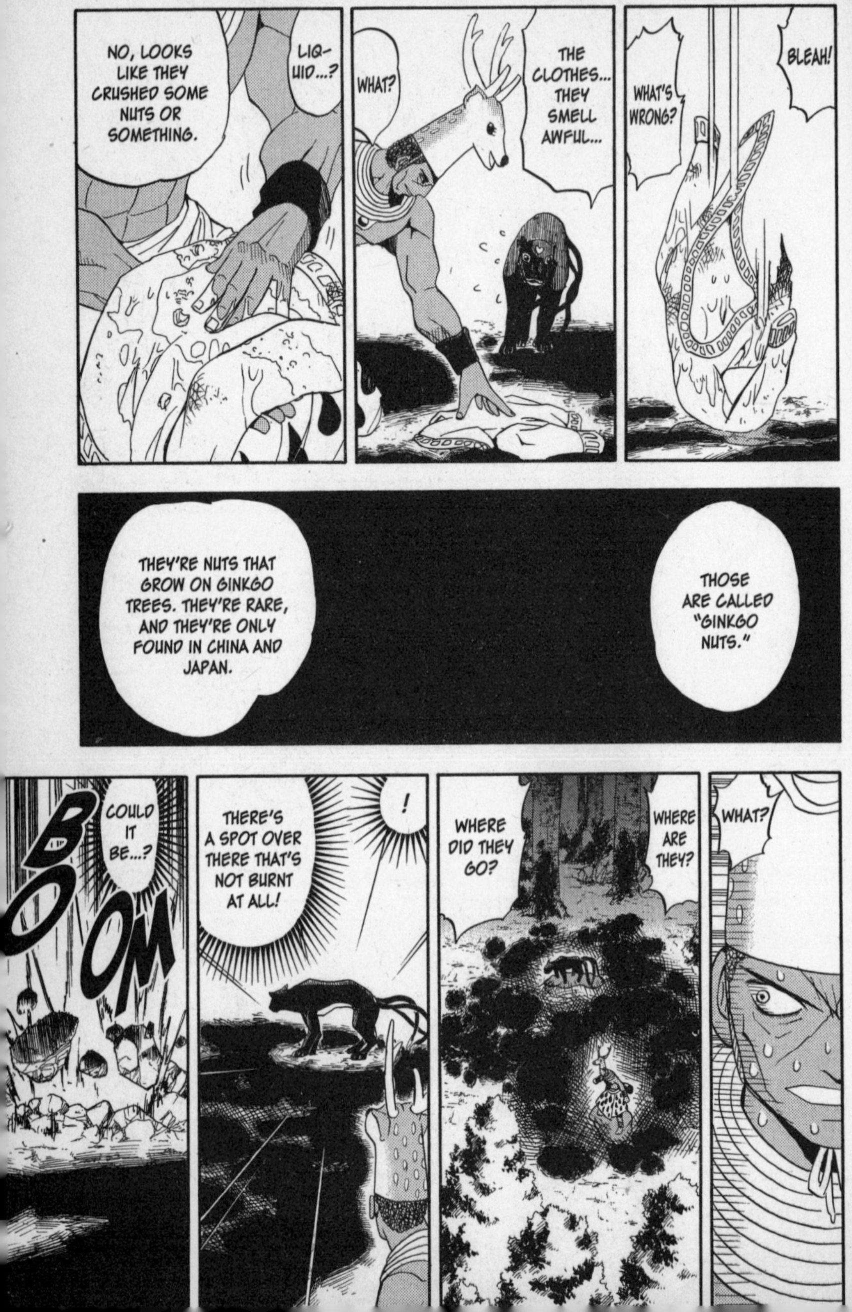
BLEAH!
WHAT'S WRONG?
THE CLOTHES... THEY SMELL AWFUL...
WHAT?
LIQ-UID...?
NO, LOOKS LIKE THEY CRUSHED SOME NUTS OR SOMETHING.
THOSE ARE CALLED "GINKGO NUTS."
THEY'RE NUTS THAT GROW ON GINKGO TREES. THEY'RE RARE, AND THEY'RE ONLY FOUND IN CHINA AND JAPAN.
WHAT?
WHERE ARE THEY?
WHERE DID THEY GO?
!
THERE'S A SPOT OVER THERE THAT'S NOT BURNT AT ALL!
COULD IT BE...?
BOOM

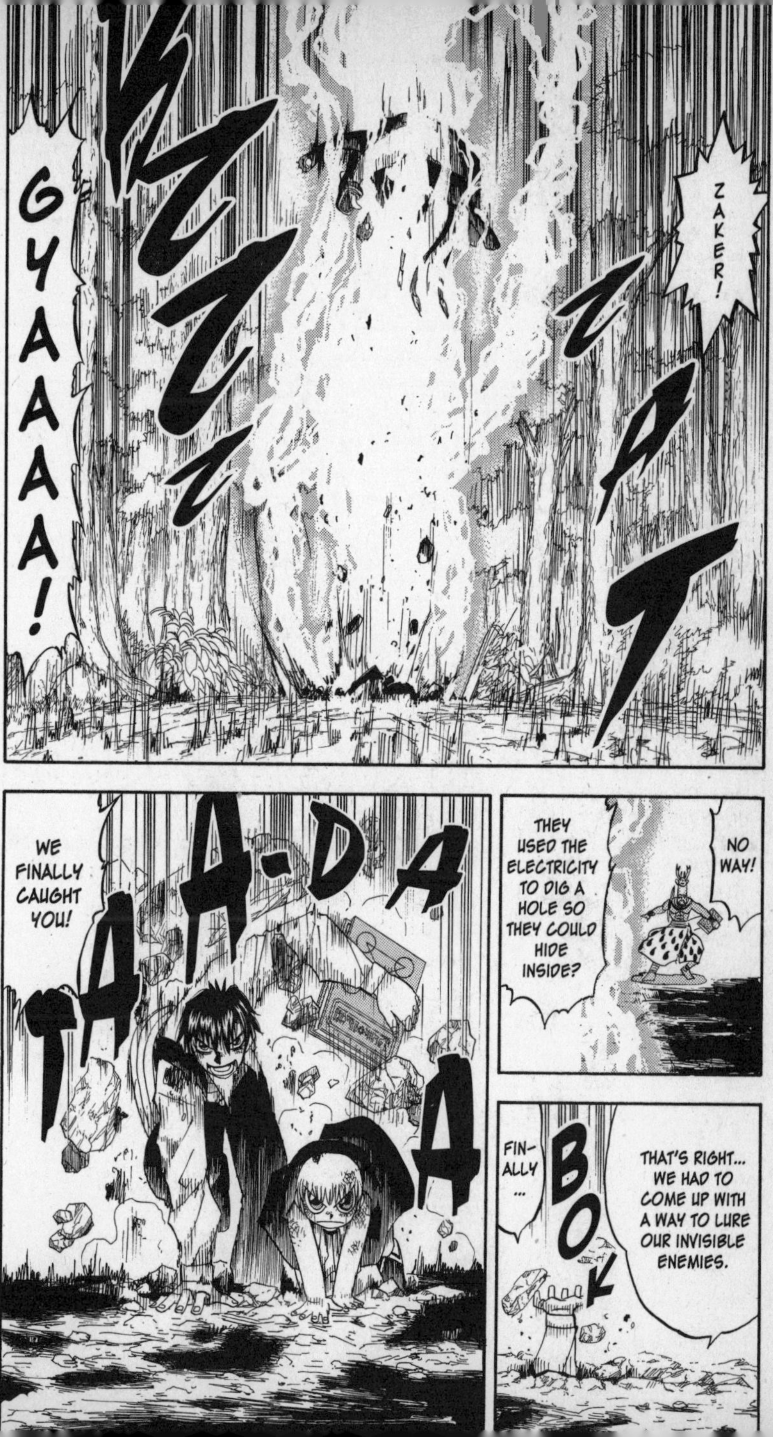
ZAKER!
GYAAAAA!
NO WAY!
THEY USED THE ELECTRICITY TO DIG A HOLE SO THEY COULD HIDE INSIDE?
THAT'S RIGHT... WE HAD TO COME UP WITH A WAY TO LURE OUR INVISIBLE ENEMIES.
FIN-ALLY...
BOK
TA-A-DA-A
WE FINALLY CAUGHT YOU!

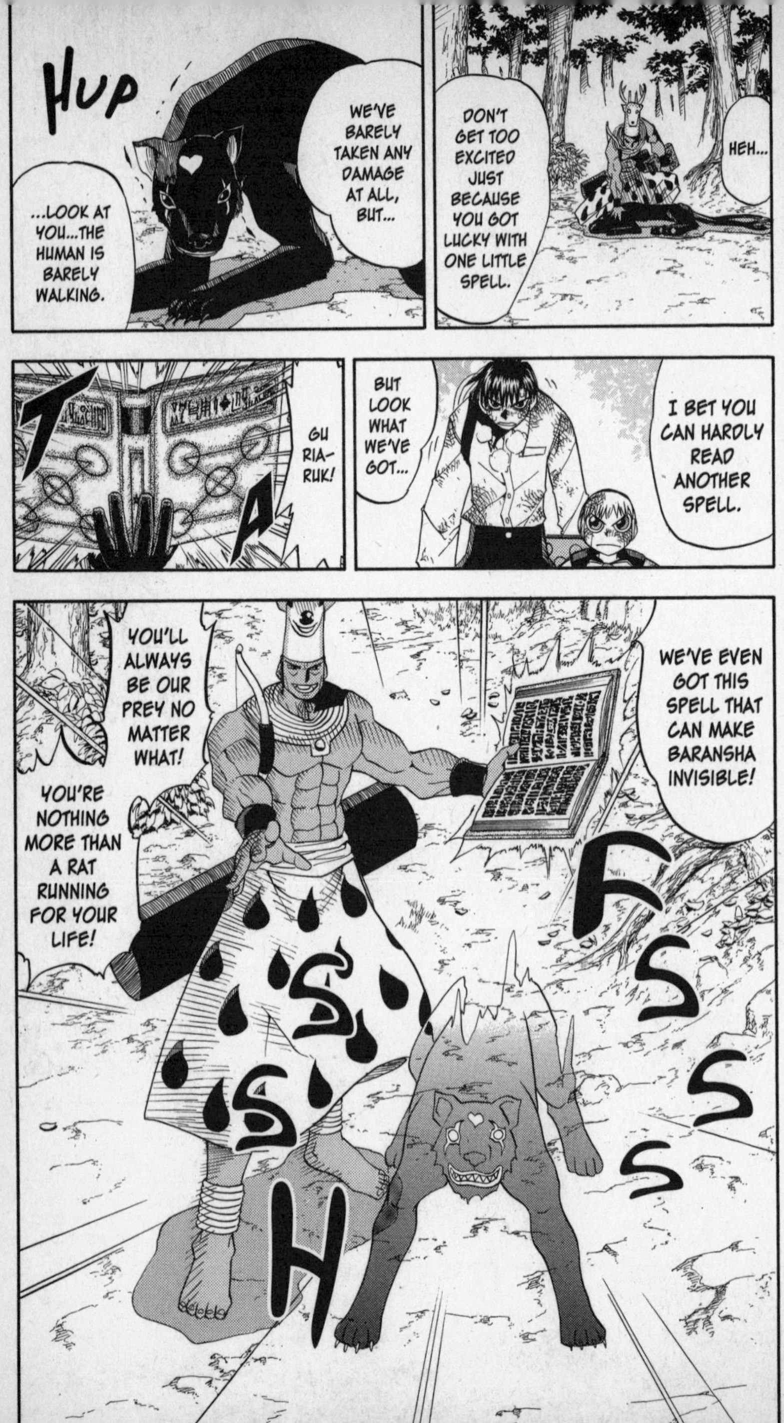
HEH...
DON'T GET TOO EXCITED JUST BECAUSE YOU GOT LUCKY WITH ONE LITTLE SPELL.
HUP
WE'VE BARELY TAKEN ANY DAMAGE AT ALL, BUT...
...LOOK AT YOU...THE HUMAN IS BARELY WALKING.
I BET YOU CAN HARDLY READ ANOTHER SPELL.
BUT LOOK WHAT WE'VE GOT...
GU RIA-RUK!
TA
WE'VE EVEN GOT THIS SPELL THAT CAN MAKE BARANSHA INVISIBLE!
YOU'LL ALWAYS BE OUR PREY NO MATTER WHAT!
YOU'RE NOTHING MORE THAN A RAT RUNNING FOR YOUR LIFE!
FSSSS
SSH

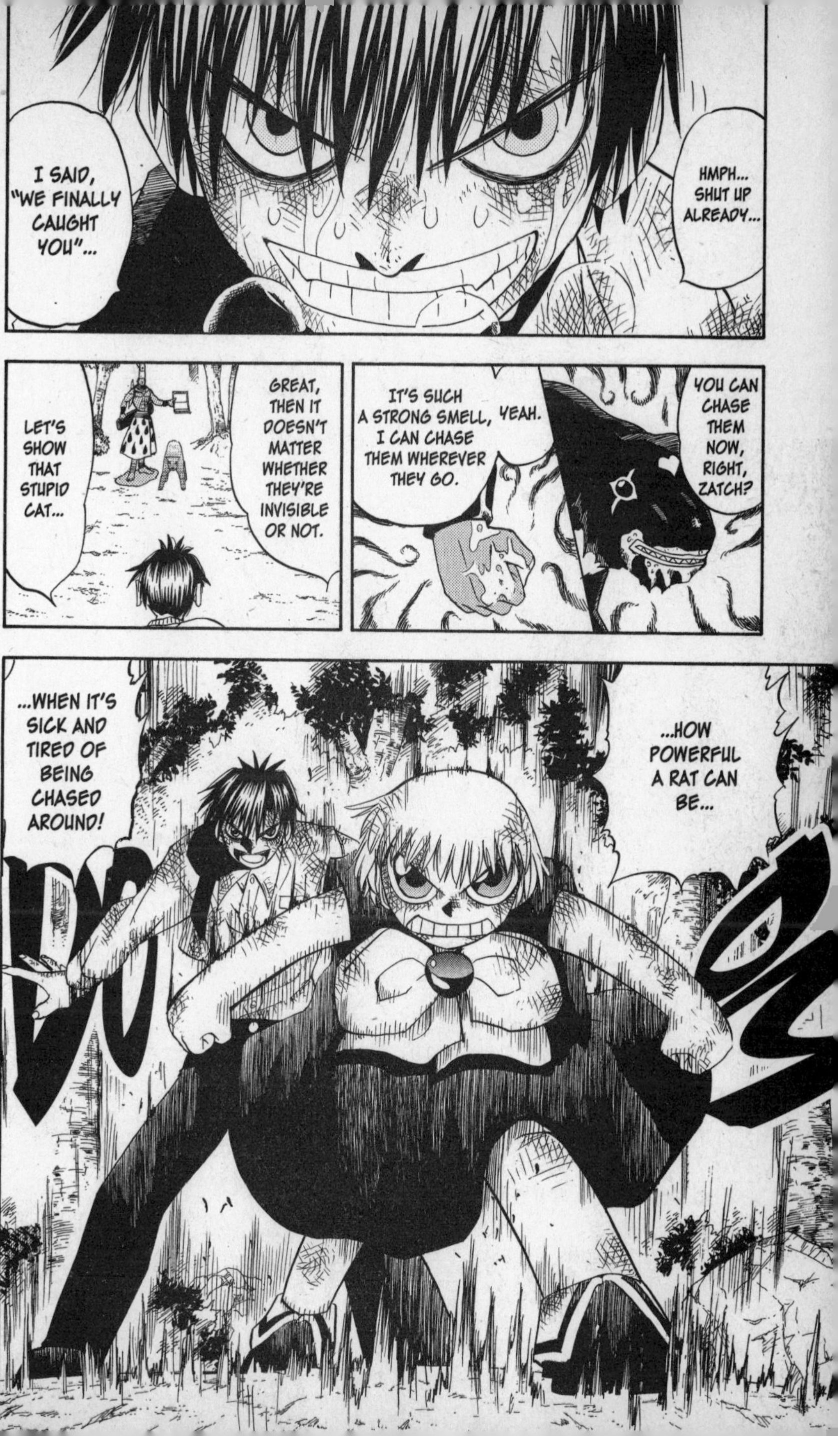
HMPH... SHUT UP ALREADY...
I SAID, "WE FINALLY CAUGHT YOU"...
YOU CAN CHASE THEM NOW, RIGHT, ZATCH?
YEAH.
IT'S SUCH A STRONG SMELL, I CAN CHASE THEM WHEREVER THEY GO.
GREAT, THEN IT DOESN'T MATTER WHETHER THEY'RE INVISIBLE OR NOT.
LET'S SHOW THAT STUPID CAT...
...HOW POWERFUL A RAT CAN BE...
...WHEN IT'S SICK AND TIRED OF BEING CHASED AROUND!

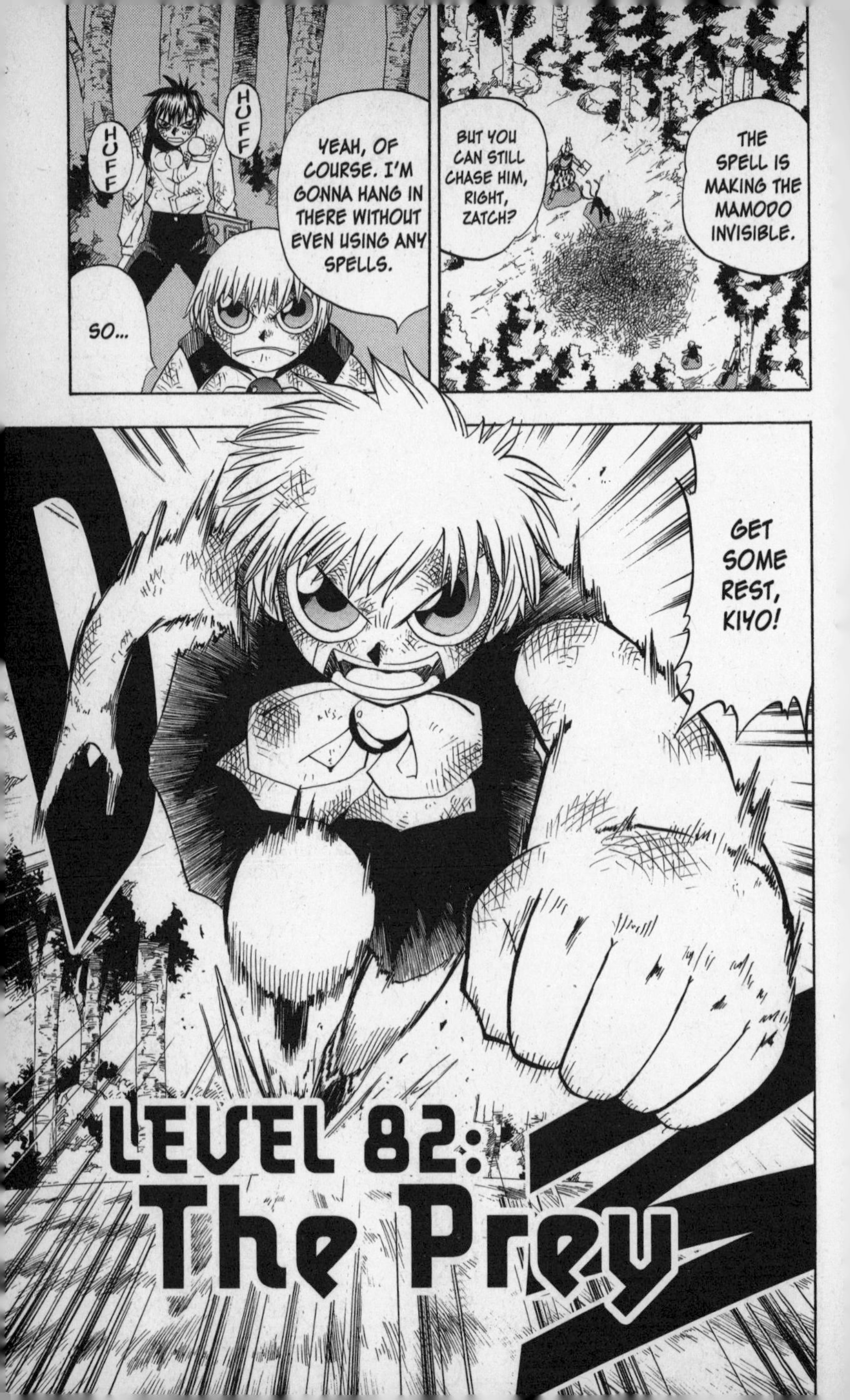
THE SPELL IS MAKING THE MAMODO INVISIBLE.
BUT YOU CAN STILL CHASE HIM, RIGHT, ZATCH?
HUFF
HUFF
YEAH, OF COURSE. I'M GONNA HANG IN THERE WITHOUT EVEN USING ANY SPELLS.
SO...
GET SOME REST, KIYO!
LEVEL 82: The Prey

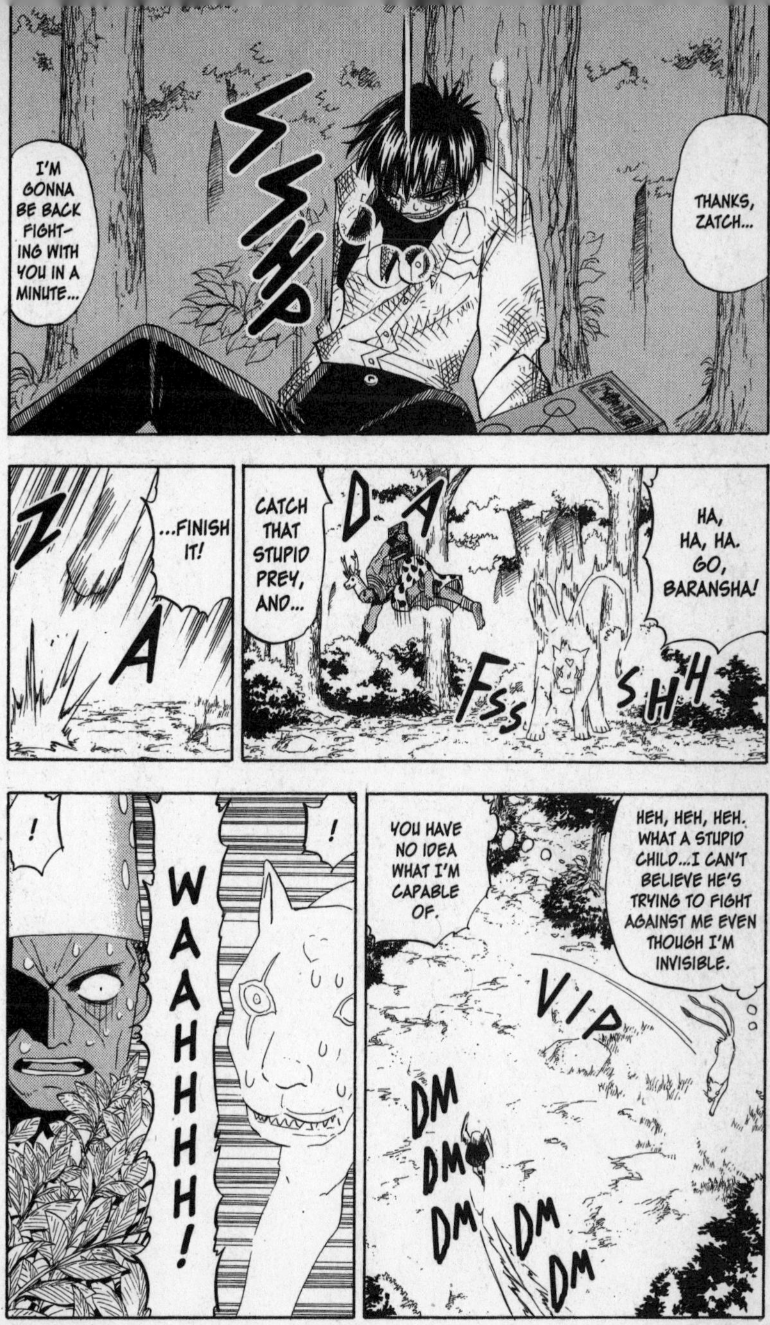
THANKS, ZATCH...
SSHP
I'M GONNA BE BACK FIGHTING WITH YOU IN A MINUTE...
HA, HA, HA. GO, BARANSHA!
DA
CATCH THAT STUPID PREY, AND...
FSS SHH
...FINISH IT!
ZA
HEH, HEH, HEH. WHAT A STUPID CHILD...I CAN'T BELIEVE HE'S TRYING TO FIGHT AGAINST ME EVEN THOUGH I'M INVISIBLE.
YOU HAVE NO IDEA WHAT I'M CAPABLE OF.
VIP
DM DM DM DM DM
!
!
WAAHHHH!

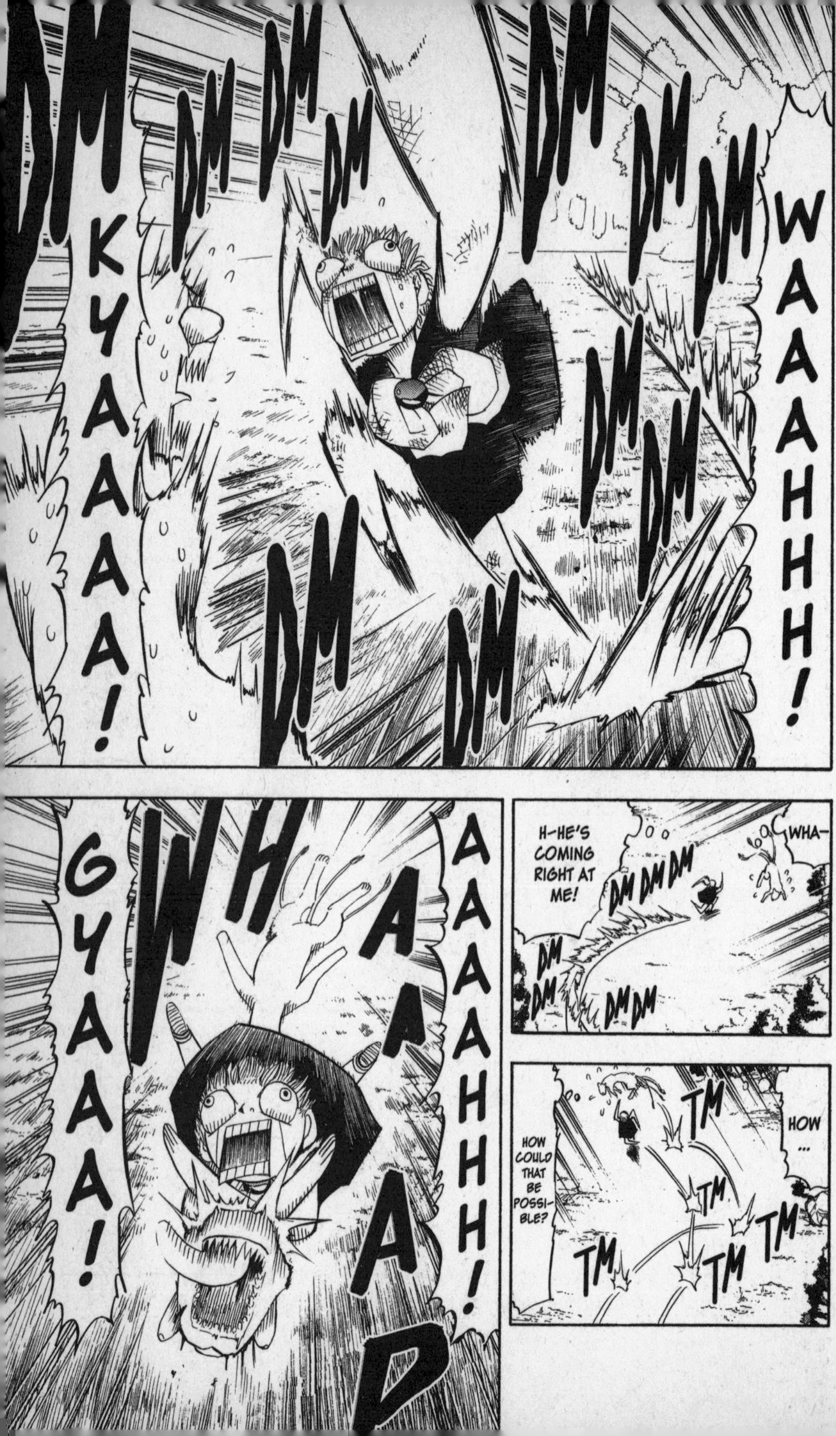
WAAAHHH!
DM DM DM DM DM DM DM DM
DM DM DM DM DM DM
KYAAAA!
WHA-
H-HE'S COMING RIGHT AT ME!
DM DM DM
DM DM
DM DM
HOW ...
HOW COULD THAT BE POSSIBLE?
TM TM TM TM TM TM
AAAAHHH!
WHAAAD
GYAAA!

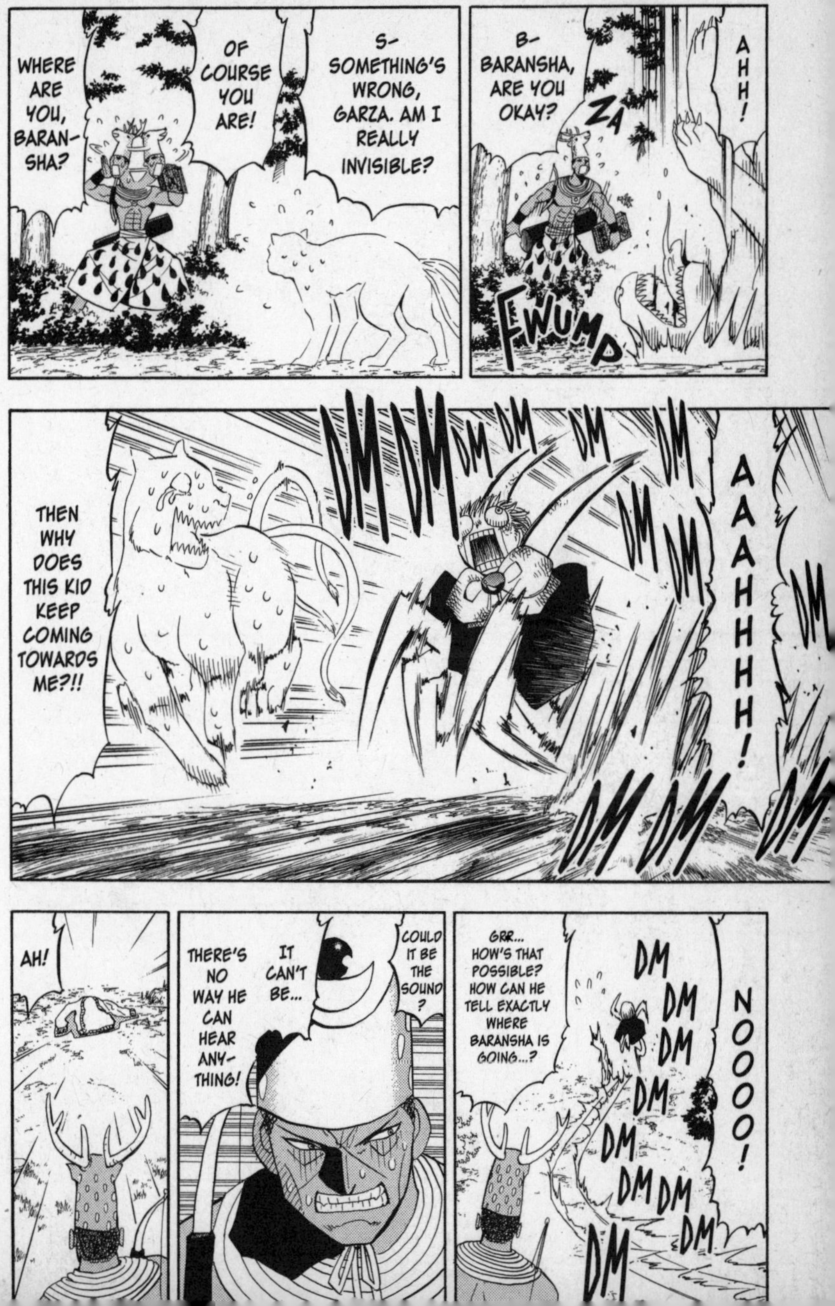
AHH!
B-BARANSHA, ARE YOU OKAY?
ZA
FWUMP
S-SOMETHING'S WRONG, GARZA. AM I REALLY INVISIBLE?
OF COURSE YOU ARE!
WHERE ARE YOU, BARANSHA?
AAAHHHHH!
DM DM DM DM DM DM DM DM DM DM DM DM DM DM DM
THEN WHY DOES THIS KID KEEP COMING TOWARDS ME?!!
NOOOO!
DM DM DM DM DM DM DM DM DM
GRR... HOW'S THAT POSSIBLE? HOW CAN HE TELL EXACTLY WHERE BARANSHA IS GOING...?
COULD IT BE THE SOUND?
IT CAN'T BE...
THERE'S NO WAY HE CAN HEAR ANYTHING!
AH!

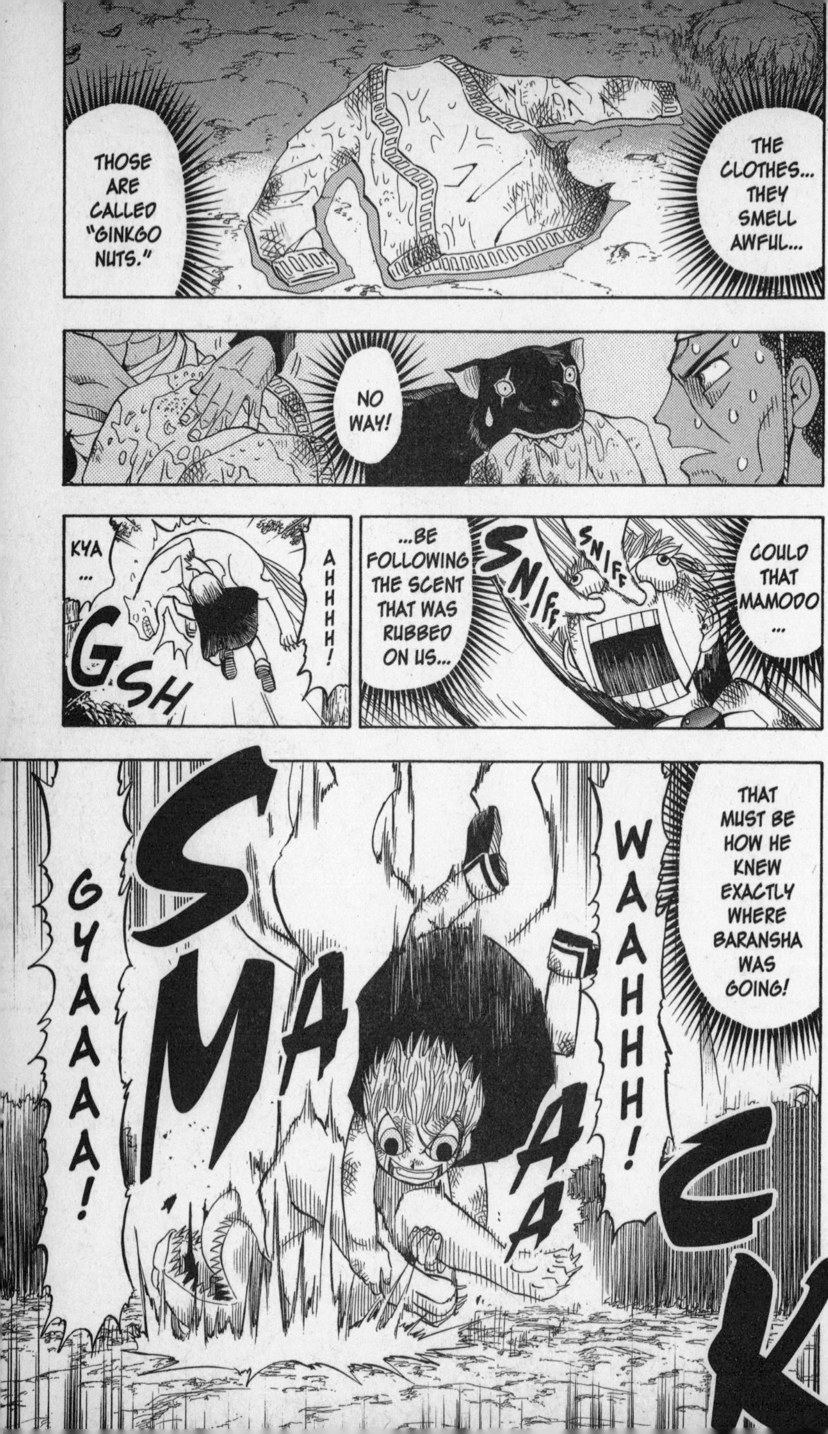
THE CLOTHES... THEY SMELL AWFUL...
THOSE ARE CALLED "GINKGO NUTS."
NO WAY!
COULD THAT MAMODO ...
SNIFF
SNIFF
...BE FOLLOWING THE SCENT THAT WAS RUBBED ON US...
AHHHHH!
KYA ...
GSH
THAT MUST BE HOW HE KNEW EXACTLY WHERE BARANSHA WAS GOING!
WAAHHH!
SMACK
AAA
GYAAAAA!

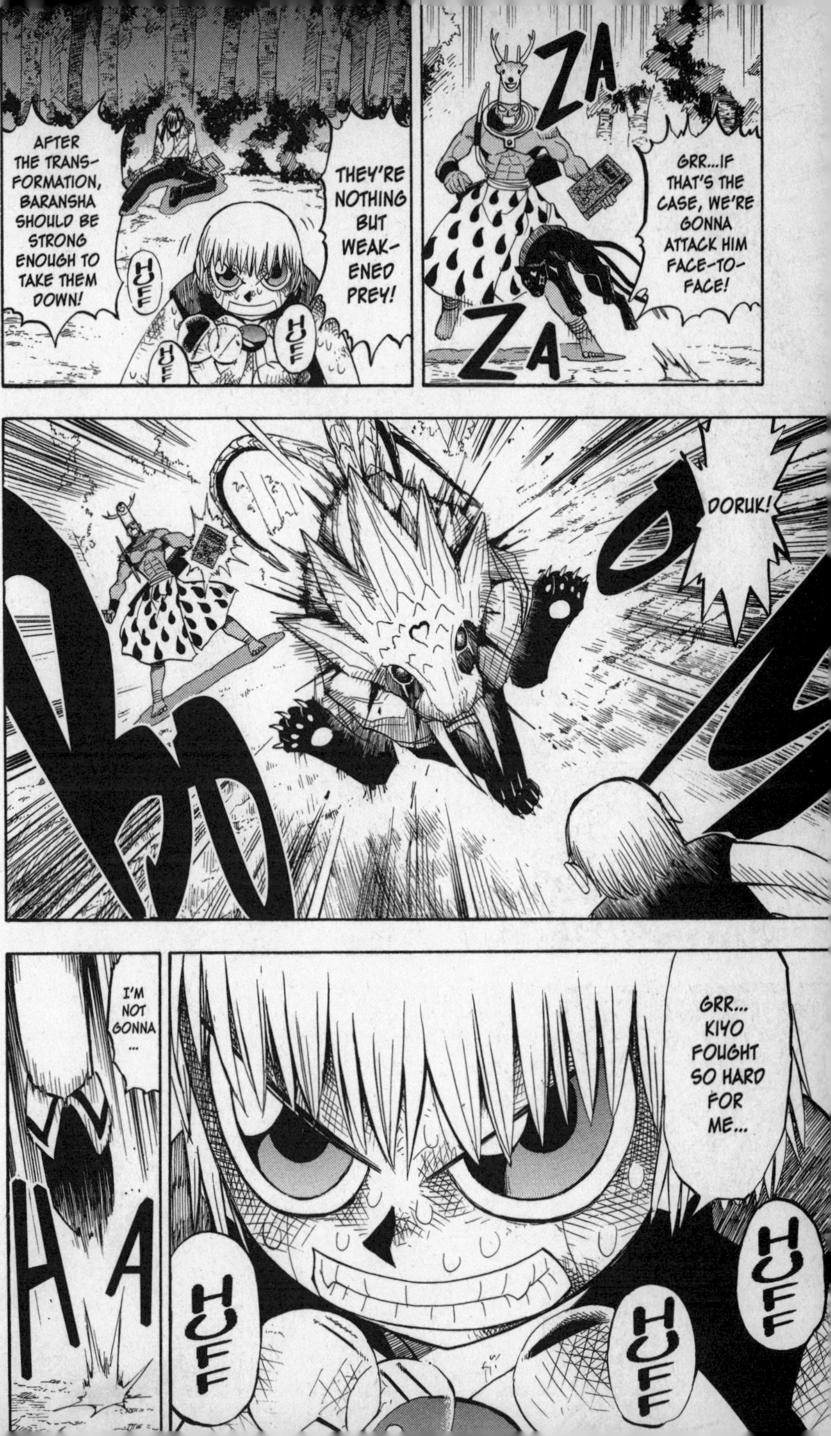
ZA
GRR...IF THAT'S THE CASE, WE'RE GONNA ATTACK HIM FACE-TO-FACE!
ZA
THEY'RE NOTHING BUT WEAK-ENED PREY!
AFTER THE TRANS-FORMATION, BARANSHA SHOULD BE STRONG ENOUGH TO TAKE THEM DOWN!
HUFF
HUFF
HUFF
DORUK!
GRR... KIYO FOUGHT SO HARD FOR ME...
HUFF
HUFF
HUFF
I'M NOT GONNA ...
HA

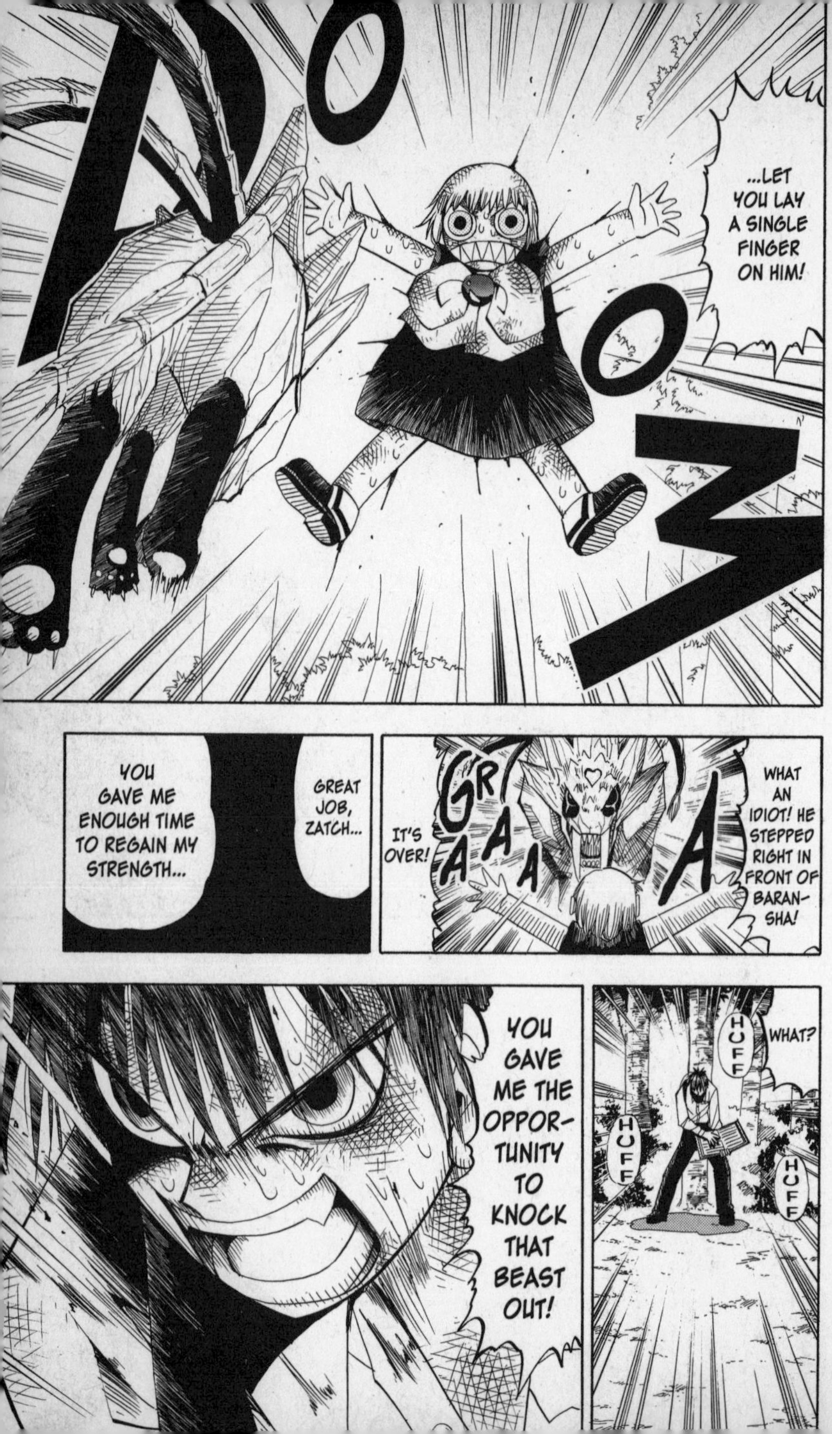
DOOOM
...LET YOU LAY A SINGLE FINGER ON HIM!
WHAT AN IDIOT! HE STEPPED RIGHT IN FRONT OF BARAN-SHA!
GRAAAAA
IT'S OVER!
GREAT JOB, ZATCH...
YOU GAVE ME ENOUGH TIME TO REGAIN MY STRENGTH...
WHAT?
HUFF
HUFF
HUFF
YOU GAVE ME THE OPPOR-TUNITY TO KNOCK THAT BEAST OUT!

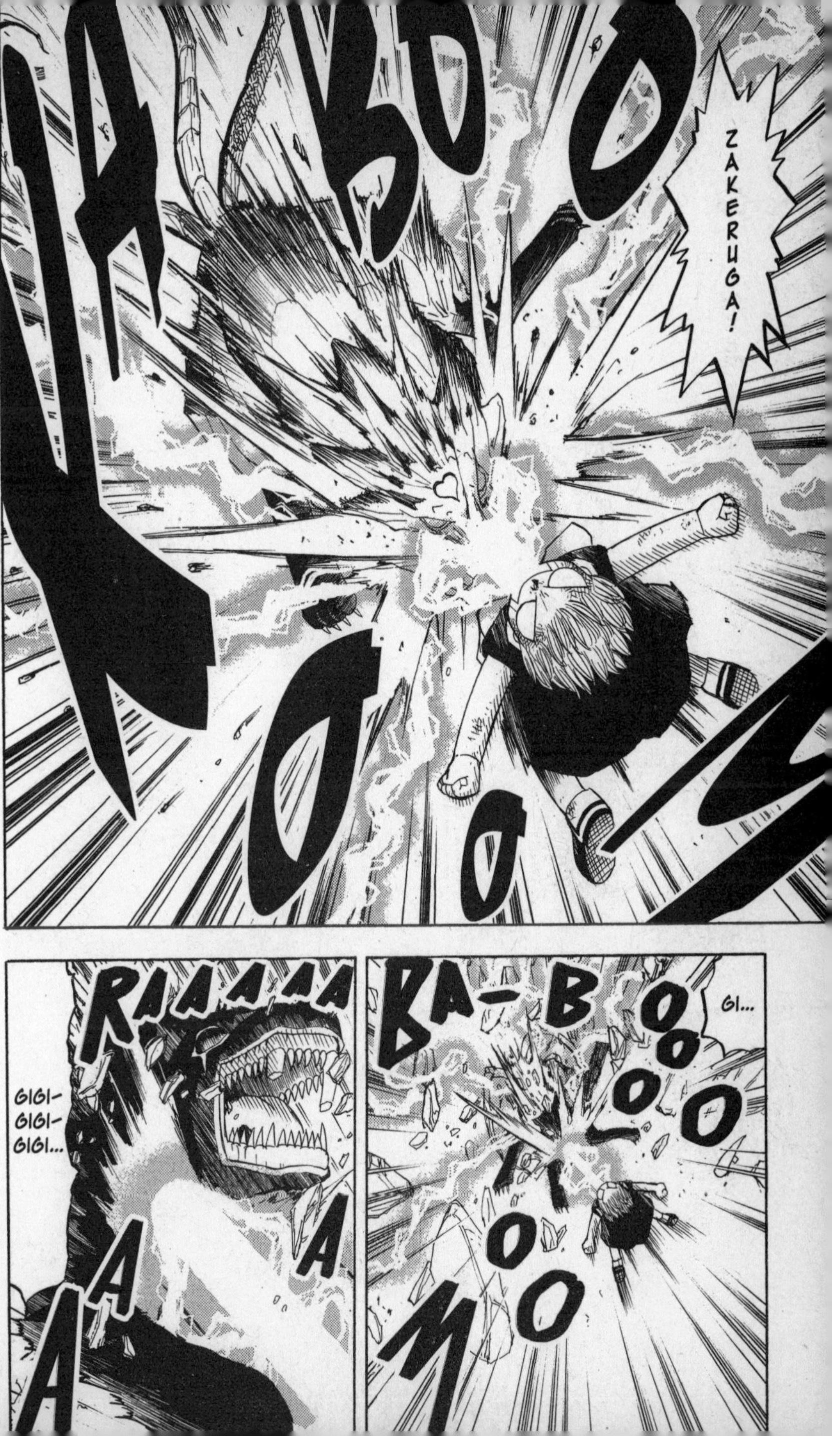
ZAKERUGA!
BA-BOOOO-OOOM
GI...
RAAAAAAAAAA
GIGI-
GIGI-
GIGI...

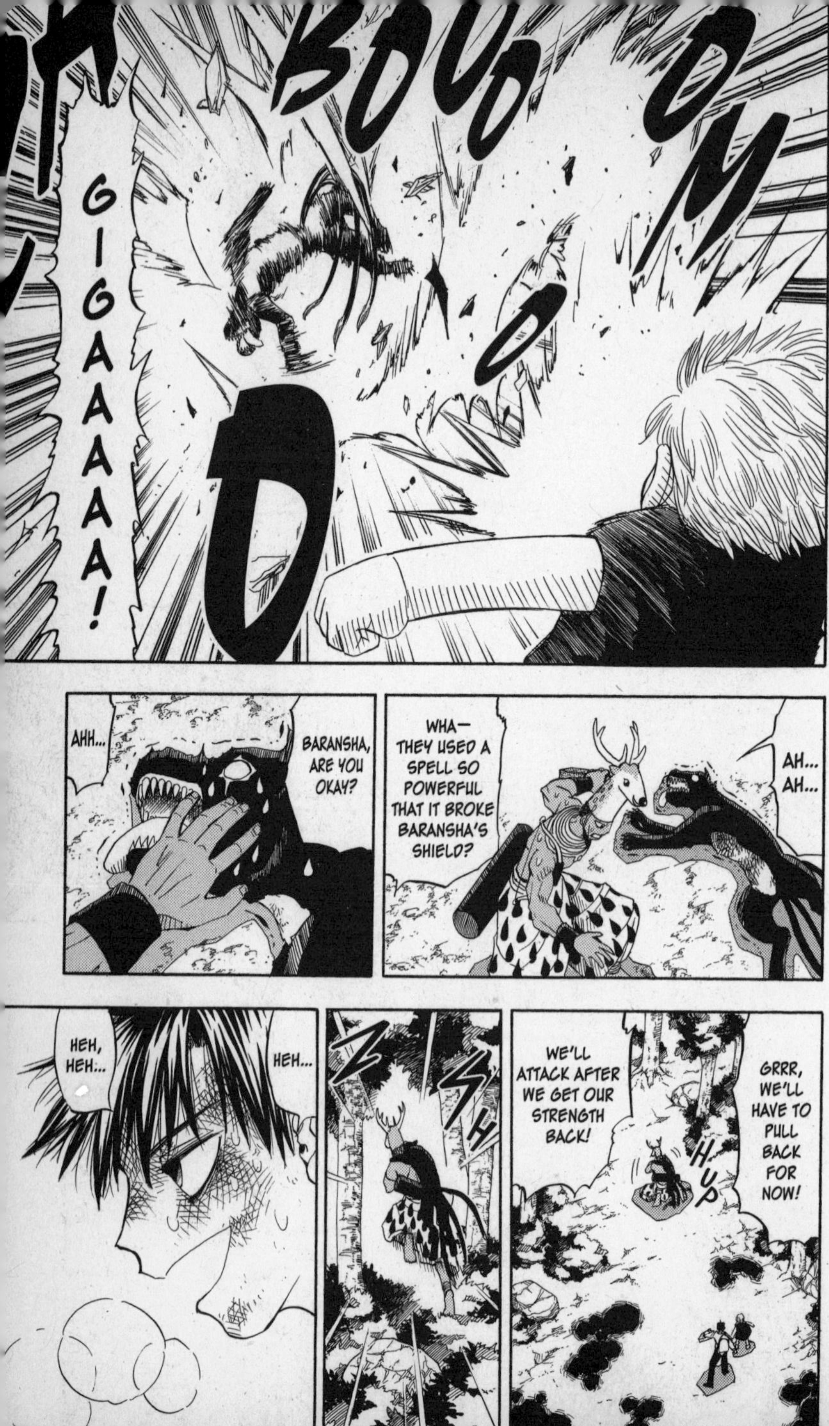
BOOOOM
D
GIGAAAAAA!
AH... AH...
WHA— THEY USED A SPELL SO POWERFUL THAT IT BROKE BARANSHA'S SHIELD?
BARANSHA, ARE YOU OKAY?
AHH...
GRRR, WE'LL HAVE TO PULL BACK FOR NOW!
WE'LL ATTACK AFTER WE GET OUR STRENGTH BACK!
HUP
ZSSH
HEH...
HEH, HEH...

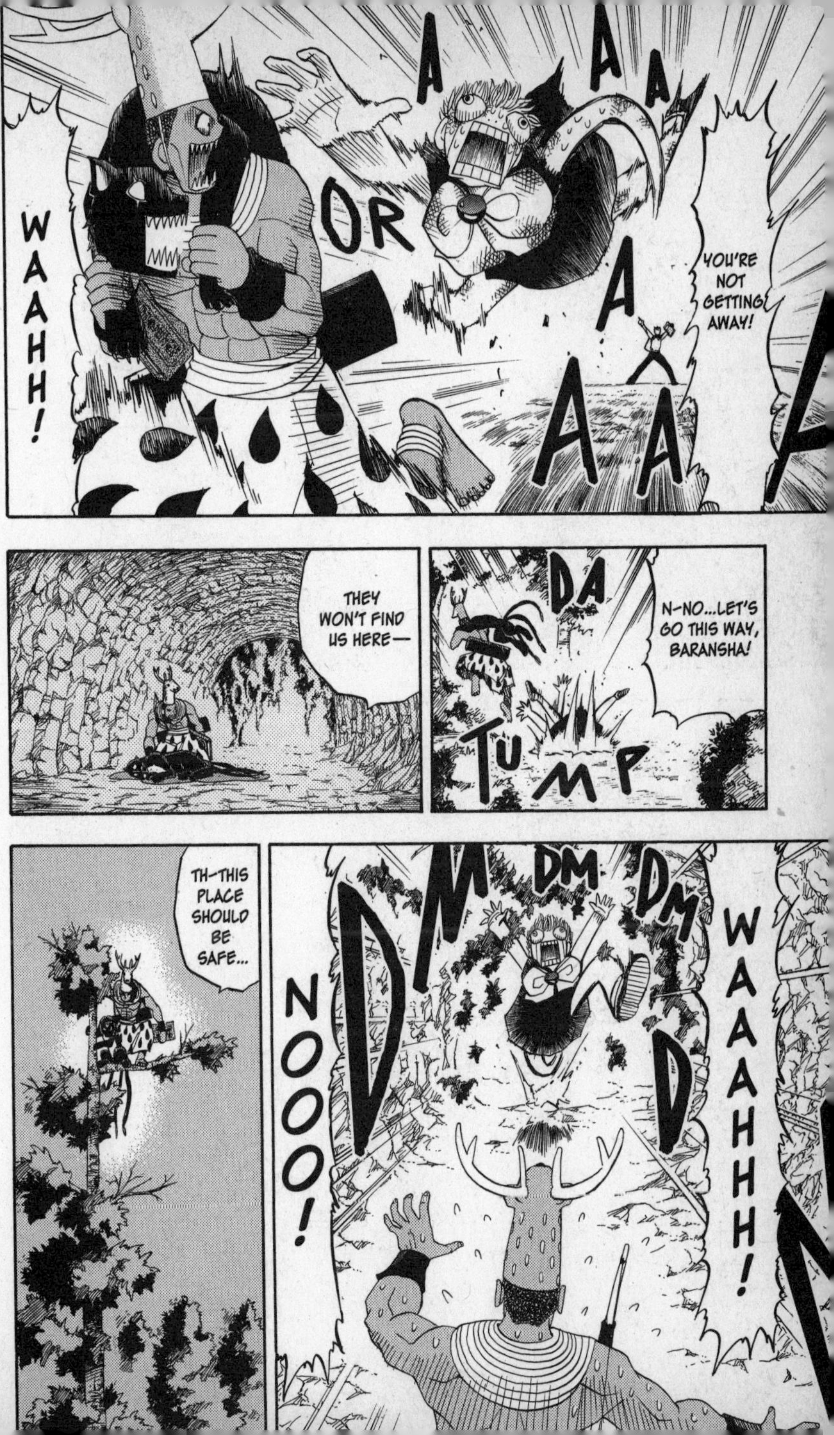
AAAAAA!
YOU'RE NOT GETTING AWAY!
OR
WAAHH!
DA
N-NO...LET'S GO THIS WAY, BARANSHA!
TUMP
THEY WON'T FIND US HERE—
DM DM DM D
WAAAHHH!
NOOO!
TH-THIS PLACE SHOULD BE SAFE...

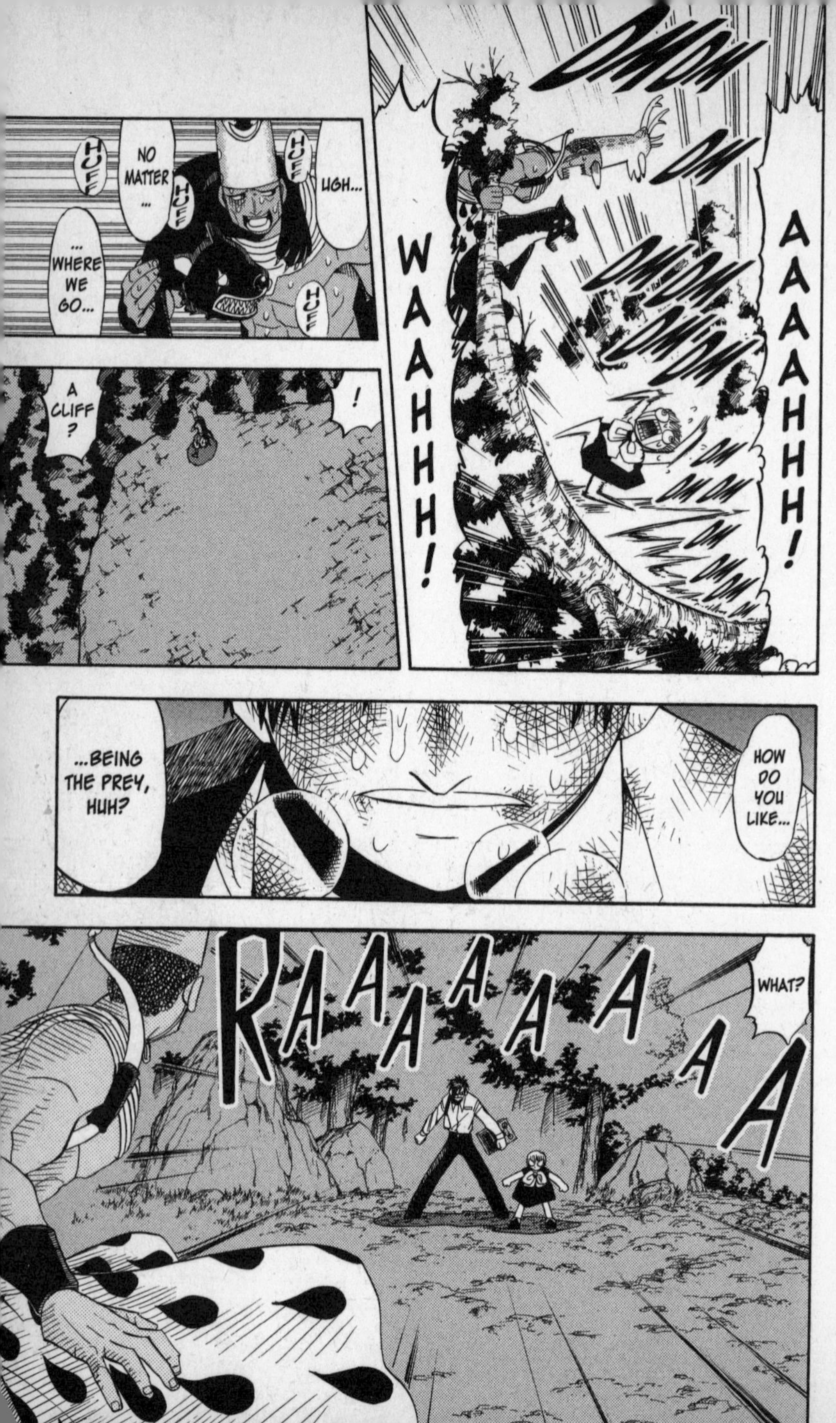
DMDM
DM
DMDMDMDM
AAAAAHHH!
WAAHHH!
UGH...
HUFF
NO MATTER...
HUFF
HUFF
...WHERE WE GO...
HUFF
!
A CLIFF?
HOW DO YOU LIKE...
...BEING THE PREY, HUH?
WHAT?
RAAAAAAAAAA

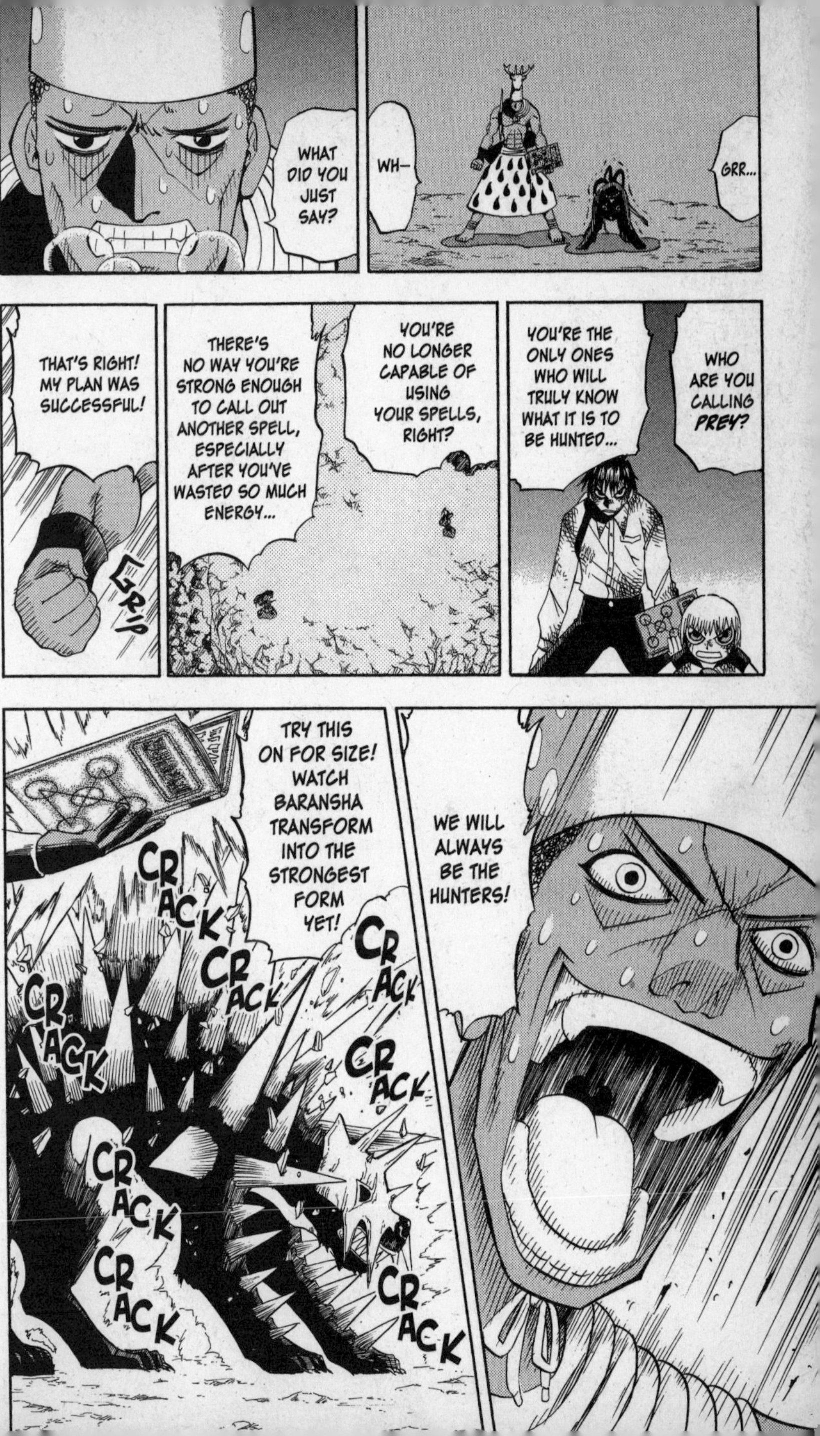
GRR...
WH—
WHAT DID YOU JUST SAY?
WHO ARE YOU CALLING *PREY*?
YOU'RE THE ONLY ONES WHO WILL TRULY KNOW WHAT IT IS TO BE HUNTED...
YOU'RE NO LONGER CAPABLE OF USING YOUR SPELLS, RIGHT?
THERE'S NO WAY YOU'RE STRONG ENOUGH TO CALL OUT ANOTHER SPELL, ESPECIALLY AFTER YOU'VE WASTED SO MUCH ENERGY...
THAT'S RIGHT! MY PLAN WAS SUCCESSFUL!
GRIP
WE WILL ALWAYS BE THE HUNTERS!
TRY THIS ON FOR SIZE! WATCH BARANSHA TRANSFORM INTO THE STRONGEST FORM YET!
CRACK
CRACK
CRACK
CRACK
CRACK
CRACK
CRACK
CRACK

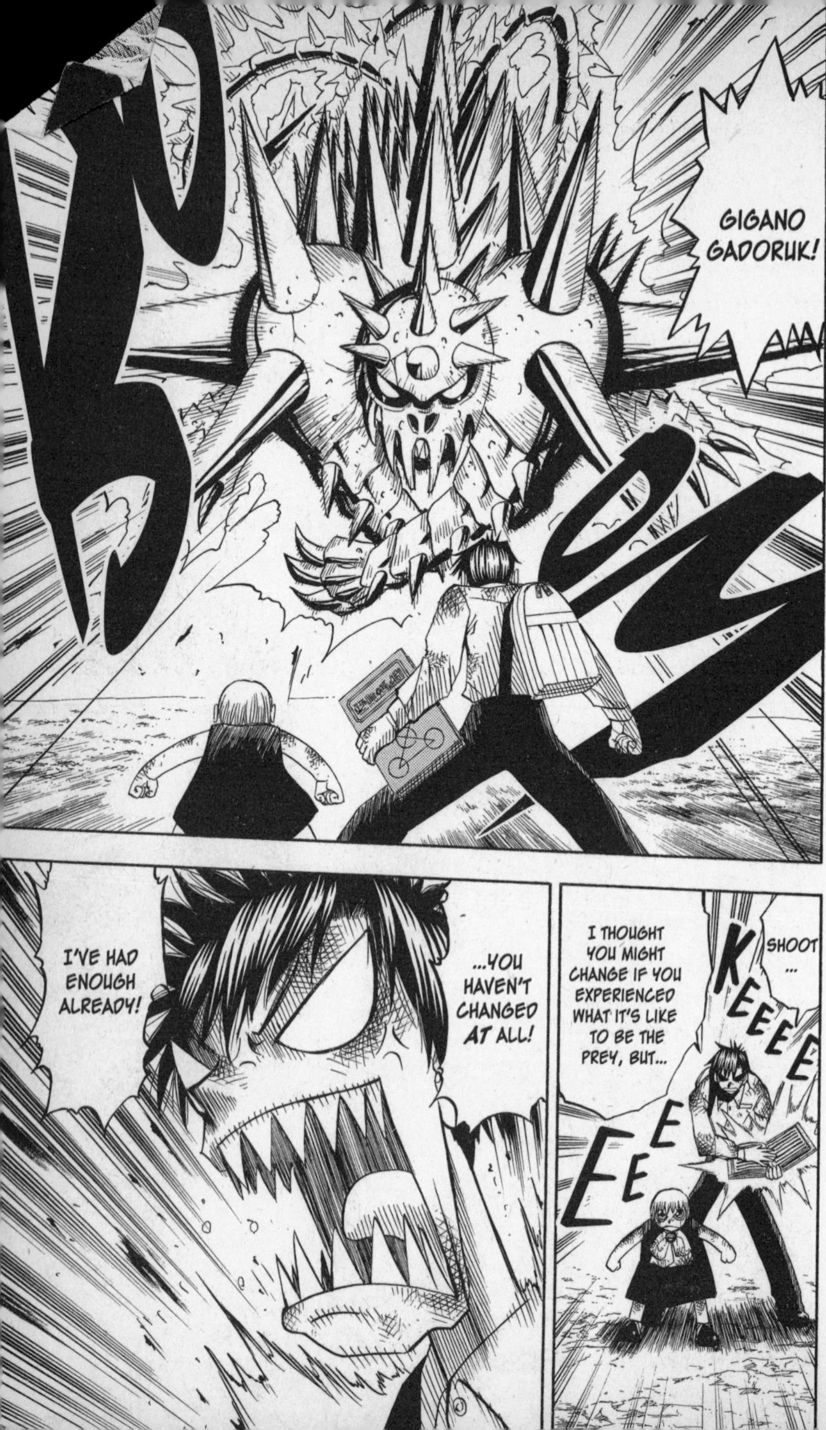
GIGANO GADORUK!
AAAA!
SHOOT ...
I THOUGHT YOU MIGHT CHANGE IF YOU EXPERIENCED WHAT IT'S LIKE TO BE THE PREY, BUT...
KEEEEEEEE
...YOU HAVEN'T CHANGED AT ALL!
I'VE HAD ENOUGH ALREADY!

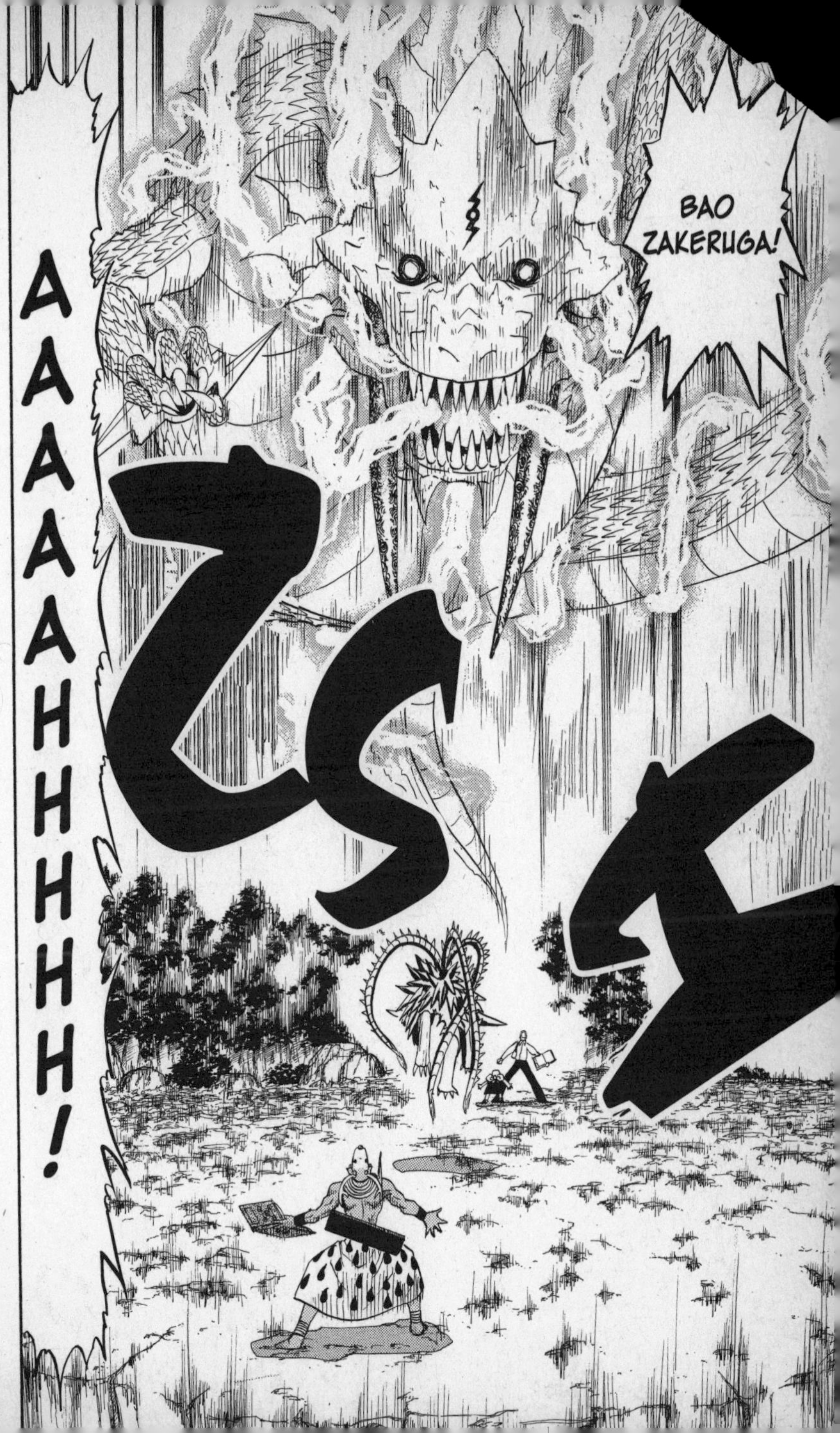
BAO ZAKERUGA!
AAAAAHHHHH!

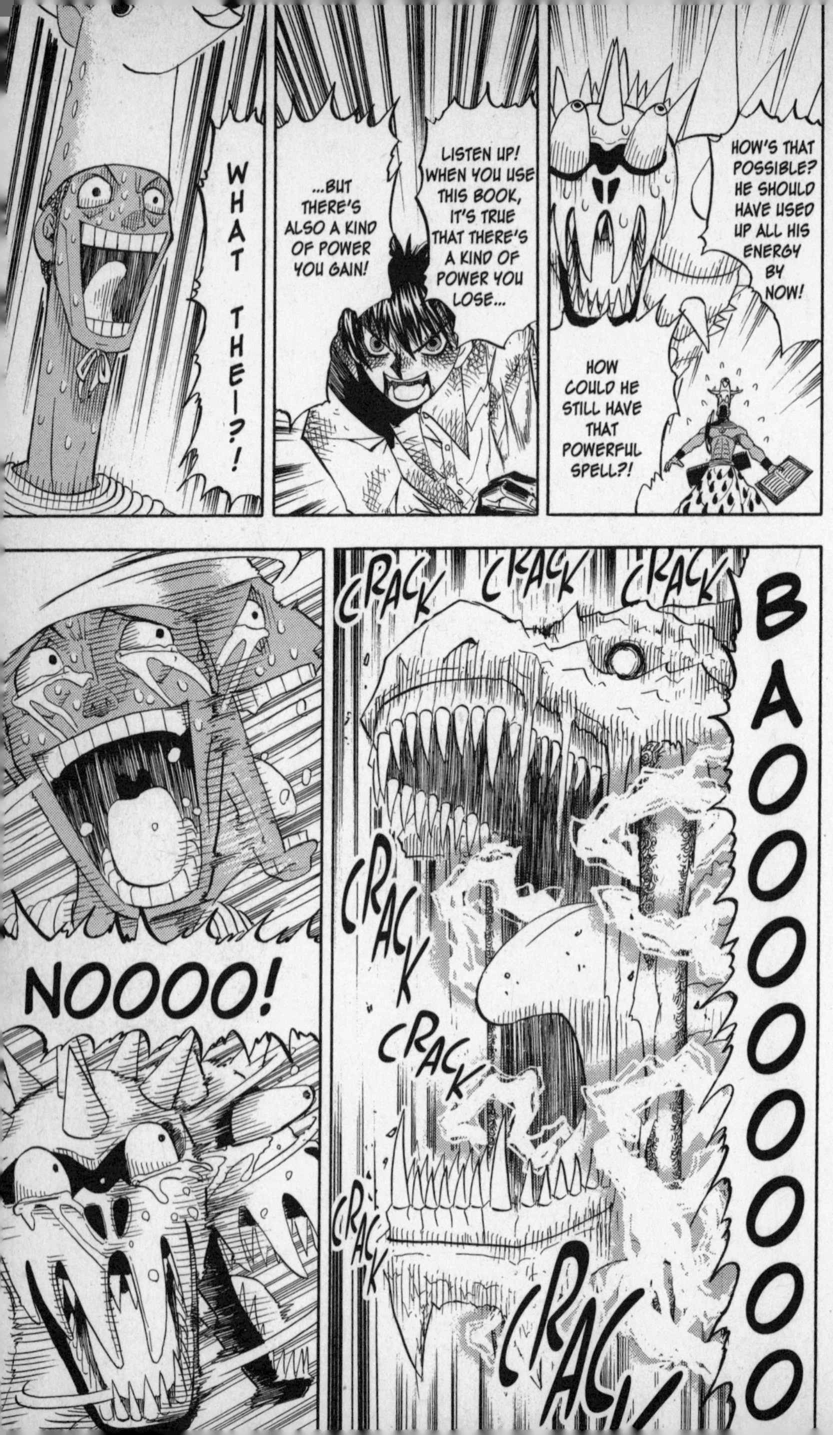
HOW'S THAT POSSIBLE? HE SHOULD HAVE USED UP ALL HIS ENERGY BY NOW!
HOW COULD HE STILL HAVE THAT POWERFUL SPELL?!
LISTEN UP! WHEN YOU USE THIS BOOK, IT'S TRUE THAT THERE'S A KIND OF POWER YOU LOSE...
...BUT THERE'S ALSO A KIND OF POWER YOU GAIN!
WHAT THE!?!
BAOOOOOOOOOOO
CRACK CRACK CRACK
CRACK
CRACK
CRACK
CRACK
NOOOO!

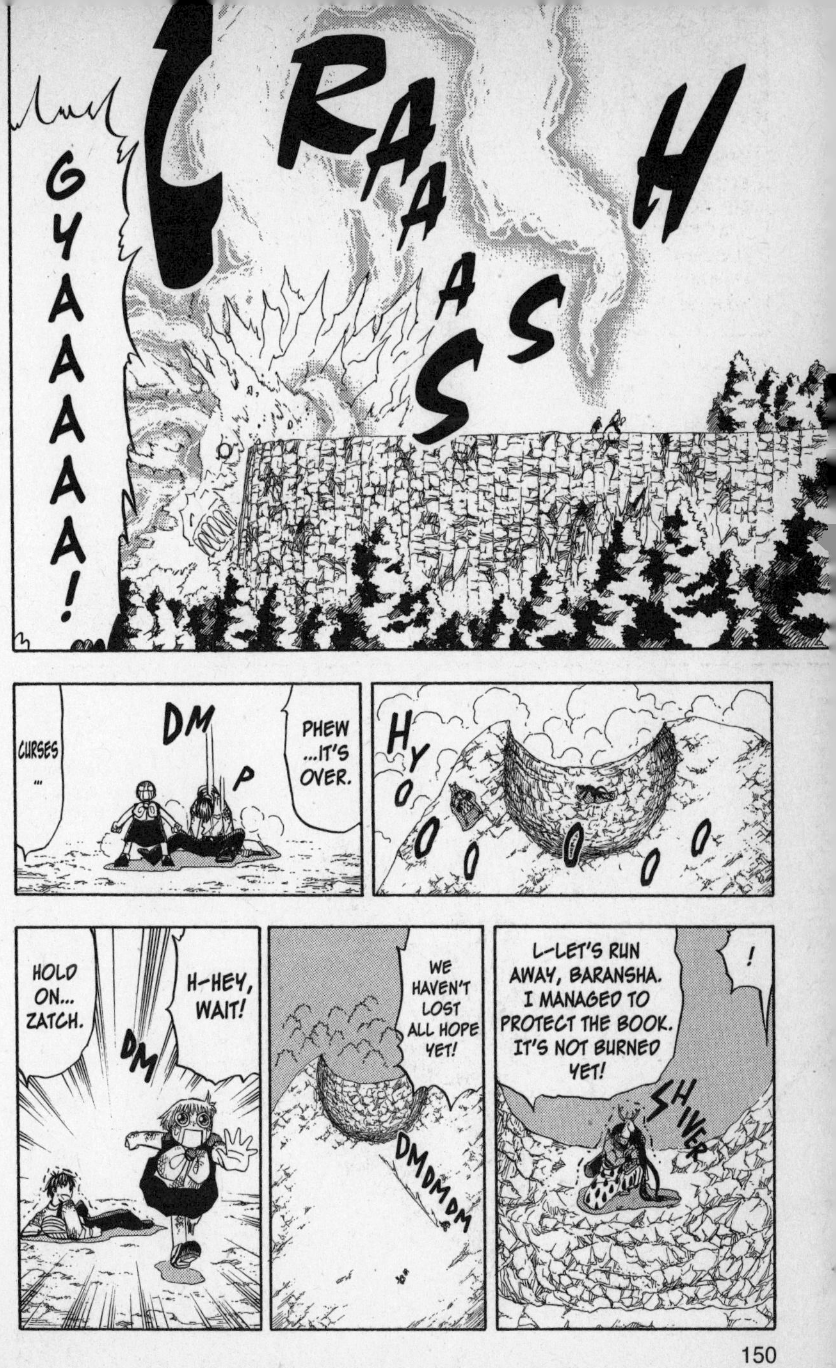
CRAAASSH
GYAAAAA!
HYOOOOOO
PHEW ...IT'S OVER.
DMP
CURSES ...
!
L-LET'S RUN AWAY, BARANSHA. I MANAGED TO PROTECT THE BOOK. IT'S NOT BURNED YET!
SHIVER
WE HAVEN'T LOST ALL HOPE YET!
DMDMDMDM
H-HEY, WAIT!
HOLD ON... ZATCH.
DM

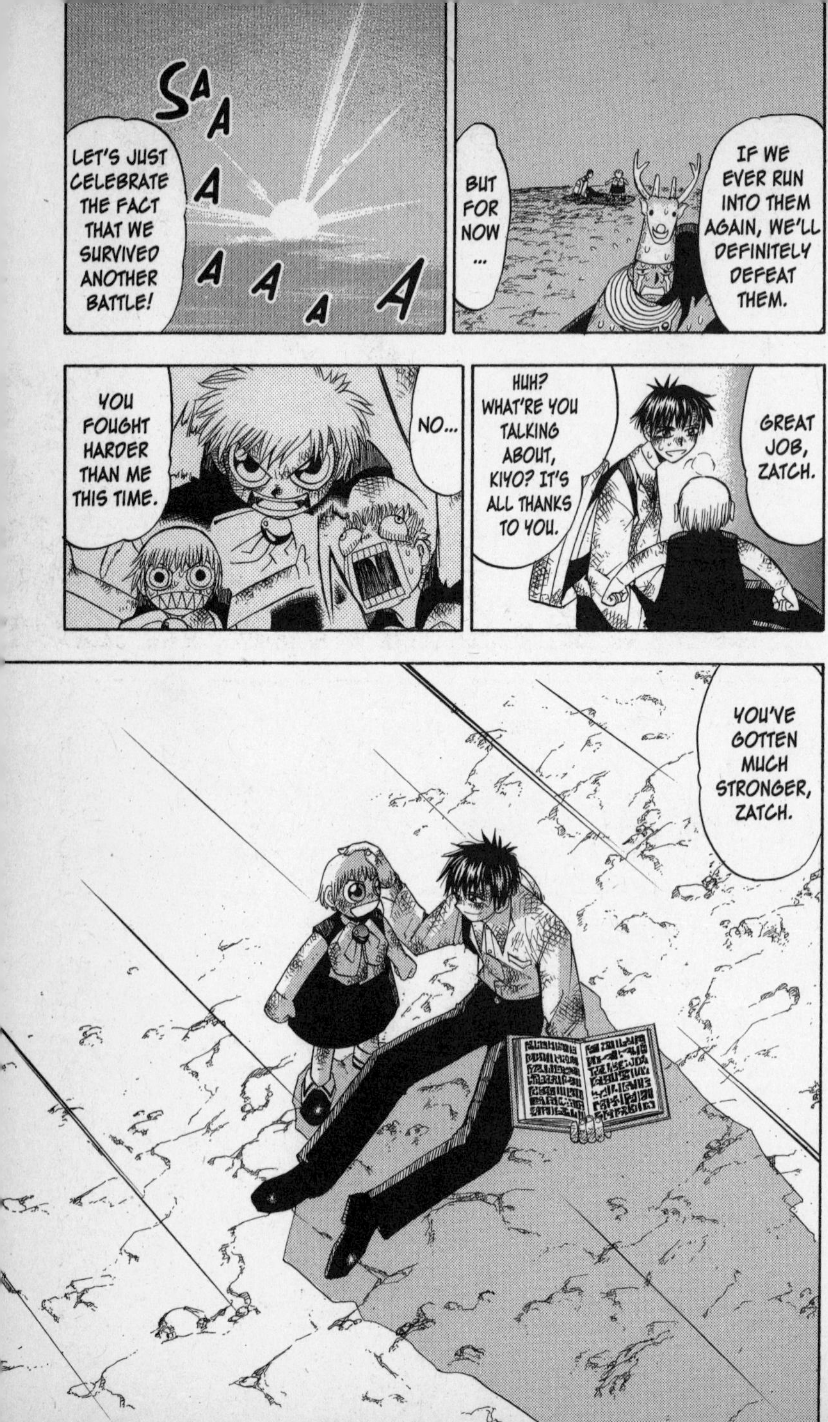
IF WE EVER RUN INTO THEM AGAIN, WE'LL DEFINITELY DEFEAT THEM.
BUT FOR NOW ...
LET'S JUST CELEBRATE THE FACT THAT WE SURVIVED ANOTHER BATTLE!
SAAAAAAA
GREAT JOB, ZATCH.
HUH? WHAT'RE YOU TALKING ABOUT, KIYO? IT'S ALL THANKS TO YOU.
NO...
YOU FOUGHT HARDER THAN ME THIS TIME.
YOU'VE GOTTEN MUCH STRONGER, ZATCH.

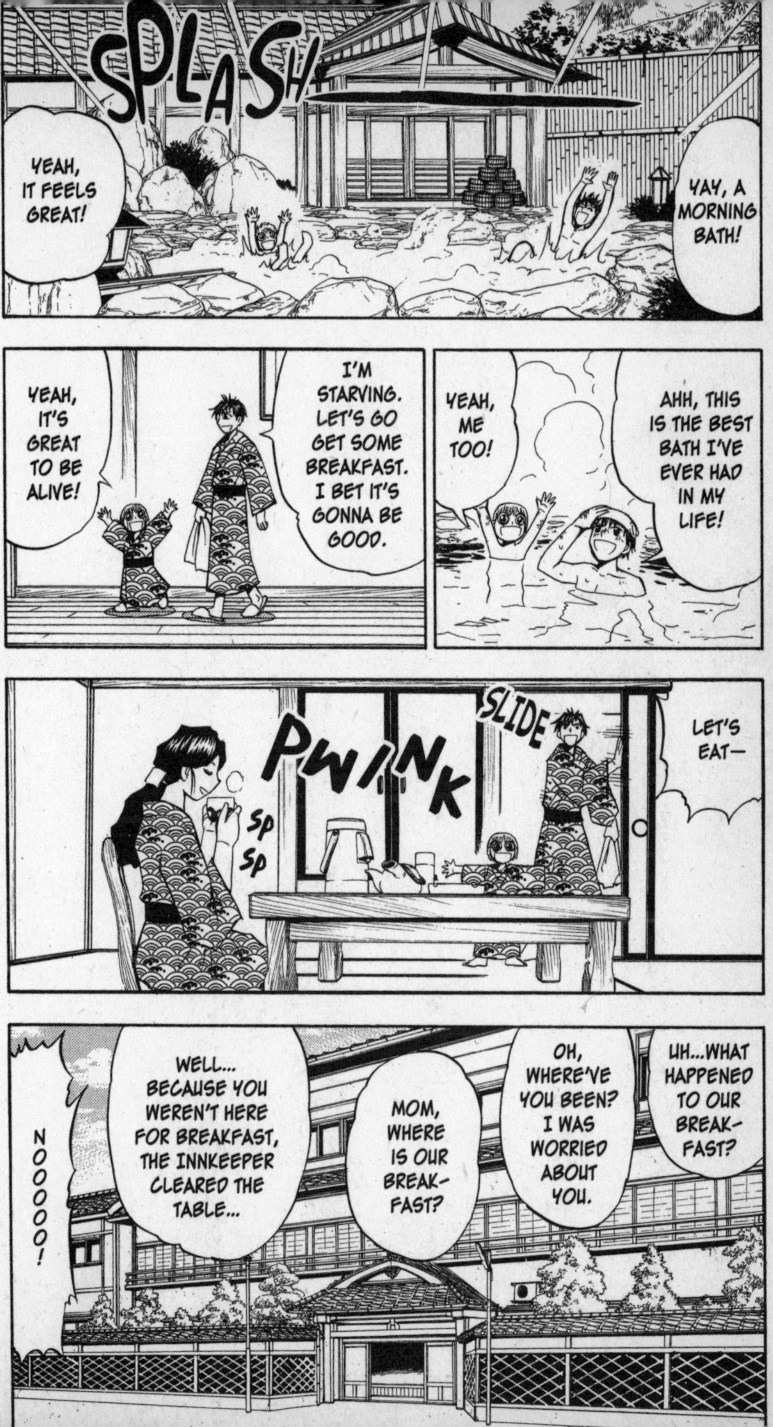
SPLASH
YAY, A MORNING BATH!
YEAH, IT FEELS GREAT!
AHH, THIS IS THE BEST BATH I'VE EVER HAD IN MY LIFE!
YEAH, ME TOO!
I'M STARVING. LET'S GO GET SOME BREAKFAST. I BET IT'S GONNA BE GOOD.
YEAH, IT'S GREAT TO BE ALIVE!
LET'S EAT—
SLIDE
PWINK
SP SP
UH...WHAT HAPPENED TO OUR BREAK-FAST?
OH, WHERE'VE YOU BEEN? I WAS WORRIED ABOUT YOU.
MOM, WHERE IS OUR BREAK-FAST?
WELL... BECAUSE YOU WEREN'T HERE FOR BREAKFAST, THE INNKEEPER CLEARED THE TABLE...
NOOOOOO!

LEVEL 83: An Unidentified Object

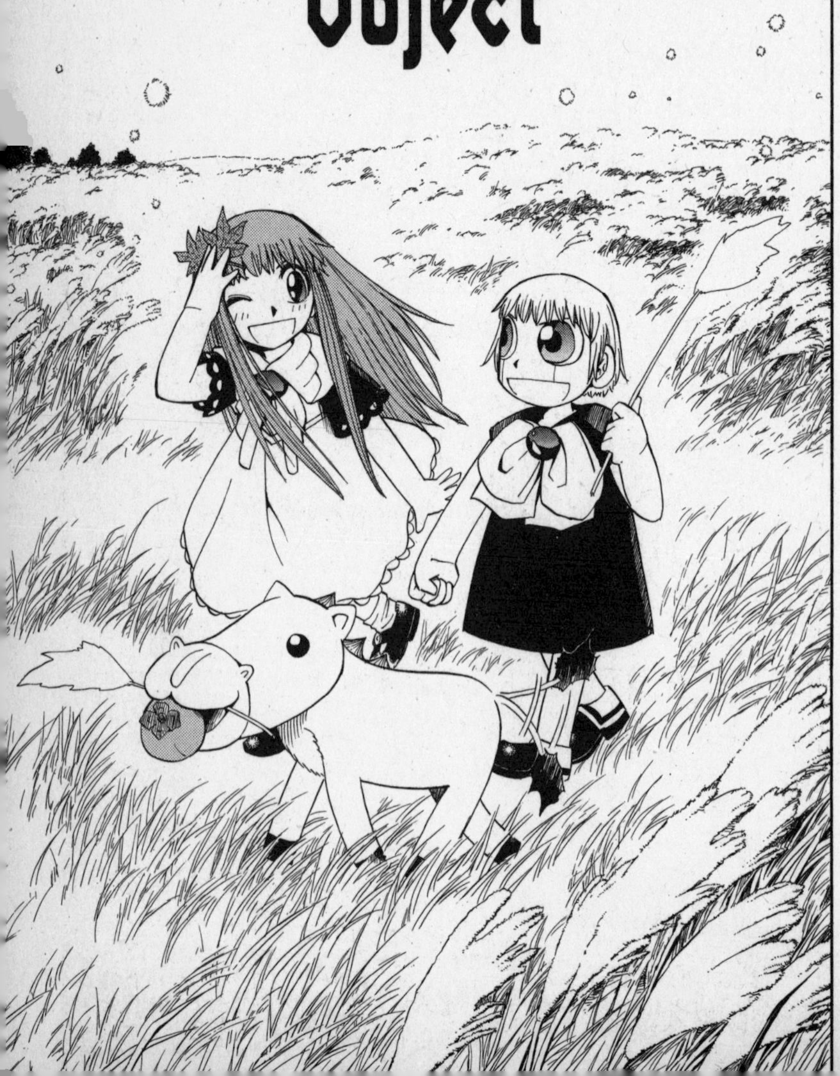

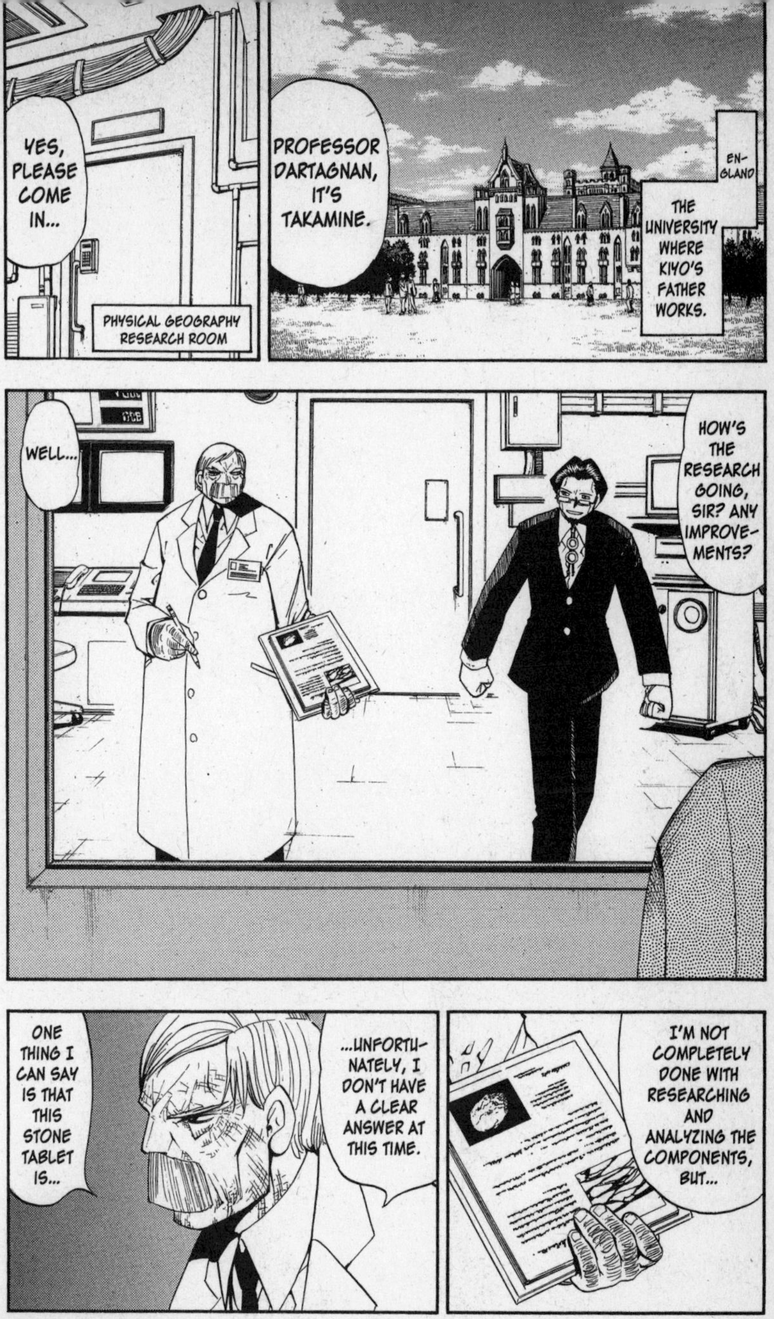
ENGLAND
THE UNIVERSITY WHERE KIYO'S FATHER WORKS.
PROFESSOR DARTAGNAN, IT'S TAKAMINE.
YES, PLEASE COME IN...
PHYSICAL GEOGRAPHY RESEARCH ROOM
HOW'S THE RESEARCH GOING, SIR? ANY IMPROVEMENTS?
WELL...
I'M NOT COMPLETELY DONE WITH RESEARCHING AND ANALYZING THE COMPONENTS, BUT...
...UNFORTUNATELY, I DON'T HAVE A CLEAR ANSWER AT THIS TIME.
ONE THING I CAN SAY IS THAT THIS STONE TABLET IS...

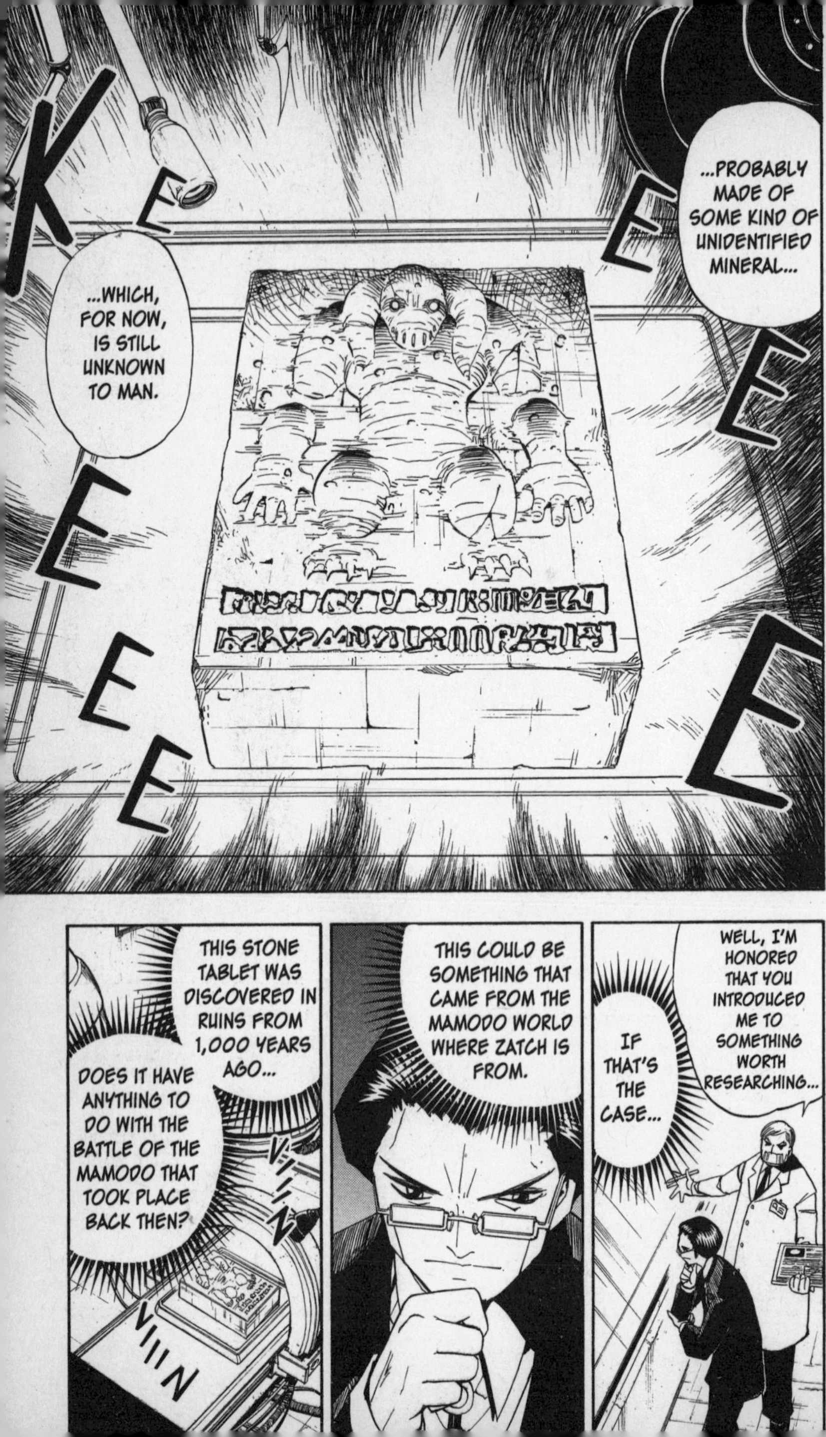
...PROBABLY MADE OF SOME KIND OF UNIDENTIFIED MINERAL...
EEE
KEEEEE
...WHICH, FOR NOW, IS STILL UNKNOWN TO MAN.
WELL, I'M HONORED THAT YOU INTRODUCED ME TO SOMETHING WORTH RESEARCHING...
IF THAT'S THE CASE...
THIS COULD BE SOMETHING THAT CAME FROM THE MAMODO WORLD WHERE ZATCH IS FROM.
THIS STONE TABLET WAS DISCOVERED IN RUINS FROM 1,000 YEARS AGO...
DOES IT HAVE ANYTHING TO DO WITH THE BATTLE OF THE MAMODO THAT TOOK PLACE BACK THEN?
VIIIN
VIIIN

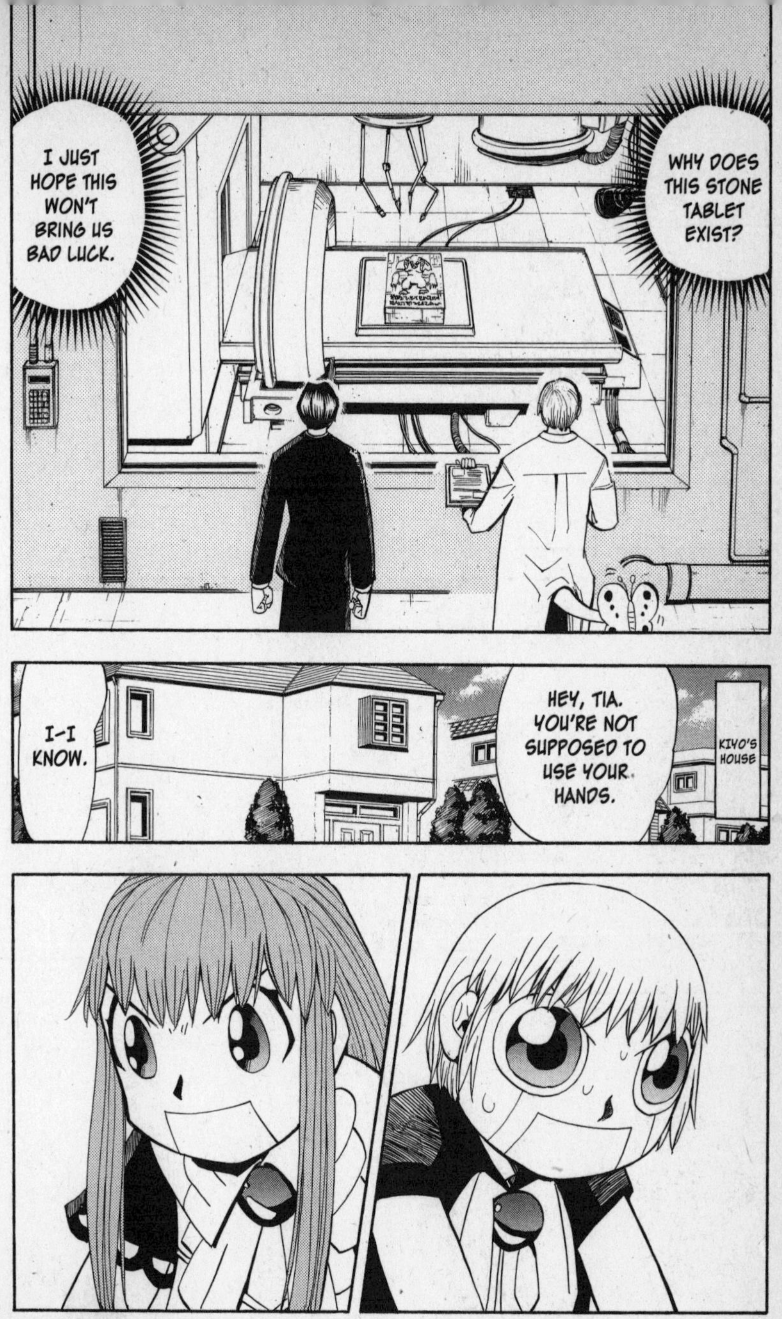
WHY DOES THIS STONE TABLET EXIST?
I JUST HOPE THIS WON'T BRING US BAD LUCK.
KIYO'S HOUSE
HEY, TIA. YOU'RE NOT SUPPOSED TO USE YOUR HANDS.
I-I KNOW.

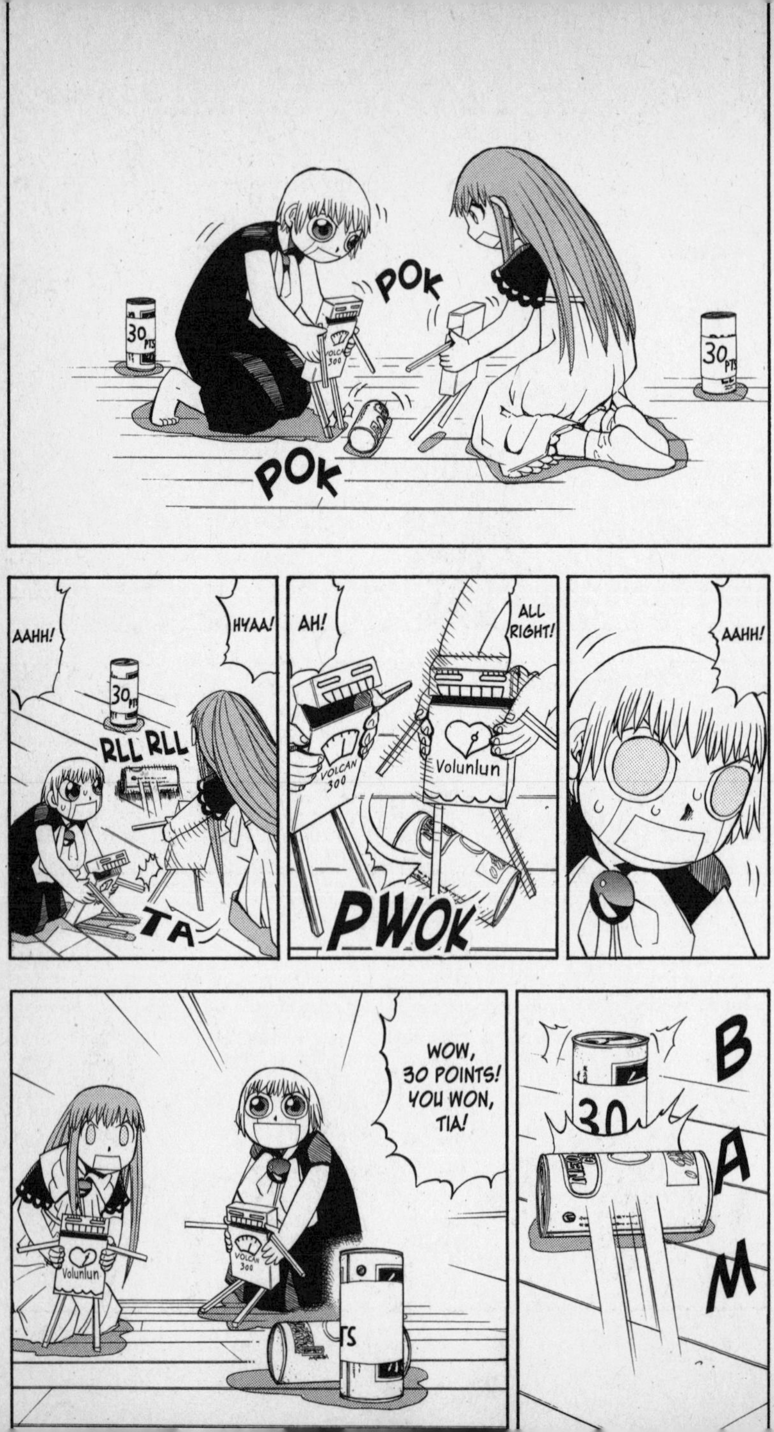
POK
POK
AAHH!
ALL RIGHT!
AH!
Volunlun
VOLCAN 300
PWOK
HYAA!
AAHH!
RLL RLL
TA
BAM
WOW, 30 POINTS! YOU WON, TIA!

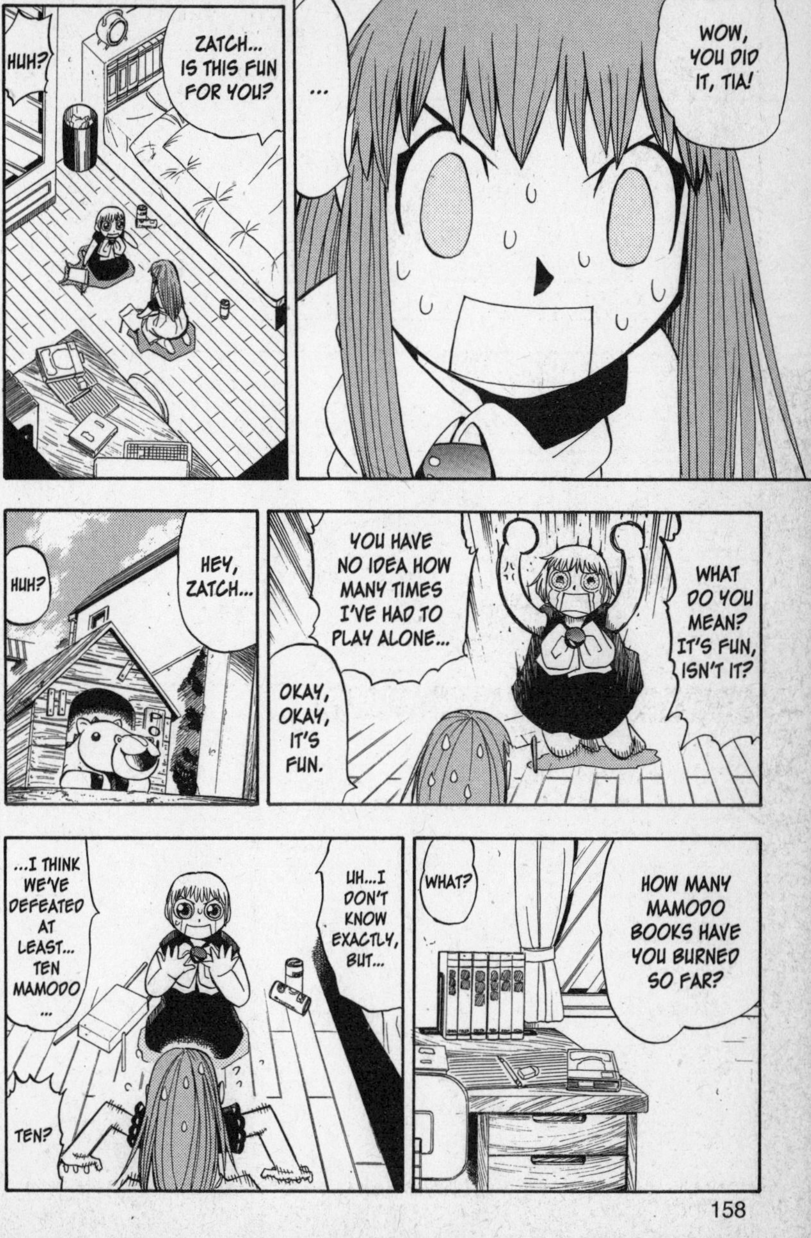
WOW, YOU DID IT, TIA!
...
ZATCH... IS THIS FUN FOR YOU?
HUH?
WHAT DO YOU MEAN? IT'S FUN, ISN'T IT?
YOU HAVE NO IDEA HOW MANY TIMES I'VE HAD TO PLAY ALONE...
OKAY, OKAY, IT'S FUN.
HEY, ZATCH...
HUH?
HOW MANY MAMODO BOOKS HAVE YOU BURNED SO FAR?
WHAT?
UH...I DON'T KNOW EXACTLY, BUT...
...I THINK WE'VE DEFEATED AT LEAST... TEN MAMODO ...
TEN?

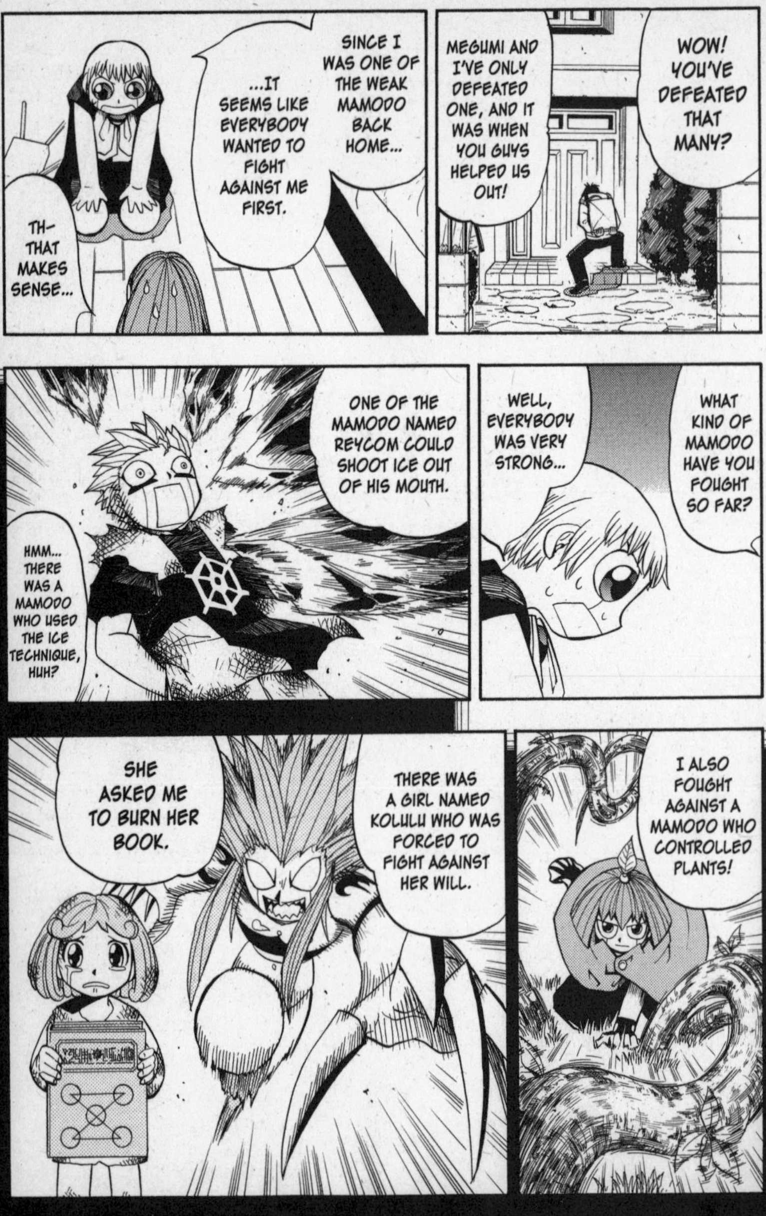
WOW! YOU'VE DEFEATED THAT MANY?
MEGUMI AND I'VE ONLY DEFEATED ONE, AND IT WAS WHEN YOU GUYS HELPED US OUT!
SINCE I WAS ONE OF THE WEAK MAMODO BACK HOME...
...IT SEEMS LIKE EVERYBODY WANTED TO FIGHT AGAINST ME FIRST.
TH-THAT MAKES SENSE...
WHAT KIND OF MAMODO HAVE YOU FOUGHT SO FAR?
WELL, EVERYBODY WAS VERY STRONG...
ONE OF THE MAMODO NAMED REYCOM COULD SHOOT ICE OUT OF HIS MOUTH.
HMM... THERE WAS A MAMODO WHO USED THE ICE TECHNIQUE, HUH?
I ALSO FOUGHT AGAINST A MAMODO WHO CONTROLLED PLANTS!
THERE WAS A GIRL NAMED KOLULU WHO WAS FORCED TO FIGHT AGAINST HER WILL.
SHE ASKED ME TO BURN HER BOOK.

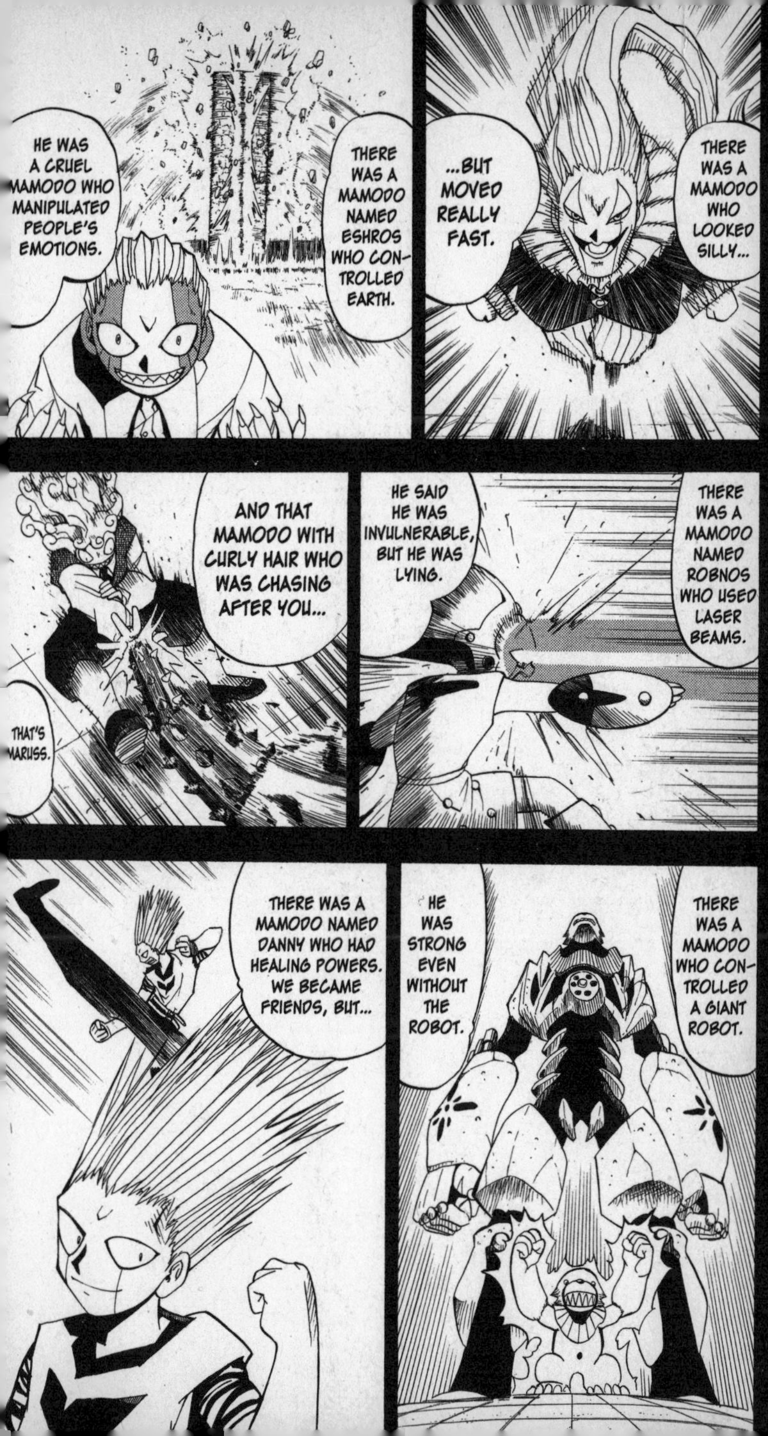
THERE WAS A MAMODO WHO LOOKED SILLY...
...BUT MOVED REALLY FAST.
THERE WAS A MAMODO NAMED ESHROS WHO CONTROLLED EARTH.
HE WAS A CRUEL MAMODO WHO MANIPULATED PEOPLE'S EMOTIONS.
THERE WAS A MAMODO NAMED ROBNOS WHO USED LASER BEAMS.
HE SAID HE WAS INVULNERABLE, BUT HE WAS LYING.
AND THAT MAMODO WITH CURLY HAIR WHO WAS CHASING AFTER YOU...
THAT'S MARUSS.
THERE WAS A MAMODO WHO CONTROLLED A GIANT ROBOT.
HE WAS STRONG EVEN WITHOUT THE ROBOT.
THERE WAS A MAMODO NAMED DANNY WHO HAD HEALING POWERS. WE BECAME FRIENDS, BUT...

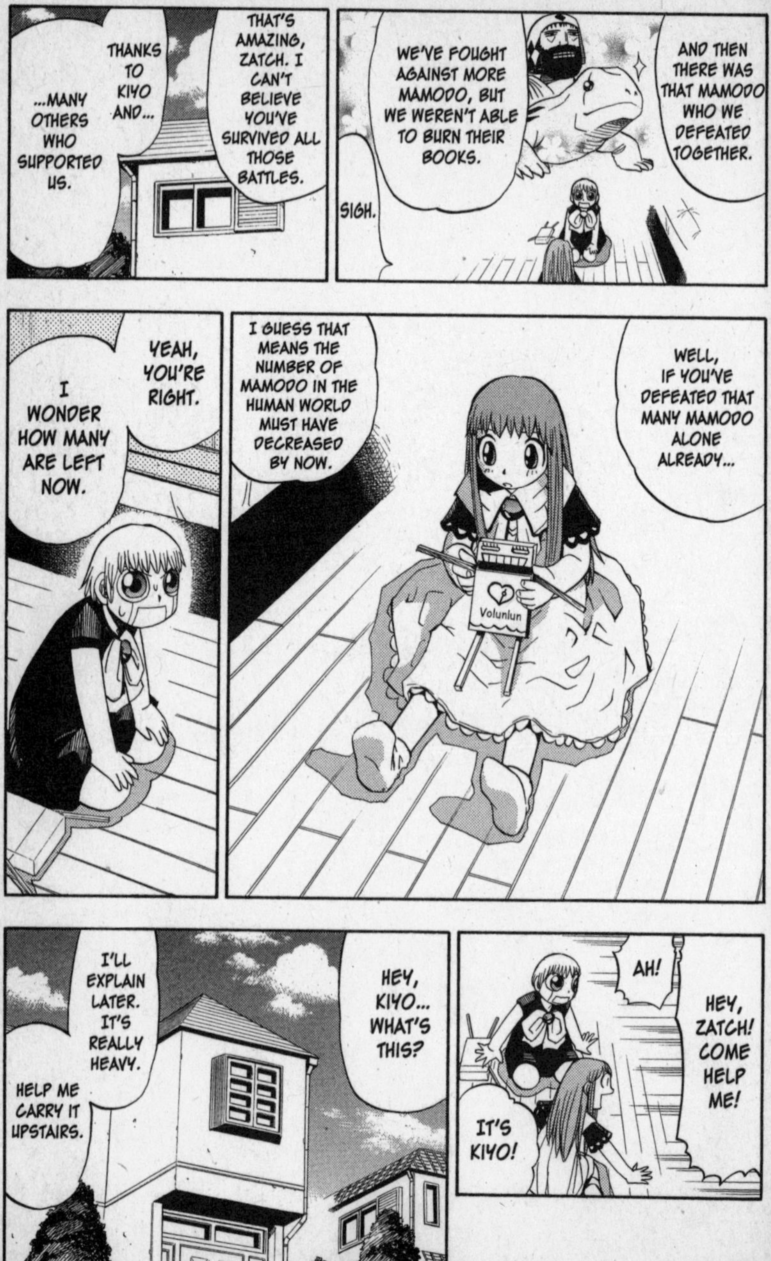
AND THEN THERE WAS THAT MAMODO WHO WE DEFEATED TOGETHER.
WE'VE FOUGHT AGAINST MORE MAMODO, BUT WE WEREN'T ABLE TO BURN THEIR BOOKS.
SIGH.
THAT'S AMAZING, ZATCH. I CAN'T BELIEVE YOU'VE SURVIVED ALL THOSE BATTLES.
THANKS TO KIYO AND...
...MANY OTHERS WHO SUPPORTED US.
WELL, IF YOU'VE DEFEATED THAT MANY MAMODO ALONE ALREADY...
I GUESS THAT MEANS THE NUMBER OF MAMODO IN THE HUMAN WORLD MUST HAVE DECREASED BY NOW.
Volunlun
YEAH, YOU'RE RIGHT.
I WONDER HOW MANY ARE LEFT NOW.
AH!
HEY, ZATCH! COME HELP ME!
IT'S KIYO!
HEY, KIYO... WHAT'S THIS?
I'LL EXPLAIN LATER. IT'S REALLY HEAVY.
HELP ME CARRY IT UPSTAIRS.

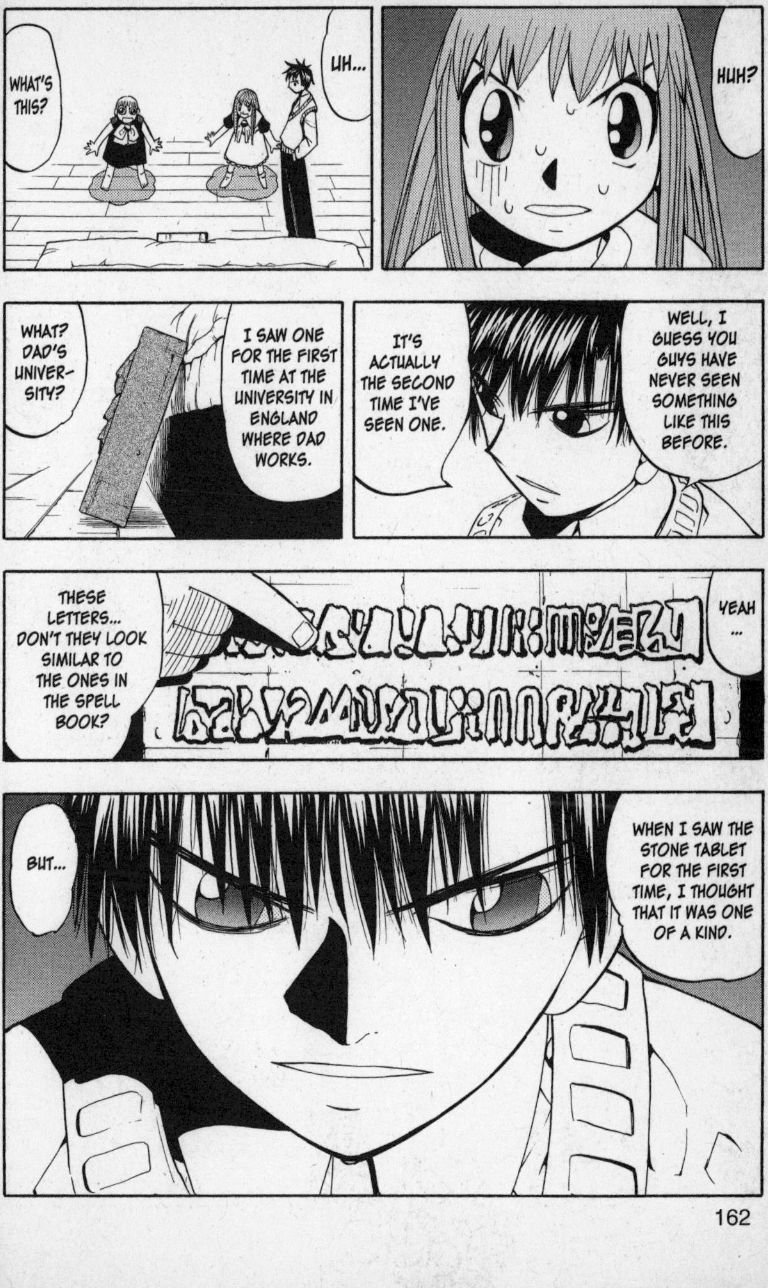
HUH?
UH...
WHAT'S THIS?
WELL, I GUESS YOU GUYS HAVE NEVER SEEN SOMETHING LIKE THIS BEFORE.
IT'S ACTUALLY THE SECOND TIME I'VE SEEN ONE.
I SAW ONE FOR THE FIRST TIME AT THE UNIVERSITY IN ENGLAND WHERE DAD WORKS.
WHAT? DAD'S UNIVER-SITY?
YEAH ...
THESE LETTERS... DON'T THEY LOOK SIMILAR TO THE ONES IN THE SPELL BOOK?
WHEN I SAW THE STONE TABLET FOR THE FIRST TIME, I THOUGHT THAT IT WAS ONE OF A KIND.
BUT...

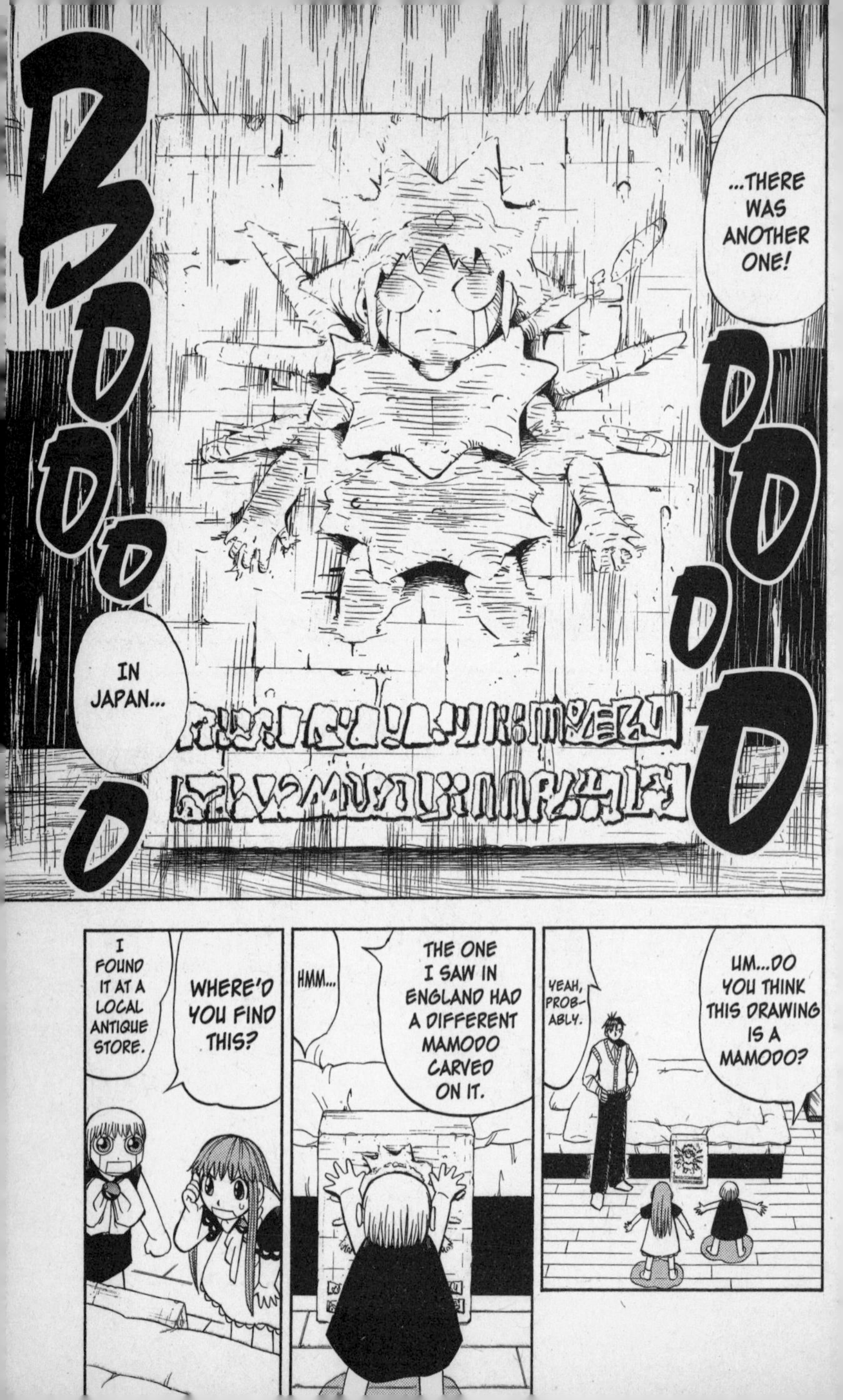
...THERE WAS ANOTHER ONE!
DDDD
IN JAPAN...
ZDDDDD
UM...DO YOU THINK THIS DRAWING IS A MAMODO?
YEAH, PROB-ABLY.
THE ONE I SAW IN ENGLAND HAD A DIFFERENT MAMODO CARVED ON IT.
HMM...
WHERE'D YOU FIND THIS?
I FOUND IT AT A LOCAL ANTIQUE STORE.

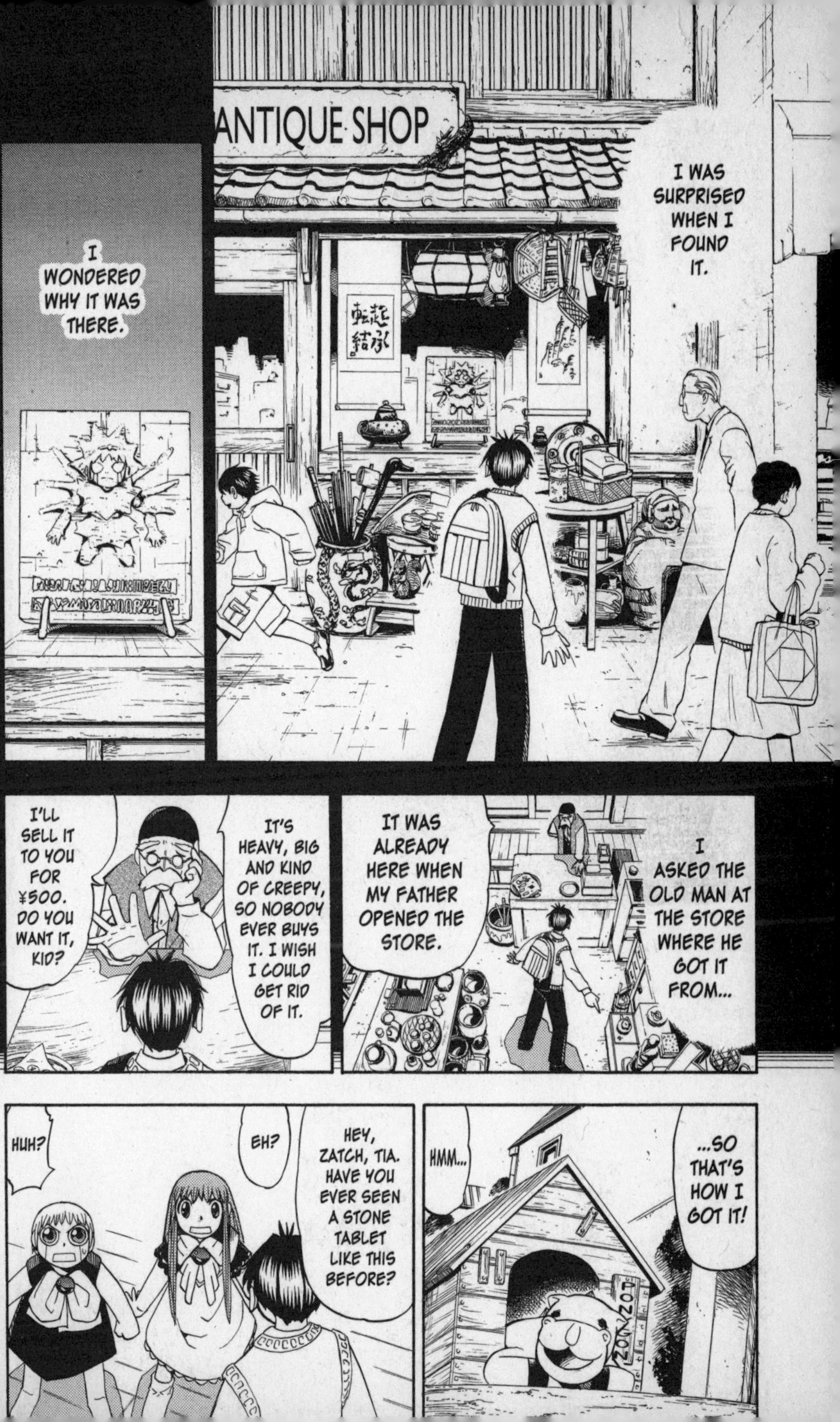
ANTIQUE SHOP
I WAS SURPRISED WHEN I FOUND IT.
I WONDERED WHY IT WAS THERE.
I ASKED THE OLD MAN AT THE STORE WHERE HE GOT IT FROM...
IT WAS ALREADY HERE WHEN MY FATHER OPENED THE STORE.
IT'S HEAVY, BIG AND KIND OF CREEPY, SO NOBODY EVER BUYS IT. I WISH I COULD GET RID OF IT.
I'LL SELL IT TO YOU FOR ¥500. DO YOU WANT IT, KID?
...SO THAT'S HOW I GOT IT!
HMM...
HEY, ZATCH, TIA. HAVE YOU EVER SEEN A STONE TABLET LIKE THIS BEFORE?
EH?
HUH?

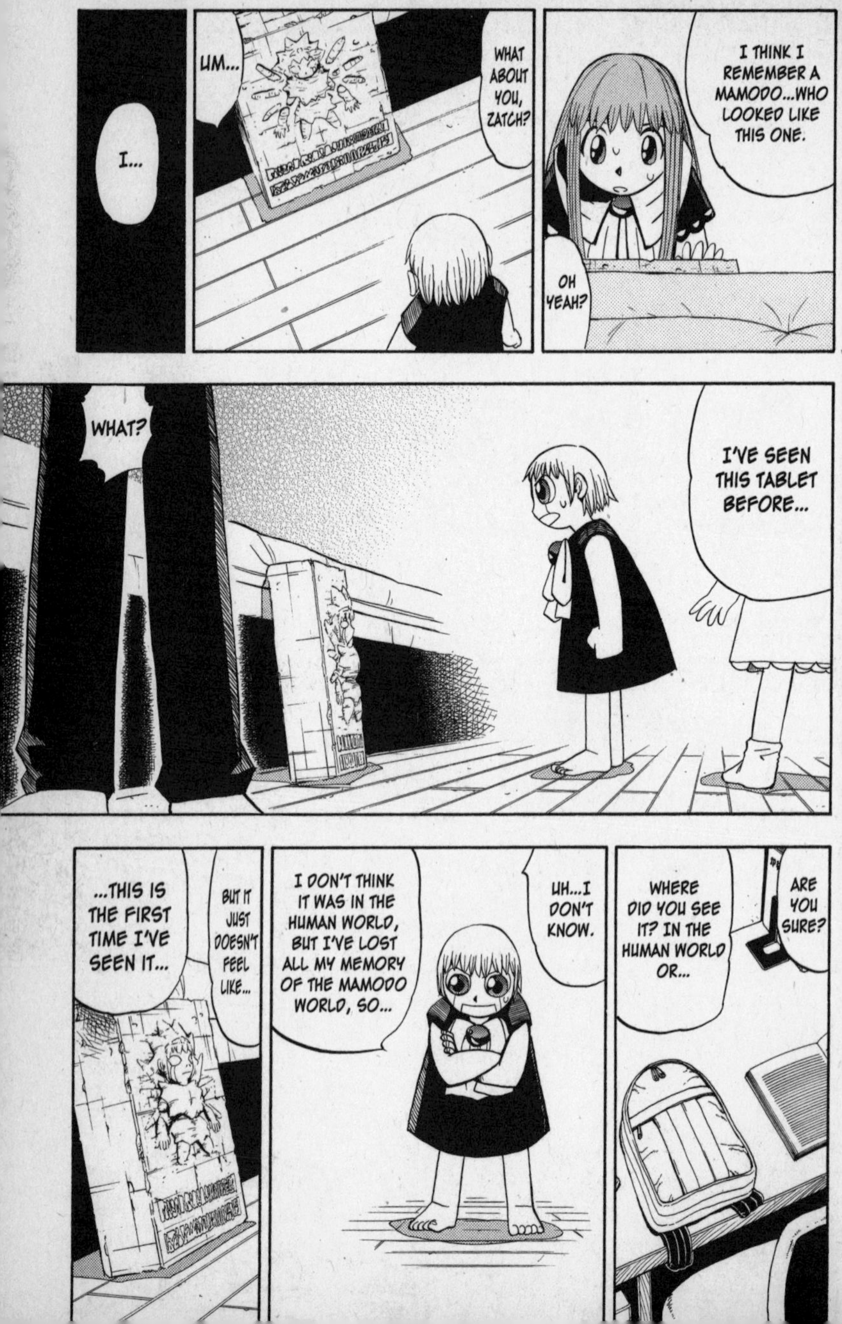
I THINK I REMEMBER A MAMODO...WHO LOOKED LIKE THIS ONE.
OH YEAH?
WHAT ABOUT YOU, ZATCH?
UM...
I...
I'VE SEEN THIS TABLET BEFORE...
WHAT?
ARE YOU SURE?
WHERE DID YOU SEE IT? IN THE HUMAN WORLD OR...
UH...I DON'T KNOW.
I DON'T THINK IT WAS IN THE HUMAN WORLD, BUT I'VE LOST ALL MY MEMORY OF THE MAMODO WORLD, SO...
BUT IT JUST DOESN'T FEEL LIKE...
...THIS IS THE FIRST TIME I'VE SEEN IT...

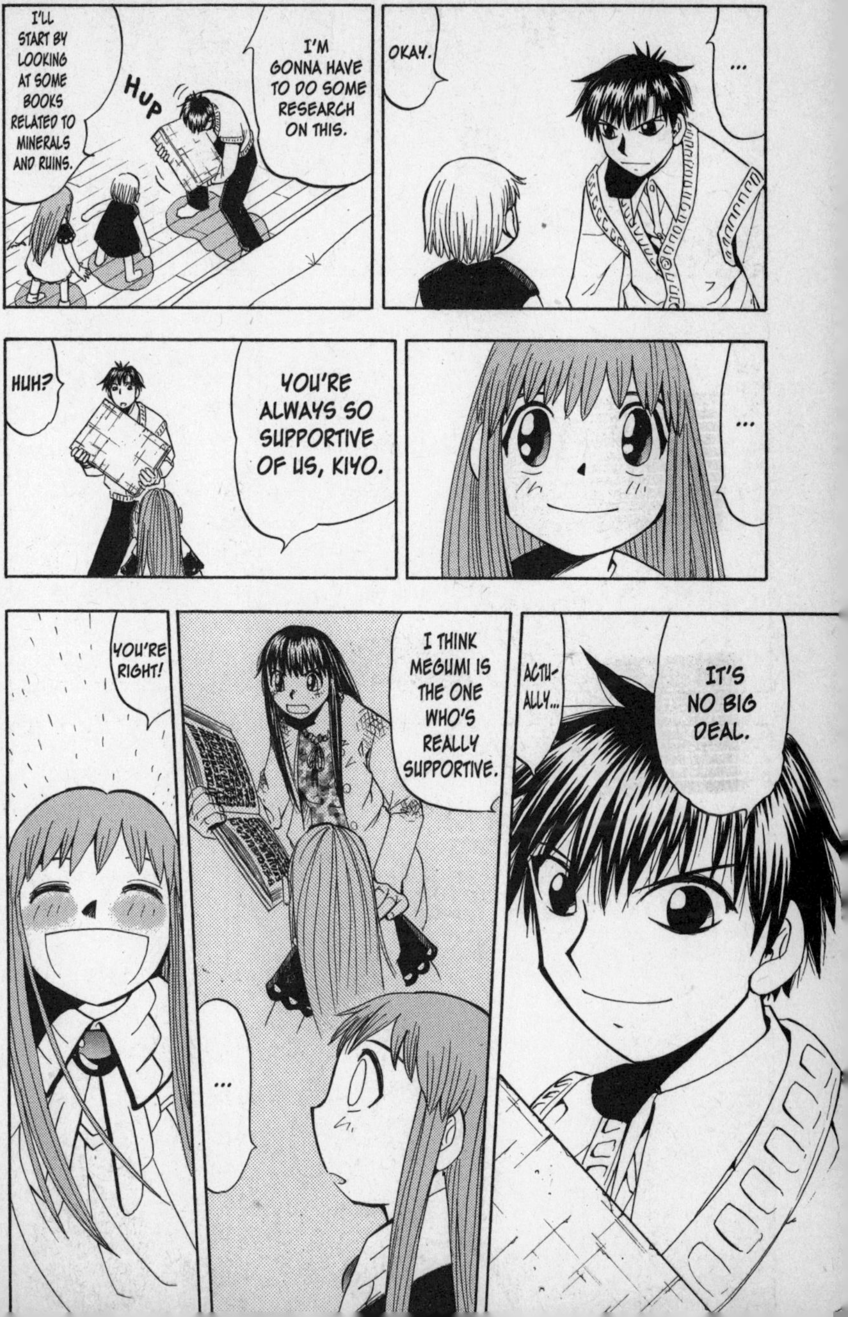
...
OKAY.
I'M GONNA HAVE TO DO SOME RESEARCH ON THIS.
HUP
I'LL START BY LOOKING AT SOME BOOKS RELATED TO MINERALS AND RUINS.
...
YOU'RE ALWAYS SO SUPPORTIVE OF US, KIYO.
HUH?
IT'S NO BIG DEAL.
ACTUALLY...
I THINK MEGUMI IS THE ONE WHO'S REALLY SUPPORTIVE.
...
YOU'RE RIGHT!

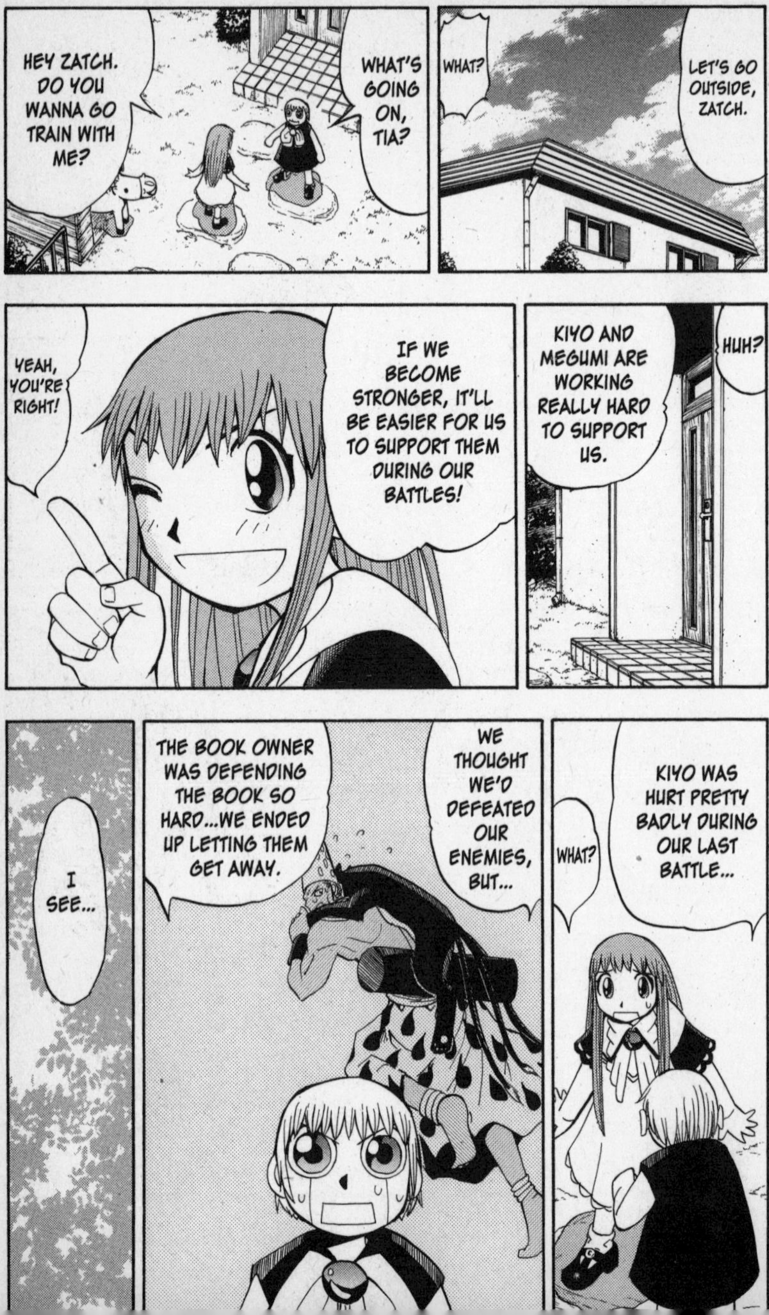
LET'S GO OUTSIDE, ZATCH.
WHAT?
WHAT'S GOING ON, TIA?
HEY ZATCH. DO YOU WANNA GO TRAIN WITH ME?
HUH?
KIYO AND MEGUMI ARE WORKING REALLY HARD TO SUPPORT US.
IF WE BECOME STRONGER, IT'LL BE EASIER FOR US TO SUPPORT THEM DURING OUR BATTLES!
YEAH, YOU'RE RIGHT!
KIYO WAS HURT PRETTY BADLY DURING OUR LAST BATTLE...
WHAT?
WE THOUGHT WE'D DEFEATED OUR ENEMIES, BUT...
THE BOOK OWNER WAS DEFENDING THE BOOK SO HARD...WE ENDED UP LETTING THEM GET AWAY.
I SEE...

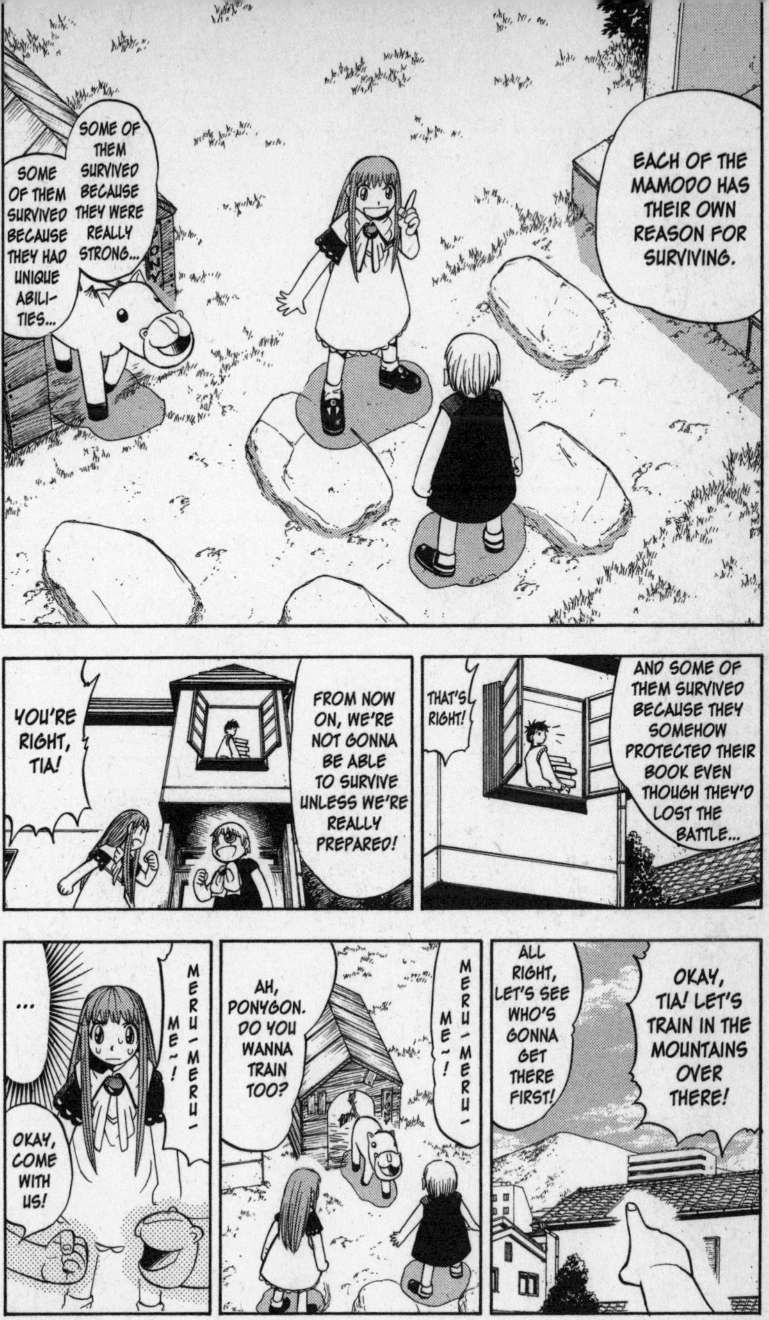
EACH OF THE MAMODO HAS THEIR OWN REASON FOR SURVIVING.
SOME OF THEM SURVIVED BECAUSE THEY WERE REALLY STRONG...
SOME OF THEM SURVIVED BECAUSE THEY HAD UNIQUE ABILITIES...
AND SOME OF THEM SURVIVED BECAUSE THEY SOMEHOW PROTECTED THEIR BOOK EVEN THOUGH THEY'D LOST THE BATTLE...
THAT'S RIGHT!
FROM NOW ON, WE'RE NOT GONNA BE ABLE TO SURVIVE UNLESS WE'RE REALLY PREPARED!
YOU'RE RIGHT, TIA!
OKAY, TIA! LET'S TRAIN IN THE MOUNTAINS OVER THERE!
ALL RIGHT, LET'S SEE WHO'S GONNA GET THERE FIRST!
MERU-MERU-ME~!
AH, PONYGON. DO YOU WANNA TRAIN TOO?
MERU-MERU-ME~!
...
OKAY, COME WITH US!

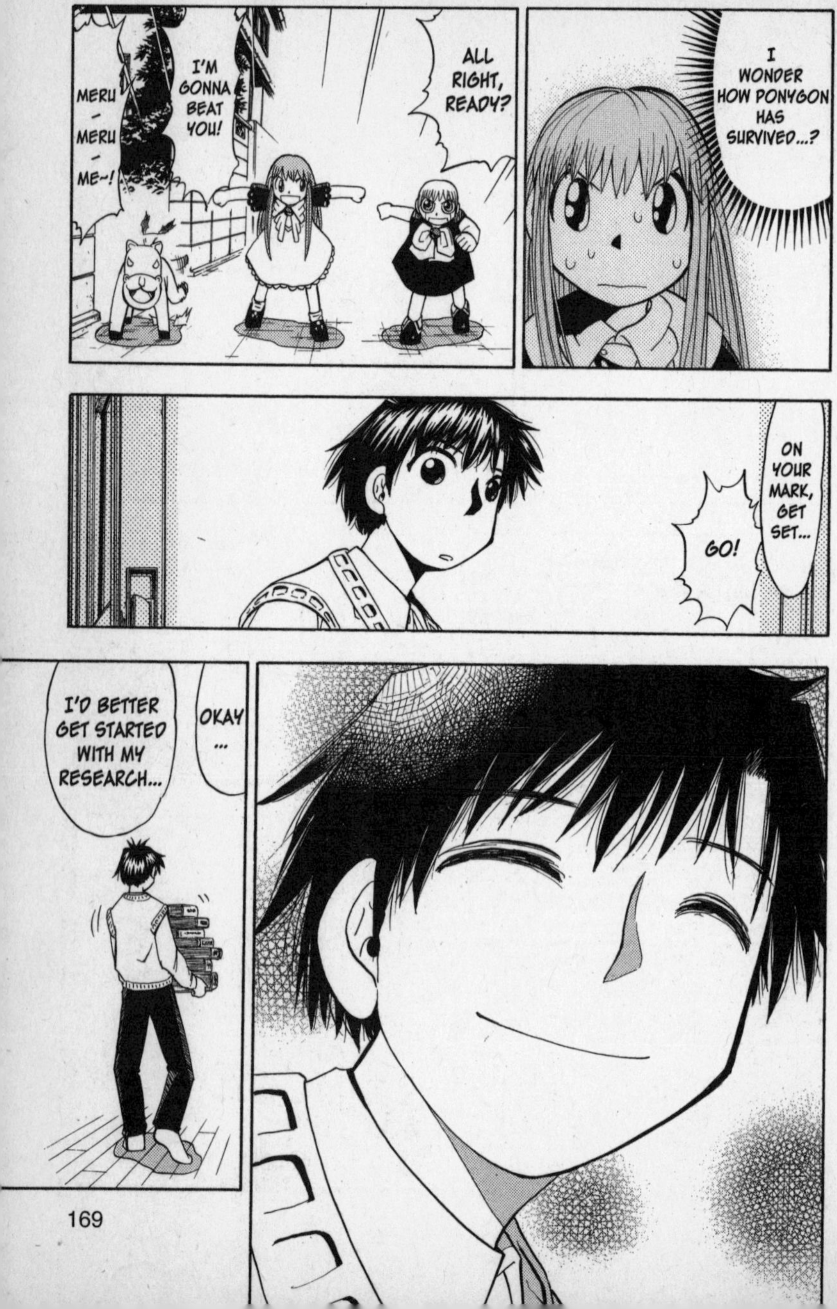
I WONDER HOW PONYGON HAS SURVIVED...?
ALL RIGHT, READY?
I'M GONNA BEAT YOU!
MERU - MERU - ME~!
ON YOUR MARK, GET SET...
GO!
OKAY...
I'D BETTER GET STARTED WITH MY RESEARCH...

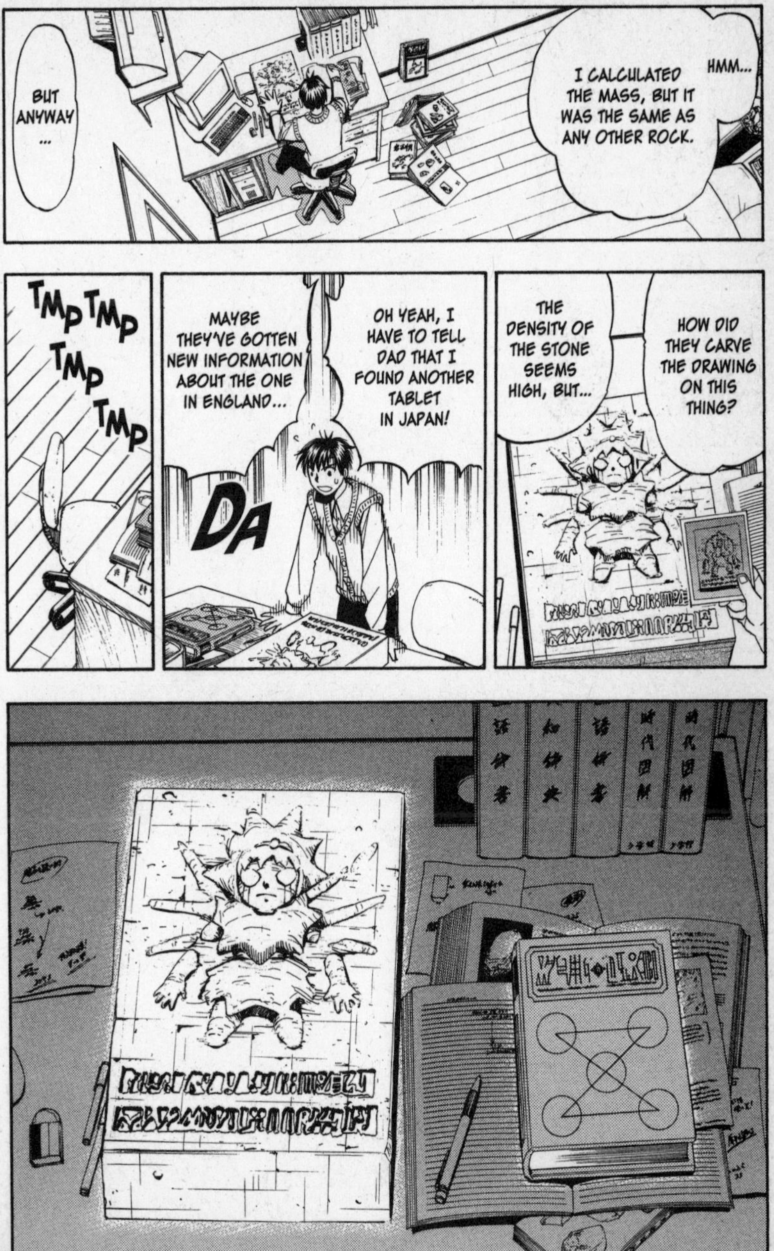
HMM...
I CALCULATED THE MASS, BUT IT WAS THE SAME AS ANY OTHER ROCK.
BUT ANYWAY...
HOW DID THEY CARVE THE DRAWING ON THIS THING?
THE DENSITY OF THE STONE SEEMS HIGH, BUT...
OH YEAH, I HAVE TO TELL DAD THAT I FOUND ANOTHER TABLET IN JAPAN!
MAYBE THEY'VE GOTTEN NEW INFORMATION ABOUT THE ONE IN ENGLAND...
DA
TMP TMP TMP TMP

LEVEL 84: The Mystery of the Stone Tablet

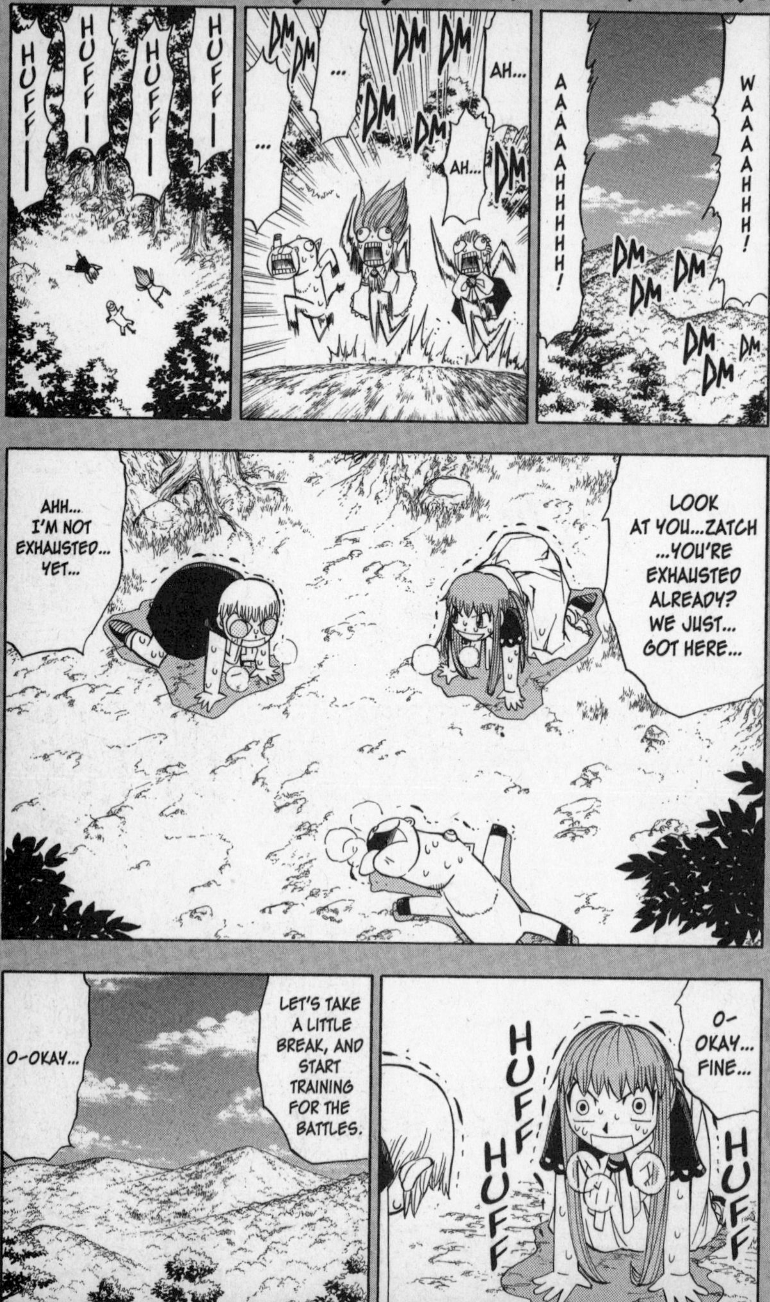

WAAAAAHHHH!
AAAAAAHHHHHH!
DM DM DM DM DM DM
AH...
AH...
DM DM DM DM DM DM DM
...
...
HUFF!
HUFF!
HUFF!
HUFF!
LOOK AT YOU...ZATCH ...YOU'RE EXHAUSTED ALREADY? WE JUST... GOT HERE...
AHH... I'M NOT EXHAUSTED... YET...
O-OKAY... FINE...
HUFF HUFF
HUFF HUFF
HUFF HUFF
LET'S TAKE A LITTLE BREAK, AND START TRAINING FOR THE BATTLES.
O-OKAY...

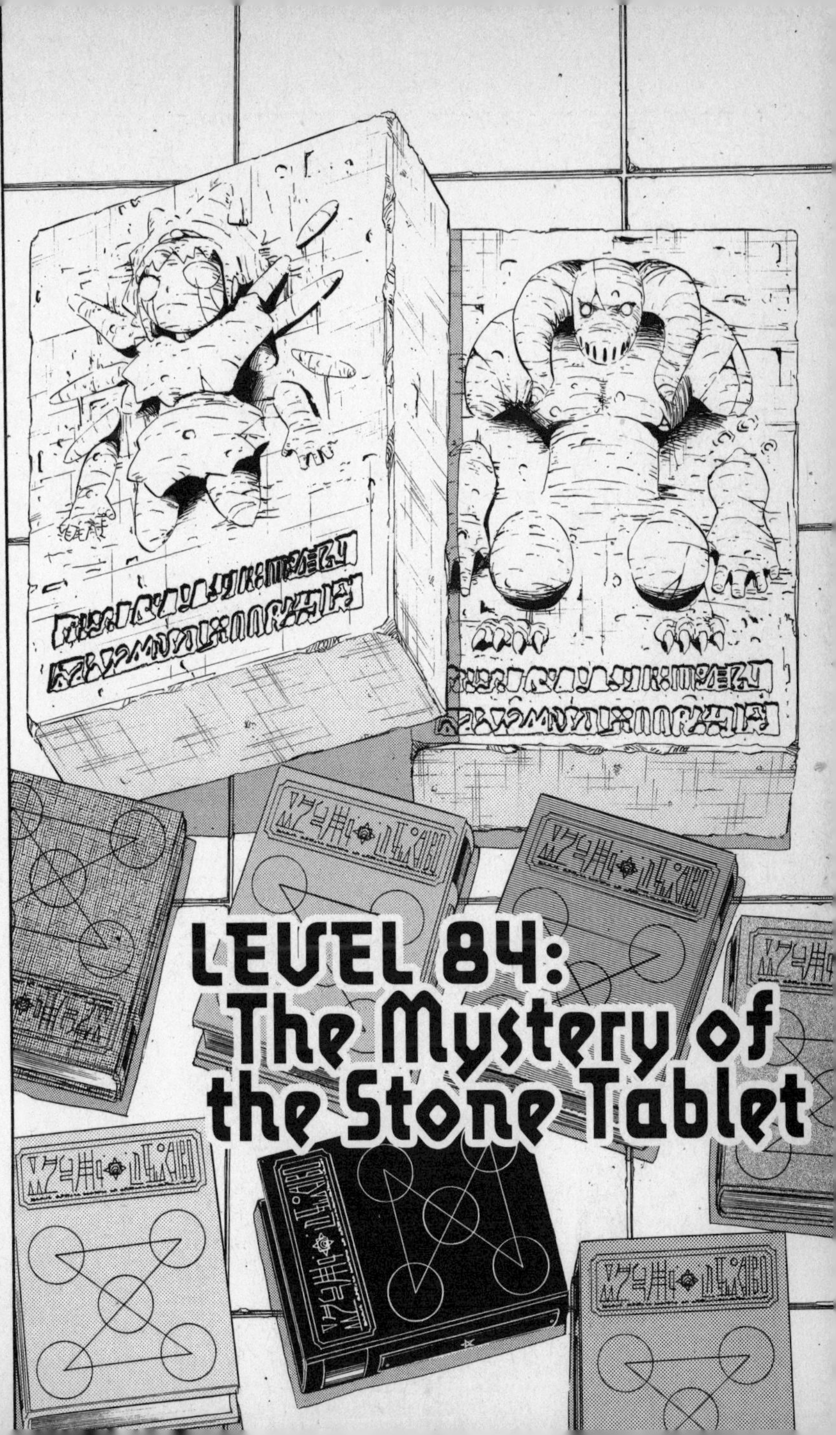
LEVEL 84:
The Mystery of
the Stone Tablet

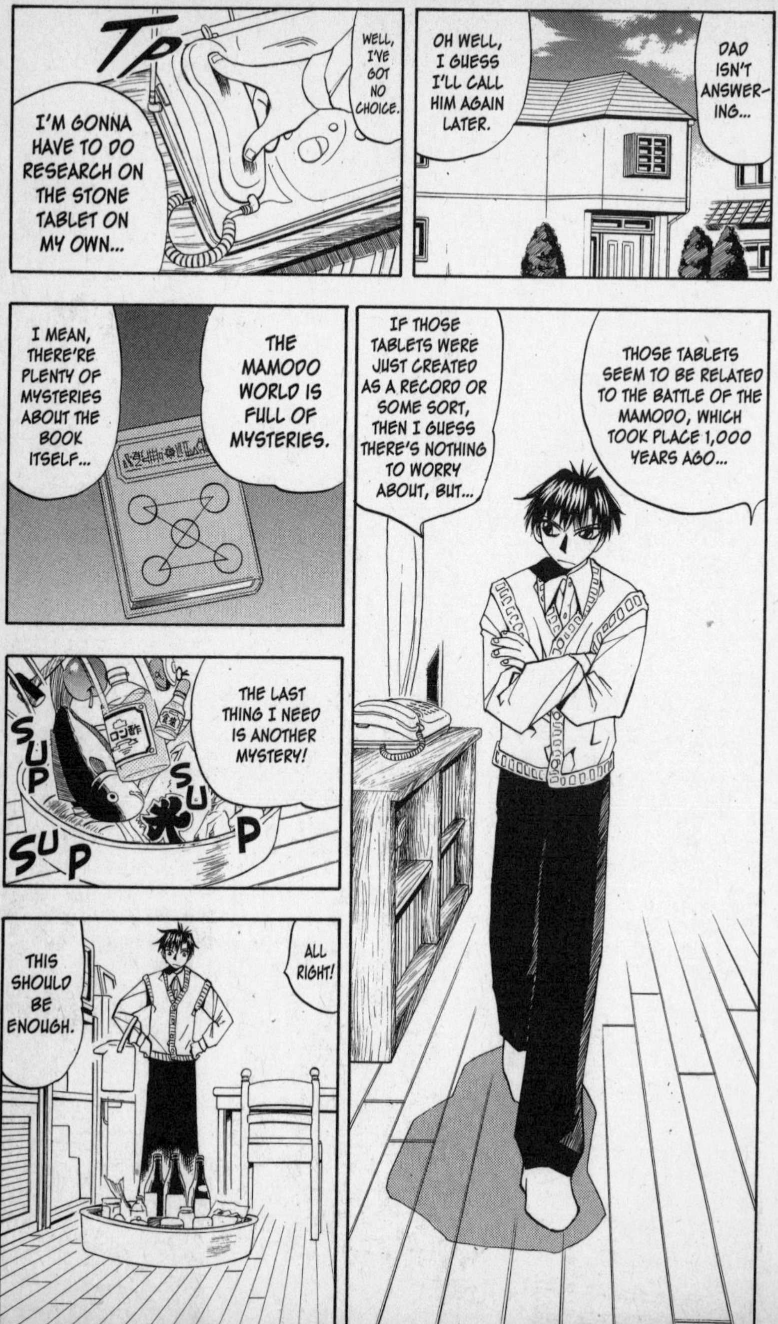
DAD ISN'T ANSWERING...
OH WELL, I GUESS I'LL CALL HIM AGAIN LATER.
WELL, I'VE GOT NO CHOICE.
TP
I'M GONNA HAVE TO DO RESEARCH ON THE STONE TABLET ON MY OWN...
THOSE TABLETS SEEM TO BE RELATED TO THE BATTLE OF THE MAMODO, WHICH TOOK PLACE 1,000 YEARS AGO...
IF THOSE TABLETS WERE JUST CREATED AS A RECORD OR SOME SORT, THEN I GUESS THERE'S NOTHING TO WORRY ABOUT, BUT...
THE MAMODO WORLD IS FULL OF MYSTERIES.
I MEAN, THERE'RE PLENTY OF MYSTERIES ABOUT THE BOOK ITSELF...
THE LAST THING I NEED IS ANOTHER MYSTERY!
SUP
SUP
SUP
ALL RIGHT!
THIS SHOULD BE ENOUGH.

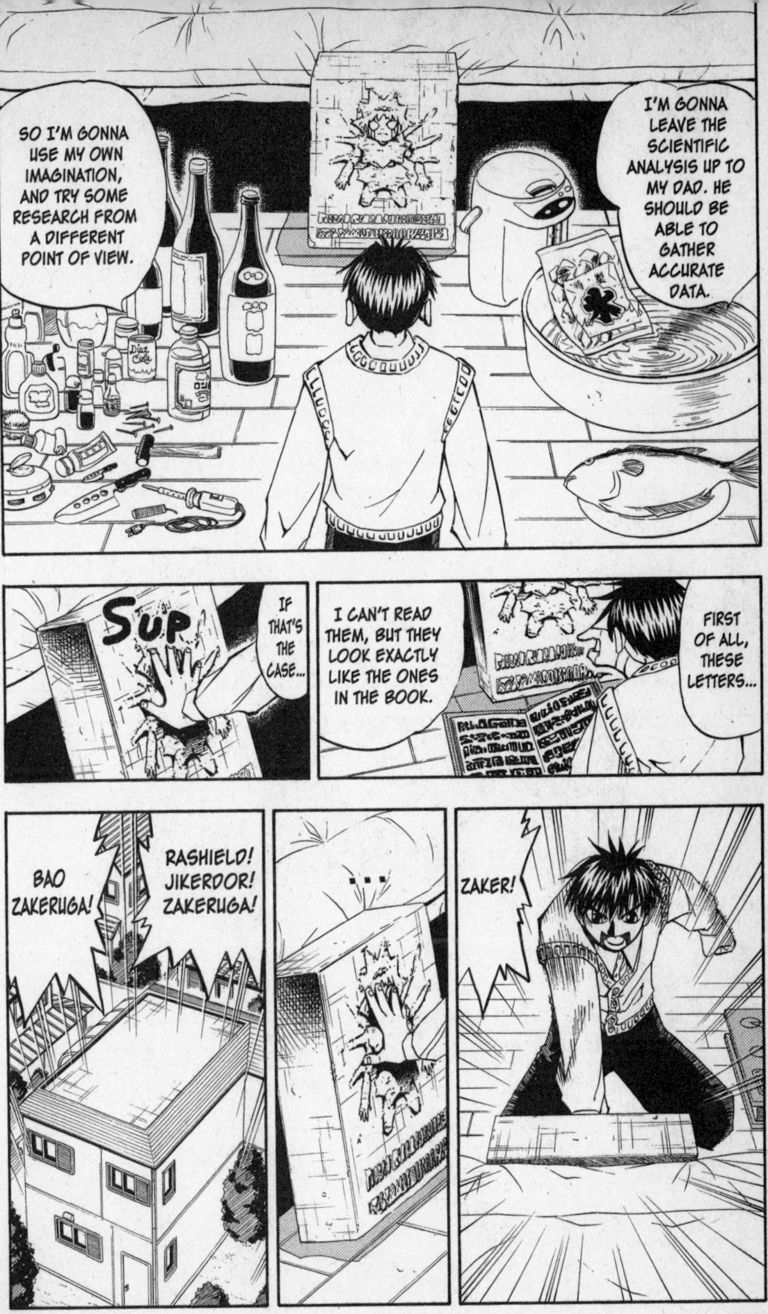
I'M GONNA LEAVE THE SCIENTIFIC ANALYSIS UP TO MY DAD. HE SHOULD BE ABLE TO GATHER ACCURATE DATA.
SO I'M GONNA USE MY OWN IMAGINATION, AND TRY SOME RESEARCH FROM A DIFFERENT POINT OF VIEW.
Diet Cola
FIRST OF ALL, THESE LETTERS...
I CAN'T READ THEM, BUT THEY LOOK EXACTLY LIKE THE ONES IN THE BOOK.
IF THAT'S THE CASE...
SUP
ZAKER!
...
RASHIELD! JIKERDOR! ZAKERUGA!
BAO ZAKERUGA!

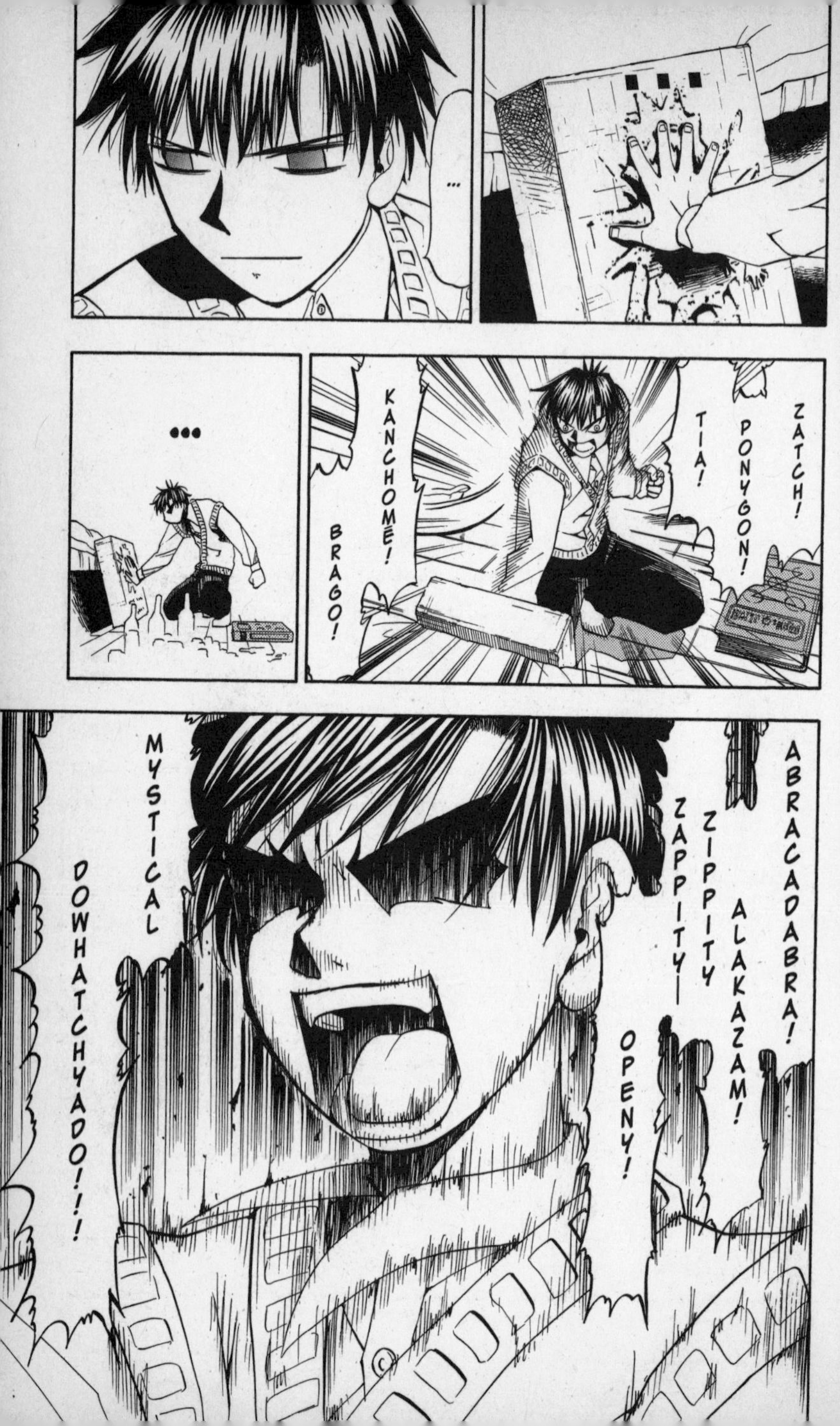
...
ZATCH!
PONYGON!
TIA!
KANCHOME!
BRAGO!
...
ABRACADABRA!
ALAKAZAM!
ZIPPITY
ZAPPITY-
OPENY!
MYSTICAL
DOWHATCHYADOO!!!

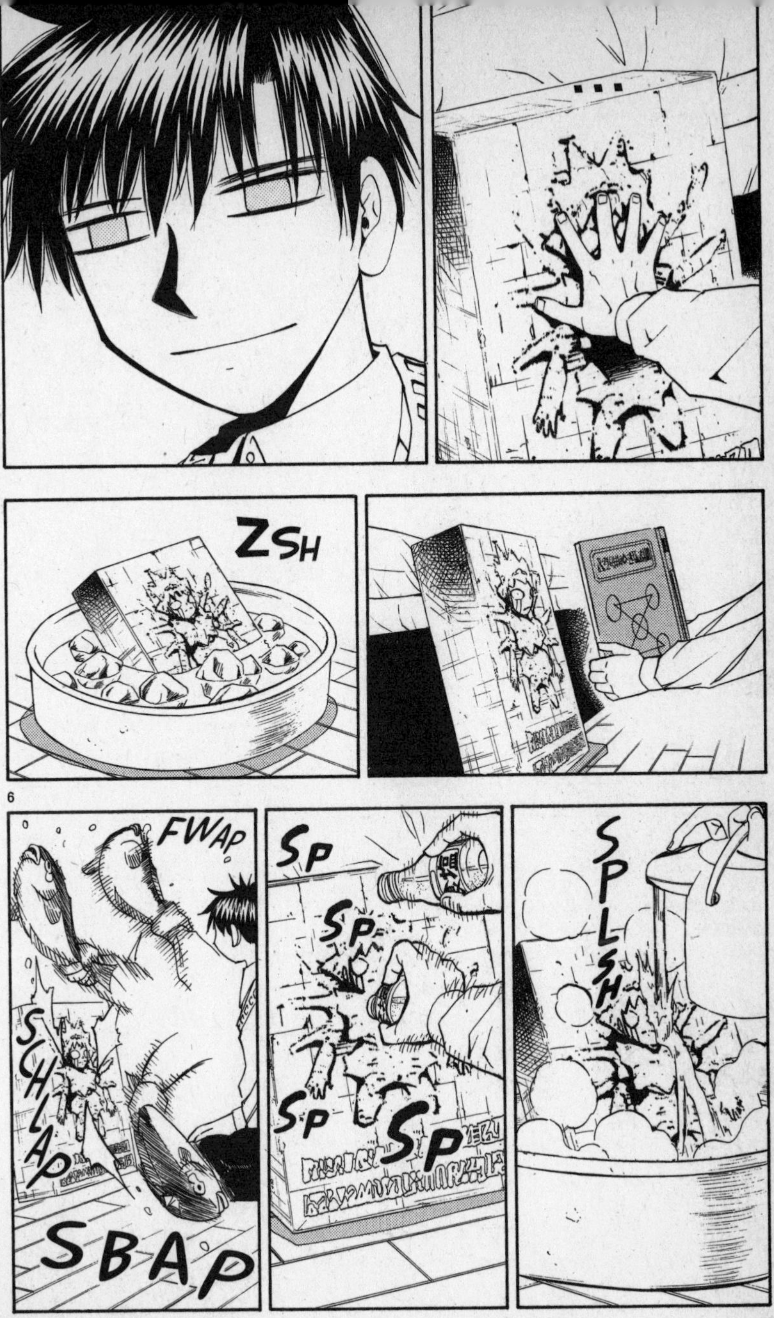
ZSH
SPLSH
SP
SP
SP
SP
FWAP
SCHLAP
SBAP
6

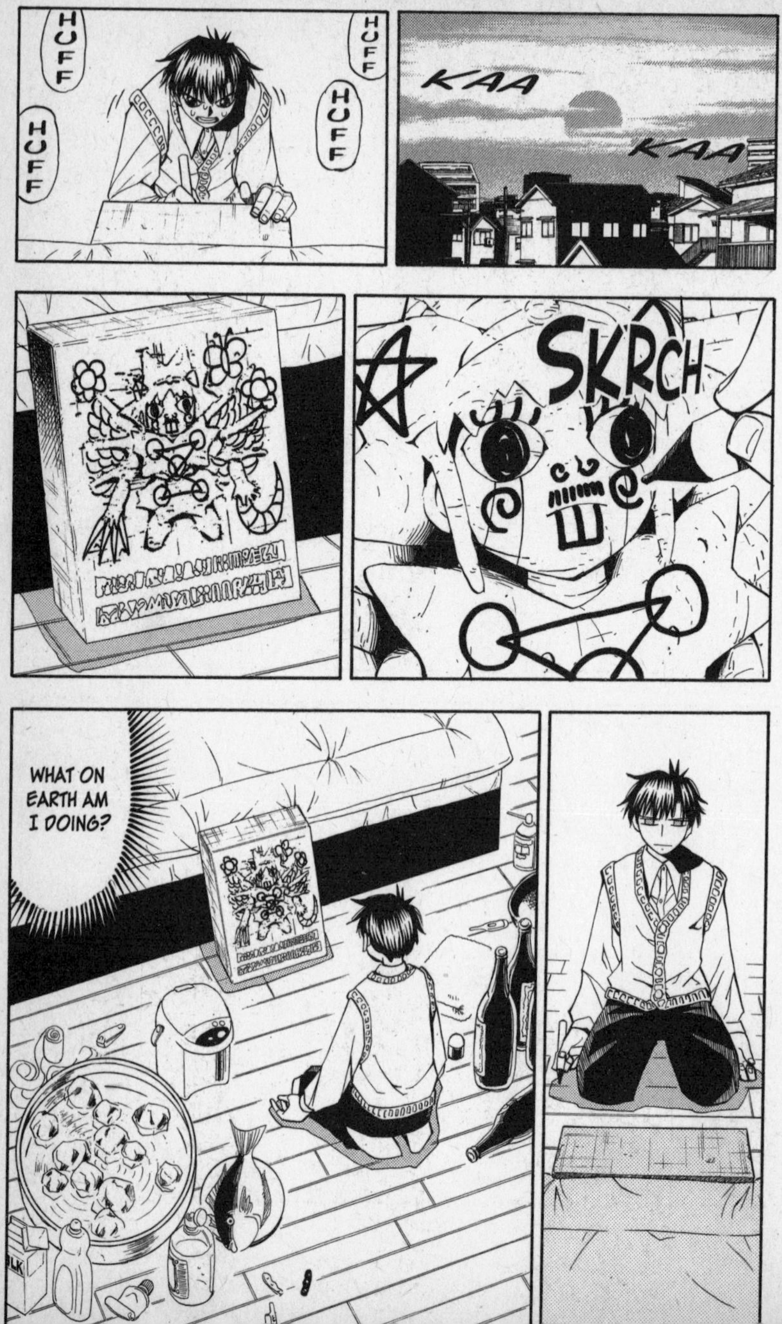
KAA
KAA
HUFF
HUFF
HUFF
HUFF
SKRCH
WHAT ON EARTH AM I DOING?

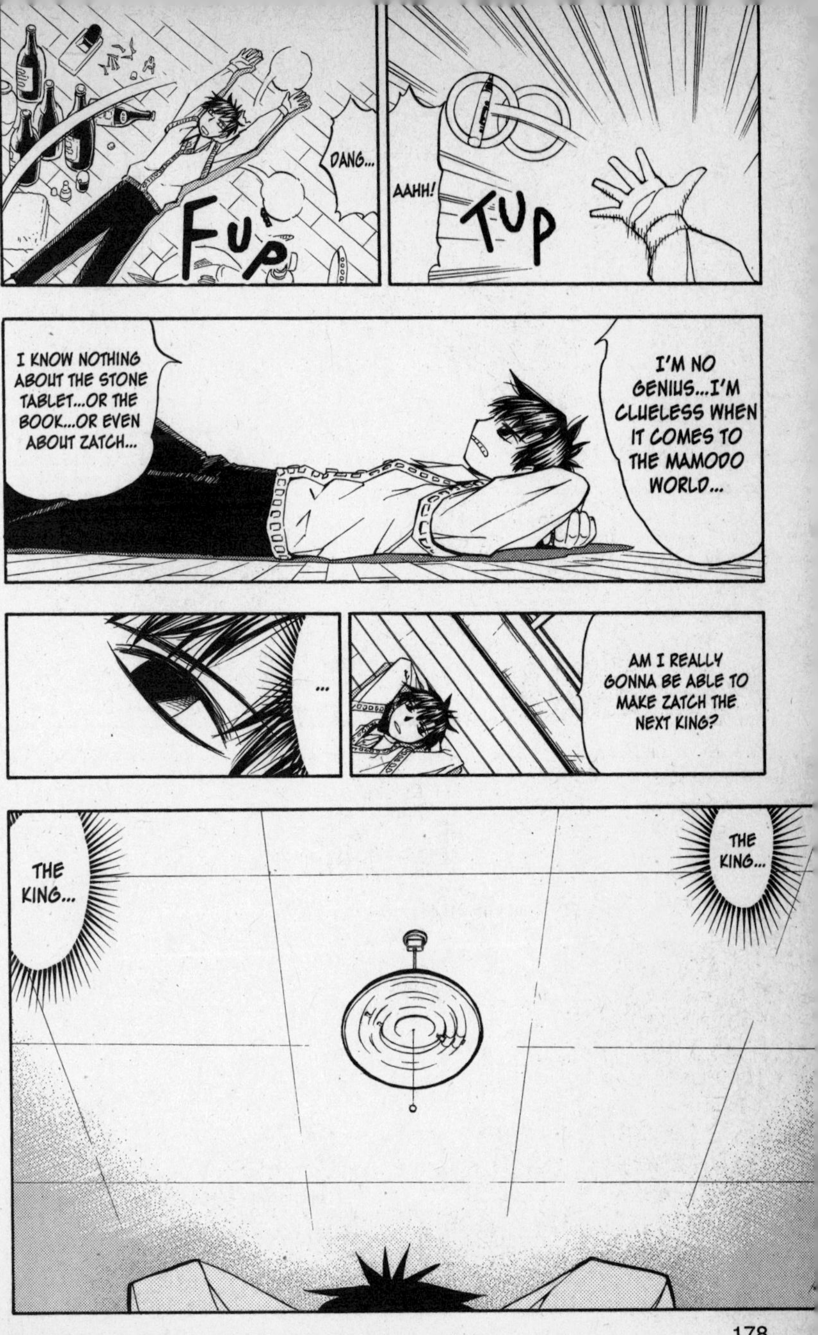
AAHH!
TUP
DANG...
FUP
I'M NO GENIUS...I'M CLUELESS WHEN IT COMES TO THE MAMODO WORLD...
I KNOW NOTHING ABOUT THE STONE TABLET...OR THE BOOK...OR EVEN ABOUT ZATCH...
AM I REALLY GONNA BE ABLE TO MAKE ZATCH THE NEXT KING?
...
THE KING...
THE KING...

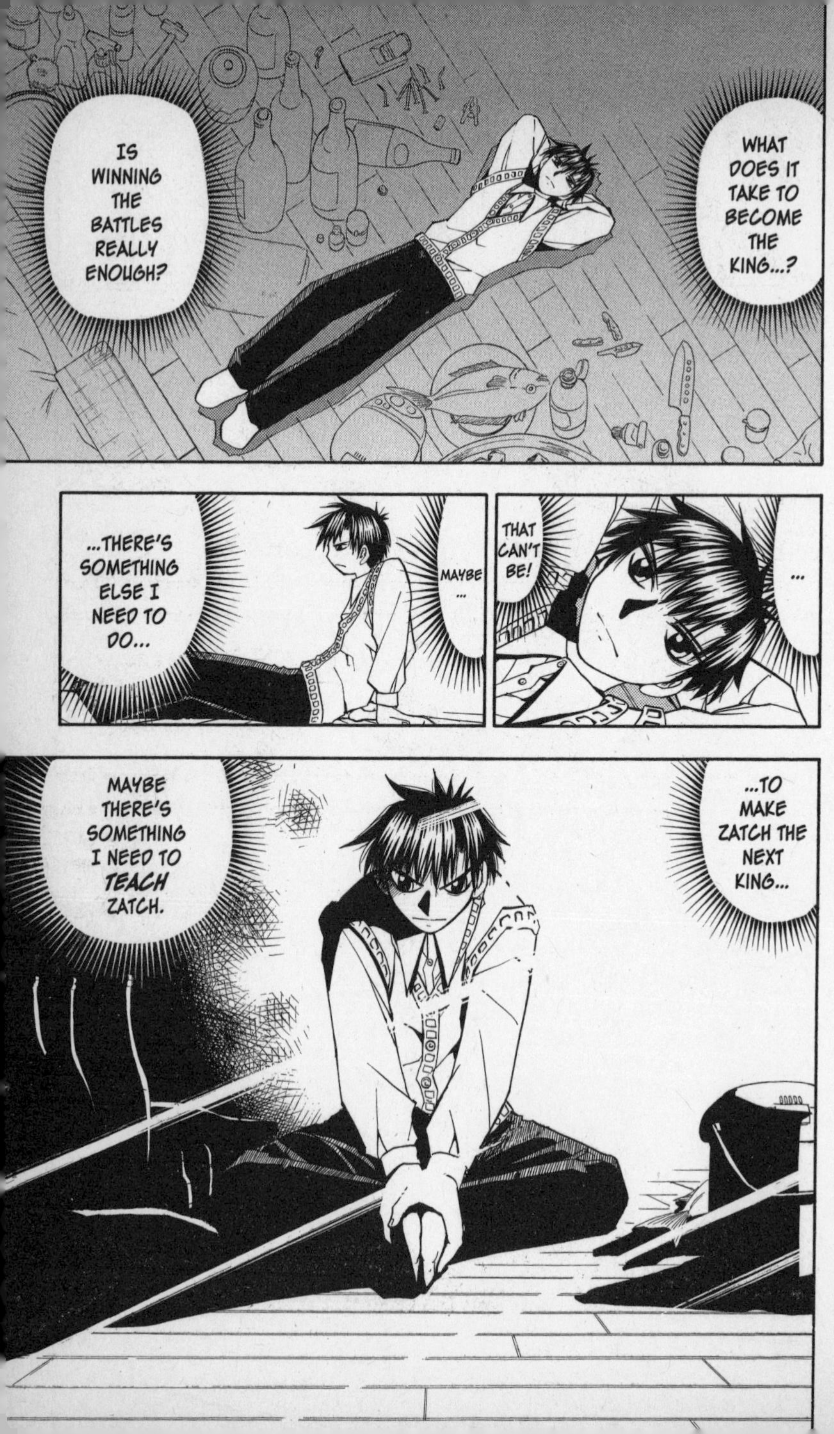
WHAT DOES IT TAKE TO BECOME THE KING...?
IS WINNING THE BATTLES REALLY ENOUGH?
...
THAT CAN'T BE!
MAYBE ...
...THERE'S SOMETHING ELSE I NEED TO DO...
...TO MAKE ZATCH THE NEXT KING...
MAYBE THERE'S SOMETHING I NEED TO *TEACH* ZATCH.

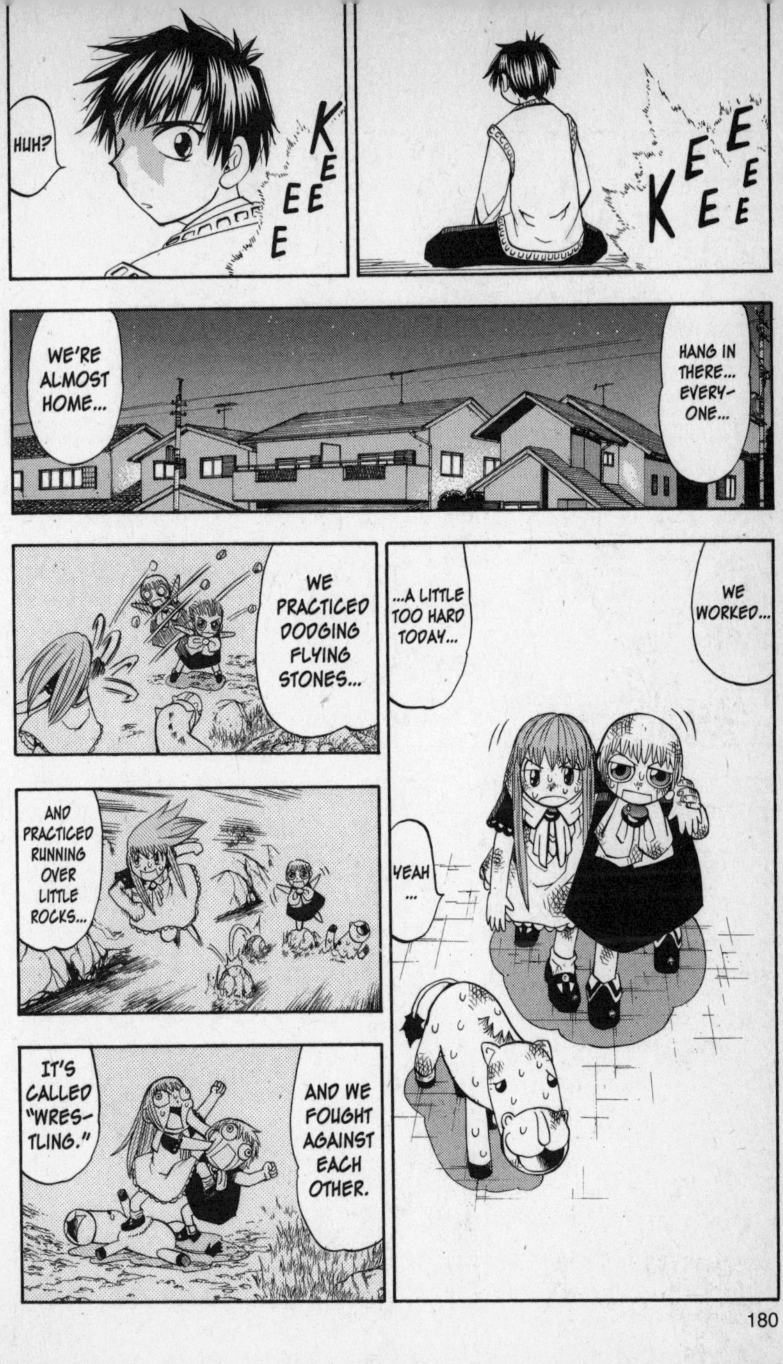
KEEEEE
KEEEE
HUH?
HANG IN THERE... EVERY-ONE...
WE'RE ALMOST HOME...
WE WORKED...
...A LITTLE TOO HARD TODAY...
YEAH ...
WE PRACTICED DODGING FLYING STONES...
AND PRACTICED RUNNING OVER LITTLE ROCKS...
AND WE FOUGHT AGAINST EACH OTHER.
IT'S CALLED "WRES-TLING."

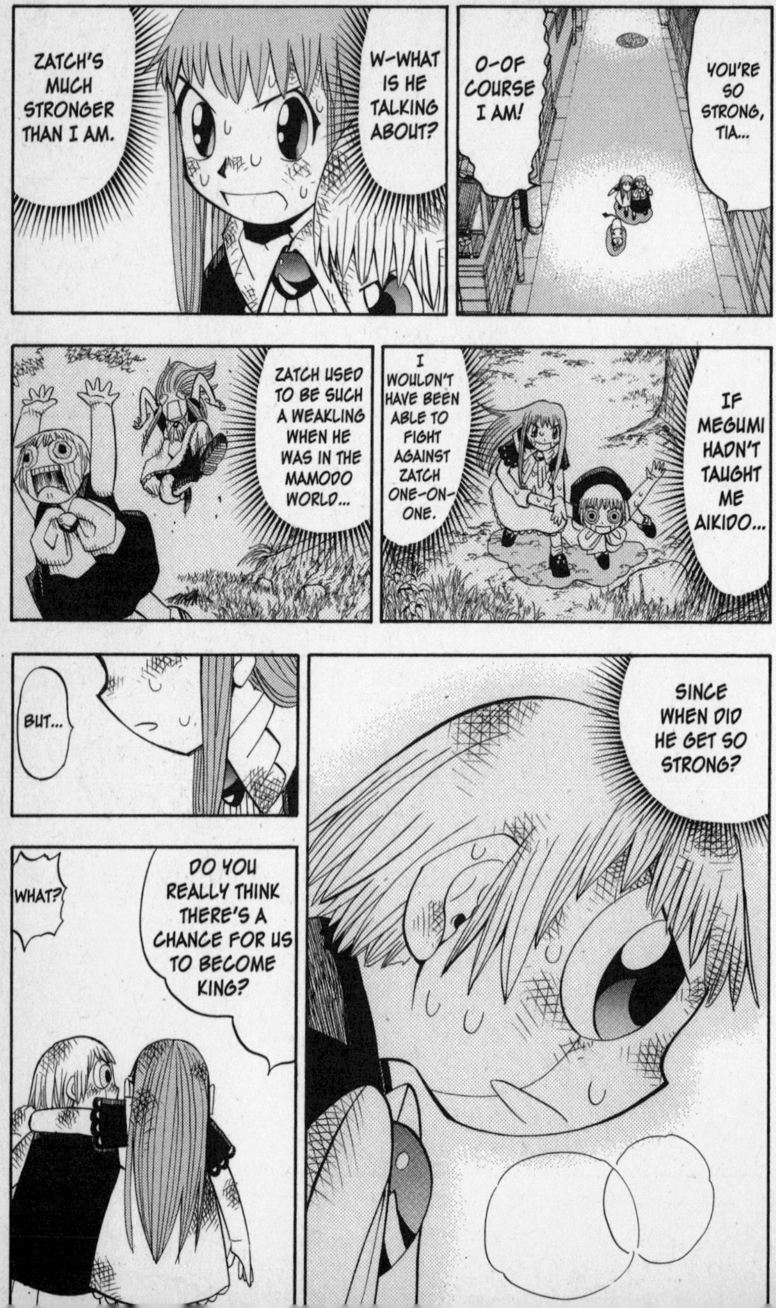
YOU'RE SO STRONG, TIA...
O-OF COURSE I AM!
W-WHAT IS HE TALKING ABOUT?
ZATCH'S MUCH STRONGER THAN I AM.
IF MEGUMI HADN'T TAUGHT ME AIKIDO...
I WOULDN'T HAVE BEEN ABLE TO FIGHT AGAINST ZATCH ONE-ON-ONE.
ZATCH USED TO BE SUCH A WEAKLING WHEN HE WAS IN THE MAMODO WORLD...
SINCE WHEN DID HE GET SO STRONG?
BUT...
DO YOU REALLY THINK THERE'S A CHANCE FOR US TO BECOME KING?
WHAT?

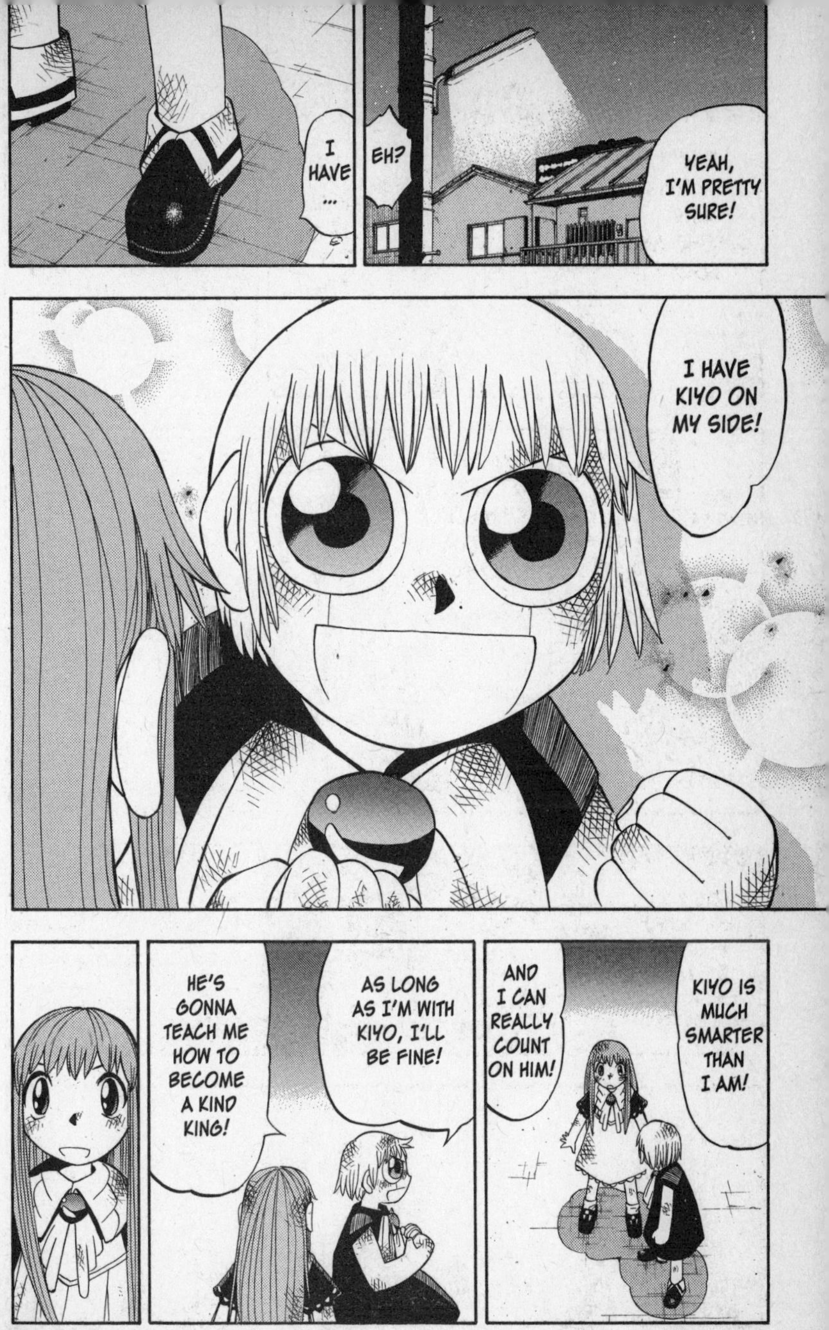
YEAH, I'M PRETTY SURE!
EH?
I HAVE ...
I HAVE KIYO ON MY SIDE!
KIYO IS MUCH SMARTER THAN I AM!
AND I CAN REALLY COUNT ON HIM!
AS LONG AS I'M WITH KIYO, I'LL BE FINE!
HE'S GONNA TEACH ME HOW TO BECOME A KIND KING!

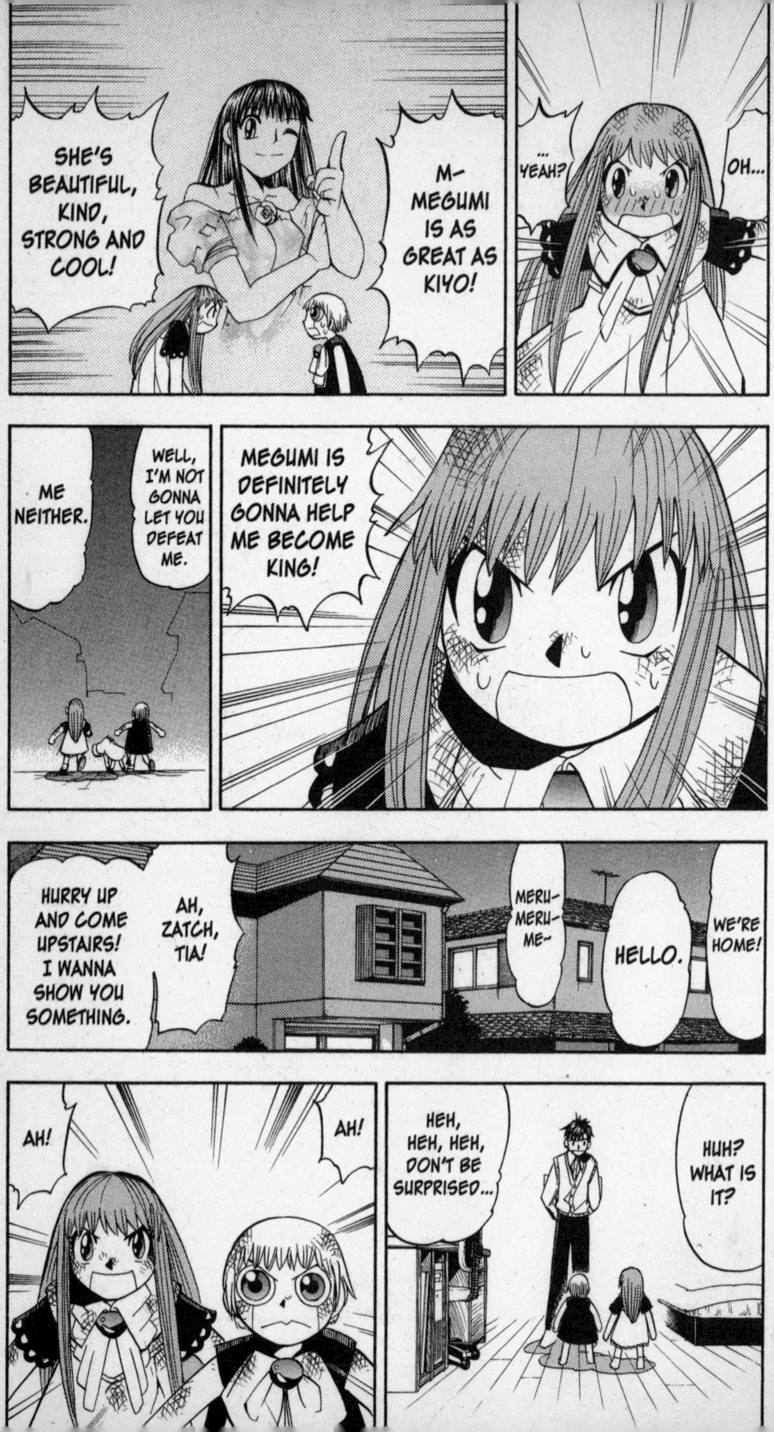
OH...
...YEAH?
M-MEGUMI IS AS GREAT AS KIYO!
SHE'S BEAUTIFUL, KIND, STRONG AND COOL!
MEGUMI IS DEFINITELY GONNA HELP ME BECOME KING!
WELL, I'M NOT GONNA LET YOU DEFEAT ME.
ME NEITHER.
WE'RE HOME!
HELLO.
MERU-MERU-ME~
AH, ZATCH, TIA!
HURRY UP AND COME UPSTAIRS! I WANNA SHOW YOU SOMETHING.
HUH? WHAT IS IT?
HEH, HEH, HEH, DON'T BE SURPRISED...
AH!
AH!

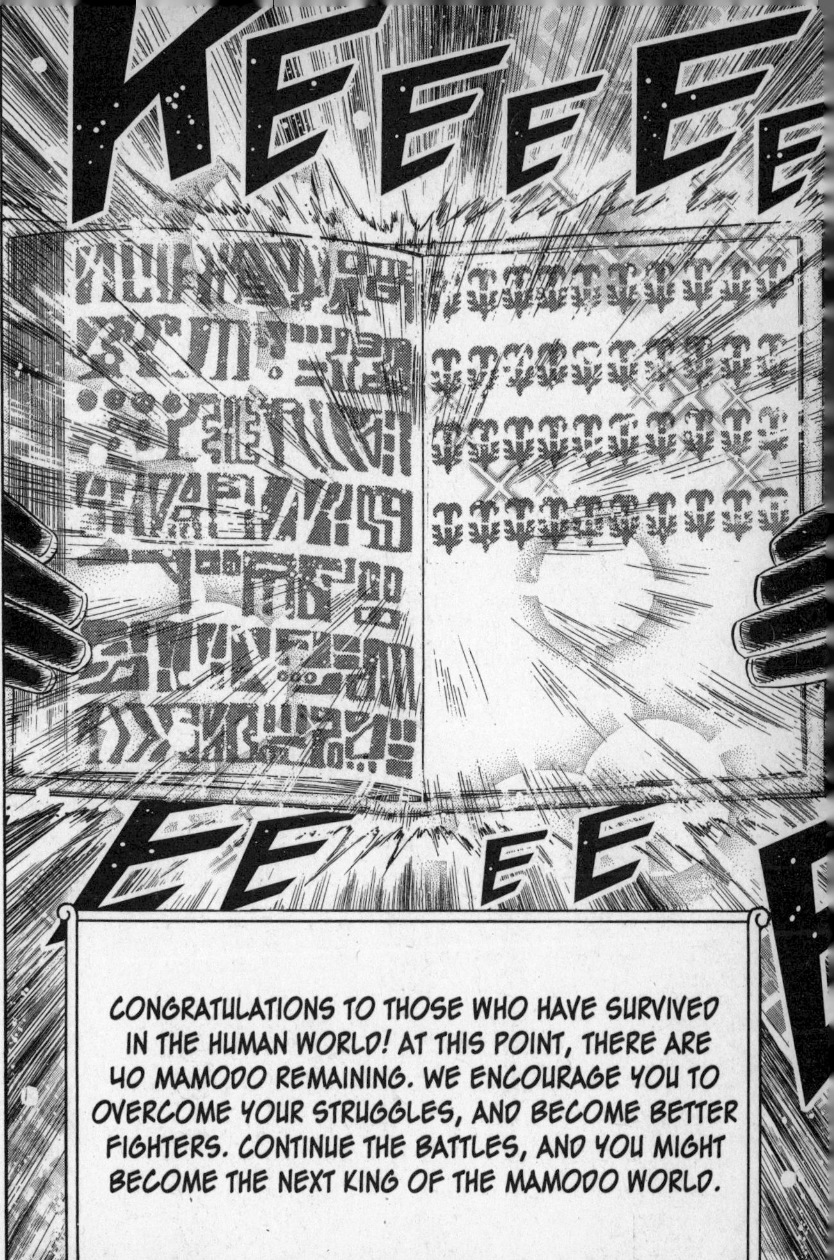
KEEEEE
KEEEEE
CONGRATULATIONS TO THOSE WHO HAVE SURVIVED IN THE HUMAN WORLD! AT THIS POINT, THERE ARE 40 MAMODO REMAINING. WE ENCOURAGE YOU TO OVERCOME YOUR STRUGGLES, AND BECOME BETTER FIGHTERS. CONTINUE THE BATTLES, AND YOU MIGHT BECOME THE NEXT KING OF THE MAMODO WORLD.

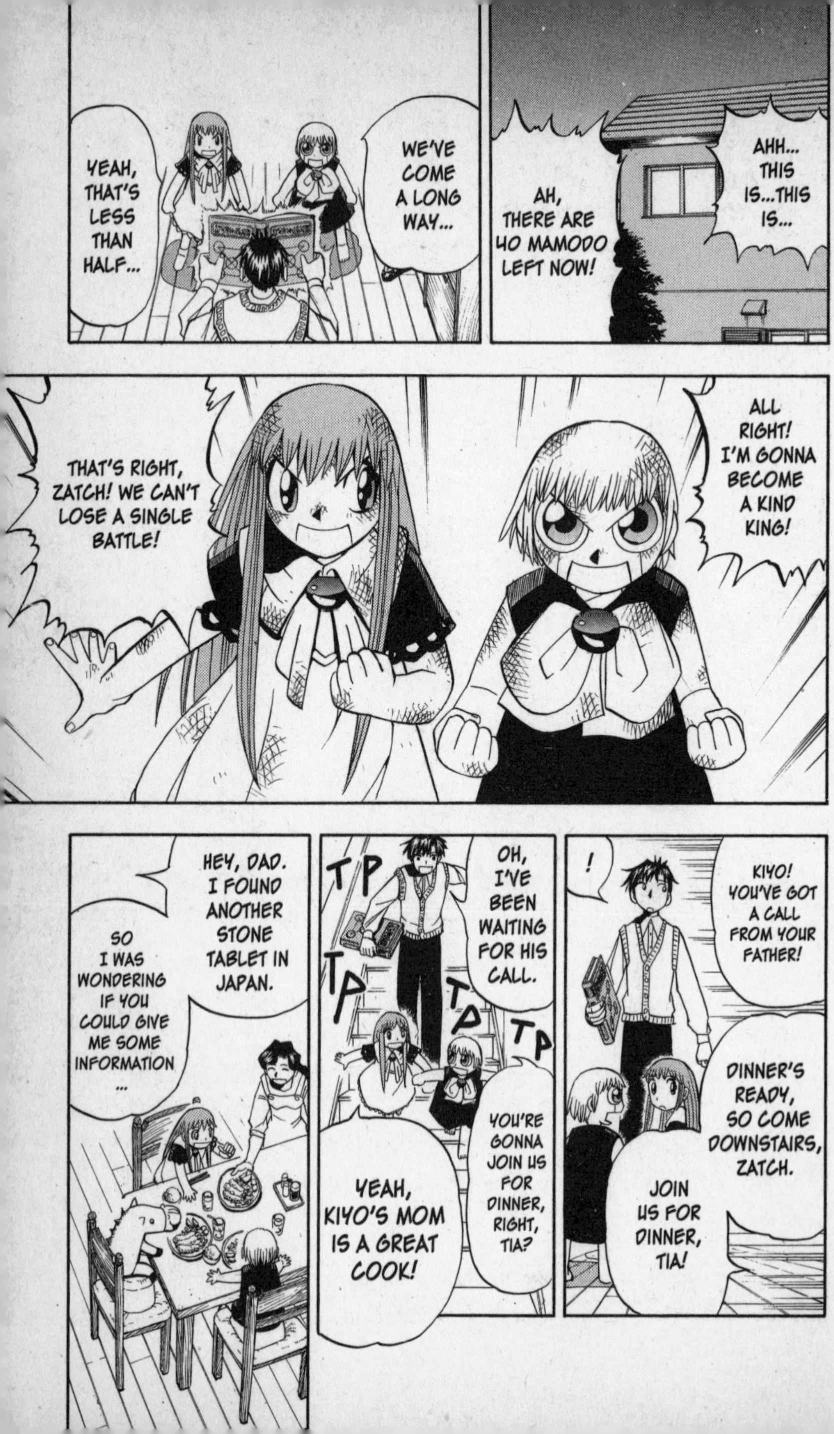

AHH... THIS IS...THIS IS...
AH, THERE ARE 40 MAMODO LEFT NOW!
WE'VE COME A LONG WAY...
YEAH, THAT'S LESS THAN HALF...
ALL RIGHT! I'M GONNA BECOME A KIND KING!
THAT'S RIGHT, ZATCH! WE CAN'T LOSE A SINGLE BATTLE!
KIYO! YOU'VE GOT A CALL FROM YOUR FATHER!
!
DINNER'S READY, SO COME DOWNSTAIRS, ZATCH.
JOIN US FOR DINNER, TIA!
OH, I'VE BEEN WAITING FOR HIS CALL.
TP
TP
TP
TP
YOU'RE GONNA JOIN US FOR DINNER, RIGHT, TIA?
YEAH, KIYO'S MOM IS A GREAT COOK!
HEY, DAD. I FOUND ANOTHER STONE TABLET IN JAPAN.
SO I WAS WONDERING IF YOU COULD GIVE ME SOME INFORMATION...

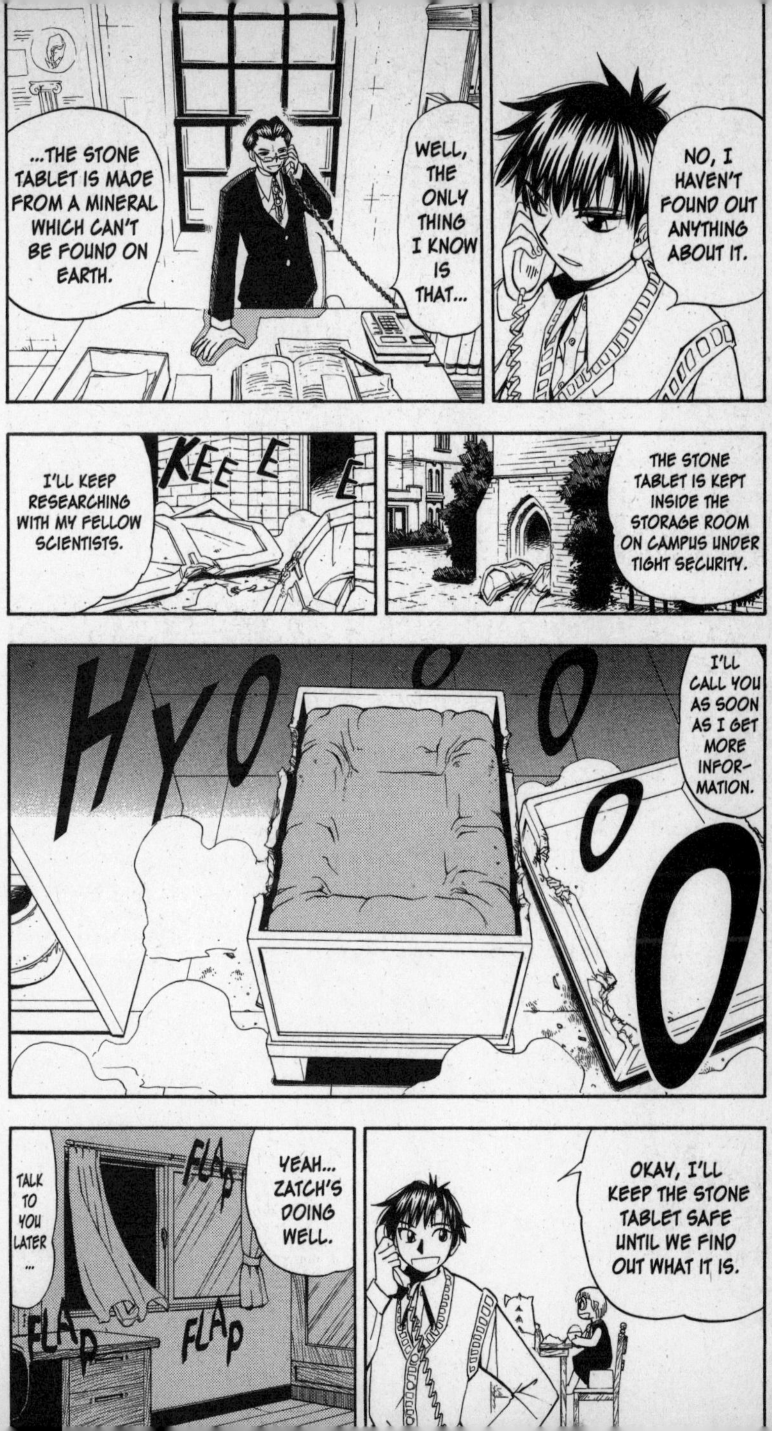
NO, I HAVEN'T FOUND OUT ANYTHING ABOUT IT.
WELL, THE ONLY THING I KNOW IS THAT...
...THE STONE TABLET IS MADE FROM A MINERAL WHICH CAN'T BE FOUND ON EARTH.
THE STONE TABLET IS KEPT INSIDE THE STORAGE ROOM ON CAMPUS UNDER TIGHT SECURITY.
KEEEE
I'LL KEEP RESEARCHING WITH MY FELLOW SCIENTISTS.
I'LL CALL YOU AS SOON AS I GET MORE INFORMATION.
HYOOOOOO
OKAY, I'LL KEEP THE STONE TABLET SAFE UNTIL WE FIND OUT WHAT IT IS.
YEAH... ZATCH'S DOING WELL.
FLAP
TALK TO YOU LATER ...
FLAP
FLAP

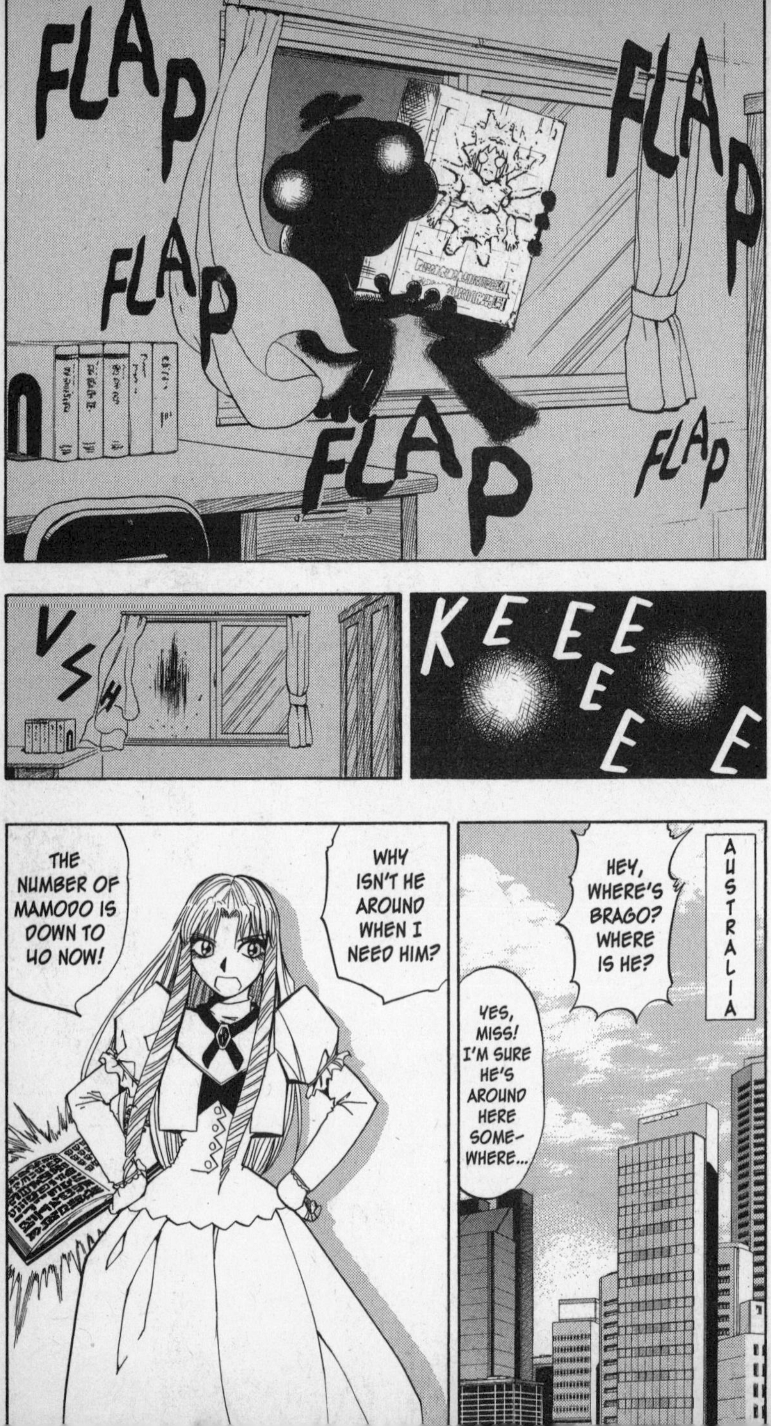
FLAP
FLAP
FLAP
FLAP
FLAP
KEEEEEE
VSH
AUSTRALIA
HEY, WHERE'S BRAGO? WHERE IS HE?
YES, MISS! I'M SURE HE'S AROUND HERE SOME-WHERE...
WHY ISN'T HE AROUND WHEN I NEED HIM?
THE NUMBER OF MAMODO IS DOWN TO 40 NOW!

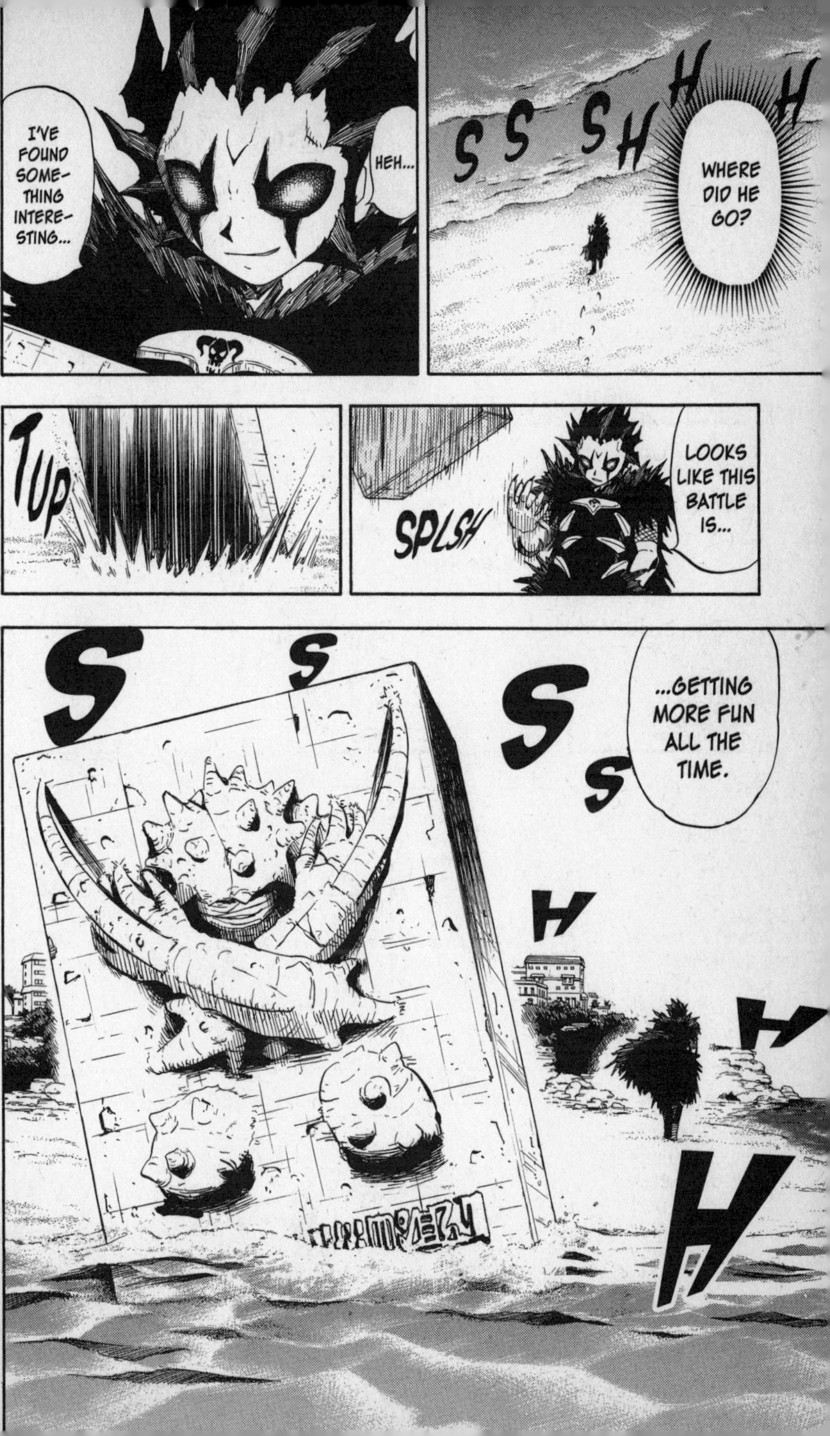
SSSHHHH
WHERE DID HE GO?
HEH...
I'VE FOUND SOMETHING INTERESTING...
LOOKS LIKE THIS BATTLE IS...
SPLSH
TUP
...GETTING MORE FUN ALL THE TIME.
SSSSHHHH

TO BE CONTINUED!!

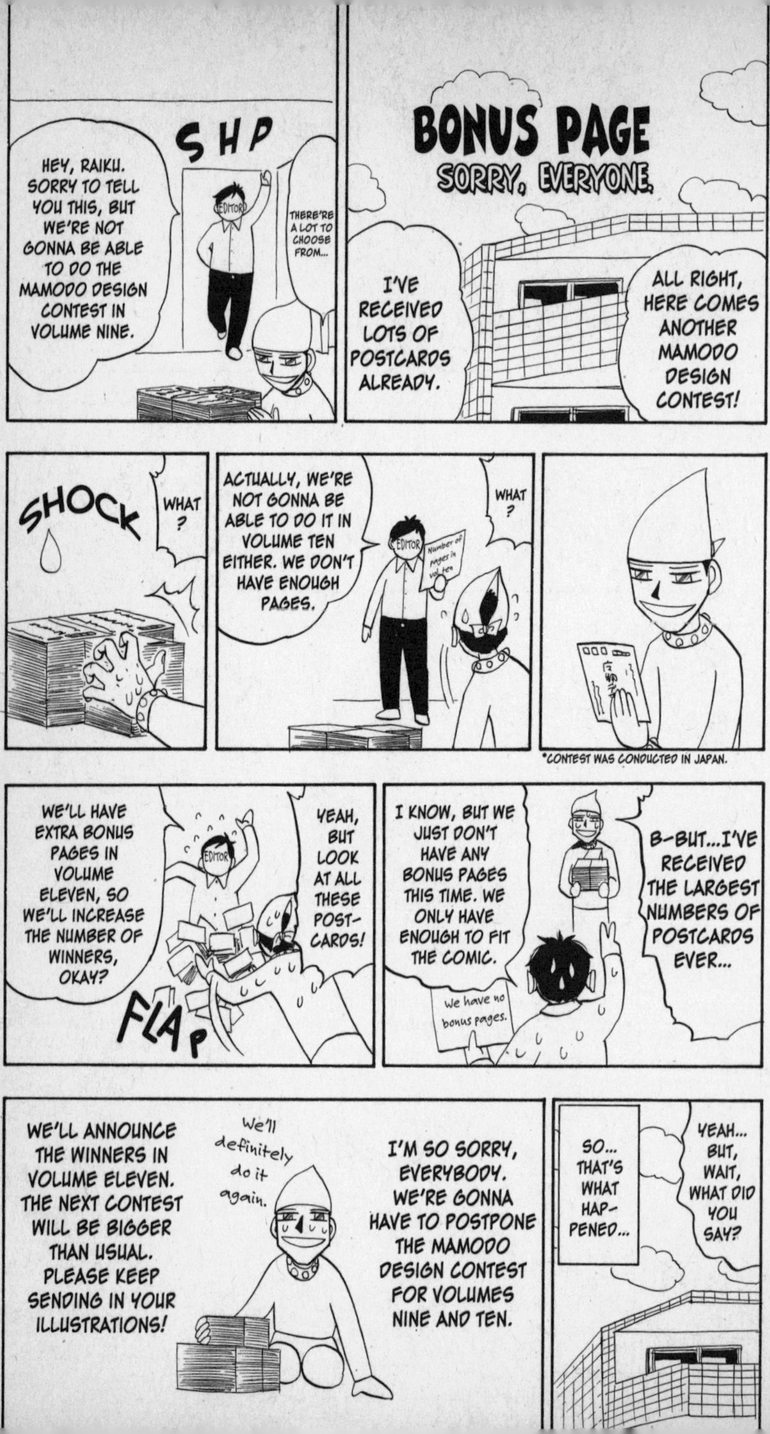
BONUS PAGE
SORRY, EVERYONE.
ALL RIGHT, HERE COMES ANOTHER MAMODO DESIGN CONTEST!
I'VE RECEIVED LOTS OF POSTCARDS ALREADY.
THERE'RE A LOT TO CHOOSE FROM...
SHP
EDITOR
HEY, RAIKU. SORRY TO TELL YOU THIS, BUT WE'RE NOT GONNA BE ABLE TO DO THE MAMODO DESIGN CONTEST IN VOLUME NINE.
WHAT?
ACTUALLY, WE'RE NOT GONNA BE ABLE TO DO IT IN VOLUME TEN EITHER. WE DON'T HAVE ENOUGH PAGES.
EDITOR
Number of pages in vol. ten
WHAT?
SHOCK
*CONTEST WAS CONDUCTED IN JAPAN.
B-BUT...I'VE RECEIVED THE LARGEST NUMBERS OF POSTCARDS EVER...
I KNOW, BUT WE JUST DON'T HAVE ANY BONUS PAGES THIS TIME. WE ONLY HAVE ENOUGH TO FIT THE COMIC.
We have no bonus pages.
YEAH, BUT LOOK AT ALL THESE POST-CARDS!
WE'LL HAVE EXTRA BONUS PAGES IN VOLUME ELEVEN, SO WE'LL INCREASE THE NUMBER OF WINNERS, OKAY?
EDITOR
FLAP
YEAH... BUT, WAIT, WHAT DID YOU SAY?
SO... THAT'S WHAT HAP-PENED...
I'M SO SORRY, EVERYBODY. WE'RE GONNA HAVE TO POSTPONE THE MAMODO DESIGN CONTEST FOR VOLUMES NINE AND TEN.
We'll definitely do it again.
WE'LL ANNOUNCE THE WINNERS IN VOLUME ELEVEN. THE NEXT CONTEST WILL BE BIGGER THAN USUAL. PLEASE KEEP SENDING IN YOUR ILLUSTRATIONS!

ZATCH & SUZY

BY MAKOTO RAIKU

WAH.
HEH, HEH, HEH, HEH.
YAY!
KYAAA!
HEH, HEH, HEH, HEH...I'M SO HAPPY! I'M SO GLAD...
I FOUND OUT THAT MEGUMI IS TIA'S GUARDIAN.
SHE'S NOT TAKAMINE'S GIRLFRIEND.
HEH, HEH, HEH, HEH, HEH...

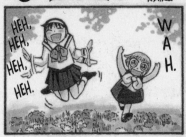

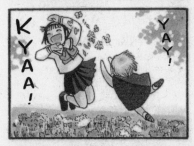

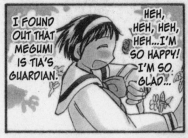

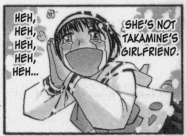

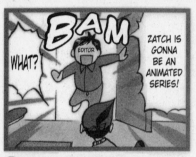

ZATCH IS GONNA BE AN ANIMATED SERIES!
BAM
EDITOR
WHAT?
EVERYBODY FROM THE EDITORIAL DEPARTMENT
CONGRAT-ULATIONS ON RECEIVING THE SHOGAKUKAN MANGA AWARD!
DM
DM
DM
EDITOR
WHAT?

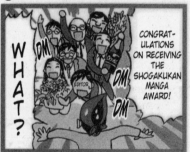

MAKOTO RAIKU

It was like Christmas and New Year's arriving at once!
I want to thank everybody who supported me, everybody who encouraged me, and everybody who read my manga.

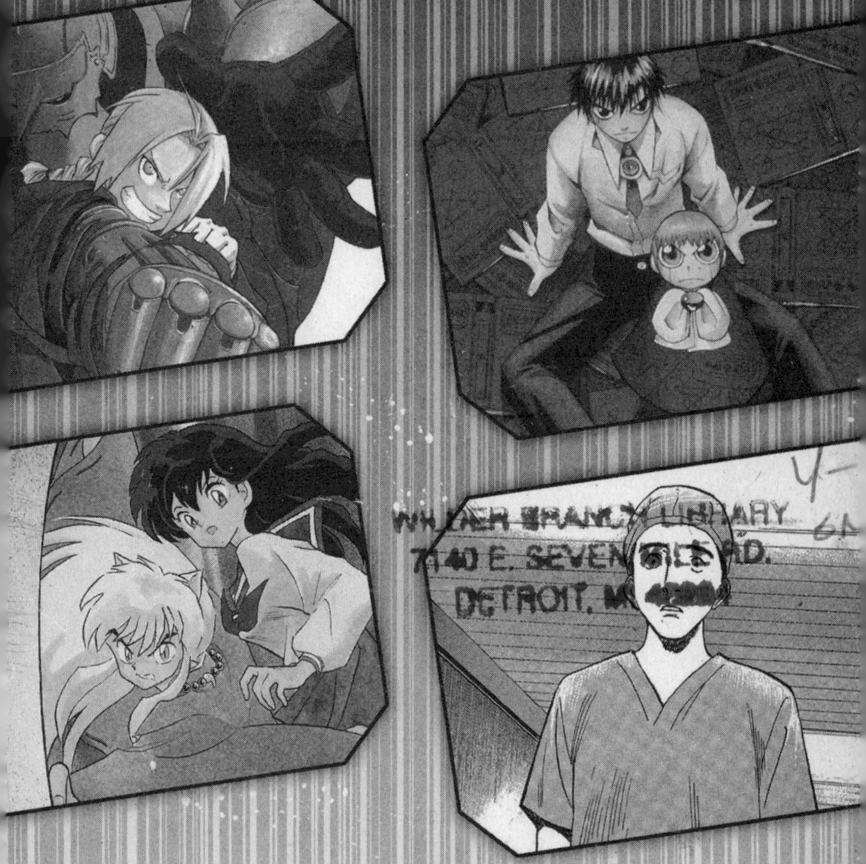